ROADS TO UTOPIA

ROADS TO UTOPIA

The Walking Stories of the *Zohar*

David Greenstein

STANFORD UNIVERSITY PRESS
STANFORD, CALIFORNIA

Stanford University Press
Stanford, California

Printed in the United States of America on acid-free, archival-quality paper

Library of Congress Cataloging-in-Publication Data
Greenstein, David, 1951- author.
Roads to utopia : the walking stories of the Zohar / David Greenstein.
pages cm
Includes bibliographical references and index.
ISBN 978-0-8047-8833-5 (cloth : alk. paper)
1. Zohar. 2. Cabala. 3. Mysticism--Judaism. 4. Walking in literature.
5. Jewish literature--Themes, motives. I. Title.
BM525.A59G735 2014
296.1'62--dc23 2013039097

ISBN 978-0-8047-8968-4 (electronic)

Typeset by Bruce Lundquist in 11/16 Bembo

For Zelda

In Memoriam
Susan Goodstein Lerner,
1940–2013

Contents

For appendices 2, 3, and 4, see www.sup.org/roadstoutopia

Acknowledgments

I am fortunate to have studied with one of the great scholars of our time, Professor Elliot R. Wolfson. He and the other wonderful members of the faculty at New York University made my time there one of great excitement and exhilaration. I am grateful for their generous teaching and support.

I thank all my students at rabbinical seminaries and adult education programs where I have taught for helping me learn, feel, and see more. Since 2005, I have been privileged to hold a weekly study session in the *Zohar* with devoted congregants from New Hyde Park and Forest Hills, New York, and now Montclair, New Jersey. Each member of those groups has been a dear companion in our quest to experience the riches that the *Zohar* offers. Using Daniel Matt's magisterial Pritzker edition, we began at the beginning and now, eight years later, we are on page 1:69a. I pray that I will merit many more years of such delicious and wondrous study.

I owe a great debt of thanks to Danny Matt for his steadfast faith in this project. Without his support I doubt that I would have been able to persevere. To Norris Pope, Stacy Wagner, Mariana Raykov, and the entire staff at Stanford University Press, my deepest gratitude. I thank the anonymous readers of this work for their helpful suggestions and Peter Dreyer for his superb work, which goes beyond good copyediting. To Dr. Laurence Lerner, and Susan Goodstein Lerner, of blessed memory, my heartfelt thanks for your friendship and for arranging for the support from the Elmar Fund, Inc., that made this publication possible.

Finally, I acknowledge the gift of my family's love. Our son, Yonah, is the best. To Zelda I owe everything.

Blessed be the Compassionate One, Who has aided us all along the way.

Zoharic Texts Discussed in This Study

This list does not include texts cited in passing. Numbers in square brackets refer to the numbering of walking texts found in Appendix 1 to this book.

1:49a–50a [#3]	chapter 1 (entire)
1:69b–70a [#9]	chapter 2, pp. 33–36
1:74a–75b	chapter 5, pp. 173–178
1:76a [#10]	chapter 2, pp. 36–39
1:92b–96b [#12]	chapter 5 (entire)
1:155b [#20]	chapter 2, pp. 43–44
1:178a–b [#26]	chapter 6, pp. 199–202
1:224b–225b	chapter 6, pp. 188–190
2:2a	chapter 3, pp. 82–84
2:17b (*Midrash ha-Ne'elam*) [#50]	chapter 2, pp. 44–46
2:151b–152b	chapter 6, pp. 191–197
2:183b–184a [#72]	chapter 6, pp. 209–212
2:198a–217b [#74]	chapter 2, pp. 46–55
2:241a–244b	chapter 3, pp. 63–65
2:248a–254b (*Heikhalot*)	chapter 3, pp. 66–68
3:45b–46b [#87]	chapter 6, pp. 205–207
3:149a–b [#108]	chapter 3, pp. 96–105
Zohar Ḥadash (*Rut*) 77b [#24]	chapter 5, pp. 166–168

ROADS TO UTOPIA

Two Introductions

Studying the Zohar*: A Unique Book and a Unique Motif*

The *Zohar* is a work of radiant illumination and murky mysteriousness. It is unarguably the most precious and significant work of Jewish mysticism, but it has undergone periods of both prominence and obscurity. As Gershom Scholem noted, its "place in the history of Kabbalism can be gauged by the fact that alone among the whole of post-Talmudic rabbinical literature it became a canonical text, which for a period of several centuries actually ranked with the Bible and the Talmud."[1] Yet, from the beginning, it has encountered skepticism and opposition as well as homage and reverence. Its very origins are disputed. Even the most traditional view sees the *Zohar* as a text that was lost or hidden for over a thousand years before it miraculously reappeared in late thirteenth-century Spain. And the *Zohar* went into another period of eclipse during the modern period, only to enjoy a renewed upsurge of devoted attention and study, by various groups and individuals with varying interests and agendas, in our own time.[2]

We are privileged to live at a time of flourishing scholarly attention to this great work. The *Zohar* is being studied for its theosophical teachings, its literary qualities, its approach to mystical experience and thinking, its psychology and anthropology, its hermeneutics, its halakhah, and its historical references. It has been or is in the process of being translated and retranslated into Hebrew, European languages, and English. No other kabbalistic classic has elicited so much devoted and intensive study.

The purpose of this book is to focus on a unique feature—for a kabbalistic work—of this unique composition: it introduces its teachings with statements such as: "Rabbi A and Rabbi B were walking along the road. Rabbi A opened: . . ." What follows is the disclosure of the zoharic teachings that are the basic substance of all study and research into the *Zohar*'s treasures. But why does the *Zohar* choose to present its teachings in this seemingly unnecessary way? What is the function or meaning of its recurrent "stories" of this kind?[3]

To a degree, this question is related to the issue of the role of narrative in the *Zohar*. Alongside of and interwoven with its mystical teachings, it contains many strange, moving, and enchanting stories. Why are they included? One of the first to notice this question was Rabbi Judah Aryeh de Modena (1571–1648), who suggested that the stories be read as "entertainments," intermezzos partaking of the aesthetic and the humorous. They afford some relief from the intensity of the *Zohar*'s more profound concerns. Of the author and composition of the *Zohar*, de Modena wrote:

> I mean that he acted shrewdly [*hitḥakem*] so that the reader would not get fed up with the heavy riddles and mysteries bound and bunched together. Therefore, he mixed in with these . . . stories to no purpose, such as Rabbi Pinḥas and Rabbi Shim'on were walking on the road, they came to a field, they saw an animal, they saw a snake, and many miracles and wonders—not that the matter is unworthy of being believed—that God did wondrously for His devotees in what happened. . . . How beautiful, how pleasant they are! So that I therefore praise and extol the composition of the *Sefer ha-Zohar* as to its style over everything composed in our nation from three hundred years ago until now. Indeed, they show and inform everyone that they are not the work of either Tannaites or Amoraites, but rather are by a sage, beloved later stylist.[4]

While this comment is fascinating as an example of de Modena's talent for ambiguity, inasmuch as he succeeds in both praising and diminishing the stature of the *Zohar* at the same time, what is of interest for the present are his two insights: he is perhaps the first clearly to express the idea that the narrative approach of the *Zohar* is a problem for critical readers, and he intuits that understanding this problem can shed light on the question of the composition of the *Zohar*.[5] For him, the introduction of this playful element is a sure indication of the late composition of the work.

Let us focus on de Modena's first insight. It is important to appreciate that by saying that the stories of the *Zohar* are a problem, he is not making an obvious claim. In the history of the study of the narrative portions of the

Zohar, and of the walking motif in particular, the explicit questions: "What are these stories and narrative fragments *doing* in this mystical text? Why are they there?" are conspicuously absent.

Of course, many zoharic stories have been noticed and commented on. But it must be said that the fact that the *Zohar* is, in its narrative proclivities, very different from other mystical works, whether prior, roughly contemporary with it, or even subsequent, was not regarded as a concern by traditional commentators. When we turn to modern scholarship, we see that it has only gradually put the issue of the zoharic narratives on its agenda. Scholem was interested in the matter for the evidence that it might give regarding the *Zohar*'s knowledge of Israel and its place of composition. Otherwise, he was content to subsume the issue under the topic of pseudepigraphy—a common tack taken by esoteric writers; it was thus not to be considered a problem at all.

It is not necessary here to review the important contributions of such scholars as Yehuda Liebes, Ronit Meroz, Michal Oron, Mordekhai Pachter, Naomi Tene, Isaiah Tishby, Aryeh Wineman, and Elliot Wolfson to the study of zoharic narratives. The fundamental discoveries and insights of these scholars notwithstanding, none of them has given sustained attention to the commonest, best-known element of zoharic narrative—its recurrent use of the walking motif. The element of recurrent "walking stories" occupies a paradoxical place in studies of the *Zohar*. Everyone knows that it is there, but no one until now has subjected the phenomenon to sustained interrogation. The motif has been taken for granted. In general, it can be said that traditional and critical readers of the *Zohar* have shared the assumption that the meaning of the walking motif is to be found within the array of the *Zohar*'s pietistic and theosophical concerns.

Undoubtedly, these are the important concerns of the *Zohar*. But, in addition, Yehuda Liebes has highlighted the celebratory approach of the *Zohar* toward innovation and creativity. And contemporary scholars such as Daniel Matt and Arthur Green have emphasized the vitality expressed through the walking motif. It is seen as indicative of the *Zohar*'s delight in elusive creativity and openness to spiritual inspiration from all sources. In a way this approach can be seen as a more sophisticated and internalized application of de Modena's entertainment model.

These valuable scholarly interpretations should be taken primarily as appreciations of the walking motif rather than as analyses of it.[6] The motif has not been isolated as a problem, but has been subsumed within the known agendas of the *Zohar*.

But when we turn our attention to the motif itself, we cannot escape its paradoxical and problematic nature. In order to properly analyze this motif in the *Zohar*, we must ask certain fundamental questions: How should the motif be defined? How many times does it occur? Where in the *Zohar* is it found?

To better understand what we are looking for, it may be helpful to begin with stating what we are *not* looking for. For example, a text that tells us, "Rabbi A went to see Rabbi B and heard some teaching there," is not relevant to our topic.[7] The walking serves to get us somewhere. This is a conventional literary device and is not problematic. Our concern is aroused when this motif appears even though it could just as well not be there.[8] Then we encounter the paradox of the insistent presence of a literary gesture that seems to have no meaning. In a certain sense, the presence of the walking motif as a meaningless element has contributed to its invisibility; once it is noticed, its apparently meaningless presence is all the more troubling.

In this light, it is paradoxical to call the walking motif a "motif" at all. Consider the work done in folklore studies regarding motif categorization. Stith Thompson describes what makes for a motif: "A *motif* is the smallest element in a tale having a power to persist in tradition. In order to have this power it must have something unusual and striking about it."[9] How special is the act of walking? By this criterion, can it be a motif? What salience endowed it with significance and led it to be retained as a narrative element in the *Zohar*? Thompson says:

> It must be more than commonplace. A mother as such is not a motif. A cruel mother becomes one because she is at least thought to be unusual. The ordinary processes of life are not motifs. To say that "John dressed and walked to town" is not to give a single motif worth remembering; but to say that the hero put on his cap of invisibility, mounted his magic carpet, and went to the land east of the sun and west of the moon is to include at least

> four motifs—the cap . . . , the carpet . . . , the magic air journey . . . , and the marvelous land. . . . Each of these motifs lives on because it has been found satisfying by generations of tale-tellers.[10]

Thompson explicitly rules out "walking to town" as a motif because it is too commonplace an activity. Why would anyone feel the need to preserve such a superfluous detail in a larger narrative?[11] For example, there are many places where the *Zohar* emphasizes how important it is to learn Torah while on the road. Yet the Torah that is taught "while Rabbi A and Rabbi B were walking on the road" is more often than not isolable and quotable without any reference to the walking itself.

The walking motif is thus fraught with paradox. It really should not be a motif at all. And it really should not be in the *Zohar* in the first place. Still, the zoharic authorship insists on employing this negligible motif over and over. Furthermore, the "walking stories" are not really stories or narratives either. As we shall see, they do not commonly function to further the instruction or the plot of the drama being told. To be precise, to refer to the *Zohar*'s "walking stories" is not to refer to a collection of narratives, but to narrative shards or slivers found liberally embedded throughout the main body of the *Zohar* (the *guf ha-Zohar*). By embedding these storytelling phrases in its chain of mystical homilies and discourses, the *Zohar* turns the latter into speeches embedded in these "walking stories," rather than free-standing teachings. Are these narrative fragments to be seen as alien trace elements in this strange corpus of works called the *Zohar*, or are they integral to defining it? By inadvertence or intention, readers have often ignored or even dislodged these slivers from the zoharic body, apparently without concern for causing pain or damage to it. But, in doing this, can we be sure that no injury has been inflicted, or that something vital has not been lost?

Where are these narrative shards located? As a body of work, the *Zohar* should be thought of as a library, rather than as a book. It comprises many literary units whose delineation, correlation, and composition into "the *Zohar*" is a matter of continuing scholarly discussion.[12] In cataloguing the walking texts throughout the *Zohar*, it becomes clear that there are certain gaps in its pages, where the motif is not found. These gaps include some of the most significant sections of the *Zohar*. Stories of traveling associates do not appear in the *Idrot*, the *Sifra de Tzeni'uta*, the *Heikhalot* sections, *Raza de Razin*, *Rav Metivta*, or the *Sabba de Mishpatim* sections.[13] The many walking texts of the *Zohar* are thus concentrated in only a few of the literary units that comprise the zoharic library. Chiefly, they are found in the main body of the *Zohar*. But they are also found in relative abundance in the *Midrash ha-Ne'elam* and other sections in *Zohar Ḥadash*. In that volume the walking narratives are absent from the sections on the Chariot Vision and the Song of Songs, *Qav ha-Middah*, and *Sitrei Otiyyot*.

The paradoxical nature of the motif, its ubiquity and invisibility, is reflected in this pattern of its distribution. The *Sifra de Tzeni'uta*, *Idrot*, and *Heikhalot* texts have been seen as the defining sections of the zoharic project.[14] Yet the motif is absent from these most significant, profound, and central portions of the *Zohar*. On the other hand, the motif is centrally located as a constant element in the main body of the *Zohar*, and its presence is already abundant in the earliest layer of the *Zohar*, the *Midrash ha-Ne'elam*. This dichotomy conveys a message about the place and meaning of the walking motif. When dealing with the most sensitive and esoteric theosophical teachings, especially those bearing on the divine image and structure, the zoharic authorship has no use for the walking motif. But the use of the motif is frequent and abundant outside of these sections. Furthermore, the hypothetical separation between the *Zohar*'s mystical content and the walking motif is strengthened when we notice that the motif is common in the *Midrash ha-Ne'elam*, the early layer of *Zohar*, which is characterized by a less mystical approach than later strata. This would indicate that the impulse to use this motif does not initially come from a desire to attach it to the transmission or experience of esoteric theosophical or theurgical truths. Perhaps, then, the inclination to subsume the walking stories into the known concerns of this mystical encyclopedia should be resisted.

If this is so, what alternative truths, great or small, are we meant to discover when we delicately examine the zoharic corpus for these glancing slivers of narration? Toward what new apprehension, prosaic or sublime, might we be led if we follow these shards along the way?

Spatiality and the Zohar*: Places, Spaces, and Movement in and through Them*

Rabbi Isaac of Acre, an early kabbalist, came to Spain in 1305.[15] He heard of the recent appearance of a wondrous work, purportedly by the second-century sage Rabban Shim'on bar Yoḥai, but copied by Rabbi Moshe de Leon. Rabbi Isaac tells us that his attempt to see the manuscript was thwarted by the demise of Moshe de Leon. He reports that another person who had desired to acquire the original manuscript subsequently told him that de Leon's widow had denied that it was a copy of a book by Rabban Shim'on, saying:

> Thus and more may God do to me if my husband ever possessed such a book! He wrote it entirely from his own head. When I saw him writing with nothing in front of him, I said to him, "Why do you say that you are copying from a book when there is no book? You are writing from your head. Wouldn't it be better to say so? You would have more honor!" He answered me, "If I told them my secret, that I am writing from my own mind, they would pay no attention to my words, and they would pay nothing for them. They would say: 'He is inventing them from his own imagination.' But now that they hear I am copying from Rabbi Shim'on son of Yoḥai through the Holy Spirit, they buy these words at a high price, as you see with your very eyes!"[16]

This work has become known as *Sefer ha-Zohar*—The Book of Splendor. It seems from Rabbi Isaac's story that the *Zohar* has been a book of magnetic attraction and mysterious elusiveness from the outset, and it remains one to this very day. But this story tells us even more. Various scholars have probed it for whatever it may say about the identity of the *Zohar*'s author. But that is not my interest. Neither is my focus, as it has been for some scholars, on the nature of Rabbi Moshe de Leon's act of writing. Was it some kind of mystical act of automatic writing or prophecy?[17] Or was the reproduction of the ancient sage's words a task of sacred discipleship? Or was the dull work of copying from one page to another a daily act of drudgery? It will have to suffice simply to note the questions.

For our purposes, the interesting aspect of this story is what it suggests about the spatial world inhabited by the thirteenth-century mystic Rabbi Moshe de Leon, since he was regularly engaged in what was very possibly a profound religious and mystical experience.

Where are such experiences meant to take place? Traditionally, they are located in the real or imaginal Temple, in the *beit midrash* (house of study), the master's private room, near a natural or artificial body of water, on a mountain, or in a secluded spot in the forest. We are used to thinking about these intense experiences as "taking" place in—that is, gravitating toward or producing—sacred spaces.

Yet, as described in this story, Moshe de Leon's practice of writing out the *Zohar*—whether as a boring pecuniary act, or as the exalted expression of mystical illumination—took place in the de Leons' cramped apartment, while Mrs. (not Ms.) de Leon did the cooking and the cleaning. A different spatial reality is presented here. We are forcibly reminded that mystics live in real time and space. While we are convinced that the essential thrust of mystical thought and practice is to transcend, sanctify, or transform mundane reality, this scenario reminds us that Moshe de Leon's activity was undertaken within the familiar domestic world of clutter and grime, of clearing away a clean space for writing against the encroachments of one's own stuff and that of others. Moreover, this is a space that is hardly imbued with a sacred aura. Instead, it is filled with conversations and even arguments and misunderstandings between the writer and his spouse. The subjects of their disagreements were not theosophical doctrines and the kabbalist's desire for *unio mystica*. They were the very mundane issues of reputation and finances, themselves perhaps expressions of more intimate frustrations, disappointments, and exasperations.[18]

The story serves here to trigger consideration of a question regarding religious and mystical cultures in general, and specifically the religious culture exemplified by the *Zohar*.[19] Is it possible for such cultures to account—to themselves—for the vast realm of human experience that is not controlled by religious values—the realm of the mundane as such? And if it is possible, in what ways might they do this? This is a serious question for a religious culture, because it is in the nature of a religious culture such as mystical Judaism to conceive of itself as containing the true and all-encompassing understanding of and relationship to reality—that is, the total truth about all reality.

Another way to ask this question is to explore the ways in which such a religious culture might account for the spatial dimension of living. Mircea

Eliade proposed that religions map out space in a very specific way. He conceived of all truly religious experience as definitive and transformative of space and gave us the very powerful model of the sacred center:

> When the sacred manifests itself in any hierophany, there is not only a break in the homogeneity of space; there is also revelation of an absolute reality, opposed to the unreality of the vast surrounding expanse. The manifestation of the sacred ontologically founds the world. In the homogeneous and infinite expanse, in which no point of reference is possible and hence no *orientation* can be established, the hierophany reveals an absolute fixed point, a center.[20]

This is counterposed to profane experience, described by Eliade in this way:

> The profane experience, on the contrary, maintains the homogeneity and hence the relativity of space. No *true* orientation is now possible, for the fixed point no longer enjoys a unique ontological status; it appears and disappears in accordance with the needs of the day. Properly speaking, there is no longer any world, there are only fragments of a shattered universe, an amorphous mass consisting of an infinite number of more or less neutral places in which man moves, governed and driven by the obligations of an existence incorporated into an industrial society.[21]

Eliade thus contrasts the premodern religious person with the modern profane person, "*living in a desacralized cosmos*."[22] While the latter moves about among neutral places, *homo religiosus* desires "to move about only in a sanctified world, that is, a sacred space."[23]

This has been a useful and very influential conceptualization of the spatial orientation of religious people, but it is patently inadequate as a description of historical religious experience. Every person, no matter how religious or mystical, cannot help but live in the homogenized, desacralized cosmos of mundane space. Though such a situation may be explicitly viewed as a scandal to be overcome, or, perhaps, simply as an existential perversity better skipped over in silence, it never does go away. Is there, then, even in the totalizing project of the religious mystic, room for an acknowledgment of the vast stretches of nonsacralized, homogeneous, humdrum space that we all live in.

It cannot be easy for a religious culture such as that of the Spanish Jewish mystics to sustain such an acknowledgment for any length of time. This is because, given their totalizing thrust, cultures such as this will try either to co-opt such spaces or to expunge them. Mundane space is both ontologically unreal and temporally fleeting. The eschatological dream is for the disappearance of the horizontal dimension of mundane space—or its collapse—into the sacred center, along with the further collapse of this sacred vertical axis into a point. The end result of this tendency is the necessary abolition of the horizontal and, finally, of spatiality itself. It would require an exceptional religious culture to allow for the mundane horizontal to coexist with the sacred vertical dimension. Indeed, in Eliade's model this would seem to be impossible.

J. Z. Smith has challenged Eliade's religious typology and topography. Instead of limiting the sense of the sacred to a vertical axis, Smith suggests that we distinguish

> between those cultures which affirm the structures of the cosmos and seek to repeat them; which affirm the necessity of dwelling within a limited world in which each being has its given place and role to fill, a centrifugal view of the world which emphasizes the importance of the "Center" as opposed to those cultures which express a more "open" view in which the categories of rebellion and freedom are to the fore; in which beings are called upon to challenge their limits, break them, or create new possibilities, a centripetal world which emphasizes the importance of the periphery and transcendence . . . between a *locative* vision of the world (which emphasizes place) and a *utopian* vision of the world (using the term in its strict sense: the value of being in no place).[24]

According to Smith, there is a more complicated play between notions of the sacred and the spatial dimensions of horizontal and vertical. Locative cultures work with sacred centers, but they operate horizontally. Meanwhile, the vertical thrust is powerfully evident in utopian cultures that do not privilege a sacred center. They express discomfort with orderliness and definitive placement. Instead, they valorize the adventurous, the disruptive and, ultimately, the explosion of all limitation, including, indeed, the cosmos itself.

Just as Smith denies that the concern for defining sacred spaces must derive from an exclusively vertical orientation to the sacred, he also allows the horizontal experience of everyday life to play a more positive function in constituting ritual.

For Smith, the significance of ritual is not, as Eliade thought, that it creates an opening to the realm of the sacred, the real and the powerful. Smith's notion of power is much more problematized: "Ritual relies for its power on the fact that it is concerned with quite ordinary activities, that what it describes and displays is, in principle, possible for every occurrence of these acts. But it relies, as well, for its power on the perceived fact that, in actuality, such possibilities cannot be actualized."[25] Ritual does not connect its practitioners and spectators with a truer realm of power. Rather, ritual serves, by antithesis, to open up a more focused, attentive way of experiencing the significance of the mundane and the ordinary, "a significance which rules express but are powerless to effectuate."[26] Ritual is not an erasure of the profane, but its displacement: "*ritual represents the creation of a controlled environment* where the variables (i.e., the accidents) of ordinary life may be displaced *precisely* because they are felt to be so overwhelmingly present and powerful."[27]

This dimension of ritual that provokes consideration and thinking about the limits of mundane existence is characterized by Smith as "gnostic."[28] This suggests the possibility that salvation may be found, not necessarily in either the security of location or the excitement of escape, but in a combination of the two. The locative view of salvation seeks to confer on its perceived limits a quality of finality and stasis. The utopian view of salvation depends on the outright denial of limitation and stasis in the name of total freedom. The gnosis of ritual is in the untrammeled contemplation of difference, of the limits of possibility. Rightly, I think, Smith perceives that if the elements of paradox, of absolute puissance and flat-footed impotence, are essential to ritual, then the realm of ritual must be understood to be closely related to the realm of the joke.

The question is whether this alternative conception can have any relevance to understanding a serious and intense mystical culture such as that which produced the *Zohar*? I would venture to say that most understandings of the religious aspects of zoharic culture—its theosophy, cosmogony, ritual theory, ethics, and so on, have been dominated by an Eliadian approach. The realia of the lives and actions of the *ḥevrayya* (fellowship)—their gatherings,[29] learning,[30] ways of speech,[31] or eating[32]—have been shown to have multiple associations with the deepest esoteric concerns of the *Zohar*, so that all these actions have been conceived of as rituals of illumination, of ascent, of unification and theurgy. These studies and insights are compelling, even revelatory. But is it possible that there is something else involved as well? I ask this question specifically regarding the walking motif of the *Zohar*.

In discussing one instance of this motif, Noami Tene, in her study of zoharic narrative, offers a nuanced version of Eliade and speaks of the transcendence of the horizontal through ascent into the vertical. She writes:

> The action in the fellowship takes place while walking together in the paths of the Torah. "Being on the way" is the main existence of the figures in the *Zohar's* stories, and is the great topic of the stories. The road is the main fabulatory thread of the stories, the mission and the destination both, in the sense of "way-arousal-fellowship." Much beyond the picaresque element, walking on the road facilitates the encounter with matter and its elevation . . . as an encounter without separation from the world.
>
> The "road" cuts across accepted coordinates of space and time; for the figures live a priori in a reality with a dual foundation: in this world and, withal, in the upper worlds. For a brief moment the human is detached from earthly existence and passes over to survey the upper worlds with his body or his soul.[33]

While this analysis is a valuable beginning, it makes assumptions that need to be questioned. It assumes that the roads walked by the Companions can be accurately labeled and valorized as "paths of Torah." It assumes that the walking motif alludes to a metaphorical situation of "being on the way," and it assumes that the walking is for the purpose of detachment from and transcendence of this world. It is through such assumptions that readers of the *Zohar* have tended to try to place the walking of the Companions into the category of mystical ritual practice. But what if their walking signals a utopian resistance to such a placement? Let us examine the plentiful, if fragmentary, material of the walking stories by dispensing with those assumptions and by beginning with a much simpler one: walking is our primary means of moving physically through space. Before it may become anything else, walking is a spatial practice. If we proceed with that premise as our guiding assumption, it is my hope, our journey will take us to new understandings.

CHAPTER I

The Dregs of Tar

> Rabbi Shim'on was traveling to Tiberias, and with him were Rabbi Yose, Rabbi Yehudah, and Rabbi Ḥiyya. Meanwhile, they noticed Rabbi Pinḥas, who was approaching. Once they joined as one, they came down and sat under [one of] the mountain trees.
>
> Rabbi Pinḥas said, "Now that we are seated, I wish to hear some of the excellent words that you say every day."
>
> Rabbi Shim'on opened and said: "And he [Abraham] went on his journeys from the south to Bethel, until the place where his tent had been originally, between Bethel and the Ai" [Gen. 13:3]. 'And he went on his journeys,'—it should have been 'on his journey.' What [is the meaning of] 'on his journeys'? Rather, there are two journeys, one that is his and one of the Shekhinah."[1]

Thus begins one of the first of the many "walking stories" of the *Zohar*.[2] It calls for examination both on its own merits and in terms of what it may teach about the use of walking stories in the entire zoharic corpus. Such an examination should focus on the story's content and stylistic elements, of course, and, also, on its literary context or placement within the preceding and following zoharic texts.

As presently constituted, the *Zohar* goes on for many pages and adopts a number of literary approaches to presenting its teachings before offering a walking story.[3] In one long stretch, its teachings are successfully presented by the anonymous authorial voice. It also couches them as lessons taught by named sages. Why the resort to a story about walking comrades to introduce more such statements? Furthermore, it may be asked whether the *Zohar* understands itself as shifting gears when it adopts this motif as the container for its teachings. But these questions of authorial choice will have to wait until after the walking story itself is studied.

The story begins by picturing Rabbi Shim'on bar Yoḥai (Rashbi) traveling with a few of his disciples.[4] They encounter another sage of their acquaintance, Rabbi Pinḥas.[5] They halt their journeying and come to sit together under a tree. At the invitation of Rabbi Pinḥas, Rashbi begins a discourse whose topic is the very activity that these sages were just engaged in—traveling on the road.

The discourse follows the standard pattern: a biblical verse is highlighted (thereby apparently rendering its contextual meaning irrelevant), a textual curiosity is noticed in the verse and this apparently surprising textual feature serves as the platform for a new teaching.[6]

Rashbi's chosen text depicts the wealthy and prosperous Abraham traveling from his encampment in the south to an earlier place of encampment, Bethel, a place where Abraham had originally set up an altar to worship God. Rashbi "opens up" the verse by explaining that referring to Abraham's journeys in the plural tells us that his trip was not a solitary one, but constituted two journeys, in that he was accompanied by the Shekhinah. Similarly, Rashbi teaches, every Jewish man, when he leaves his wife and home, should make sure that the Shekhinah will accompany him on the way. "Every person must be found male and female so as to strengthen the faith. And then Shekhinah will never depart from him."[7] In order to guarantee the continuous presence of Shekhinah, the man should, while still at home with his wife, and they are thus still found as both male and female together, pray to the Holy Blessed One so as to draw God's Shekhinah upon him before he sets forth on the road.[8]

This is vitally necessary because the union of the Upper Male and Female aspects of God depends on the male's faithfully maintaining his connection to his wife below. Indeed, it is crucial for the husband to return home

> to make his wife happy, for it is his wife who has caused that Upper coupling. As soon as he comes to her he must make her happy because of two aspects: one, because the joy of that coupling is the joy of mitzvah, and the joy of a mitzvah is the Shekhinah's joy. And not only that, but he also simply increases joy below, as it is written, "Then you will know that your tent is at peace, when you visit your home and you will not sin" [*Job* 5:24]. Can it be that if one does not visit one's wife that one has sinned? That is so, indeed! Because one has lessened the honor of the Upper coupling to which she has joined, for it is his wife who has brought it about.[9]

Later in the same discussion Rashbi will boldly describe the dynamic of divine forces activated by this human union as one of "the passion of the heights of Eternity—*ta'avat giv'ot 'olam*" [Gen. 49:26]. As he and his disciples and Rabbi Pinḥas sit "under mountain trees," Rabbi Shim'on describes the divine potencies of the Upper and Lower Mothers as passion-filled "heights."

The theurgic power of the conjugal coupling of the earthly husband and wife is seen as paradigmatic of the power inherent in performing any mitzvah. Every mitzvah effects joyful union above. To know this is itself a source of joy, "the joy of a mitzvah." This is the *Zohar*'s understanding of this classic rabbinic phrase: "the joy of that coupling is 'the joy of *mitzvah*.'"[10] Such joy is made possible by the presence of one's wife in the home.

The associative and referential web in this zoharic text is thickly woven, with threads of theosophical claims, domestic instructions, and biblical explications all combined together. We may begin, as does Rashbi, with the *Zohar*'s scriptural reading. Though the *Zohar* has begun its teaching by focusing on a seemingly slight, solitary, textual peculiarity in a biblical verse, there are significant implications to be drawn from its discussion that go beyond that textual "trigger," opening up new understandings of the broader biblical story. The Abraham story is used to teach that a husband, when going on a journey and leaving his wife behind, should make sure to draw Shekhinah's accompaniment to him. Abraham's "journeys" were doubled because they were traveled together with Shekhinah. We must infer, therefore, that they were made without Sarah. Yet the previous verse tells us that "Abraham went up from Egypt, he and his wife and all that was his, with Lot accompanying him, to the Negev" (Gen. 13:1). We are led to conclude that Sarah stayed put once they reached the Negev. This was taken by the *Zohar* to constitute a return home, for Abraham had traveled to the Negev before, as related in verse 9 of the previous chapter.[11]

The two verses that mention Abraham's travels to the Negev bracket the story of Abram and Sarai's descent to Egypt, during which Sarai was abducted by Pharaoh. While the first of the Negev verses mentions Abram, but not Sarai, it is clear from the Egypt story that Abram and Sarai were traveling together, as they had been doing since leaving Haran. Yet Sarai is put at great risk once they arrive in Egypt. Elsewhere the *Zohar* would see this event as a foreshadowing of the Egyptian bondage of the Israelites. And it would see Abram's emergence from Egypt as a great spiritual victory, with Abram struggling with the forces of darkness and overcoming them.[12] Yet the discussion in this text gives a sharper point to a question that has plagued generations of readers regarding Abram's apparent willingness to sacrifice Sarai for his own safety.[13] Besides the ethical issues raised by others, the *Zohar* implicitly faults Abram with a spiritual failure of major import. Upon descending to Egypt, Abram violates the fundamental injunction: "Every person must be found male and female so as to strengthen the faith." In denying his wedded relationship to Sarai, Abram denies that he is "male and female" together. In so doing he has sundered the divine conjugal bond. This denial necessitated divine intervention, both to save Sarai from Pharaoh's intentions and to reinstate the relationship between Abram and Sarai.[14] Therefore God told Pharaoh that he was being afflicted "because of Sarai, the wife of Abram."[15]

Thus, in leaving Egypt, Abram must restore Sarai to their earlier home and settle her there, in the Negev (v. 1). This will also restore Shekhinah to their home. When he embarks on his "journeys" in verse 3, it is clear to the *Zohar* that he is no longer traveling with her. While she stays in their house, he goes toward the "house" of God—Beit El—without her, but with the journeying Shekhinah alongside him—making two journeys out of one.

Careful consideration of this midrashic point should help us better understand the relationship between Shekhinah and her traveling companion. Strictly speaking, the journey traveled by Abram and Shekhinah is one and the same. The path is identical. Yet the *Zohar* understands the Torah to be teaching that there are two journeys—*masa'av*. Thus, Shekhinah's accompanying Abraham adds a second "journey," even though they are going on the same path. The journey is not the abstract tracing of the route, a single path, whether traveled by one traveler or many. Rather, it is the actual traversal of space. Each traveler occupies and moves through space separately. Each, as it were, leaves a separate set of footprints, and it is they that constitute the "journeys." In that sense, Abram and Shekhinah are on parallel tracks; they are not united as one.

As this text proceeds, it again and again sets out alternating scenes of union and separation. With regard to one's wife, it presents the tension between joyous copulation and periods of refraining from intimacy. Examples of times of separation include times away from the house, whether on the road or in the House of Study. But even inside the home, there are times of separation or of waiting. These include, for Torah scholars, the days of the week between Sabbaths. Then there are the days following the onset of one's wife's menstrual period. During these times, so that the man shall not suffer loneliness, "Shekhinah comes with you and dwells in your home."[16]

If the constant presence of Shekhinah is necessary, even in the home, where coupling with one's wife is only a sporadic practice, then why not avail oneself of continuous, pure, spiritual conjunction by abandoning the physical and domestic realm for the open road? As the *Zohar* puts it: "And if you should say, 'If this is the case, then it is preferable[17] for a person to go out on the road rather that stay at home, for the sake of the supernal coupling that joins with him!'" But the *Zohar* answers: "Come see: When a person is at home, his wife is the essence of his home, for Shekhinah never leaves the home on account of his wife, as it is written: 'And Isaac brought her into Sarah's tent' [Gen. 24:67]—for the candle was burning. For what reason? Because Shekhinah had entered the home." While the *Zohar* explicitly discusses Shekhinah's accompaniment of the man on his travels, this last phrase, applied to the biblical episode of Rebecca entering Sarah's old tent, actually indicates that Shekhinah has been accompanying Rebecca in her journey to become Isaac's wife, for it is her entrance into the tent that restores to it Shekhinah's presence. The presence of Shekhinah in the home is not dependent on the conjugal relations enacted between husband and wife. It depends entirely on the presence of the wife in the home.

Thus there is a fundamental difference between the presence of Shekhinah in the home and Her presence as the man's traveling companion. While he is on the road, the man is challenged to exercise great restraint, since, because he is separated from his wife and also exposed to others, he is subject to numerous opportunities for sexual transgression.[18] "Come, see: As long as a person is detained on the road, he must guard his actions so that the supernal coupling not depart from him." The role of Shekhinah is to help protect him from giving in to temptation "until he returns home."[19] The constant presence of Shekhinah is in the negative role of "*sh'mirat ha-derekh*—the safeguarding of the road," to use Rabbi Moshe Cordovero's phrase.[20]

But the positive role of Shekhinah in the home is celebrated by the *Zohar*: "When the home is properly arrayed and the male comes upon the female and they join as one, then the Lower Mother pours out blessings to bless them." The divine paradigm is thus replicated below: "Thus it is that the male is adorned with two females when he is in his home, just as it is above." When the male places himself between two females below as the Divine Male is between two Females above, setting the house in order, then, just as Rebecca was able to replicate the illuminating role of Sarah, so Shekhinah is able to replicate the beneficent role of the Upper Mother and shower them with blessings. But, "when he goes out on the road, it is not like that. The Upper Mother joins with him and the lower remains [alone]."[21]

Rabbi Shim'on therefore insists that the husband must return to his wife who "remains alone," "in order to be crowned [*l'it'atra*][22] with two females, as we have said."[23] The focus seems to be solely on the male, yet the implication of the previous phrases is that the loneliness of the female, the wife, is equally important. The implication is only glancingly made visible and is then covered over by the redirection of the lesson to its standard object, the male. Nevertheless, for a moment, the *Zohar* has reread the Torah's famous dictum "It is not good for the human to be alone" (Gen. 2:18) so as to apply it to the female. This verse has just served as the backdrop for the zoharic text immediately preceding this teaching on the road. In this second text, the verse is faintly alluded to so that its import may be shifted. In the Torah, it is necessary to address the evil of the male's loneliness by bringing the female to him. Now the *Zohar* compels the male to come home to the female so as to prevent her loneliness.

In subtle ways, the *Zohar* has developed a cluster of associations and instructions that go against our expectations of how a mystical reader might read the Torah, and about what a mystical approach to human and divine relationships might entail. A rich cluster of dualities is set up by this teaching: physical/spiritual, male/female, Upper/Lower, home/road, union/separation, blessing/protection. But the valorization of each term in these dualities, and their connective arrangement, is somewhat surprising.

Where we might expect to find a celebration of mystical union, or of the transcendence of the physical for the sake of the spiritual, Rabbi Shim'on insists, instead, that the spiritual is found most fully in the physical realm of domesticity. The quest for spiritual conjunction with the Divine, free from material constraints of physical being and material obligations, that is, the spiritual quest of the road, leads to an impaired spiritual state, while the full flow of blessed union is only found at home.

The *Zohar* privileges staying home over going on the road with respect to the quality of Shekhinah's presence that one may expect to merit. Nevertheless, staying home is not an option for the man, although it is required of the woman. The man may need to travel outside the home, but the woman's role requires her presence inside the house. She does not travel. Indeed, she must not travel.[24] According to the *Zohar*'s scheme of things a man is caught between two women—one who must stay at home and one who may travel with him. Surely the man will be tempted to go with the woman who is "freer" to roam with him, and whose companionship can be constant. Yet according to this teaching, a man's union with Shekhinah can be experienced only at home; if he travels on the road, the accompaniment of Shekhinah is merely to protect him from the temptations of the road, so that he can keep faith with his housebound wife. Conjunction with Shekhinah happens in the marriage domicile. It is here that the man is enveloped in the passionate desire of the Divine Female, both Upper and Lower. These are the yearnings for divine union felt, as it were, by "the 'Hills of Eternity,' the Upper Female, so as to adorn Him and crown Him and bless Him, and the Lower Female, to unite with Him and be nourished from Him."[25] By contrast, the Shekhinah's presence on the road is only prophylactic.

Thus Rashbi's initial point is that the path of the traveler and the path of Shekhinah by his side are not one, united path, but two. They run parallel, but are not united. Moreover, ascribing the two paths to the traveler, as they are ascribed to Abram (*masa'av*—"his journeys"), does not have to mean that the traveler takes possession and unites with that other path. On the contrary, in the sense that these two journeys both belong to the traveler, the second journey, created through the accompaniment of Shekhinah, can be seen as the journey not taken—the path of temptation that is blocked to the traveler by Shekhinah in her role as the Protector of the Road.

We are presented with a problem: The *Zohar*'s stay-at-home message is clear enough. But this message is undermined in basic ways. One subversive element is the inclusion of Rabbi Pinḥas in the story. Rabbi Shim'on's teaching could just as well have been offered without introducing the episode of meeting Rabbi Pinḥas on the road. Instead, we are introduced to Rabbi Pinḥas, who travels alone—both before and after Rashbi's words of Torah. As noticed above, again and again, Rashbi's teaching sets out scenes that alternate between union and separation. In portraying this teaching as one occasioned by Rashbi's meeting with Rabbi Pinḥas, the *Zohar* applies the teaching's theme of union and separation to the teaching's narrative setting as well. First, Rashbi and his disciples meet up with Rabbi Pinḥas, but their union eventually ends and they go their separate ways. Their respective ways separate geographically and also in terms of their spatial theory and practice. Rabbi Pinḥas travels alone; the Companions travel together. This means that Rabbi Pinḥas, who does not seem to have known Rashbi's teaching before hearing it in this story, has been traveling without the intention of drawing Shekhinah to accompany him on his journey. And, even after he hears this teaching, and seems to express great admiration for it, he is not about to return home first, in order to draw Shekhinah's presence from out of his home and onto the road. Thus, though Rabbi Pinḥas delights in hearing these words from his son-in-law, he does not actually exemplify or adopt the way of life that Rashbi describes as righteous. If Rashbi's words are to be taken seriously, Rabbi Pinḥas is solitary in that he lacks traveling comrades and he is apparently solitary in lacking the companionship of Shekhinah. Yet any expression of such a judgment is absent from the text.[26]

The second and more fundamental way in which the *Zohar* upends its own teaching is by offering it within the context of a walking story. The *Zohar* insists that it is better to stay home than to abandon one's flesh-and-blood wife for the sake of Shekhinah—yet the Companions are ever on the road! Rashbi extols the passions of the "Hills of Eternity," the Upper Female, who can be found only at home, but he sits with his students under "one of the mountain trees."

To consider this second difficulty is to open up to the possibility that Rashbi's solitude, perhaps more than Rabbi Pinḥas's, is in a way the *Zohar*'s concern. And it is Rabbi Pinḥas who delivers a hint that this is so. When Rabbi Pinḥas extols Rashbi's uniqueness, the meaning of Rabbi Pinḥas's remark (along with its correct text) is difficult to determine. He says something like, "Even with the scales and fins of a knot, there are none to open an opening before you." The commentators struggle to make sense of the words. Matt translates: "Even in a skein of scales and fins, no one dares challenge you." Among other possibilities, he suggests that the mythic Leviathan is being alluded to, hinting that "Rabbi Shim'on has mastered not only the holy but also the demonic realm."[27]

Rabbi Shim'on's mastery of the demonic realm is not simply a quantitative expansion of his knowledge and power. As Yehuda Liebes has pointed out, Rashbi, by attaining this mastery, attains messianic standing. The entire world stands upon him. But this status is fraught with loneliness. Liebes reminds us that Leviathan, in the Sages' midrash, is deprived of his mate. And in the Idra, the record of the climactic meeting of Rashbi and his disciples, he greets them with the words, "Until when shall we dwell where only one pillar is our support?" It is Rabbi Shim'on himself who is this solitary pillar, for he is one of the "few who know how to interpret [the story of Creation] in connection with the great sea monster, and, as we have learned, the entire world hangs from its fins."[28]

Rabbi Pinḥas is alone, but seems unperturbed by his aloneness. Liebes reads the opening of the *Idra* as an expression of Rashbi's suffering from his loneliness. What is the solution for him? Liebes writes with reference to our text: "In the *Zohar* (I, 50a) there is a discussion of the problem of a traveler who is distant from his wife. His *tikkun* is to have an erotic union with the *Shekhina*, which is precisely Rabbi Simeon's *tikkun* in the *Idra*."[29]

But Rashbi's solution, as explained by Liebes, takes us only so far in settling the difficulties the *Zohar* has raised. I have argued that one should not characterize the relationship between the traveler and Shekhinah as one of "erotic union," although this is a common conception, shared by Liebes and others.[30] As we have seen, the relationship is rather one of a chaperone than of a lover. Furthermore, while Rashbi may have been blessed with the ultimate experience of union at his death, we are left mystified by the situation of the rest of the zoharic fellowship, who are constantly on the road rather than in their homes.[31] Something is not right with the relationship between the *Zohar*'s ideal theory and the Companions' real practice.

Is the *Zohar* aware of this dissonance? It would be strange to imagine that this text, which introduces what will become an insistent motif in the rest of the *Zohar*, is oblivious to the tension it creates as it unites its mystical teaching about the primacy of the home with such an incongruous narrative frame, on the road, under the mountain trees.

The pressure of this difficulty pushes us to seek a new understanding of the words offered right before this text begins. From the beginning of its discussion of Genesis, the *Zohar* had devoted itself to explicating the esoteric meaning of the verses about the six days of creation, of Shabbat, and of the creation of Adam and Eve. Rabbi Shim'on teaches that these verses are not about this earthly world or about human beings at all. Instead, they describe the mystery of the Divine Male and Female and their union with each other. This union is imagined as deeply erotic and fully correspondent with the human sexual experience, for which, in the *Zohar*'s view, the Divine is not a reflection but a paradigm. But, in wedding this imagery to the biblical story of human arousal and seduction, Rabbi Shim'on also must allow for the surprising possibility that these troubling propensities exist in the divine realm as well as in the imperfect human sphere. Shocked, Rabbi Ele'azar asks, "If this [series of explications] is so, by what means can we establish, Above, the evil impulse that grasps for the female?" His father, Rabbi Shim'on, assures him: "We have already been aroused [about this].

They are above and they are below, the good inclination and the evil inclination. The good inclination to the right and the evil inclination to the left. And the left, above, grasps for the Female, to bond with her as one, in body, as it is written, 'His left hand is under my head' [Song of Sol. 2:6]. . . . Thus are these matters explicated above and below."[32]

Rashbi asserts that it is entirely correct to posit the presence of some sort of evil inclination within the Godhead. Somehow this is a necessary result of the crucial role played by arousal, which is essential in the creative unfolding of the Divine, of the Divine as Torah, and of the revelation of this Torah through Rashbi and his disciples.[33] The apprehension of the presence of this shocking element within the Divine is, itself, accomplished through arousal, "We have already been aroused . . ."[34] With this statement, the zoharic discussion is brought to its climax. No further explanation is given. Our arousal is sufficient to guarantee its cogency.

The next set of teachings is our own walking text, starting with Rashbi and his students traveling on the road. But before we begin that text, the *Zohar* offers a short comment. The text and its Aramaic terms are uncertain. Matt reads the phrases as a continuation of Rashbi's last statement and translates: "So until here words are interpreted above and below. From here on, words with a residue of tar, interpretable by tiny children. By this the Companions have already been aroused."[35]

What does Rashbi means by "until here" and what lies ahead, as we proceed "from here on"? What two areas are being demarcated by Rashbi's distinction, and what is the distinction that is being made? Commentators have generally assumed that it is the Genesis text that is indicated. Matt, basing himself on traditional authorities, notes: "So until here. . . . Perhaps meaning: until this point in Genesis (3:6), the verses apply both on the earthly plane and on the sefirotic plane. From here on, they apply primarily on the corporeal level (as indicated by 'a residue of tar') and their interpretation requires no profound insight." In this reading, Rabbi Shim'on differentiates between the very first chapters of the Torah and the rest of the Torah with regard to their esoteric meaning. The first chapters, read correctly, describe the creation of the Creator, while the following verses are about human interrelationships and human relations to God. But the split is not so neat, neither in the Torah, nor in the *Zohar*'s discussions of the verses. Some subsequent verses have already been discussed in the *Zohar*. Earlier discussions sometimes deal with human matters, and the later discussions do sometimes delve into esoteric matters of theosophy. Furthermore, in what sense is the interpretation of the later verses accessible to "children"? The *Zohar*'s discussions, even if not about theosophical matters, are hardly superficial and facile. Moreover, what is the meaning of the second reference to the Companions' arousal? What is the cause of the arousal? Is it the subsequent biblical verses? Is it the perception of the distinction between the two biblical sections? And what is the result of their arousal? Where does it find expression?

But what if this statement does not refer to the biblical text, but rather to the *Zohar*'s own text? It is possible to read these lines as an editorial comment. "Until here" we have heard teachings presented in a disembodied way. From the start of the *Zohar*'s treatment of Genesis until page 31a, all teachings are mentioned anonymously. The mystical fellowship is not mentioned, nor is any spatial or temporal context given to these teachings.[36] From then on, Rabbi Shim'on is in conversation with Rabbi Ele'azar and with eight Associates, Rabbis Yose, Yehudah, Yitzḥaq, Abba, Ḥiyya, Ḥizqiyah, Aḥa, and Yeisa (Sava).[37] But their environment is never mentioned. It is only when we begin our first walking story that we have a *Sitz im Leben* for a zoharic collection of teachings. That context is the gritty world of travel on the road. It is not the home, the synagogue, the *Idra*, or the study hall.

Thus, this editorial comment does not refer to the biblical text. It refers to the *Zohar*'s own shift from a classical presentation of religious teachings, given anonymously or in formalized dialogues between disembodied sages, to a presentation that places the teachings in a landscape and in a narrative. The *Zohar* compares this new narrative material to the dregs of tar scraped from the bottom of a pot. The early commentator Shim'on Lavi explains the image:

> *Zuta* is the turbid, sedimentary bottom of a container. . . . And *zifta* is of the term *zefet* [tar]. And it is already known that tar sap is the lowliest and smelliest of all tree saps, and the blackest and most disgusting in odor, so much so

> that anyone who makes a forgery of anything and removes it from its purity is called a counterfeiter [*m'zayyef*—smearer of tar] from the term for tar [*zefet*].
>
> The intention in this is that, until here matters have derived from the Work of Creation. It is necessary to speak of them by way of mystery, in the World of Emanation. From here on it speaks of the lower world, the world of tangible nature, which is like the dregs and detritus and spoilage in comparison with the supernal. And permission to speak about it is given to the infants who suckle from their mother's breasts, to use a metaphor, for matters from here on are self-explanatory and there is no danger in them.[38]

Tar is a disagreeable material because of its dark color and bad odor.[39] This mixture is an apt reflection of negative qualities of this world. Still, as a coating it has protective qualities.[40] The protection that Rashbi affords his disciples, and all humanity, is his mastery of this dark, repugnant side for the sake of ultimate union with the side of Light and Love. While the lower world may be the topic of the rest of the verses in the biblical story of Creation, it is also the topic of Rashbi's next discourse. Moreover, it is its explicit context. The expression of these words of Torah is immediately located in a landscape, along the road, under mountain trees, the natural source of tar. And the teaching is, when thought through along with its context, a murky mix of inspiring ideals and frustrating failures to realize those ideals in this lower realm of the everyday. The Companions are extolled as "those who enter and go out," a reference to the rabbinic term used to describe successful traversal of mystical experiences.[41] Yet, on the more mundane level, they are literally the ones who do not stay at home or in the study hall. They are ever leaving, going out to walk on the road. From the point of view of the ideal, this situation can only seem faulty. To accept the situation as necessary is to recognize that our pure dreams of harmonious union are permanently tarred with the stain and smell of dissonance and separation.

The exalted status of the Companions cannot be maintained from this perspective. Instead of referring to the students who are privy to these teachings as "the enlightened," the *Zohar* calls them "tiny children."

Or does the *Zohar* mean to refer, not to the Companions themselves, but to Rabbi Pinḥas? He, along with the Companions, is the innocent and enthusiastic audience for these teachings. But he does not seem to take their import to heart. He does not adopt the lessons of the Rashbi's lecture, apparently because he is oblivious of the dregs of tar clinging to and besmirching them.

The Companions, on the other hand, live in the consciousness of this contradiction, and they pick themselves up and walk. They "have already been aroused."

CHAPTER 2

Walking with God

Orientation and Disorientation

Mircea Eliade's *History of Religious Ideas* opens with a description of how a human being, once s/he is identifiable as such, is primordially situated in the world:

> It is sufficient to recall that the vertical posture already marks a transcending of the condition typical of the primates. Uprightness cannot be maintained except in a state of wakefulness. It is because of man's vertical posture that space is organized in a structure inaccessible to the prehominians: in four horizontal directions radiating from an "up"–"down" central axis. In other words, space can be organized around the human body as extending forward, backward, to right, to left, upward, and downward. It is from this original and originating experience . . . that the different methods of *orientatio* are developed; for it is impossible to survive for any length of time in the vertigo brought on by disorientation. This experience of space oriented around a "center" explains the importance of paradigmatic divisions and distributions of territories, agglomerations, and habitations and their cosmological symbolism.[1]

The *Zohar*, following earlier rabbinic teachings, understands that this human orientation to the world must be rooted in an apprehension of an even more primal, divine reality. It sees one of Judaism's most basic ritual practices, the commandment to recite the *Sh'ma*, the declaration of the oneness of God, as a call to apprehend this unified sense of orientation: "One who prolongs saying 'One' is required to establish the Holy Blessed One as King above and below and to the four directions of the world. This is the meaning of 'One.'"[2]

The commandment to reaffirm and reestablish this apprehension and this orientation seems to both affirm and challenge Eliade's contention that "it is impossible to survive for any length of time in the vertigo brought on by disorientation." On the one hand, the importance of sustaining this orientation is clear from this command. On the other hand, the continuous need to renew it would seem to indicate that disorientation is a constant threat if not a constant reality.

The biblical record goes even further. The Bible gives an account of the first moment at which humans experienced the Divine after losing their innocence. As described in Genesis (3:8–9), it is a moment of crisis experienced by both parties through a sense of spatial disorientation. Adam and Eve hear the sound of God "taking a walk in the Garden in the breeze of the [waning] day," and, in panic, they hide. The contrast is established between God's leisurely and apparently innocent stroll in His garden, indicative of a sure, satisfied sense of ownership of the place, and the fearful scurrying of the human couple, betraying a guilty sense of trespass. The human loss of a sure sense of place is devastatingly emphasized when God asks Adam and Eve, "Where are you?"[3] The implications of that moment are drawn out in the rest of the Bible.

Medieval readers of the Torah understood that the redemptive vision of their tradition would necessitate a return to that primeval situation and its repair. Rashi paraphrases a rabbinic midrash on the biblical verse so as to highlight this point. The verse reads: "And I shall walk along in your midst, and I shall be your Almighty God and you shall be a nation of mine" (Lev. 26:12). Rashi comments: "I will stroll with you in the Garden of Eden as one of you and you will not be taken aback by Me."[4] Thus God's walk in the Garden, originally planned to proceed with human accompaniment, will finally be realized.

We find a mystical exposition of this view in the words of Joseph of Hamadan, identified by Yehuda Liebes as a member of the zoharic circle. His vision of the End of Days imagines the righteous welcoming the sound of God's skipping over the mountains and hills (from Song of Sol. 2:8): "When they see His light and that holy voice issues from the Garden of Eden, as it was with Adam, as it is written, 'I heard your voice in the Garden' [Gen. 3:10]—then the righteous, as they are aroused and hear the voice of the Holy Blessed One, will say, 'This is the voice of my Beloved Who is coming.'" Adam's moment of dread at hearing the sound of God's walking will be transformed into an eternity of joy.[5]

The image of walking with, or before, God is applied by the Torah to such exemplary and pious individuals as Noah, Abraham, Isaac, and the enigmatic Enoch.[6] It remained a yearning recited in Psalms: "I will walk before God in the land of the living."[7] For the common Israelite, the aspiration was a bit more limited. If one could not presume to walk with God, one could hope to fulfill the call to speak words concerning the love of God "while dwelling at home and while you walk on the road."[8] It is plausible, therefore, to assume that, with the final redemption as yet unattained, there would be a tendency to imbue the activity of walking with a pre-redemptive or quasi-redemptive significance. Was this the intent of the *Zohar*, as it multiplied its allusions to walking, its discussions of this act, and most pertinently, its references to the regular walking of the Companions? Is the zoharic "walking story" a reflection of a mystical practice of the medieval kabbalists who influenced or composed the discourses that were collected to form the *Zohar*?

The Walking Stories and the Traditional Commentators

A number of traditional readers of the *Zohar* have explained the Companions' perambulations as having some kind of religious, spiritual, or mystical meaning. Before examining their claims, I must first define what I mean when I refer to the *Zohar*'s "walking stories."

THE *ZOHAR*'S WALKING STORIES

The "walking stories" do not encompass all the stories of the *Zohar*, but they include stories of "meetings on the road with exalted, mythical figures, next to travel stories whose destination is actual: a *brit-milah*, visiting the sick, learning Torah. Many stories describe the potential dangers that might threaten the fellowship traveling on the road, and others describe miraculous events (stories of being saved from death) or adventures of journeys and daring ascents up a mountain or the entry into a cave."[9] Whatever the content or genre of the ensuing story, a walking story is a text that is introduced by the walking motif. The most striking manifestation of this motif is in the repetitive appearance of the phrase "Rabbi A (and Rabbi B) was (were) going[10] on the road."

But I must clarify that not every story that seems to begin in this way is an example of the "walking story" phenomenon. For example, a text that tells us, " Rabbi A went to see Rabbi B and heard some teaching there" is not relevant to our topic.[11] In such a text, the fleeting mention that Rabbi A has gone somewhere is not, in and of itself, noteworthy. That is the conventional way that texts quickly and efficiently place their characters into the context necessary to get to their point. The movement could have been from one side of the *beit midrash* to another, from one room to another, from next door or from across the country. In such a story, the report of the movement of Rabbi *X* conveys to us an intention: Rabbi A goes somewhere because he wants to hear what Rabbi B has to teach, and, presumably, so should we. Movement signals motivation. This is a conventional narrative usage that is not unique. It is also not so plentiful in the *Zohar* that we are compelled to account for it. The realization that the *Zohar* has a very unique narrative framework, and that the framework consists of depictions of Rashbi and the Associates walking around, does not derive from texts of that type. What distinguishes the walking stories is that their apparently unexceptional motif is used repeatedly in ways that subvert the conventional expectations the motif calls forth.

All in all, there are 125 "walking stories" in the *Zohar* proper.[12] There are another 33 in the other strata.[13] The statement "Rabbi A (and Rabbi B) was (were) going on the road," or something similar, appears in 72 texts in the main body of the *Zohar* and in another 14 texts in the *Midrash ha-Ne'elam* and *Zohar Ḥadash*. In addition, there are many other stories and texts that indicate that the content of the text records what transpired while Rabbis were traveling. There are 29 texts in the *Zohar* that have a sage going from one place to another, and 5 more such texts in other strata.[14] In 15 texts in the *Zohar,* the sage is going to see another sage or a family member, with another 5 in other strata.[15] Occasionally, a text relates an experience that transpires while sages travel in the wilderness.[16] There is some overlap between all these categories. Thus we find, "Rabbi Yehudah and Rabbi Yitzḥaq were walking on the road from Bet Meron to Sepphoris,"[17] mentioning both "walking on the road," and also indicating the start and goal of the trip. Or we find, "Rabbi Yehudah was going from Qapotqiya to Lod to see Rashbi,"[18] giving us the route and also the purpose of the trip.

In many zoharic texts, however, this information is lacking, so that the travel motif is present as a mere generality. Indeed, even in texts where there seems to be some specificity in describing the direction, locale, or purpose of the walking, the expectations raised by these additional elements are very often thwarted, frustrated or subverted. Of these 29 texts in the body of the *Zohar* that tell us that a sage was intending to reach a certain place, he actually reaches his destination in only three instances. No one reaches his destination in the 5 texts found in the other zoharic strata. Among stories of those who set out to visit another sage, rather more than half don't make it in the *Zohar* itself[19] (though 4 of the 5 texts found in *Midrash ha-Ne'elam* and *Sitrei Torah* report a successful arrival).[20] Moreover, the texts are not at all concerned with this situation. These are not stories from Kafka or Agnon that chronicle the frustration of the designs of their protagonists. Here there is no discussion of frustration or failure. The lack of closure seems to be of no concern to the zoharic authorship. We must conclude from this that the conventional use of depiction of motion to stand for expression of motivation is not what the *Zohar* is doing.[21]

With what, then, are the texts concerned? They depict one or more rabbis walking along. Sometimes what follows is a story that tells of actions done by the rabbi/s or of some sight they see or some experience they undergo. But such texts are a distinct minority of the total. There are only 14 texts that can be described as narratives lacking substantial content devoted to explicating the Torah. There are another 8 texts that have much Torah discussion, but that also incorporate significant narrative content. That leaves over 100 texts devoted to Torah teachings, couched within the context of the rabbis' traveling. As can be seen from parallels of zoharic walking stories cited by contemporary kabbalists,[22] it is entirely possible to extract the teachings and discussions from the context of travel. But the *Zohar*, of course, does not do this. The *Zohar* seems to be saying that there is a connection between the Associates' teachings of Torah and their walking on the road. Indeed, it reinforces this message in 28 of these texts, in which one of the traveling Associates makes an explicit appeal to say words of Torah while traveling: "Said Rabbi Abba: 'Let us open portals of Torah, for it is the hour and time to set ourselves [*le'itat'qena*] on our way.'"[23] In another instance, we find: "Rabbi Ele'azar said to his father: 'The way is set [*metuqana*] before us; we wish [need] to hear words of Torah.'"[24]

Indeed, commenting on the zoharic story introduced by this last citation, Shim'on Lavi states: "Wherever Rabbi Shim'on went, the Associates would go with him, for their walking was not for the sake of business but, rather, to be alone and be involved in Torah."[25] But the walking stories cannot be explained in this way alone, if only because Rashbi travels in only 25 texts of 125 in the main part of the *Zohar* and in 1 text of 33 in the other strata.[26] There are thus numerous texts in which the Associates walk along without Rashbi.

WALKING ALONE OR TOGETHER?

What is the purpose of their walking together? Regarding another story, Shim'on Lavi remarks: "They, peace be upon them, would always walk on the road in fellowship so as to occupy themselves with Torah."[27] The fellowship of the Associates affords them the opportunity to learn Torah together. Lavi makes this point in *Ketem Paz*, his commentary on *Zohar*, apropos of a story that opens with a rabbi apparently traveling on his own:[28]

> Rabbi Ḥizqiyah was walking from Qapotqiya to Lod.[29]
>
> Rabbi Yeisa encountered him. He said to him, "I am amazed at you for being by yourself. For haven't we learned that a person should not go out on the road alone?"
>
> He said to him, "There is a certain youth who is going with me and he is coming behind me."
>
> He said to him, "And I wonder about that. How could the one walking with you be someone with whom you cannot talk words of Torah? Haven't we learned that anyone who goes on the road and doesn't have words of Torah with him is in mortal danger?"[30]
>
> He said to him, "That is certainly so."
>
> Meanwhile the young man arrived.
>
> Rabbi Yeisa said to him, "My son, what place are you from?"

> He said to him, "From the city of Lod. And I heard that this wise person was going there and I devoted myself to his service and to walk with him."
>
> He said to him, "My son, do you know words of Torah?"
>
> He said to him, "Yes I do, for Father taught me from the portion dealing with sacrifices and I listened in on what he spoke with my brother, who is older than I."
>
> Rabbi Yeisa said to him, "My son, tell me."[31]

Lavi reads this story as a straightforward declaration of the importance of learning in a group while on the road. In his reading, the ignorant and negligent Rabbi Ḥizqiyah needs to be confronted by Rabbi Yeisa:

> But this time Rabbi Ḥizqiyah was walking alone and Rabbi Yeisa happened upon him and said, "I am astonished at you, that you are alone, for we have learned, 'A person should not go out on the road alone.'" And he thought that he said this because he had gone out all alone. So he replied that he was waiting for a lad who was coming after him, though he also had not recognized him [the lad] to be a master of Torah. And Rabbi Yeisa responded to him that he did not mean to say to him that he went out alone from a social aspect. Rather he meant that even if many ignoramuses [*rabim 'am ha-'aretz*] would now go out with him, he would still be alone, since there would be no one with whom to speak words of Torah. For we have learned, "One who walks on the road without having words of Torah with him mortally endangers himself," even if many of the ignoramuses should go with him, because it is the Torah which protects a person, not other people. He said to him, "It is certainly so," because he did not know that the lad knew any Torah and he was now happy that Rabbi Yeisa happened upon him. Meanwhile that youth arrived. Rabbi Yeisa said to him, "My son, from what place are you?" He wanted to check whether he was from a city of scholars [*sofrim*] so that he might get from him some new insight that he had heard. For that was his intention in asking him "What city are you from?" Because what would he care what his city was, whether he was from city A or city B?[32]

Lavi's dedication to his conception of the traveling Associates as a group who always go on the road together so as to learn in fellowship requires him to miss much of what happens in this text.

The first element he misses is the playfulness of the text.[33] The narrator plays with the reader. He introduces Rabbi Ḥizqiyah and gives us the detailed information of Rabbi Ḥizqiyah's route, but he withholds the fact that the sage is accompanied by another person. We watch Rabbi Yeisa, from whom this information has likewise been withheld, challenge Rabbi Ḥizqiyah on this score. Rabbi Ḥizqiyah supplies Rabbi Yeisa, and the reader, with the missing information—that there is a young man whose absence from Rabbi Ḥizqiyah's side is only temporary. This does not mollify Rabbi Yeisa, who now enunciates the principle that Lavi accepts as the basic message of the narrative, that one must have company with whom one will study on the road.

This credo of the Associates is readily, if curtly, accepted by Rabbi Ḥizqiyah. He is aware of the principle. Unexplained, so far, is how Rabbi Ḥizqiyah allowed himself to transgress this rule. The soon to be discovered fact that his traveling companion is very much a person with whom one can share Torah does not account for Rabbi Ḥizqiyah's placid reaction to Rabbi Yeisa's lecture—if we accept Lavi's comment that the lad's Torah mastery was hidden from Rabbi Ḥizqiyah as well as from Rabbi Yeisa. However, if we assume that Rabbi Ḥizqiyah has had time to get to know his companion as a Torah scholar, our reading is turned around. Rabbi Ḥizqiyah seems to be playing with Rabbi Yeisa, concealing information that he will allow to unfold in due time. We read the exchange between the two sages as a playful vignette acted out between one calm, knowing character and an ignorant, blustering foil. The playfulness of the text makes us take Rabbi Yeisa and his words a little less seriously. The rule is further undermined when we consider Rabbi Ḥizqiyah's original actions. After we learn that the exemplary lad has taken it upon himself to leave his own town—Lod—in order to meet and accompany Rabbi Ḥizqiyah, on his way from Qapotqiya, we understand that Rabbi Ḥizqiyah has knowingly embarked on this journey alone, without thinking about having any companion, let alone one he can talk with in Torah matters. Yet the text testifies, through the lad, to Rabbi Ḥizqiyah's great stature as a sage. Moreover, the contrast drawn in the first zoharic walking story, analyzed above, between Rabbi Pinḥas, who is not counted among the Companions, and Rashbi and his disciples, who travel together, does not apply here, since both sages are members of this select group. The irony is further compounded when we realize that Rabbi Yeisa himself, despite his criticizing his colleague, is also apparently walking on the road alone, without a Torah companion, for the story tells us that his meeting with Rabbi Ḥizqiyah was accidental.

But Lavi is convinced that there can be no other experience relevant to the Associates than Torah learning while walking in fellowship. Therefore he must next impose his conception upon the apparently innocuous question asked by Rabbi Yeisa of the youth: "What place are you from?" He rhetorically asks, "Because what would he care what his city was, whether he was from city A or city B?" He cannot accept that Rabbi Yeisa may have employed a simple conversational gambit to begin speaking to the lad. Note that Lavi's question is not of the narrator, along the lines of "What purpose would be served by recording an innocuous remark?" We have already noted that Rabbi Yeisa's question elicits information that the reader can use to better picture, and wonder about, the actions of Rabbi Ḥizqiyah. Given the narrative approach adopted in the text until now, we may assume that our own garnering of information is being juxtaposed to and contrasted with the sage's continuing to remain in the dark. The epistemic mastery of the sages is undermined, first—between themselves, second—by the reader, and, finally—and most clearly—by the uninvited youth, who delights them with new Torah insights. To be sure, their priority is reasserted after the youth speaks—through the bestowal of an approving kiss by Rabbi Yeisa: "Rabbi Yeisa came and kissed him and said, 'My, how much good is in your grasp, and we did not know of it!'"[34] In this way, Rabbi Yeisa can admit to his previous ignorance but also assume the role of sage and arbiter of Torah.

So we are left to wonder about the words and actions of these sages. Rather than being a predictable message reinforcing their piety and constant devotion to Torah, the story tells us that the real source of their learning Torah and speaking words of Torah derives from an unexpected young master. Everything works out in the end, but not because of the Associates' programmatic commitment to learning Torah in fellowship on the road. Rather, that commitment must follow after their solitary beginnings and their fortuitous encounters with each other and the lad. It is at that point that the fellowship can begin. Rabbi Yeisa continues: "'Let us turn from the road and join with you.' They walked on. Said Rabbi Ḥizqiyah, 'We will walk this road with the Shekhinah, for it is set before us.' He took hold of the hand of the child [*yenuqa*][35] and they went on."

Read carefully, this text tells us that the elements of traveling and Torah study do not completely overlap. Though it may lead to it, the sages' traveling is not necessarily motivated by the ideal of studying on the road. Still, Rabbi Hizqiyah's last statement tells us that their Torah study had additional significance beyond fulfilling this commandment for these sages. He looks forward to continuing the journey with his compatriots along with the accompaniment of the Shekhinah.[36]

We find the links between Shekhinah, Torah study and walking on the road expressed clearly in the following text which derives from contemplation of the figure of Noah walking before God:

> Rabbi Yose and Rabbi Ḥiyya were walking on the road. Rabbi Yose said to Rabbi Ḥiyya, "Let us open with Torah and say a word." Rabbi Yose opened: "'For God, your Almighty goes walking [*mit'halekh*] within your camp to save you and to place your enemies before you. So let your camps be holy, and let Him not see in you anything immoral [*'ervat davar*], for God will turn away from you' [Deut. 23:15]. 'For God, your Almighty goes walking [*mit'halekh*]'—'walks' [*m'halekh*] is what it should say! Rather, it is as it is said 'taking a walk [*mit'halekh*] in the Garden in the breeze of the [waning] day' [Gen. 3:8]. That is the tree from which First Adam ate.[37] *Mit'halekh* is female; *m'halekh* is male. This is who walks before Israel when they were walking in the wilderness, as it is written, 'And God[38] was walking before them by day' [*Exod.* 13:21]. . . . This is who walks before a person when he walks on the road, as it is written, 'Righteousness[39] walks before him as he sets his feet to the road' [Ps. 85:14], and this is the one who walks before a person when he is righteous. And why? 'To save you and to place your enemies before you,' to save a person on the road so that the Other cannot rule him. Therefore a person should guard against his sins and purify himself. What is this purification? That which is written, 'So let your camps be holy [*qadosh*].' Why *qadosh*? Shouldn't it say *qedoshim* [pl.]? Rather, 'your camps be holy' are these limbs of the body by which the body is held together and ordered. Therefore, 'let your camps be holy.' 'And let Him not see in you anything immoral [*'ervat davar*].' What is *'ervat davar*? This is any word about sexual immorality, for such a word God despises more than anything. Since it says *'ervat*—immorality—why [does it say] *davar*—anything/word? It refers rather to those sinners of the world who defile and besmirch themselves with their words that issue from their mouths.

> That is *'ervat davar.* And why all this? Because He walks before you and if you behave thus, right away, 'God will turn away from you.' He will not walk with you, but will turn away from you. Now we who are walking before Him on the road, let us busy ourselves in words of Torah, for the Torah is crowned upon a person's head and the Shekhinah does not leave him."[40]

Rabbi Yose invites his companion to engage in Torah study on the road. But his invitation is embellished with a lengthy explanation and justification, concluding with a reiteration of the invitation. It is as if Rabbi Yose's words of Torah do not count as part of the Torah study Rabbi Yose was calling for. Ibn Lavi, sensing the awkwardness of the text, attempted to offer a psychological insight into Rabbi Yose's state of mind, before reaffirming his conception of the meaning of the *Zohar*'s walking texts:

> Know that Rabbi Yose was always afraid of the dangers of the road, as is seen in the *Zohar* in many places, especially since sometimes he would be occupied with mundane matters, as is brought [out] in that story. . . .[41] And now, also, perhaps his heart was bothered by mundane matters. And bother prevents a person from sleeping and certainly from being occupied with Torah. But in order to meet the requirements of the road—for they, peace be upon them, always would occupy themselves with Torah along the whole way—he said, "Let us open with Torah and say a word," that is, even a little, so as to draw along with him the Shekhinah, who accompanies on the way those who occupy themselves with Torah.[42]

Lavi begins with a sensitive hunch about the mental and emotional life of one of the chief protagonists in the *Zohar*. Lavi speculates that Rabbi Yose may have had a tendency to lose his focus on matters of Torah and think about mundane matters, instead. But, in this case, he forces himself to draw his mind toward Torah, since this is imperative while walking on the road. However, we can discern that Rabbi Yose's extended invitation includes a number of statements that are not quite equivalent to the summary found in *Ketem Paz*.

Rabbi Yose explains that Shekhinah is the divine potency who walked before the Israelites in the wilderness. He then states, "This is who walks before a person when he walks on the road, as it is written, 'Righteousness walks before him as he sets his feet to the road' [Ps. 85:14], and this is the one who walks before a person when he is righteous. And why? 'To save you and to place your enemies before you,' to save a person on the road so that the Other cannot rule him." It is necessary for Shekhinah to walk before Israel in the wilderness in order to afford Israel protection from evil and danger. The wilderness is the realm of the Other Side.[43] In addition, Rabbi Yose says that this protection is necessary for any person who sets out on the road. The implication is that the Other Side inhabits the road as well as the wilderness. We shall have to return to this point. In any case, Shekhinah watches out for people, as long as they do not turn Her away through unrighteousness. We note that so far there is no statement that calls for a theurgical union with Shekhinah through Torah study. Instead, it is posited that Shekhinah will be there for a righteous person,[44] unless that person causes Her to abandon him. How does a person ensure his worthiness of the company of Shekhinah? He must refrain from unclean speech. By this act of self-control, a person will be a holy encampment for Shekhinah and She will not leave in disgust. As Rabbi Yose says, "Because He walks before you and if you behave thus, right away, 'God will turn away from you.'" In this explanation, the Divine Presence is guaranteed, unless it is pushed away by scurrilous or salacious speech.[45] No requirement is yet asserted for engaging in Torah study in order to attract the Shekhinah.

After stating these general facts, Rabbi Yose concludes his invitation by talking specifically about himself and Rabbi Ḥiyya: "Now we who are walking before Him on the road, let us busy ourselves in words of Torah, for the Torah is crowned upon a person's head and the Shekhinah does not leave him." It is only now that Rabbi Yose broaches the idea that learning Torah can play a role in cementing one's relation with Shekhinah. It seems like a suggestion, a good idea: to crown their heads with Torah while they are accompanied by Shekhinah. This is an act and experience that goes beyond the experience of ordinary travelers. It would seem to signify a state beyond mere accompaniment by Shekhinah. This is a theurgic act of unifying the female and male potencies within the Divine.[46]

We also notice that, regarding the Companions, Rabbi Yose has reversed the order of precedence in the human/divine walking. While Shekhinah walks before Israel in the desert and before the individual traveler, when Rabbi Yose refers to the Companions he says that it is they who walk before God. Perhaps this is an expression of the complex dynamic that effects a series of gender reversals in the process of the theurgical act. As Elliot Wolfson explains: "the erotic conjunction of the mystic with the Shekhinah transforms the latter from a passive female to an active male and the former from an active male to a passive female. To arouse the supernal male, the female must assume a role that is characteristically masculine. . . . The ultimate goal of the mystic's interpretive efforts is the union of the masculine and feminine aspects of the divine, but this union results in the restoration of the latter into the former."[47]

Analysis of this text, used as a basis by traditional readers to explain the walking motif of the *Zohar*, presents us, instead, with two results that make the repetitive presence of this motif obdurately problematic. First of all, we have seen that the Shekhinah is understood to be present and protective of anyone on the road, as long as the person does not drive Her away through inappropriate speech. Her accompaniment may be more in the nature of a parallel protective Presence rather than as a Presence with whom one may mystically unite. We have also seen that Shekhinah's accompaniment can be assured prior to embarking on one's journey through prayer and not on the road, through Torah study.[48]

This proposition seems at odds with the following text: "Rabbi Ele'azar, Rabbi Yitzḥaq and Rabbi Yehudah were walking on the road. Said Rabbi Ele'azar, 'It is now time to walk with the Shekhinah, for the Shekhinah will not dwell upon us except through words of Torah.'"[49] Here the necessity of Torah study to draw the presence of the Shekhinah is explicit. Apparently this effect of Torah study especially applies to the Companions, for they can exceed the experience of most people. They can go beyond the experience of being accompanied by Shekhinah in that they are uniquely able to have and produce a higher spiritual experience, the unification of upper and lower, male and female aspects of God, accomplished through their own transformational ability to constitute the "face of Shekhinah."[50] To effect this transformation, the Companions must study Torah.

Yet the question remains: This activity may be supremely significant, but what has it to do with walking? More precisely, although this activity may take place while the Companions are on the road, in what sense is it necessary to be on the road in order to engage in this theurgic unification? We have not yet understood from this text in what sense being on the road plays a part in the unification.

It seems, rather, that the study of Torah, itself, is the crucial element to this practice. Indeed, the *Zohar* often extols the practice of rising at midnight to study Torah in order to effect divine union. Wolfson refers to this practice when he writes that it is necessary, in order to fully appreciate the *Zohar*, to recognize the lived reality that produced it, a reality that included certain rituals performed by the group of kabbalists who produced the *Zohar*:

> On[e] such ritual—indeed, perhaps the central one, which informed the entire mystical community—involved the midnight study of Scripture in light of the emerging theosophy.[51] This was the stage for the narrative drama that unfolds in the pages of the *Zohar*. The mythology of the *Zohar* is anchored in a historical reality. The study group produced the anthology of texts called *Sefer ha-Zohar* on the basis of the claim that the ones who were in the group were ecstatically illuminated by the divine splendor in the moment of interpreting scriptural verses. The common bond of this mystical fraternity was the inspired exegesis of Scripture. Furthermore, the study meetings were endowed with theurgical significance, inasmuch as the masculine and feminine aspects of the Godhead were unified by means of kabbalistic discourse.[52]

The ritual of midnight Torah study makes the walking stories problematic because it shows us that it is possible to separate the strands of the presence of the Shekhinah, theurgic unification, and Torah study from walking on the road. But it also is suggestive of another possible perspective through which to consider this phenomenon. A kabbalist and commentator on the *Zohar* who struggled with this question was Rabbi Moshe Cordovero (RaMaK). Like Lavi, RaMaK saw a strong connection between going on the road and effecting divine unification. He writes "that the special quality of the road [*s'gulat ha-derekh*] is to couple the Shekhinah with the wayfarers—in the *Tiqqunim* they explained that this is called 'guarding the path [*sh'mirat ha-derekh*]'- and, of course, those who study Torah, as it is written, 'Righteousness walks before him as he sets his feet to the road'" (Ps. 85:14).[53] Commenting on a walking story about Rabbi Ele'azar, he writes, "And regarding Rabbi Ele'azar going out on the road, that was not for worldly matters, but rather travelers went for the sake of unification [*l'shem yiḥud*]."[54]

These ideas are repeated in another comment by RaMaK. The *Zohar* incorporates a number of teachings within a walking story about Rabbi Yose and Rabbi Ḥiyya. It begins: "Rabbi Yose and Rabbi Ḥiyya were going on the road and a donkey driver was driving behind them.[55] Said Rabbi Yose to Rabbi Ḥiyya, 'We should devote ourselves to studying words of Torah, for, indeed, the Holy Blessed One walks before us. Therefore it is time to effect a repair [*tiqqun*] for Him through us on this road.'"[56]

RaMaK repeats that walking on the road is an act of unification, writing, "'The Holy Blessed One walks before us,' this is the protection of the path [*sh'mirat ha-derekh*]. And it is written, 'Righteousness walks before him' [Ps. 85:14], so that She should unite with the righteous one through words of Torah, and this is what they meant when they said 'It is time . . .'" But then he broaches a new idea as he continues: "and possibly they were wandering on the roads [*mitgarshim ba-d'rakhim*] for no purpose [*lo l'shum takhlit*] except to wander in the exile ['*ela l'hitgaresh ba-galut*] that atones for sins. And therefore their Torah on the road became primary for them."[57]

RaMaK sees the Companions engaged in a ritual practice that became a significant part of his own mystical life, the practice of *gerushin*.[58] However, impelled by the personal and hermeneutical requirements of his own mystic quest, RaMaK, in his own development of this practice, moved away from the zoharic model. As Wolfson writes, "Cordovero effectively inverted the zoharic teaching—which, incidentally, provides the mystical backdrop for the narrative of the *Zohar*—that the Shekhinah accompanies the righteous in all their wanderings in exile. Paradoxically, according to Cordovero, by means of the *gerushin*, the 'banishments' or 'exile wanderings' from place to place, the kabbalists were elevated above their own state of exile, for they gave support to the weakened Shekhinah and received mystical illumination in the form of innovative scriptural interpretations."[59]

This inversion of the zoharic teaching is the result of Cordovero's attempt to be faithful to the *Zohar* as he read it. For Cordovero, the practice of wandering begins with an initial acceptance of suffering and privation by the kabbalist in the hope of ameliorating the divine suffering, and in so doing, ending up in the unlocking of new insights into Torah. The emphasis on suffering as a basis for *gerushin* derives from the influence of the *Tiqqunei Zohar* on Cordovero's reading of the *Zohar.*[60] But the walking motif in the *Zohar* itself is lacking in that basic element of suffering. On the contrary, the texts are imbued with a sense of excitement, enjoyment and liveliness.[61]

In practice, as well, Cordovero's version of *gerushin* departed from the *Zohar*'s model. Cordovero and his companions embarked on walks, as did their zoharic predecessors. But their walks tended towards a culmination at a sacred location—a grave of a saint, a synagogue or study hall.[62] It was in these sanctified places that the kabbalists were granted their illuminations. But the *Zohar* knows of no such itinerary. As indicated above, the zoharic texts are emphatically characterized by their lack of a culminating terminus. It is in the frequently repeated phrase "as they were walking [*'ad de-havu azli*]"[63] that the narrative and kabbalistic content of the walking texts is revealed, and it is there that the motif's significance must be sought.

Nevertheless, while RaMaK's own ideological and spiritual drives propelled him out of the zoharic framework, there lies within his tentative comment, cited above, what may be a truer intuition into the meaning of the walking motif in the *Zohar*. What if RaMaK had slowed down, as it were, and paused after his speculation that the Companions went out wandering "for no purpose, but just to wander"? Perhaps, in not being able to find the proper symbolic or mythic purpose or equivalence for this motif, we have stumbled on its essential lack of symbolic or mythic purpose. Perhaps the meaning of the motif must be sought in a more literal, physical realm. This would mean that the *Zohar* sought to record, alongside the mystical and spiritual teachings of the Companions, the recurrent fact that all this transpired as these men traversed space, earthly space, in the most earthly way. Instead of trying to subsume this motif into the zoharic complex of kabbalistic myth, symbol, and praxis, a complex to which this motif has clearly been appended, perhaps we should try to accept the motif on its own terms, as a statement of spatial orientation and production.

The Repression and Resurgence of the Mundane

Let us entertain the possibility that the walking stories are in some way an acknowledgment of the stubborn persistence of the mundane realm in spite of the sanctifying, all-encompassing power of the Divine, and in spite of the intense and exclusive devotion of the mystic to that vision. It must be acknowledged, however, that it has been difficult to accept such a possibility. This difficulty is reflected both in commentaries on the *Zohar* as well as in the *Zohar* itself.

For example, we read:

> Rabbi Shim'on went out to take care of his estate business.[64] He happened upon Rabbi Abba, Rabbi Ḥiyya, and Rabbi Yose. When he saw them he said, "New insights in Torah are necessary here." The three sat.[65] When he wanted to go, each one opened a verse.[66]

The text is explicit in telling us that Rashbi went on his trip alone. It also says that the purpose was to deal with mundane matters. By chance he meets some of the Companions, and he declares the need for new Torah insights. But when the Associates sit down, no Torah is reported. When Rashbi has to leave them, each one explicates a verse in praise of their master. The continuation of their journeys is not reported.

Lavi was struck by the way this text upended his conceptions regarding Rashbi and his disciples. His response was to explain:

> This means that few were the times that Rashbi, peace be upon him, would go out to walk outside the city. For he was always occupied with Torah in the *beit ha-midrash*. So the one time he went out was mentioned in their discourse as a wonder. And it said that immediately his three comrades happened upon him, so that his heart would not turn to vanity. . . . And undoubtedly Rabbi Shim'on told them new insights while at that place, since he said, when he saw them, "New insights in Torah are necessary here," but they did not expostulate here on what transpired among them from those

> new insights that he told them. Instead it only mentioned what each one said at their farewell, because "a person should not depart from his master without permission and from words of Torah."[67]

Lavi feels forced to project his own amazement onto the zoharic text. The picture of a solitary Rashbi embarking on a business trip could not be accepted as usual. But, in reaction, Lavi's explanation leads him to undermine his own construct of the traveling Master and disciples by stating that Rashbi hardly ever left the study hall.[68] Is every walking text an exception then?

Lavi's remarks show how a truly sensitive reader may falter when he attempts to make differing texts adhere to an all-encompassing explanatory theory. There is no doubt that the traveling Associates' theurgic Torah study is reported by the *Zohar*. There is no doubt that the presence of the Shekhinah is a major concern of theirs in many texts.[69] But none of this is necessary or adequate to explain this walking text and others. Were it the function of this motif to convey the theurgical significance of Torah study while on the road, we would still remain mystified by the overabundance of the motif, repeated too many times to be making a point that could adequately be communicated in far fewer than 125 instances.

The fleeting mention of the mundane purpose of Rashbi's trip is quickly passed over by the rest of the zoharic text, and it was easily suppressed by its traditional commentators. But the mundane is ubiquitous. If given the chance, it will immediately reappear. In the mystic quest, it will be necessary to engage those reappearances again and again.

The Case of Rabbi Yose

In general there is very little material in the *Zohar* from which to draw any character portraits of the Associates. Nevertheless, as we have seen,[70] Rabbi Lavi felt able to call attention to a personality trait of one of the prominent Companions, Rabbi Yose, claiming that he was prone to losing his focus on matters of Torah. This suggestion is based on the following walking story:

> Rabbi Yose went on the road and Rabbi Aḥa bar Ya'aqov went with him. While they were walking, Rabbi Yose was silent and thought about mundane

> matters. But Rabbi Aḥa thought about matters of Torah. As they were walking, Rabbi Yose saw a snake running after him.
>
> Rabbi Yose said to Rabbi Aḥa: Do you see that snake running after me?
>
> Rabbi Aḥa said to him: I don't see it.
>
> Rabbi Yose ran, the snake after him. Rabbi Yose fell and blood spurted and flowed out of his nose. He heard that they were saying, "Only you have I known of all the families of the earth, [therefore I will hold you accountable for all your sins]" [Amos 3:2].
>
> Said Rabbi Yose: If this is how it is for only one moment, how much more so for one who abandons Her completely!
>
> He opened and said: "For God your Almighty has blessed you in all the works of your hands; He knows your walking" [Deut. 2:7]. . . . "Who had you walk along . . . snake, viper, and scorpion . . . " [Deut. 8:15]. Why are "snake, viper" here? It is for them to mete out punishment on Israel any time they separate from the Tree of Life, as it is written, "for that is your life and the length of your days" [Deut. 30:20].[71]

This story is told in order to support the teaching that immediately precedes it. Rabbi Yitzḥaq explains that the suffering of the Jewish people is actually a sign of divine favor. It is only because God cares enough to expect Israel to observe the Torah that, when they do not, they are punished. The prooftext is the verse from Amos: "Only you have I known of all the families of the earth, [therefore I will hold you accountable for all your sins]." The story is then told of Rabbi Yose, who had to learn this lesson the hard way. His traveling companion Rabbi Aḥa bar Ya'aqov walks along while pondering matters of Torah. But Rabbi Yose walks along thinking of everyday things. He is attacked by a poisonous snake. Meanwhile, his friend is secure because of his Torah study. After he is saved from the snake, he repeats the verse from Amos mentioned right before the story began. The story ends with the citation of other verses that mention walking and snakes. The lesson is clear: walking with God by engaging in Torah study protects one from danger, while abandoning the Torah exposes a person to the perils of the road.

This short and didactic story[72] has a number of humorous elements that belie its simplicity and complicate its message. Rabbi Aḥa is, indeed, safe from the snake. In fact, he does not even see the snake! We find this out by a small pause in the action. Rabbi Yose, who sees the snake "running" (!) after him, does not immediately run away from it. First he asks his companion whether he sees the snake, too. This pause serves in the same way as does the pause in modern cartoons, in which a person mistakenly runs off a cliff but does not fall down immediately. First, he hovers in midair in order for his predicament to fully register in his mind and for the viewer to savor it. Of course, in the cartoon, the end result of the fall will not be fatal. The cartoon character will crash to the ground only to get up, much bruised, but alive enough to go on to the next adventure. In our case, the danger of the snake is highlighted and mitigated by this pause. Because Rabbi Aḥa does not see the snake, he cannot come to Rabbi Yose's assistance. Rabbi Yose is all alone. But the reader may also wonder whether our daydreaming sage is also dreaming up the snake itself, for only he can see it. We might suspect that his fear of the snake is unfounded and his flight unnecessary. But, since the snake is real to him, Rabbi Yose must run away from it. In the end, the snake does not hurt Rabbi Yose. Has he been saved by God? He falls and bloodies his nose all by himself.[73]

While, overall, Rabbi Yose is a major figure in the zoharic oeuvre, experiencing visions,[74] discovering ancient mystical texts,[75] and continually offering important teachings, he serves here as a comic character.[76] Like many comic characters, despite his interactions with others he is essentially alone. Not only is he left alone by Rabbi Aḥa in his time of danger, but he is alone from the start, for, as he walks beside Rabbi Aḥa, each is lost in his own thoughts. The two sages are not walking and studying Torah together. Each is silent and preoccupied with his own concerns. Though this is not the *Zohar*'s ideal, nevertheless, for a moment, Rabbi Yose is alone in the realm of the mundane.

This short and relatively early tale should be coupled with a much later walking story, one of the longest, and richest of them all. It includes extensive homilies and discourses on ethical, religious, and esoteric matters. These teachings, offered by Rabbi Abba and the various sages present, are interrupted with narrative comments. In contrast to traditional and standard treatments of zoharic teachings, our attention will be focused primarily on these narrative elements, rather than on the discourses. The following is an edited quotation, citing and locating certain lines as written, while paraphrasing much of the material of the Associates' teachings:[77]

> [198a] Rabbi Hiya and Rabbi Isaac and Rabbi Yose were walking together on the road when Rabbi Abba met them. Said Rabbi Hiyya—"Certainly the Shekhinah is now among us."

We are not told whence the three friends came. Nor do we know Rabbi Abba's starting point. And we do not know where they are walking to. We may assume that they are walking from different directions, and so it is not clear that they were originally headed in the same direction, let alone going to the same destination. But now they have met and join together. Apparently, the chance meeting of these sages immediately conjures the Divine Presence.[78] We are jolted out of our leisurely stroll by the sudden certainty that, though Shekhinah may not have been present among the three sages until now, Rabbi Abba's fortuitous appearance must now make it so. The exalted and unique status of the Companions is evident.

> When Rabbi Abba met them, he said, "It is written . . ."[79]

The first discourse is Rabbi Abba's. It is a moralistic homily about the dedication of true leaders, upon whom the welfare of the rest of the people depends. Through this simple homily, he gives an embellished expression to his celebration of the Companions, the disciples of Rashbi. There is an evident contrast between the purposeful nature of the Companions' travels, as described in Rabbi Abba's homily, and the open-ended walking, without any specified purpose or destination, of these Companions in this scenario. After Rabbi Abba's salute to them the narrative continues:

> [198b] They walked along together.
> He opened and said . . .[80]

First, through a tiny narrative fragment, the *Zohar* chooses to tell us that the next discourse is not spoken at rest. It is delivered during their walk. We are not told why we must know this. The discourse follows without further pause. Utilizing a verse from the Torah portion in which this zoharic text has been placed, a verse concerning gifts for the Tabernacle, Rabbi Abba again offers a short sermon whose purpose is to sweeten his praise of the Companions with midrashic creativity.

> Rabbi Ḥiyya said, "Let the one who has begun to raise up this gift continue to uplift!" Rabbi Abba opened and said: . . . [81]

There is an artificial quality, reminiscent of courtier-like formality, to Rabbi Hiyya's invitation. Punning on the term for the uplifted gift—*t'rumah*—Rabbi Ḥiyya urges Rabbi Abba to engage in a more uplifting, and apparently more complex discourse. Rabbi Abba's next teaching is five times longer than his previous homily. It could have been a free-standing teaching, easily excerpted from its narrative context of the walking Associates, to stand alone. Instead it is embedded in a jocular exchange between mutually admiring friends.

> [199b] The Companions approached and kissed him on his head.

Again our chain of homilies is halted. The narrator insists on pausing to record the gestures of camaraderie employed and enjoyed by this special fellowship.[82] Furthermore, the words of Torah are insistently not allowed to stand alone. Rather, it is imperative to show that these words are being shared, and that this act of sharing is being appreciated by those receiving the pleasure and illumination of the teachings. Thus these homilies are never allowed to become abstract texts. They are displaced from the rarified realm of Wisdom to become complexes of interpersonal acts of intense speech and intent listening. The interaction recorded so specifically by the *Zohar* is not the intellectual give-and-take of talmudic argument, but, through these narrative interruptions, it becomes an emotional "giving-and-taking" to which the narrator wishes to testify. Thus we are continually drawn away from the timeless record of homiletical teaching and back to the fleeting record of momentary human reactions, which are sometimes collective and sometimes, as we shall see, particular and personal.[83]

> Rabbi Hiyya opened . . . [84]
>
> [201a] Rabbi Abba raised his voice and said: "Woe, Rabban Shim'on! You are alive and I cry for you. I do not cry for you, but I cry for the Companions and I cry for the world. Rabbi Shim'on is like a light of a lamp that

> burns above and below. And with the light that burns below all people of the world are illumined. Woe to the world when this lower light will rise up into the upper light. Who will illumine the Torah's light to the world?"
>
> Rabbi Abba then rose and kissed Rabbi Hiyya, saying: "You were in possession of these thoughts. Hence the Holy Blessed One sent me here to become one of your company. Happy is my portion!"

Having heard Rabbi Ḥiyya credit his teacher, Rabbi Shim'on, as the source of his teaching and as the ultimate arbiter of when and to whom it could be revealed, Rabbi Abba expresses a fear for the future preservation and promulgation of this knowledge after Rashbi is gone.[85] But there is consolation and excitement in the realization that these sages have been vouchsafed these esoteric teachings. This is not only a guarantee of their preservation. It also confirms the exalted status of the Companions. They will be able to illumine the world on their own after Rashbi's passing. If our text has insisted on interrupting its flow of discourses with its narrative miniatures, it also uses such an outburst to certify that this revelatory flow of illumination will not be interrupted permanently by death, not even by the death of Rashbi. The relationship between this world and the divine realm is viewed dialectically. Who stands to lose by Rashbi's death? Will there be a loss to the theurgic unification that only he and his disciples can effect? Or is it this lower world that will be deprived of his insights? Rashbi's power over the Divine is fatally compromised by his mortality. And, despite the importance of the intentional project of the Companions to affect the upper worlds, we are reminded that the Heavens are still in control of the mundane, for the seemingly chance encounter of these Companions has, in fact, been providentially arranged.

> Rabbi Yose opened the verse after him and said: . . .[86]

Rabbi Yose's discourse continues the theme of exalting the Companions even as it adds independent esoteric teachings. In addition, the theme of death, feared by Rabbi Abba as an obstacle to the continued flow of esoteric revelation, is extolled by Rabbi Yose as the goal to be desired by the righteous. This echoes and pushes beyond the opening remarks of Rabbi

Abba, who praised the Companions for their self-sacrifice. The emphasis is shifted away from this world and back up to the world above.

> [203a] Rabbi Abba went and kissed him. After him, Rabbi Isaac opened . . . [He begins a very lengthy exposition of the mystery of Shabbat, "known only to the supernal sages, the Companions."[87] This exposition continues to page 209a.][88]

Rabbi Isaac's discourse continues in the vein established by Rabbi Yose, privileging the spiritual over the mundane, seeking to suffuse and transform the mundane through and into the holy, seeking to collapse spatial extension into mystical concentration.[89]

> [209a] Rabbi Abba and the other Companions rose up and kissed his head. They wept and said: "Happy is our portion in that the Holy Blessed One has prepared this path for us."

This section of the narrative continues to highlight the special status of the Companions. Their self-understanding includes a sense of gratitude for the privilege of having access to the most profoundly esoteric wisdom, as well as delight in that very self-awareness.[90] Weeping, they are emotionally overtaken by this double portion of good fortune.[91]

> Said Rabbi Abba: "The Lord prepared this way for me so that I might join your company. Happy is my portion in having been thus privileged."
>
> Rabbi Abba said to them: "Let me relate to you what I saw. When I set out on my journey today, I saw a light ahead of me, which split into three separate lights. They all went in front of me and then disappeared. I said to myself: 'Assuredly, what I saw was the Shekhinah. Happy is my portion.' And now—those lights that I saw were actually you! Indeed, you are the supernal lights and lamps to shine in this world and the coming world."
>
> Said Rabbi Abba: "Until now I had not known that all these hidden pearls were within your hands. Now that I have seen that these words were said with the positive approval of your master, I know that all these words will ascend today into the Supernal Throne to be taken by the Master of the Countenance[92] to make of them a crown for his Master. And today holy chariots are crowned for the glory of the Throne with these words that were spoken this day."

Rabbi Abba has been the chief dispenser of spiritual wisdom in this colloquy. Now he is impressed when he hears the contributions of the other

Associates. His expression of surprise may mean that he has only recently made their acquaintance. Thus, this story may serve as an account of a constitutive moment in the history of the Fellowship. Rabbi Abba's stature alternates between poles of leadership and discipleship as we swing between noticing his obvious knowledge of esoteric teachings and his interest in joining the circle of Rashbi. We also hear of Rabbi Abba's powers of mystical vision. Yet he and we find out that the meaning of his vision initially eluded him. It was only after and through the accidental meeting of our story that the true interpretation of the vision becomes apparent. The vision was not a theophany, but a prophecy pointing to a divine revelation in human form.

> At this point, he raised his eyes and noticed that the sun had gone down. Said Rabbi Abba, "Let us proceed to that village yonder, as it is the nearest to us in this desert."
>
> So they went there and stayed there overnight.
>
> At midnight Rabbi Abba, with the other Companions, arose in order to study the Torah. Said Rabbi Abba: "Now let us weave discourses that will be made into crowns for the righteous in Paradise, as now is the hour when the Holy Blessed One, and all the righteous in Garden of Eden, listen to the voices of the righteous on earth."
>
> Rabbi Abba opened and said: . . .[93]

While Rabbi Abba praises their unique gift of access to the most esoteric secrets of the Torah, as granted by their teacher, Rashbi, it is he who speaks more than any of the other Companions, despite his explicit invitation to them all to participate. His chance encounter with the other Companions has developed into an opportunity for him to take charge of the group. At the same time that his discourse continues to add dimensions that build the case for the special status of the Companions, the ones who "enter and exit" unharmed,[94] it is he who orchestrates the Companions' movements, their entrances and exits, in response to his awareness of the passing of time and the surrounding geography. Through his offhand remark, we learn that the Companions happen to be walking through a wilderness that is sparsely settled. No explanation is offered for their wandering. Moreover, their Torah discussion continues through the night in the inn, just as it had transpired outside, on the road. The thread of Torah study is continuous, unaffected by its locale. If there is a connection between Torah study and traveling on the road, it is not defined here.

> [214a] Meanwhile, day had dawned. Rabbi Abba said: "Let us rise and walk and offer up praise to the Master of the World." They arose and went and prayed. Afterwards, the Companions returned to him and said to him: "Let him who began conclude the praise. How fortunate is our portion in this road for having merited all this, to crown the Holy Blessed One with secrets of wisdom."

With the dawn, Rabbi Abba calls the Companions to prayer. But an additional element is subtly added. Both in his invitation and in the description of the Comrade's fulfillment of that call to prayer, the *Zohar* adds words meaning "walk" and "go." These words are seemingly dispensable. Rabbi Abba could have said: "Let us rise and offer up praise to the Master of the World." And the story could have continued: "They arose and prayed." Yet the narrator insists on adding this small element of movement through space. Did they each go off to a separate place to pray? Did they all embark upon their journey and start walking?

> Rabbi Abba opened and said: . . .[95]
>
> [214b] Rabbi Abba wept and said,[96] "Alas for the plain folk who do not know about this shame! Alas for the punishment to all who wish to go into a coffin. For no one should go into a coffin except for the righteous person who knows of himself, and it is known of his body, that he did not sin regarding the covenant . . ."[97]

This is another expression of the unique status of the Companions. Only they are eligible to be placed within a coffin for burial. The six-sided spatial enclosure echoes the Ark of the Covenant, a manifestation of Shekhinah. Burial in a coffin signals one's meriting entrance into the embrace of Shekhinah. If weeping has a mystical effect in some places in the *Zohar*, this does not seem to be one of them. This appears to be a more mundane expression of sorrow on behalf of Shekhinah, shamed and misused by the ignorant plain folk whose desire to be buried in a coffin derives from prosaic, solely physical, material, and social concerns.

> All the Companions came and kissed him.
>
> When they came to Rabbi Shim'on[98] and repeated to him all the expositions [*sidru milin*][99] they had heard during that walk, he opened and said:

> "'But the path of the righteous is as the light of dawn, that shines more and more unto the perfect day'" (Prov. 4:18).
>
> [215a] "This verse," he said, "has been already expounded in a way, but there is still a deeper truth underlying it."[100]

Rashbi expounds upon the meaning of the biblical phrase "path of the righteous." The contextual meaning of that phrase is in the metaphorical use of the term "path." As is common, the word does not refer to a physical road but to a "way" of life.[101] Yet Rashbi's choice of this topic is inspired by the purely physical meaning of the term. The trigger for his teaching is literally the path walked by the Companions.

> And to you, supernal righteous ones, the holy supernal way happened [was prepared] for you and your [visiting] path was on it and excellent supernal words were presented before the Ancient of Days. How fortunate is your portion!"
>
> Rabbi Shim'on opened and said: . . .[102]
>
> [215b] "And you, supernal holy ones, each one of you has been filled with the spirit of Wisdom, set in wholeness through mysteries of Wisdom. For the Holy Blessed One desired you and laid His hands upon you. How fortunate is my portion that my eyes have seen this and seen the wholeness of Wisdom's spirit within you!'
>
> He opened and said: . . .[103]
>
> [217b] "And you, Companions, behold, the Holy Blessed One frolics now with those words you uttered, crowned in that way. And you are standing now before your Master as represented by your own holy images. For when I saw you and looked well at your visages, I saw that you were stamped with the secret essence of Adam.[104] And I know that your visage is destined for Above. So are the righteous invited in the time to come to become known to all with their own eyes, and to see the Holy Face, before the entire world. This is as it is written, 'All that see them will recognize them, for they are the blessed seed of God' [Isa. 61:9]."

Rashbi's discourses are an affirmation and culmination of all that has transpired among the Companions. He validates their mystical teachings on the various topics they have explored. He shares their sense of joy and appreciation for the great good fortune they have been blessed with on their seemingly random walk. He celebrates the friendship and the spiritual uniqueness of this remarkable group. His own positive embrace of the

Companions is in correspondence, he explains, with the joy and acceptance evinced by the King above. Moreover, he teaches them that even in their group cohesion, they have merited individual fulfillment, each attaining his own version of the image of the Primordial Adam.

This would be a beautiful consummation of this incredibly rich text. But it is not quite the true ending. The narrator feels compelled to proceed:

> At this point Rabbi Shim'on saw that Rabbi Yose was thinking about worldly matters. Said he to him: "Yose, arise and make your image complete, for one letter is missing in you."
>
> Rabbi Yose arose up and rejoiced in words of the Torah. He stood before him. Rabbi Shim'on looked at him. He said: "Rabbi Yose, now you are whole before the Ancient of Days, and your image is complete."

After such an elaborate and complex interweaving of narrative and spiritual teaching along a meandering path that somehow leads to its meaningful end, before Rashbi, who is given the last, inspiring word, the reader, who has been held in rapt attention by this virtuosic text, is shaken to hear that not everyone has been captured by Rashbi's charismatic power. The zoharic narrator punctures its own creative bubble by briefly noting that Rabbi Yose's mind has been wandering. While we had imagined that we had joined together with the Companions to hear the fitting fulfillment of this adventure in the words of Rashbi, we find out that Rabbi Yose has not been listening, we know not for how long. He is drawn to other things. These are not higher matters of esoteric mystery but are quite mundane. And this is not simply a case of a wayward student failing to pay attention to his teacher. This is the same Rabbi Yose who, on this journey, praised his fellow Companions and discoursed so deeply and beautifully about the ultimate value of mystical martyrdom as the most complete expression of this-worldly renunciation for the sake of spiritual reality.

Rashbi is able to notice the quiet inattentiveness of Rabbi Yose. He calls him back to his presence and challenges him to make up for this lapse. Rabbi Yose acquits himself well. He delivers a discourse with joy. But, after expending many pages recording the various discourses delivered on the road and by Rashbi, the narrator can no longer be bothered to tell us what marvelous words of Torah Rabbi Yose said. We are simply assured that Rabbi Yose's defect has been repaired. He is complete and the story is complete.[105] But there is another final message lurking beneath this neat ending.

We need to notice that a sage has momentarily stepped out and away from so many mutually reinforcing bonds. For a brief moment he has escaped the sacred realm of the *Zohar*'s mystical mysteries, stepped out of the mutually supportive and self-celebratory coterie of his friends, out of his exalted and humbling station as disciple of the great Sacred Lamp of God, and out of the quest for ideal spiritual self-realization. His action—was it forced upon him or was it entirely his own choice?—is the very opposite of that of the four sages in the classic tale who attempted to peek into the mystical Paradise. Three of them peeked and were damaged in some way. Only Rabbi Aqiva entered and emerged unhurt.[106] Rabbi Yose is the anti–Rabbi Aqiva. He has peeked into the mundane realm and emerged unscathed.

CHAPTER 3

The Spatial Orientation of the *Zohar*

Before proceeding toward a fuller understanding of the significance of the walking motif in other texts of the *Zohar*, it is necessary to recognize the seriousness of the problem with which the *Zohar* had to cope. In turn, this can lead us to appreciate the magnitude of its seemingly modest achievement. To do this, we must turn now to the question of spatiality itself.

The Problem of Space and Divinity

Space is a fundamental rubric of human, mundane existence. All actions, emotions, conceptions or other experiences "take place," that is, they transpire in a spatial environment. Thus, even when humans strive for transcendent experiences or understandings, these strivings are inescapably "grounded." Humans, as they experience or conceive of the Divine, do so within a spatial world, a world that encompasses so much that partakes of the mundane rather than the religious or transcendental realms.

One effect of the experience of spatiality as inextricably connected to the mundane world is the tendency to identify spatiality as a property of the mundane realm, exclusively. But for the traditional religious Jew, this exclusive identification proves untenable, for it must lead to either of two unacceptable conclusions. One unacceptable conclusion is the total exclusion of God from the spatial realm, from spatiality itself. Such an approach tends to create a chasm that is difficult to bridge, conceptually or experientially, between God and the world. The other option is to completely identify God with this world. But pantheism seems to be excluded by deeply rooted Jewish traditions about God.[1]

The struggle, then, is to elucidate a relation between God and the spatial world, a relation that would hold without collapsing into an identity set. Since all relations are conceived within a spatial context, spatiality is a strong force in shaping the concepts themselves. Even when ostensibly speaking about issues of ontology or value, one inevitably speaks in spatial terms—higher and lower, inside and outside, narrow and wide, close and far. How are the implications of this situation manifested in the *Zohar*'s approach to God, reality and the holy life?

While the zoharic literature evinces this phenomenon, some of the spatial influences operating in its thought and values are more apparent than others. This study tries to show that once attention is paid to it, the spatial dimension can be seen to suffuse zoharic discourse about God and the world. Furthermore, it works out an elaborate system of liminal entities to bridge between the divine realm and the mundane spatial realm of human, living entities that partake of spatial qualities even as they may also be taken to lead away from mundane spatiality.[2] In the end, however, as long as there are people engaged in this quest, living in this world, the realm of mundane spatiality will refuse to disappear. The motif of the walking Companions is an expression of this realization, a realization that mandates a particular spatial orientation, an orientation that addresses the nature of space itself as an inescapable category.

The paradoxical aspects of the walking motif that we have discerned in the *Zohar* are reflections of the paradoxical role that spatial concepts and terms play in the religious tradition of which the *Zohar* is a part. It is possible to discern the ways in which biblical and rabbinic Judaisms have integrated horizontal elements into a predominantly vertically oriented religious model. The mystical culture of the German Pietists can also be shown to include expressions of a recognition of spatial reality, on the most sublime and the most mundane levels.[3] Still, the project of maintaining a spatial orientation is especially difficult for the mystic. The fundamental issues of the Judaic tradition, as charted by its mystical streams, concern considerations of the deepest truths about God and the human soul. In pursuit of these truths, this-worldly spatial reality can seem irrelevant. Indeed, even as the tradition turns its attention to cosmogonic and cosmological issues, a move necessary in order to "fill in the gaps"[4] between the Creator and humans living in a mundane space, the mapping out of the created universe is initially conceived of in spiritual terms. Thus issues of spatial reality tend to be subsumed within and coopted by concerns viewed as more properly religious. This approach is described very well by Isaiah Tishby. He explains that the cosmogonic theory of the kabbalists had to deal with two aspects of reality:

> The first facet is the process of expansion and departure from the concealed to the revealed in the realm of the divinity itself, that is, the movement and turning from the placid being of *Eyn Sof*, Who dwells in the depths of His hiddenness, toward creative activity by developing His hidden powers and in establishing the divine cosmos of the system of *sefirot*. The second facet is the construction of the non-divine cosmos, that is, the system of worlds and entities—spiritual and material—that are outside the realm of the divinity. The kabbalist's eyes, searching for the highest and innermost principles, are raised, first and foremost toward contemplating the divine realm of *Ma'aseh Bereshit*, and the coming into being of the external world does not enter his consideration except as a secondary occurrence that is intertwined with and enfolded into the emanation of the *sefirot*.[5]

The kabbalist thus begins from a pronounced lack of attention to the reality and meaning of space. Indeed, after Tishby sorts through the various cosmogonic theories in the zoharic literature, he notes that the lived space of humans is not found on any map! "The earth, which is really the lower world, is not mentioned at all."[6] Efraim Gottlieb writes in a similar vein: "In the kabbalistic literature in all its various layers, the lack of discussion about the coming into being of the material world is a striking phenomenon."[7] Nevertheless, the intrusion of spatial terminology occurs quite early in cosmogonic teachings, so that the issue of spatiality lurks patiently within the religious discourse, awaiting its discovery. The language of spatial dimensionality is never absent for long from these themes, though they may seem initially to be conceptually unrelated. As the kabbalist tries to express the nature of the divine and non-divine realms of reality and their relations to one another, the resort to spatial terminology becomes unavoidable. This has been the case since the biblical revelations about God. Not only was anthropomorphic imagery essential and indispensable in talking about God, but so was spatial terminology, as Solomon recognized in wonder,[8] and Maimonides with patent disapproval.[9]

One of the fundamental images of the divine for Jewish mystics was of the enthroned deity within a palace. While the image was often described as one of frightening splendor, majesty, and mystery, it also sustained the essential paradox of an awesome god who is enclosed within a spatial container, a space sometimes elaborated, as was the case with the Jerusalem Temple, into a system or network of spaces.[10] The desire of the devotee was to enter that space. Thus, spatial terms and spatial concepts were used to support the problematic of access to the divine—intellectually, spiritually, and physically. The devotee wished to draw nearer to his god. As Eliade would have it, a vertical axis was established between a terrestrial palace, or *heikhal*, and its celestial counterpart. Different religious temperaments focused on entrance into one or the other of these places. The psalmist seems content with entering and abiding in the earthly House of God,[11] while apocalyptic visionaries and their mystical heirs strove for a heavenly translation.[12]

Whatever theories contemporary scholars advance regarding the genealogical kinship lines linking these traditions—including rabbinic tradition—with Jewish esotericism,[13] the *Zohar* is the heir to these sometimes conflicting traditions.[14] It pictures the classical rabbis as intense participants in this mystic quest, subject to the mystic struggle. The mystic is caught in a bind, desiring the abolition of distances and boundaries—spatiality itself—and yet continually being recalled by his own embodied, spatially conditioned imagination to conceiving of ultimate realities in spatial terms. Mystics diverge in their decisions on how to evaluate this conflict. Apophatic mystics decide that the pull to imagery and spatiality is a tempting illusion to be overcome. But kataphatic mystics accept their imagings as ultimately meaningful. At issue is not only the possibility of saying something about the deity, but also the possible relevance of the spatial category. The orientation of the apophatic mystic is clearly stated by the anonymous author of *The Cloud of Unknowing*: "Leave aside this everywhere and everything in exchange for this nowhere and this nothing. . . . A man's affection is remarkably changed in the spiritual experience of this nothing when it is achieved nowhere."[15] The apprehension of nothingness entails an abolition of spatiality. The *Zohar*, on the other hand, as an expression of kataphatic mysticism, must choose to credit the spatial characteristics of its mystical images. But it does so only after much struggle.[16] The Chariot imagery inherited by the *Zohar* is an illustration of this. The *Zohar* tries to push those cosmic elements that may be non-divine, and, hence, constituent of a physical, spatial world, back into the divine realm. Tishby writes:

> In the *Sefer Ha-Zohar*, within which the visual character predominated to a much greater degree as compared to the deliberative-contemplative kabbalah of the Gerona circle, we again find comprehensive and variegated descriptions of *Ma'aseh Merkavah*. But it is specifically here that the breakup of systems that occurred in kabbalah in this area becomes exceedingly clear. The inclination in the *Zohar* to visualization and to the proliferation of aspects in the symbolic speculum of the divine reality turned the sefirotic system into the actual Chariot, with all its parts and populace, and thus was created the dual image of the Upper Chariot and Lower Chariot, also called *Merkevet Ha-Mishneh*.[17]

In this the *Zohar* manifests tendencies apparent in earlier mystical cultures. As the mystic pushes toward ascent, there is a doubling and stacking of cosmic and divine elements, creating an ever higher ladder of being, pushing the ultimate theophanic terminus ever higher, just out of reach. Ironically, the apex of the vertical axis takes on the aspect of a horizon.[18]

Spatial terms are essential in the *Zohar*'s mysterious conceiving of the very beginnings of divine manifestation. Divine emanation is described as an anthropomorphic process of insemination and conception, but it is also described as a spreading out and a creating of space: "*Zohar*, Concealed of the Concealed, struck its aura. The aura touched and did not touch this point. Then the Beginning emanated [*itpashat*—spread out] and made itself a palace [*heikhala*] for its glory and its praise."[19] This palace is like the cocoon of the silkworm, allowing the chrysalis within it to gestate before it is ready to burst forth. The continuing spreading forth (*itpashtuta*) of divine energy creates this palace called "house," made for dwelling. The house is prepared for dwelling through further, fruitful expansion, engendering the manifestation of *Elohim*. Then the house can bring forth children—the letters of the Torah.

The vertical, hierarchical, theosophical structure of the *Zohar* was thus augmented and thickened with spatial attributes. The interweaving of the vertical with the horizontal can be seen in the *Zohar*'s image of the next stage of emanation—the cosmic tree, which the *Zohar* identifies with the Torah. It combines biblical and rabbinic associations with those it inherited from the earlier mystical classic *Sefer ha-Bahir*.[20] Commenting on the biblical command to light the menorah in the Tabernacle, the *Zohar* analyzes the image of the candelabrum into the associated images of sun and tree: "Come, see: The Tree of Life holds together [*aḥid*][21] from above to below and this sun that shines on all, its light begins from the top and spreads in the trunk of the tree [*be-gufa de-'ilana*] in a straight path. Two sides are held together in her, one to the North and one to the South, and one to the Right and one to the Left. When the sun shines, as was said, from the trunk of the tree, strength goes to the Right arm that shines by its strength, and from its strength the Left shines and is included in its light."[22]

Much as her parents do when, at the end of Kafka's "The Metamorphosis," they watch Grete Samsa stretching in the sunlight, we take in this image as an affirmation of health, life, and promise, expressed through the vital movements of the Tree's expansion and contraction—its comfortable embrace of space—as the sefirotic effluence courses through it from top to bottom and side to side.[23] But it is necessary that the spatial extension of the Tree be countered by being brought back inward through the enfolding of Left into Right. The divine unification[24] is accomplished through the collapsing of spaciousness. The embrace of space begins with an outward, welcoming move, but only in order to draw spatial extension back into a compressed vertical column.

The ideal spatial state is that of enclosure, not expansion. Yet we are given a world that has expanded outward from the self-contained divine realm. This opening outward was effected through the liminal, last divine potency, *Malkhut* or Shekhinah. The *Zohar* locates in the *sefirah* of Shekhinah some of its most fundamental meditations on the vicissitudes of a reality that is spatial. We shall return to the Shekhinah after examining some of the other areas in the *Zohar*'s discourses on this problem. The other two realms we must explore are the areas of the mundane world and the world of evil. These are two spaces located outside the Divine. Shekhinah will interact with both of them.

Space and Struggle

SPACE AND EVIL

By pushing the act of Creation back into the divine realm,[25] the kabbalist made it difficult for himself to account for the existence of a space or realm outside of God. Yet the *Zohar* affirms that there are realms outside God. One realm, which the *Zohar* could not help but acknowledge, is the mundane universe in which humans live, appropriately sometimes referred to as "the world of separation" (*'alma de-peruda*).[26] Discussion of this realm will be deferred until after some consideration of another realm that was conceived of as outside of God, a realm not below God, but next to God, existing alongside and parallel to the divine realm—the *Sitra Aḥra*—the Other Side.[27]

The *Zohar* is quite clear in discussing its presence: "Just as there are, on the side of holiness, palaces and appointees, all for good, and holy spirits and all sides that are holy, so, too, there are on the defiled side, palaces and appointees, all for bad, and defiled spirits are appointed, and all sides are defiled." Still, it would seem that even the *Zohar* is taken aback by this dualistic reality, so that it immediately concludes this description by saying, "This and that correspond, like the good inclination and the bad inclination. And all is in one mystery."[28]

The mystery of unifying this dualism is most profound, since, given that God is one of the antithetical terms in the duality, one must wonder what extra-divine unifying principle there might be. The mitigation of this problem has usually been accomplished by giving priority and primacy to the divine realm.[29] This may be effective in temporal or ontological terms, but when conceived of as a spatial problem, these solutions do not work. The implication remains that there seems to exist a dimension, spatially conceived, that is outside the divinity, not only as the opposing realm to the divine, but as the encompassing realm in which the primary and prior divine realm and the subsequent and subsidiary demonic realm abide side by side. The nature of this spatial reality will have to remain imperfectly understood. Focusing only on one component of this spatial complex, the Other Side, another question arises: If both realms, God and the Other Side, inhabit one overarching space, does this mean that the spatiality of the Other Side is essentially the same as that of the Divine, or is its spatiality different?

The dualistic picture presented by the zoharic text cited above indicates that the two realms are parallel to each other, with spatial characteristics that correspond to each other. Tishby cites many sources that describe "the precise parallelism between the forces of defilement (*tum'ah*) and the forces of holiness."[30] The Other Side recapitulates the *sefirot* and *heikhalot* in number and structure. "The correspondence is so complete that from studying the *sefirot* of the *Sitra Aḥra* it is possible to know and understand the system of the divine *sefirot*."[31]

The *Zohar* charts the correspondence between the holy realm and the Other Side and describes them in terms of palaces, but also as bodies. It is here that a fundamental difference between the two parallel systems is discernible. Describing the Other Side, the *Zohar* speaks of the joints of the legs, the limbs associated with movement, and explains:

> There are three joints [*qishrin*] to the right and three to the left. And these joints and those joints we mentioned all face [*mistaklan*] behind. For those supernal, holy joints all face inward, to the body, as it is said, "and all their hind quarters were inside" (1 Kings 7:25), while these all face behind. What is the difference between this and that one? It is that these are supernal, holy joints, all in the secret of Adam. And since they are all in the secret of Adam, it is written, "and all their hind quarters were inside." While these other joints that we mention, these central joints all face behind, and they are in the secret of Animal, and therefore, all their hind quarters are to the back side.[32]

The *Zohar* accomplishes a number of things with this set of statements. It expresses its disgust for the Other Side by calling it animal, not a person.[33] It also conjures up an image of physical deformity, suggesting that the joints of *Sitra Aḥra* do not function in the same way as the holy joints. This imagery is not mainly about the functioning of the joints, but about the way all the joints are related to each other and to the space around them. The verse cited refers to the twelve oxen that supported Solomon's Great Sea. Elsewhere, these twelve beasts are taken to be lower chariot figures that support Shekhinah.[34] The *Zohar* uses the verse to extol the locative propriety of these supernal forces. They work inward together, toward unity. But the forces of *Sitra Aḥra* have a corrupt spatial orientation. Their rear quarters face backward, that is, outward.[35] This spatial orientation is a defining distinction between the two systems.

We can find this expressed a bit earlier in that section, where the *Zohar* explains the meaning of the building of the Tabernacle. It explains why the Tabernacle was only a stopgap until the Temple could be built. This temporary, secondary quality was due to the accommodational nature of the structure. It was built to move about, "to tie each [potency] together so as to shine, but not to rest [*l'nayḥa*], for there is no rest except when the Temple was built in the days of King Solomon, for then there was rest above and below, for the power of resting, and not to move from place to place, is there."[36] The locative preference is for everything to find its place and not move from it. This tranquil state was achieved temporarily when Moses erected the Tabernacle. "And once that Point[37] was established and was illumined, then all the rest of the other arrangement [*tiqquna*] was arranged and settled in its place. And about this [is written] 'And Moses set up the Tabernacle [and he put down its bases and he placed its boards, and he put in the rods, and he set up its columns.]' [Exod. 40:18]—this is the Point that was dark and sunken in its place."[38] This process, by enforcing a locative hegemony of holiness, subdues the Other Side: "Come and see—'And Moses set up [the Tabernacle,]'—this is the Side of Holiness, and the Other Defiled Side sunk down; 'and he put [down its bases]'—this [is the] Side of Holiness, and the Other Side of Defilement weakened; 'and he placed'—this [is the] Side of Holiness and the Other Side of Defilement was subdued, and afterwards he went back and 'he put in its rods.'"[39]

The *Zohar* continues by emphasizing that this locative process establishes a vertical axis: "And after that, 'And he set up [*va-yaqem*] [its columns]'—What is the reason? In order that the start and finish be through standing erect [*be-qimah*]. Because standing up is necessary with all, beginning and end. In the beginning, so that the Other Side is weakened, and that is the erection of the Side of Holiness, so that it may be established and go up above, to become one tying-together, as is proper. Because as long as Holiness rules and ascends, Defilement is brought down low."[40]

But the Other Side is programmed for movement. In anger and vehemence, the dark forces move about. If the erection of the Tabernacle effected a locative peace, where nothing moved from place to place, "the second joint [of the Other Side][41]—it is called Rage [*za'am*]. This joint moves from place to place."[42] Its job is to lead all the other forces and bring misfortune to the world.

The *Zohar*'s conception of the disruptive nature of the Other Side is rooted in an earlier teaching by Rabbi Isaac Ha-Kohen in his "Essay on the Left Emanation." Rabbi Isaac was one of the "gnostic kabbalists" who prided themselves in having knowledge not available to other kabbalistic schools, and who were a strong influence on the *Zohar*.[43] Rabbi Isaac writes:

> Now I shall set forth another set, the set of names of the princes, princes of jealousy and hatred. Indeed, their foundation and service is in truth and innocence, without falsehood in their mouths, and there is no lying or falsehood among them. The first accusing prince, the Head of Jealousy, is Sama'el the Wicked and his entire camp. He is not called wicked from himself, but because he wishes to cleave to and approach with great intimacy the emanation that is not of his type, as we shall explain in its proper place, with the Blessed God's help.[44]

Thus, Sama'el's evil is not essential. Rather, it lies in his desire to cross boundaries, to go where he should not go, to shatter the locative tranquility of God's emanative scheme. As Scholem explains, "The evil in Sama'el is thus only in his desire to leave his place and enter and take hold of the emanation of holiness, which is not of his kind."[45] Sama'el refuses to "abide" by God's will that there be a strict separation—*masakh mavdil*[46]—between constructive and destructive forces. He refuses to stay in his assigned place.[47]

This results in a state of constant battle between the Godly forces of the Right Emanation and the Other Side. The antithetical strife between both realms takes place in a number of spaces. First, it takes place at the border that separates the two. As we shall see, the Other Side tries to interpose itself within the divine precincts, causing a separation between the *sefirot*. The protective Godly forces charged with fending off these invasions are called by Rabbi Isaac "the Guardians of the Walls."[48] Their job is not to destroy the Other Side, but to keep it in its place.

The battle is engaged in the realm of the mundane world as well. The *Zohar*'s concern is that the *Sitra Aḥra* will attempt to take over this realm. In the *Heikhalot* section in *Pequdei*, the *Zohar* charts the uneasy relationship between the divine forces and the Other Side. Since the *Sitra Aḥra* has a legitimate place in the cosmic structure, it has a role to play in the lower world. For example, in the *Zohar*'s elaborate system of heavenly palaces, *heikhalot*, the third holy palace of executing judgment is connected with the evil palace and cooperates with it regarding a negative judgment, handing to SNGDI"EL, a spirit summoned from the Other Side, the notes carrying the sentence of punishment.[49] Thus, innocent young children who are condemned to die are killed by SNGDI"EL, who does the bidding of the officer of the third holy palace, 'IRI"EL. Only after they are killed are they taken by the Holy Side and nourished in the fourth palace.[50]

But, despite this cooperation, the *Sitra Aḥra* cannot be trusted to occupy its place:

> From the secret of the third palace of the Other Side there issue two spirits, called Anger—*A"ph*—and Ire—*Ḥema"h*. From these two, all the agents go out who go to deflect people from the true path. It is they who stand by and hasten toward a person who walks toward the path of mitzvah. Therefore these *ofanim* stand against them, in order to give protection to humanity so that they not be injured. Moses was afraid of those two spirits when he came down from the mountain, as it is written, "For I was frightened of the Anger and Ire." (Deut. 9:19)[51]

The relationship continues to alternate between collaboration and conflict. In the fourth palace, where judgment is pronounced, any judgment pertaining to the rulers of the world is communicated first to the officials of the Other Side, "and they announce that matter to the world rulers, for they are on their side."[52] Collaboration with the Other Side is based on the Right Side accepting the locative propriety of each realm's jurisdiction. But, beyond this, it accepts the different natures of the two sides. The divine realm operates under a unitive principle, the Secret of Faith, while the Other Side operates under a disruptive principle of Rage. The divine realm realizes that the Other Side is a reckless partner, but this is the way it must be:

> From these palaces, which are the Side of Holiness and the Secret of Faith, levels [*dargin*] spread out downward, all in the Secret of Faith, and they descend level by level until they fly in this world and are appointed in it. Some [are appointed] to protect people from the Other Side and from harms of the world, and on the roads they walk. Some are to help people when they come to be purified. And some to make signs and miracles in the world, and some are set to watch over the actions of people to bear witness. And so they spread out, many levels to their sides, and all in the Secret of Supernal Faith in the Supernal Holiness. It is just so with the *Sitra Aḥra*, the Side of Impurity. Levels spread out from those lower palaces, all levels to do evil and to lead the world astray. Some are set to lead people astray from the good path to the bad path. And some are set to defile people who are trying to become defiled, since we learn, "if a person comes to be defiled, they defile him in this world and they defile him in that world,' and they are called boiling excrement, as it says, "you will call it excrement" [Isa. 30:22], and those levels that are set to defile even more. Therefore these are always arrayed against those, and all are at known levels, as is proper.[53]

The *Zohar* finds the root of this difference expressed in the higher palaces. The principle of acceptance is called Love (*ahavah*), located in the fifth *heikhal*. It is a principle that acts to protect the divine realm from attack even as it endeavors to spread its influence: "This spirit is the one who guards everything above that must be guarded, and it is called 'the Guardian of Israel' [Ps. 121:4], 'the Guardian of the Covenant' [Deut. 7:9]. For here is the guarding of all the hidden supernal treasures, so therefore all the treasures of his Master are here. From this go out paths and roads to those below, in order to arouse in them the spirit of love."[54]

It is potentially dangerous to enter into a space without this element of love, for even if the space is appropriate to the person, without love the person is in danger of drowning there, unable to move on. This is the way the *Zohar* explains the case of the four who entered the *Pardes*. Though each was bound to his rightful place, each sunk down and was lost, except for Rabbi 'Aqiva, who came from the Right Side and clung to the Palace of Love. "Therefore he died in Love and his soul departed with that verse,

'And you shall love [the Lord your God]' [Deut. 6:5]. How meritorious is his portion!"[55]

The force of Love is the median axis that holds all the divine forces together. It is the pillar that joins upper and lower central potencies, running from *Tiferet*/Jacob to *Yesod*/Joseph, the tzaddiq. When we arrive at the sixth palace, the Palace of Will (*Ratzon*), we learn that this spirit of love, itself, acts a bit like the Other Side in that it does not remain content with occupying its own place.[56] Sometimes it encroaches on the role of the *Sitra Aḥra* and executes judgment on its own, so as to mitigate the judgment: "In the North Side there is another light, the one that is set to cancel [*le-vatla*][57] a judgment from the house of the fourth palace, and gives a note to the appointee of the doorway, for at that doorway are set other appointees who are from the Side of Defilement, waiting for that appointee to take up judgment. And sometimes that light from the North side executes the judgment itself, so that it not be given into the hand of the *Sitra Aḥra*, because any judgments done by it have a healing remedy, and the Holy Blessed One acts graciously in those places."[58] Just as the divine realm is held together, maintained and invigorated by the median force, here called Love, so the Other Side is animated and motivated by a median entity, the Snake.

THE SNAKE

The Gnostic kabbalist Rabbi Isaac ben Rabbi Ya'aqov Ha-Kohen set forth the parallel realms of divine and other forces. Originally meant to exist in stable correspondence, the forces of the Other Side initiated a relationship of enmity and strife. Rabbi Isaac indicates that "the cause of all the jealousies between all these aforementioned princes . . . is one form unique to Sama'el, she being Lilith."[59] Lilith and Sama'el were created as an androgyne (*du partzufin*), just like Adam and Eve. Lilith causes the destabilization of the Throne, under which both she and Sama'el were emanated, in the same way that Eve brought about the fall of the first human couple. In recapitulative correspondence, the agent for this catastrophe was Gamali'el and the primordial Snake, Naḥashi'el, who acted as the intermediary to draw male and female together.[60]

Numerous mythic strands from antiquity were woven together in the kabbalistic teachings about the Snake. Ancient biblical traditions about the Serpent in the Garden of Eden were conflated with other biblical hints about a primordial sea creature, the *tanin* or *livyatan*, and combined with the astronomical/astrological being called *teli*. All these creatures afforded images that were conducive to incorporation into a set of mythologoumena with significant spatial implications.

The Bible supplies a number of characteristics that would be influential in any subsequent analysis of the Serpent. It tells us that the Serpent was cunning and that it was able to speak shrewdly and persuasively. This is how it succeeded in seducing Eve to give in to her desires. As punishment, the Torah declares, the Serpent was condemned to crawl on the ground, eating dust, and be ever ready to attack humans at their heels, just as the humans would return the same enmity.[61]

The midrash follows up on these verses, noting that the Serpent originally "stood [up] like a rod and he had legs,"[62] but that after the sin "the ministering angels descended and cut off his hands and legs."[63] The Serpent was punished by being transformed from a vertical into a horizontal being. The Talmud explains that this was because "he cast his eyes upon what was not appropriate for him."[64] Todros Abulafia, one of the Gnostic kabbalists, characterizes this presumptuousness as a breaking of boundaries, "and they said about him that he broke through the fence of the world because he cast his eyes upon someone inappropriate for him, and therefore, 'one who breaks through a fence will be bitten by a snake'" (Eccles. 10:8).[65]

The same conception is held by a kabbalist who is not identified with the Gnostic circle, Rabbi Yosef Giqatilla. In his treatise "The Secret of the Serpent and Its Sentence [Destiny]," he writes:

> And know that from the beginning of his creation, the Serpent served an important and necessary purpose for the harmony of Creation, so long as he remained in his place. He was a great servant, created to bear the yoke of mastery and service, and his head reached to the heights of the earth, and his tail reached into the depth of Hell. For he had a suitable place in all the worlds, and constituted something extremely important for the harmony

of all levels, each in its place. And that is the secret of the heavenly Serpent, known from *Sefer Yetzirah*,[66] who sets all the spheres of Heaven into motion and makes them orbit from east to west and from north to south.[67]

Like Rabbi Isaac, Giqatilla also sees that the original state of the world was meant to have a necessary place for the creature who would subsequently become its evil force. He also couches the change in terms of spatial stability and upheaval. Giqatilla goes further in positing that the Serpent was actually a positive, not neutral, force in maintaining the spatiality of the world. Like Rabbi Isaac, he also conceives of protective walls, called *masakh* (as with Rabbi Isaac) and *pargod*.[68] He describes the original state of the Serpent with the same phrase used for the oxen who supported Solomon's Sea, "while its face was turned toward the outside."[69] He continues, "Know that regarding all of God's works, when they are in their place, each one in the very place that He prepared for it and set it in at its creation, it is good. And this is [the meaning of the verse] 'and the shrewd will be crowned with knowledge' [Prov. 14:18], but if the opposite [is the case] and it leaves its place, it is absolutely evil."[70]

We should notice that, no matter how these kabbalists may differ with regard to explaining why evil eventually appeared, they all concur in characterizing its essence in terms of its spatial practice—its propensity to disturb the locative perfection of the earliest moments of Creation.[71] To convey this, Giqatilla, like Abulafia, cites Ecclesiastes 10:8: "One who breaks through a fence will be bitten by a snake."[72] In addition, the irruption of evil into the cosmos is characterized by a movement from the vertical to the horizontal. The Serpent begins as the axis that ensures the proper spatial distribution of the cosmic forces, only to fall flat to the ground.[73] Giqatilla ends his treatise with faith that the Serpent will be lifted back up at the ultimate redemption. This restoration is hinted at in the closing words of the treatise, God's words to Joshua, "Pick yourself up, why are you fallen on your face?" (Josh. 7:10).[74] The redemption is conceived of as the restoration of the horizontal to the vertical. It should be noted that Rabbi Isaac similarly foresees a redemptive era in which a messianic Snake will devour the evil Snake, much as Moses' snake devoured the snakes of Egypt and afterwards returned to its vertical state.[75] Horizontal spatiality is conceived of as an unredeemed state. Spatiality and history are intertwined.

Rabbi Moshe de Leon links the traditional picture of the villainous Esau with the evil Serpent, "for Esau is 'the crooked serpent [*naḥash 'aqalton*]'" (Isa. 27:1).[76] Esau's nature was to be a roaming hunter. He goes out to hunt for souls and punish them to fulfill the bidding of his father, Judgment and Darkness, personified by Isaac, whose eyes were darkened. This activity derives from the Serpent: "Judgment does not apply to the world without the arousal of Satan who, a man such as he, will act like a real snake [*naḥesh yenaḥesh*],[77] And he goes out to hunt prey and to wander about the whole world, as it says, 'from wandering the land and walking along in it' [Job 2:2]."[78]

The role of the Serpent in the zoharic historiography cannot be fully dealt with in this study.[79] However, it is relevant to point out that as the *Zohar* conceives of the historic conflict between Esau and Jacob, identifying Esau with the Serpent, it follows through with its identification of the Serpent as a spatial activist, as opposed to Jacob, who is a figure of sedentary stability. The *Zohar* describes the confrontation between Jacob and the Prince of Esau as a wrestling match between the evil figure who rides the evil Serpent and the perfect person, perfect "because he sits in the tents."[80] The night that they struggled together, Jacob was compelled to stay in his place, alone: "That night was the night of the birth of the moon and Jacob remained alone, for no one else was with him, as it is taught, 'a person should not go out alone at night,' surely not on a night in which the lights were created, for the moon was defective, as it is written, 'Let there be luminaries [*m'rt*],' [the word written] defectively, and that night he remained alone because when the moon is defective the evil Serpent is powerful and reigns."[81] The struggle between Jacob and Esau can be seen as a competition over spatial control to be exerted through free spatial movement. The mobile Prince of Esau therefore tries to incapacitate Jacob's own ability to move about by attacking his thigh. But Jacob eventually prevails, in some sense, by temporarily impeding his adversary's plans to move on, at least until he can wrest a blessing from him.

The attack by the Prince of Esau is quite deliberately directed at Jacob's thigh, since, for the *Zohar*, the thigh served as a point of convergence for some of its most important concerns. Physically, the thigh, as the uppermost section of the leg, the instrument for human locomotion, is, of course, situated next to the genital area. The *Zohar* pointedly states, "The way of the thigh is to go in and go out [*le-nafqa u-leme'al*]."[82] When the *Zohar* expounds upon the structure of the *heikhalot*, it combines spatial, architectural, and biological images. Openings to the divine potencies are said to allow for prophetic and quasi-prophetic access to these realms by way of the thighs (*Netzaḥ* and *Hod*). This is because the thighs occupy a place that protects and supports both the male and female genitalia, that is, the divine potencies, *Tiferet/Yesod* and *Malkhut*.[83] These potencies are identified with two aspects of divine communication, the Written and Oral Torah. "Just as there are supports for the Torah teaching [*'orayta*] that is the Written Torah, so there are supports established for the Torah teaching that is the Oral Torah, and they are included in each other."[84] So communication with the Divine must first be through these limbs. Focusing on the male physiognomy, the *Zohar* says that the thighs are the external supports for the Divine Name (the circumcised phallus), which must be kept concealed inside. "Even though we said that it is within the sign of the Holy Covenant [*qiyama qadisha*] that the Name dwells, since all forces issue forth from that sign, the thighs, which are set outside, we [nevertheless] call by that Name, and they are called outsiders [*baryatei*], for a *baraita* is outside of Mishnah. Our Mishnah stays inside of *baraita*, and the thighs are called the outside houses, just as above."[85] The *Zohar* combines spatial, physiognomic, and hermeneutical categories. The inner Mishnah is brought out through the thighs, to become exoteric teaching. "Woe if it is revealed; woe if it is not revealed."[86] Then the *Zohar* moves to the historical dimension, identifying the thighs, as "outer houses" with the Second Temple, its exoteric nature caused by the sins that destroyed the enclosed, unified First Temple.[87] We again encounter the idea that inside is good and outside is bad, that stasis is good and movement is bad. Because it was in an exposed state, the Second Temple was vulnerable to the Other Side, the outer skin (*'orlah*). It, too, was destroyed by sins, and exile ensued. The privileged state of interiority and self-sufficiency was lost. The punishment was to be condemned to walking outside. "Whosoever knows how to measure the length of the *Qav ha-Middah*, the length of distance from the thighs to the feet, can know how long the exile will endure."[88]

The *Zohar* expresses herein a number of elements of its spatial orientation. Spatiality is tied to history. History is not merely a temporal unfolding; it is a spatial unfolding, or unraveling. Interiority could not be maintained. The outside realm was able to encroach upon and open up enclosed space, forcing a move outward. For the *Zohar*, however, the tragedy of history is coextensive with the Torah's revelation in its disclosure through the Oral Law, one of the forms of Shekhinah. The self-enclosed Mishnah, identified with the Mother's House, the Holy of Holies, must be painfully revealed ("Woe if it is revealed; woe if it is not revealed") through the "external teachings," the *baraitot*. The image used to convey the process through which these teachings are promulgated is the growth of the legs: "Therefore all the outer teachers [*baraytei*] and all the [inner, mishnaic] teachers [*tana'ei*] and all *amora'im* are set in their places, as it should be, these within and these outside in the curves of the thighs and below the knees. It is called the Oral Torah in all of them, and in all of them Israel descended and went out [to exile—*ve-itgalu*]."[89]

This process is also expressed as a process of displacement with regard to the sexual organs. Sexuality itself is turned inside-out. First the outer membrane—*'orlah*—was, instead of being eliminated, empowered. The genitals, instead of remaining shielded within the protective zone of the thighs, are supplanted by them. The external limbs take the place of the functioning of the private parts. The term for the central, phallic axis—*Qav ha-Middah*[90]—is now transferred to signify the thighs and legs. Walking outside supplants the private union of the male and female potencies. "And then, when the exile will be concluded with the drawing in [*bim'shikhu*] of the legs, then 'his legs will stay standing on that day' (Zech. 14:4). And the Spirit of *'Orlah* Defilement will pass away from the world, and Israel will return to rule alone, as is proper."[91]

Following this interpretation of the meaning of the legs, it is possible to draw a distinction with regard to the spatial significations of legs and hands. The legs, as we have seen, are agents of motion and (sexual) activity. The hand is a more localizing limb. It signifies the state of being in one place.[92] To be set in a place is to be delimited by that which is "at hand." The *Zohar* bases this idea on a verse from Ezekiel's Chariot Vision:

> "And human hands were under their wings" [Ezek. 1:8]. All these human hands—we have indeed established that they are Seraphs and Creatures and Ophanim, all with wings, and with hands under their wings to receive prayers and to accept those who repent. The human hands are places and locales [*atrin ve-dukhtin*][93] for accepting people with their prayers and petitions, and to open doors to receive them. To unite and tie together [*u-leqashra qishrin*] and to do their will. And these places and locales that are called "human hands," ["hands"] that exist for [the sake of] humans, are those holy names that rule in every grade, for it is through them that people enter with their prayers and pleas into all supernal gates. And thus the lower ones rule above. This is the secret of "Your hands made Me and established Me" [Ps. 119:73]. And these are the holy names. "And God said to Moses, 'Raise [*n'teh*] your hand over the heavens'" [Exod. 9:22]. But how can he raise his hand over the heavens? Rather, *n'teh*—incline, as you say, "And He inclined heaven and descended" [Ps. 18:10], drawing from above to below. "Your hand"—your place, the place of your grade in which you dwell. And this is the secret of the holy name. And all, supernal and lower ones, travel and stand through the secret of the names. And through them people enter the supernal palaces, and there is no one who can prevent them. How fortunate are those who know how to arrange the unification of their Master as is proper, and to walk in the true path, so as not to be mistaken in the secret of the faith.[94]

A hand is a place in that it is an agent for holding, for holding together. The *Zohar* applies this image to the process of unification. Rabbi Moshe Cordovero, commenting on another part of this zoharic discussion, puts it well: "The issue is to answer how a person can unify worlds. What can he do [lit., What is in his hand to do]? And how can he effect repair to what is so very far away from him?"[95] Unification requires the overcoming of space. The agent for unification is the utterance of the Divine Names. So these names must be considered hands. In numerous texts the *Zohar* presents unification as the contraction of spaces, to the point of spatial collapse. All places are to be united into one place. The issue is manifest in a number of areas. The unitive quest through prayer is for the sake of divine unification, but also to raise the human up into the divine space.[96] The path of unification is a "straight path" because it collapses all spaces together into one place.

In these texts we have discerned connections between walking, the unredeemed state of the world, sexual transposition and the exposition of the Torah and spatial and divine unification. To more fully understand these connections, it is necessary to explore some aspects of the *Zohar*'s understanding of space as gendered, and then continue to explore some aspects of the nexus between the *Zohar*'s cosmogony and historiography in its depictions of the coming into being of the mundane world.

Roads: Space and Gender

General and Jewish (religious) cultures have long posited a relation between gender and space. Images, analogies, and concepts are drawn from the physical attributes and biological processes generally attributable to either males or females, as well as from the spatial practices adopted and affirmed within the social contexts and religious traditions of different groups and times. The kabbalists inherited a long tradition that identified the female with interior spaces and that sought biblical warrant for restricting the spatial parameters of female activity. The biblical image of Sarah in her tent was valorized,[97] while Dinah's decision to go outside Jacob's encampment was seen as the cause of her tragic suffering.[98] These assumptions carried weight in the rabbis' legal and exegetical discussions.[99] The household activities of the wife led the rabbis to declare that "'His house' [Lev. 16:6]—that is his wife."[100]

The identification of the female with interiority and enclosure is confirmed in the most basic way on the biological level, through the experience of heterosexual intercourse[101] and through the direct and indirect experience of pregnancy. The Song of Songs' erotic identification of the female beloved with a locked garden (*gan na'ul*)[102] reinforced the identification of Shekhinah as a cloistered garden.[103] Receptivity and enclosure were gendered as female, while bestowal and dispersal were gendered as male, no matter what the sex of the agent might be. Thus, the *Zohar* concludes that beings can flip their gender, depending on their relation to another being. The *Zohar* explains this drawing on 1 Kings 9:1, "And it happened when Solomon had finished building the House of God and the House of the King," saying: "This King, even though He is the Supernal King, is female with regard to the Supernal Point, most hidden of all. And even though He is female, He is male with regard to the Lower King. Therefore everything is in this manner, and thus the lower ones are according to this secret. So it is written of them, 'they came each man and his house' [Exod. 1:1]."[104]

The bridging of these spaces is made necessary and made possible by the force of desire. Speaking of *Yesod*, the *Zohar* explains: "Joseph the Righteous is the most perfect of all. He takes up everything, for everything was established for his sake, all feel intense desire because of him."[105] He takes all by taking the seventh palace, "the palace of desire, the palace of pleasure, the palace for the Upper [Realms] and the Lower [Realms] to delight in each other [*le-ishta'asha'a*] as one."[106] But how is the state of desire's consummation to be reached?

THE OPEN ROAD

The path or road makes all movement, all activity—all life—possible. It is the channel of desire. So Rabbi 'Azriel of Gerona mixes spatial concepts with theosophical ones and writes, "'And moral admonitions are the path of Life' [Prov. 6:23]. Teshuvah is called Life, for the sources of life issue from her. And it says [it is a] 'path,' like something that enters something else and gives it power."[107] The path allows for the making of connections. It penetrates the landscape and conveys influences from place to place.

This is clearly a sexually charged understanding of the image of the path. It is seen as the term for penetration and bestowal. This may be understood as relating to the conception of space as container.[108] The road is counterposed to the fixed place. The place is the point of enclosure, facilitating accumulation and reception. The path is the non-place, and hence, the opposite of the place: the vital, outward-directed energy of giving, but also of breaking through boundaries.[109] Gendered spaces are related erotically. As the erotic channel linking male and female spaces, the road may partake of both natures. The mystical treatise *Ma'ayan Ha-'Hokhmah* distinguishes between various types of pathways. It asks how God created the world, whether by one path or many, and what type of path: "What was it? That is to say, [was it] either a road [*derekh*], lane [*netiv*], or path [*shevil*]?—for the paths are narrow and short, the lanes are bigger, and the roads are wider still. The paths are like children, the lanes are like mothers, and the roads are engraved in the [primal] image of male and female."[110]

Rabbi Yosef Giqatilla alludes to matters of sexual desire and activity by referring to the term *derekh*. In his treatise about the Serpent, he identifies Amaleq with the Snake. He establishes an elaborate chain of associations that link biblical events and personalities with the idea of the road as a sign for earth and magic, sex and sin:

> And know that Amaleq is the Primordial Serpent's head, and he is attached by whisper and the Serpent is his mount [*merkavto*]. It is written, "I am standing before you there [on the rock]" [Exod. 17:6], and this was in Rephidim, and in that very place the Serpent and Amaleq were copulating together, and it is written, "the way [*derekh*] of the snake upon a rock" [Prov. 30:19], and it is written, "and Amaleq came and battled [Israel at Rephidim]" [Exod. 17:8], and surely rock and snake united, and regarding Amaleq, it is written, "Amaleq is the head of nations" [Num. 24:20]. It is written regarding Amaleq, "who put it to him on the road when they came up from Egypt" [1 Sam. 15:2]—in the place that is called road—*derekh*—he waited in ambush for Israel, for that was where Adam left him when Sama'el fell. It is written, "Upon your belly shall you go" [Gen. 3:14]. And he is always found by the female. However, he can be struck on his head. It is written, "He will attack you by head" [Gen. 3:15].[111] Because all kinds of magic [*neḥashim u-me'on'nim ve-qosmim*] are by means of falling with open eyes,[112] it is written, "The fallen ones were in the land [in those days] and also afterwards, when [the sons of God] came [to the daughters of man and they had children for them], they are the mighty ones [*ha-gibborim*]" [Gen. 6:4]—they were from the side of *Gevurah*. It is written about Amaleq, "Who happened upon you on the road" [Deut. 25:18]—in the place of Yesod, which is the road—*ha-derekh*—"and he tailed you" [ibid.]—actually with his tail, at the place he had fallen. "Where he knelt, there he fell, bereft" [Judg. 5:27]. And it is written regarding Balaam, "and God happened [*va-yiqar*][113] to Balaam" [Num. 23:4]. And it is written, "And the angel of God stood in the road to oppose [*le-satan*] him and he

was riding his ass" [Num. 22:22]—actually riding.[114] And it is written, "the way of the snake on a rock, the way of a boat in the heart of the sea and the way of a man with a young woman."[115]

The identification of the road with sexual activity derives from the cluster of associations that the word and the phenomenon evoke. It is linked to the earth, the most material of substances. The Serpent fell to the ground, its legs cut off, after his sin. So it is linked to falling, in the sense of postcoital exhaustion and also in the sense of degradation. Falling also effects a change from verticality to horizontality, returning to the sense of earth and landscape. The verse from Proverbs connects the road with the bobbing up and down of the boat at sea, the repetitive, churning motion of the legs as they walk along, and the erotic pursuit of woman by man. Later, Giqatilla will make explicit the connection between the road and the limbs used for walking—the thighs—with the space between them ever directing the walker to the empty space between the thighs of the female.[116] Additionally, the road is the place of total freedom and lack of boundaries, the open space of erotic possibilities. It is therefore understandable that, in terms of divine potencies, the *Zohar* sees the road—*derekh*—as either male or female. Like Rabbi Azriel and Rabbi Yosef Giqatilla, it sometimes identifies *derekh* with *Yesod*, the road that penetrates and enters *Malkhut*, as in Isaiah 43:16: "Who puts a road into the sea."[117] But it can also apply the term to Shekhinah.[118]

The *Zohar* tells a dramatic story that illustrates the explosive erotic potential of the road:

Rabbi Yitzḥaq and Rabbi Yehudah were going from Usha to Lod. Yose the merchant [*tay'a'a*][119] was with them with a caravan of camels, with packs on their backs.[120] As they were walking, Yose the merchant found a gentile woman who was picking greens in a field. He left them and attacked her and came into her. Rabbi Yitzḥaq and Rabbi Yehudah were amazed. They said, "Let us turn from that path, for the Holy Blessed One wished to show us not to keep company with him. They returned from the road. They checked after him and found that he was the son of the gentile woman [*bat 'el nekhar*] and his father was of disqualified seed. They said, "Bless the Merciful One for saving us."[121]

The outrageous behavior of the merchant is the way of the road. The Companions must turn away from that road. The behavior could only have been enacted by someone who was the product of similar acts of licentiousness. The couple in the story are both non-Jews. The merchant, despite his Jewish name, turns out to be a non-Jew, the product of a sinful union, with his father also being such a product. The connection to the lascivious Serpent is made clearer through one more analogical step. Yose the merchant is like the "mixed multitude" that accompanied Israel out of Egypt and induced them to worship the Golden Calf. "Come and see," says Rabbi Yitzḥaq, "If not for the mixed multitude who joined up with Israel, that act would not have been done and all those from Israel who died would not have died, and all that was caused them wouldn't have been caused."[122] The acceptance of the Torah from Sinai would have repaired the mortal sin caused by the Serpent. But the penalty of death was reapplied because of the influence of the mixed multitude who accompanied Israel on the way.[123]

The danger of sexual chaos on the road is a product of the road's nature as an open space accessible to all. In one walking text, the *Zohar* offers an extended meditation on what it means to walk a path. It offers examples of people following old customs without thinking, of deliberately choosing to do evil to others, of obstructing the ways of the unsuspecting, of gossiping and of acting vengefully, or—alternatively—of choosing to walk in God's ways. At its conclusion it differentiates between two types of paths: "It is written 'road' [*derekh*] and it is written 'way' [*oraḥ*]. What is the difference between this and that? Rather 'road' is that upon which the soles of other people['s feet] have gone. 'Way' is that which has been opened only a short time ago. And it is about such a path that it is written 'And the way of the righteous, like a glowing light [*k'or nogah*], goes on and shines until the day's end' [Prov. 4:18].[124] Amen, so may it be willed."[125]

These concepts are not unique to medieval kabbalists. They have been remarked as characteristic of medieval European culture in general. In a collection of essays on medieval spatial practices, the editors remark: "The realization that people divided space by gender is becoming more apparent; women occupied rooms, houses, quarters in the cities and villages, while men's activities took them farther abroad to streets, highways, fields, cities, oceans, battles and council tables."[126] Another scholar notes: "Entrances and interiors are female, especially churches, and even whole cities. If sacred and enclosed space was coded feminine as a number of studies have shown, the unexplored area of the street, I would argue, was masculine. Not only because it was where public men went out to do business leaving wives and daughters at home, but because its very signs were the art of a network of phallic significations; the only women who could roam freely in Paris were the 'women of the streets,' the 'filles de joie,' and then only in certain regulated and prescribed areas."[127]

The identification of the female with enclosed space attains poetic and erotically charged expression in the courtly motif of the maiden in the tower. The desire of the knight for his lady could be depicted as an assault on a castle, defended by fair damsels.[128] The "Sabba de-Mishpatim" section of the *Zohar* uses this image to depict the desire of the kabbalist to apprehend Torah.[129] The zoharic picture of the tzaddiq is, accordingly, the picture of the virtuous male, the one who knows how to walk on straight paths and who avoids the "licentious woman," the woman who does not stay in her place.[130] The zoharic Companion is the valiant and free male who walks on the road, leaving behind a wife at home. He can avoid temptation because he is accompanied by the Shekhinah.[131]

Yet, in light of the gender assignments made for enclosed and open spaces, the role of the feminine Shekhinah as the companion of the man on the open road is problematic and paradoxical. Furthermore, there seems to be a clash between the sets of oppositions adopted by the *Zohar* as it worked out its gendered spatial orientation. We have seen repeatedly that the *Zohar* values enclosed, contained, interiorized space over exteriorized, open, expansive space. But the gender assignments for these spaces would seem to produce a valorization of the feminine over the masculine, a stance explicitly negated in many places by the *Zohar*, the product of an exclusively male religious culture and tradition. This apparent paradox may be better appreciated when we consider the paradoxical role of Shekhinah in the creation of the mundane world itself.[132]

THE TRAVAILS OF SHEKHINAH

As noted above, the *Zohar* is very reticent about the cosmogony of earthly space, but it contains various statements that could cohere with concepts of creation or emanation.[133] Statements depicting the mundane world as the product of an act of creation are concentrated in the more philosophically oriented zoharic stratum *Midrash ha-Ne'elam*.[134] But if, as the *Zohar* indicates in its boldest statements, the creative and emanative processes were processes internal to the Godhead, what act or mechanism was available to break out of that closed circle and produce a non-divine realm?

The *Zohar* offers a solution to the problem with the image of a secondary emanative process that issues from Shekhinah.[135]

> Come and see: When the Holy Blessed One created the world, He cast a precious stone from under His Throne of Glory and it sank into the depth. One end of that stone was stuck in the depth and the other above. And that other, supernal end is the one point that is set in the center of the world. And from there the world expanded out to the right and to the left and to all sides, established through that central point. And that stone was called *Sheti'ah*—Foundation—for it was from it that the world was planted [*ishtil*] to all sides. Moreover, *Sheti'a"h* is *sha"t Ya"h*—the Holy Blessed One designated it to become the foundation [*yesoda*] of the world and the planting of all.[136]

In this text, standard terms for emanation are used to describe how the mundane world issued from Shekhinah, here imaged as a stone.[137] The mystery of the transition from the Divine to the mundane is expressed through the contradictory transformation of Shekhinah from inanimate stone to source of plantings. But, more pertinent to our discussion is the clear statement that in order to effect this act of transformation it was necessary to transform the feminine Shekhinah into the engendering, male force, *Yesod*.[138]

Another important image in this text is that of God casting His stone down into the depths. This is a dramatic image of rejection or ejection, that is, exile.[139] The making of a mundane world necessitated a forceful act that must be seen as involving pain and suffering.[140] We are familiar with the image of the exiled Shekhinah after the destruction of the Temple. But this myth posits exile and rejection as inherent in the life story of Shekhinah. Since

Shekhinah is the feminine principle, the principle of enclosed space, it would be a violation of her nature to become the source for spatial expansion. Her claim to remain within the enclosed divine system must be rejected if the world is to come into being. To make the world, She must become male Herself and, thereby, She must suffer a separation from the male divine realm. She must leave home. She must suffer exile.

We encounter this theme in another description of the cosmic Tree, at the start of the *Zohar* to the Book of Exodus. The first verse of the book refers to the Israelites' descending into Egypt. The *Zohar* begins its comments on this verse by appealing to Daniel 12:3, the same verse cited at the beginning of its comments on Genesis: "And the enlightened shall shine like the splendor of the firmament."[141] The firmament is the light that issues from Eden, the medium holding the celestial luminaries. The *Zohar* declares:

> *Zohar*—[The Splendor] of that firmament shines with light on the Garden. And the Tree of Life stands in the middle of the Garden, with its branches covering all the images [*diyuqnin*], trees and fragrances in the Garden with appropriate garments. And all the creatures of the field take shade under it and all the birds of the sky live under those branches.
>
> *Zohar*—The fruits of the Tree give life to all. It's existence is eternal. The Other Side does not dwell in it, but only the Side of Holiness. Meritorious is the portion of those who taste of it, they live for ever and ever. They are called "enlightened," and their life is fortunate in this world, and they live on in the coming world.
>
> *Zohar*—This tree stands straight very, very high, 500 parasangs in walking distance, 600,000 in its spread. In this tree there exists one shining light in which all the colors exist. These colors ascend and fall without settling in any other place but that tree. When they go out of it in order to appear in the splendor that does not shine, they settle but don't settle, exist but don't exist, since they do not exist in any other place. From this tree issue twelve tribes [*shevatin*][142] that appear in it. They descended in that splendor that does not shine into the exile of Egypt with numerous supernal camps. This is what is written, "And these are the names of the children of Israel" [Exod. 1:1]. . . .[143]

The *Zohar* creates a rhetorical tour de force around the term *Zohar.*[144] Beginning with the image of light, it shifts to considering how refreshing the shade from that light must be, shade created by the luxuriant, horizontal spread of the branches of the Tree. While the origin of the light might have us expect that it should be welcomed as a source of divine warmth, we find, instead, that all the creatures of the Garden actually stay away from the light, shielded by the Tree that alone basks in its radiance. Yet, by absorbing this light, the Tree itself becomes a source of light.[145] But this new light, displaced from the firmament, is localized within the precincts of the Tree. We are told that there are other spaces, such as the "Other Side," that are not direct beneficiaries of this light. The light of the Tree does not leave its home, nor can the Other Side derive anything from that light. The *Zohar* has described a complex interplay between the vertical and the horizontal, upper and lower, inside and outside, light, shade and dark. Each of these terms' values has been relativized. Each can be seen as positive and negative. There is the realm of the firmament, that beneficent source that is too powerful not to require that its light be absorbed by the protective shade of the Tree. Then we have a sense of two spatial realms, one that is good and one that is not. The self-contained spatial realm of the Tree is good and desirable. Outside the Tree are the realms of exile and the Other Side.

And then we are told that there is an intermediate entity, characterized as a "splendor that does not shine." This is a place of sorts, a place that the Tree's light visits, but in which that light does not feel comfortable. This is an image of the Shekhinah. The Shekhinah serves as the Godhead's liminal force for going between the divine and non-divine realms. To enter that space is already, in some measure, to go outside the Tree. Also, it is somehow capable of leaving the divine space to go "outside." From the perspective of the self-contained space of God, this means going into exile. This liminal quality makes the Shekhinah an uncomfortable space for other divine energies. But this image of the unsettled quality of the divine influx into Shekhinah must be understood against the oft-described and extolled model of unification of upper potencies with Shekhinah. It can be assumed that in this text the reason for the discomfort is unhappiness with the possibility that the twelve tribes will descend from the Tree into that zone of *Malkhut* so as to go outside, into prolonged exile.[146] It would have been preferable for the divine potencies to circulate within a closed system. The effluence of blessing described in many other texts is implicitly seen here as a leakage problem. The spatial orientation expressed here strongly prefers that space be enclosed and sealed.[147] If that space is secured it can be enjoyed. The outside is to be feared and avoided. The ideal state of space is enclosure, not expansion. But the Shekhinah, whose feminine nature determines her identity as an enclosing space, must turn outward. The source of this necessity must be seen as having theosophical and cosmogonic as well as historical dimensions.

The interplay between rejection and devotion, between Her femaleness and maleness is particularly paradoxical in the event that brings about full human engagement in this mundane world, the Expulsion from the Garden of Eden. In reading the Garden of Eden story the *Zohar* had to find a way to continue the identification of the Shekhinah with the enclosed garden while accepting that the story tells of the expulsion of humans from the garden as a result of actions by a female. Its solution was to conceive of Adam's sin as an overdedication to Shekhinah, so that he separated Her from the other divine potencies and effected Her expulsion from the garden just as surely as he suffered his own.[148] The paradox of the Shekhinah's separation from the other divine potencies is that, by Adam's focusing on the female too intently, he condemns her to play the role of the male.

This transformation causes Shekhinah pain. The idea is most pointedly confirmed for the *Zohar* by the biblical decree that, ever since the sin of Adam and Eve, women shall give birth in pain. As Elliot Wolfson has shown in numerous studies, the act of giving birth is valenced by the *Zohar* as a male act.[149] The pain of childbirth is the pain of the female acting as a male. Thus, the *Zohar* explains that the pain of childbirth comes from the bite of the snake, the instigator of spatial boundary crossing.[150] This image is expanded upon in the longer version of this discourse, the homily of the "Hind of the Morning [*Ayelet Ha-Shaḥar*]."[151] The image of the Shekhinah as the source of sustenance for the mundane world is expressed in spatial terms. She is, like the "Woman of Valor" of Proverbs, the one who, instead of fulfilling the female role of staying inside, must travel distances in order to collect the food for the creatures who depend on Her. And the act of dispensing food, requiring a spatial activity appropriate to the male,[152] is identified as the act of giving birth in pain. Here, also, the *Zohar* expresses ambivalence regarding the Serpent. Is it the facilitator of this process or its obstacle? First, the Serpent is summoned by God to bite Her in "that place" twice.[153] But then, after Her womb is opened through the snake bite, releasing sustaining waters for all creatures, God takes away the Serpent. It has a role to play, but must be kept under control.[154] After it is pushed aside, Shekhinah "may be revealed among them in order to walk on [*u-le'itgalya hahi ḥayah beynayhu l'mehakh*]." The Shekhinah's outward-directed spatial practice of walking, below, is acknowledged above by the celestial retinue in God's palace, who declare that "God's Glory has flowed from His Place.[155]

We find a similar expression linking God's Glory and God's Place as an explanation for the Shekhinah's spatial predicament in Rabbi Moshe de Leon's *Sheqel Ha-Qodesh*:

> They asked me: If the Shekhinah has her dwelling in the lower realms, as the early authorities told us, and at the time that the Holy Temple stood, the Shekhinah would descend and remain above the two cherubs, and Her dwelling was in the lower realms, and after that, in the same way, the Shekhinah's dwelling was in the lower realms in the synagogues and study halls—if so then Her place is not above. And it is not right for Her to lose Her place among the upper realms. How will they be supported and how can they stand? Response: This is a matter about which there is no need for a person to try to inquire. For we already know with clear knowledge that "the whole earth is full of His Glory" [Isa. 6:3], and behold, "the heavens and heavens' heavens cannot encompass Him" [2 Chron. 2:5]. No matter how small this world is, there is no place empty, above or below, from the Shekhinah, for She is the Glory of His Place. Indeed the dwelling of the Shekhinah is above and below, all at the same time.[156]

De Leon's interlocutor is troubled by issues of spatial logic and divine justice. How can Shekhinah be sent to dwell down below when She is supposed to be above. She cannot logically be in both realms together, and it is unjust to deprive Her of Her rightful place. De Leon's answer is that there is no logical problem for God. Shekhinah can be in both places, for She is the manifestation of God's spatiality. To answer the charge of injustice, de Leon reviews Israel's history to show how Shekhinah was content to be united above and yet be drawn down to dwell with Israel below, in the modest shelter of the Temple, until Israel's sins sent Her into exile. "Now

She walks in exile after them to all the places where they settle. And She continuously walks in exile with Israel to protect them and defend them. And now, above and below and from all sides, She is in exile."[157]

For the *Zohar*, the pain of Shekhinah, as She remains in this world (as a male), is recounted in the biblical story of the death of Rachel as she gives birth to Benjamin:

> It is written: "And it was, as her soul departed as she died" [Gen. 35:18]. Come and see—in this world below, the righteous enters it and leaves it. When he enters it, he is of the mystery of Joseph the Righteous. When he leaves, he is of the mystery of Benjamin. This is what [is meant when it] is written, "And it was, as her soul departed as she died." Who is "her soul"? This is the tzaddiq who goes out from her. And this is Benjamin, called *ben 'oni* [the son of my sorrow], for she thought that she had given birth for the [world] below, the world of separation, and [only] eleven [tribes] were left among those above. What is written? "And his father called him 'Benjamin.'" [That is] *ben yamin* [son of the Right], for he ascended upward to the higher world, for when Joseph was lost, Benjamin took his place.[158]

Rachel, the personification of Shekhinah, calls her son "child of my sorrow" because she mistakenly thinks that she has given birth to a being of this lower world. Since the act of giving birth is valenced as a male activity in the zoharic system, Shekhinah's pain issues from being in the state of having to change into a male for the sake of this world of separation. Since She cannot, of Herself, initiate a move toward the upper realms, it is necessary for Jacob to do so, restoring Her offspring to the upper realm by renaming the child Benjamin—son of the Right—and in so doing, apparently restoring Rachel to herself as the female partner of the higher potencies. But this is not quite so. Rachel, as Shekhinah, nevertheless continues to be tied to this mundane world.[159]

In his responsum on the relations between the Matriarchs Leah and Rachel and their husband, Jacob, de Leon explains that Leah represents the potency *Binah*, the "happy mother of children," while Rachel represents Shekhinah. The implication is that Rachel is the unhappy mother of children. He distinguishes between the concealed nature of Leah and the revealed nature of Rachel. "According to this approach Leah was hidden in the secret spaces within the Cave of Makhpelah because she is a hint of the Hidden World, while Rachel [was buried] at the crossroads on the way, because she is the hint for the Revealed World. And so all of Rachel's affairs, concerning her match and all her matters and her burial, are revealed, so as to hint at the Revealed World."[160]

The *Zohar* takes this one step further. It asks why Leah merited being buried with Jacob, hidden away in the Cave, while Rachel was condemned to be buried in the open, by the road. Its answer is that each was rewarded or punished for their behavior before uniting with Jacob. "Rabbi Yehudah said: 'Leah would stand all her days at the crossroads, crying for Jacob's sake, when she heard that he was a tzaddiq, going out to him in prayer. And this is what is written, 'And Leah's eyes were soft' [Gen. 29:17], as we established, for she first sat at the crossroads to plead. Rachel did not ever go to the roads. Therefore Leah merited to be buried with him and Rachel's grave was set to be at the crossroads and there she was buried."[161] Because Leah was willing to go out to the roads in her yearning for Jacob, she was rewarded by becoming the representative of the Concealed World. But because Rachel was unwilling to leave her place, to go out to the road for Jacob's sake, she was destined to remain buried apart from Jacob, in the open intersection of the roads. Shekhinah's painful struggle over Her spatial nature is given a grim sense of inevitability. In this world it is necessary to go out onto the road, no matter how much this may violate one's nature. Only after such a sacrifice may one contemplate the possibility of union with the Divine Beloved.

There is no denying that the theme of bringing about divine unification is a pervasive one in the *Zohar*. But in our investigation so far, we can discern a quieter countertheme, the necessity for the outward turning of the Divine to sustain this world in its separate, mundane existence, the necessity of maintaining spatiality rather than reasserting unity.

Letters, Names, Words, Creation

Another approach adopted by the *Zohar* to explain how this lower world came about was to assign the creative function to a letter or to letters of the Hebrew alphabet or of God's Name.[162] This linguistic approach is rooted in traditions going back to the Torah's own depiction of Creation. Language is a good example of a creative medium that issues from the creative agent and then takes on a life of its own. The act can be conceived of as one of speaking, of writing or of combination.[163] We find that even in this approach, which tends toward abstraction, the spatial element asserts itself nonetheless:

> Come and see—Through forty-two letters the world was engraved[164] and established. And all are the diadem [*'ateret*] of the Holy Name. When all these letters collected together above and descended below, diadems were crowned in the four directions of the world,[165] and it could stand. And afterwards the letters went out and created the world above and below, in the World of Unity and the World of Separation, which were called "the mountains of *Bater* [splitting]" [Song of Sol. 2:17]—mountains of separation—that are watered when the South side begins to approach it.[166]

The letters, in order to create the world, first must establish a spatial realm, in which the horizontal directions are as important as the vertical. The original space-creating role of the letters persists as a sustaining activity into the present. Thus the *Zohar* instructs: "He who wants to go out on a journey should get up at the break of day, and look momentarily in a mirror [*b'istakluta*] towards the east. And he will see the appearance of letters that strike in the sky, one goes up and the other goes down. These are the sparks of the letters through which heaven and earth were created."[167] The *Zohar* pictures the letters in constant movement through space. They constitute a "chariot work" (*ma'aseh merkavah*) for the "holy celestial creatures," as the *Zohar* shows by explicating Isaiah 7:11, "Ask for yourself a sign [letter -*'ot*] from God, deep down to the Depths or raised up high."[168] The space-creating letters are thus also instrumental in facilitating successful motion through space and angelic and human activity in space.[169] Therefore, the traveler, to prepare for his journey, utters prayers with these very letters, ensuring that "Shekhinah certainly starts out with him."[170]

We are reminded of the zoharic Heikhalot text discussed above,[171] in which the *Zohar* ties the continued revelation of the Torah with the unfolding of history. The development of the Oral Torah after the historical crisis of the destruction of the Temple was simply another manifestation of the inherent identity obtaining between the life of the letters and the ramification of space. The *Zohar* connects this concept with the activity of Companions who are constantly creating new Torah. We saw earlier that their innovative way is what differentiates their path from that of the masses. The expansive nature of the cosmogonic letters is paralleled by the world-creating faculty employed by the constant utterance of new words of Torah. "Those words measure out upper dwellings and lower dwellings. From those are made firmaments and from those earth, out of that praise. And should you say that those words are in one place, [they are, rather] roaming the world—[as it says] 'their words are from the end of the earth' [Ps. 19:5]."[172] The *Zohar* explicitly opposes the idea that words of Torah must be kept in one place only. Their very nature is to be creative, expansive, and spatially active.

This bright, early morning imagery contrasts with the darker aspects of pathos and pain that characterize the image of Shekhinah in labor, tied as that image is to the historical context of destruction and exile. In the linguistic approach, the role of Shekhinah in making the mundane world is exuberantly loquacious rather than tragic. Shekhinah is Speech itself.[173]

Accepting Spatiality

The transition from the divine to the mundane worlds is not merely explained by means of intermediary spaces, agents and media. These elements also serve to mitigate the abruptness of the transition. This is necessary so that the mundane world may attain some level of acceptance. To this end, the transition between the two realms is softened by means of a buffer zone. Such a liminal function is performed by the set of *heikhalot*—a spatial/spiritual construct. More profoundly, Shekhinah Herself is charged with serving as the liminal divine force—that potency within the Godhead that, in sorrow or in joy, enables the bridging of the Godly and the mundane worlds. Finally, a third liminal area is provided by the letters and words of divine speech by means of the biblical text itself, in the form of story or instruction. The figures and events of Israel's sacred history, as well as her sacred laws, serve as the practical bridge between God's space and the space of human activities. The Patriarchs and Matriarchs, Moses, Israel, and other biblical personalities and events serve in both a historical and a mythic capacity. They take place in mundane space and yet participate in theosophical realities. The Torah's laws constitute models of significant actions. These are all the liminal entities called *dugma*—a term equivalent to "form" "exemplar," or "paradigm"[174]—and *'uvda* (*'uvada*)—equivalent to the Hebrew term *ma'aseh* and carrying the meanings of "act," "story," or "geste." The actions and events of the Torah—both mandated and narrated—allow for future human actions to "take place"—that is, to meaningfully transpire—within a seemingly meaningless spatial context.

If the implication of the concept, *dugma*, is that there is a straightforward correspondence and mutuality between objects, spaces and actions below and above, the concept *'uvda* is involved in a more complicated attitude toward the realm of human activity. After all, the term's connotations range from the most serious to the most playful and frivolous. This will be touched upon below. For the present our subject demands that we focus on one particular issue. The value by which actions are usually judged for kabbalistic significance, as pointed out in any number of discussions and studies of these questions, is the value of unification. In spatial terms, this indicates a tendency to try to contract space and reenclose reality, as I have shown above. But there is another value that runs counter to this unitive, space-annihilating tendency. This is the value of spatial maintenance, the support and reaffirmation of the already expanded realms of the cosmos, this mundane world included. This secondary source of significance is invoked by the *Zohar*, sometimes explicitly and sometimes less clearly. First, we shall examine some aspects of the zoharic theory of sacrifice. Then we shall consider other types of *'uvda*.

SACRIFICES

Unlike the philosophers, who could allegorize, historicize, or otherwise mitigate the sacrifices' importance, the kabbalists believed that the sacrifices performed indispensable operations of cosmic moment. Most discussions about sacrifices in kabbalah focus on sources that emphasize the unificatory function of these rites.[175] But this is not the only function that sacrifices play. Sacrifices also perform the important function of spatial maintenance. This point is very important because, with the Temple and its cultus lost, the kabbalists had to transfuse their understanding of the sacrificial system into a set of substitutes. Furthermore, the more intensive and convincing the kabbalists' explanations for the necessity of the sacrifices, the more acute the crisis caused by their disappearance.

As elucidated by Seth L. Brody and others, the zoharic solution is based on kabbalistic traditions that singled out the element of intention and consciousness as the source of meaning in actions, especially rituals. This was beneficial for the kabbalists in three ways. One gain was that it allowed for the preservation of the essence of the sacrificial system, since even if the cultus was destroyed, it would still be possible to continue the requisite intentions, albeit in a new context. Moreover, through the notion of parallelism—*dugma*—by preserving sacrificial intentions and grafting them on to other actions, the sacrificial system as it obtains to the divine realm could continue. The final gain was the elevation of mystical experience to primacy, since kabbalah was the fullest and deepest source for understanding and executing the requisite intentions. And these intentions were overwhelmingly those of *tiqqun* and *yiḥud*—repair and unification of the divine realms—and *devequt*—unification of the kabbalist with the Divine.

But the kabbalists acknowledged that there was another function to the sacrifices. Sacrificial acts were also directed toward the Other Side.[176] These offerings were seen either as a distraction of the evil forces, allowing Israel and Shekhinah to be saved,[177] or as a gesture of appeasement to that Side.[178] The scapegoat ritual of Yom Kippur entailed the ritual disposition of two goats, one offered on the Temple's altar and one sent away to the wilderness. Based on earlier traditions, this was interpreted as a simultaneous offering to God and to the Other Side.[179] But this idea was not exclusively limited to the scapegoat. In some sense all sin offerings could be seen as gifts to the *Sitra Aḥra*.[180] Or else the innards of all sacrifices were seen in this light.[181] Similarly, the act of circumcision was seen as a sacrificial act, the foreskin, discarded in the dust, being a gift to the Other Side.[182] This striking concept, which even the *Zohar* had to question,[183] nevertheless follows from the cosmogonic map adopted by the *Zohar*. The Other Side, as long as it was held at bay, had its rightful space, a space that had to be maintained.

Indeed, while the unitive significance of the sacrificial act (and its substitutes) has been studied in depth, the recognition of the need for spatial maintenance within the kabbalistic theory of sacrifice has been somewhat elided in the scholarly discussions. Sacrifices are intended to effect the union of male and female, upper and lower divine potencies. But the intended result of this unificative act is the release of divine energies back into the lower regions, including the mundane world, in order to sustain them and help them thrive. In his treatment of the sacrifices, Tishby devotes barely a line to this idea.[184] In one place, however, Brody writes about this quite clearly:

> Although de Leon defines personal and cosmic reintegration as the teloi of halachic praxis, Israel's service ultimately fulfills three essential goals. The observance of the commandments firstly enables the soul to attain devekut, communion or adhesion to God. Secondly, Catalonian tradition depicts halachic praxis as unifying the Sefirot—drawing the entirety of the emanational pleroma back to its ultimate source in Keter, so that it might be charged with energies of blessing and renewed life. It is from this unitive function that the final telos of praxis emerges, the invocation of meshekh or shefa—creative energy into the phenomenal universe. Upon their reemergence from their ultimate ground, the Sefirot radiate their light into the cosmos.[185]

But Brody fails to keep this concept distinct. In his development of these points, Brody gives attention to Baḥya's explanation of the significance of the four species used on Sukkot. Baḥya makes the comparison between this practice and offering a sacrifice, "which (served) to draw forth divine energy."[186] Brody comments that "the 'mitzvot are Divine Glory' and thus tools for the reconstitution and reunification of the divine and phenomenal cosmoi."[187] Unfortunately, Brody does not differentiate here between divine unification and maintenance of the non-divine realm. Thus, at the end of his discussion, the three teloi of halakhic praxis he enumerated at the start are reduced to two. He writes: "The array of sources collected and analyzed in this chapter reveals that halachic praxis fulfills two essential purposes. Its first end is the spiritual transformation of the Kabbalistic adept, who is brought into a state of devekut or mystical adhesion to Divinity. Its second end is theurgic, directed towards the maintenance of Sefirotic unity and the invocation of beneficent and life infusing energies into the cosmos."[188]

But these two issues should not be combined into one.[189] As this study has argued, there is a tension between the two. The maintenance of spaces that remain outside of the Divinity, whether the *Sitra Aḥra* or the mundane world, requires a turning outward by the Divine that is antithetical to the unitive process. The push to unification would ultimately wish to eliminate these cosmic spaces. The divine embrace must be broken and reopened for the mundane world to continue to exist. To recognize this tension is to recognize the strain placed on the unitive idea as well as the nature of divine sacrifice in acceding to spatiality.

In one text the *Zohar* teaches that these two aspects of spatial maintenance—the distancing of the *Sitra Aḥra* and the evocation of blessing into the mundane sphere—are involved in Noah's sacrifice and God's response after the Flood. Commenting on God's promise never to curse the earth again, the *yenuqa* reports: "I heard that since it is written 'the earth is cursed because of you' [Gen. 3:17], that at the time when the earth was cursed because of Adam's sin, permission was given to the Evil Snake to rule over it, for he is the wrecker of the world and destroys people. From the day that Noah offered the sacrifice and God smelled it, permission was given to the earth to get out from under that Snake and it left defilement. Therefore Israel offers sacrifices to the Holy Blessed One, in order to illuminate the face of the earth." A bit further we read this comment on God's blessing to Noah and his children to be fruitful: "Rabbi Abba opened and said, 'God's blessing will enrich and He will not add pain with it' [Prov. 10:22]. 'God's blessing'—this is the Shekhinah Who is charged with the world's blessings and from Whom blessings issue for all."[190]

The *yenuqa* teaches that the purpose of sacrifice is to distance the Other Side so that the mundane world can flourish without harassment by the forces of evil. Rabbi Abba develops this point, alluding to the abolition of the pain that must accompany the enjoyment of the earth's produce, as God ordained after the sin. This pain is eliminated through the giving of gifts to husband and wife, the divine couple, through the medium of sacrifices. But their union is for the sake of releasing blessings into the mundane world. If the loving relationship between husband and wife is enhanced, the wife will be able to "send the guest out"[191] without pain. Is it possible that the pain that is at issue is not only the pain of eating from the earth, but the pain of childbirth, as well? One possible allusion to this is the concluding teaching of Rabbi Abba: "'In pain'—the pain and rage without the illumination of the Faces, when the moon is darkened and blessings are not found."[192] He connects the pain with the absence of divine union, signaled by the darkening of the moon, a manifestation of the moon's diminution. This symbolism is explicitly tied to the Shekhinah's pain during the birth process in the texts that relate the myth of the Hind, mentioned above.

If we recognize that one purpose of sacrifices is spatial maintenance, and that creating and vouchsafing extra-divine spatiality, specifically through the reorientation of Shekhinah, entails a painful divine accommodation, we may perhaps have a better understanding of the *Zohar*'s veiled explanation for the New Moon sacrifice.[193] The *Zohar*, based on an earlier midrash, hints that the New Moon offering is a sin offering to expiate God's decision to diminish the moon.[194] This enigmatic teaching is somewhat elucidated by Rabbi Moshe de Leon's remarks in his *Sefer Ha-Rimmon*:

> But, indeed, this atonement does not have to do with [*eyn kaparah zu etzel*] the moon or the sun, but only with regard to Above, so that the intention should be toward the High Place to draw from there the Bright Light by way of the channels, to illuminate the moon for her being the least grade of all. And that is [the meaning of] "because I reduced the moon" and she has no light from herself. And in order to draw light from the Bright Light, "bring an atonement for Me"—because it is from there that all life issues forth—by focusing the proper intention with this sacrifice. And the secret is that [the intention in] all the sacrifices is from below to above, in order to join all together. But now "bring [atonement] for Me" so that the intention shall be from above to below, so as to illuminate her and to walk in her light day and night.[195]

Relating this text to other texts in the *Zohar* proper, Brody explains this teaching as follows:

> As the interface between the noumenal and phenomenal realms and the point of divine self-limitation giving rise to differentiated reality, the Shechi-

> nah is impaired and thus vulnerable to the depredations of cosmic evil. The bestowal of this vulnerability constitutes the "sin" for which God must render atonement through the sin offering of the New Moon. This act of atonement does not simply invoke the unificative energy of the Clear Light into Malkhut. The sin offering literally rescues the Shechinah from the clutches of the Sitra Aḥra.[196]

This explanation does not go far enough. Brody suggests that the economy of divine forces is harmoniously restored once Shekhinah is rescued from *Sitra Aḥra*. But our understanding is that, conceived as an act of spatial maintenance, the sacrifices merely reset the cosmos within its intractable paradox of divine and non-divine spatial existence. Rather, the underlying message seems be that God takes responsibility for making a decision that both deprives Shekhinah of Her own light, and yet requires that She be the source of light for the world. This paradox produces an inherently unstable condition. The erotic, boundary-crossing nature of the Other Side must be brought under control. But doing so merely allows Shekhinah to continue in Her self-negating condition. While this decision is fundamentally necessary for the world's sustenance, the painful nature of the predicament that God has decreed for Shekhinah requires that God ask for atonement from Israel, whose very life derives from this situation. It is only because of God's painful decision that Israel is able "to walk in Her light."

Or, to put it another way: Ostensibly the defeat of the evil forces threatening Shekhinah brings the drama to a happy ending. But, as we have seen above, the control of the Other Side is not equivalent to its obliteration. That Side is a spatial requirement of the cosmos, as is the mundane world. Shekhinah will be united within the Divine, but not so happily that the mundane world demanding Her care will disappear. In truth, the more fundamental plot line of this drama—or *'uvda*—has it that both the "villain" (*Sitra Aḥra*) and the "damsel" (Shekhinah) are equally involved in the maintenance of the conditions necessary for the existence of our "hero" (Israel). In fact, it is really not the hero who is rescuing the damsel from the rapacious villain, or her "elderly father" (*Keter*) from the foolish mistake that put his daughter in jeopardy. Actually, once these "characters" are put in their proper places, it emerges that it is they who are saving the hero.

The offering of atonement is thus an offering of acceptance from the hero, acknowledging that this drama must nevertheless be enacted.

SPACE AND STORY

The sacrificial system was interpreted by the kabbalists in such a way that it served as a paradigm for meaningful action. The destruction of that system had raised the question of the possibility of meaningful action in other ways and, just as important, in other places. The kabbalists inherited a long tradition devoted to sacrificial "displacement" and "replacement." "Displacement" of the cultus meant finding personae, places, and actions that could be seen as being of a cultic nature. In this vein, for example, kabbalists saw circumcision as a sacrificial act, synagogues as sacred spaces and kabbalists as priestly adepts of theurgic intentionality. "Replacement" meant finding other means of accomplishing the same purposes of the cultus, without being restricted to its personnel, structures, or locales.

The rabbis suggested that sacrifices had been replaced by prayer, Torah study and acts of goodness. Their approach raised the value of words to the level of deeds. The tradition that the world was created through divine speech gave the best justification for this belief. But the question of the power or efficacy of words and actions is a fundamental one, so the kabbalists had to struggle with it also. They, too, wanted to know: Are all human actions significant, or only some? What about human speech? Are only the mitzvot meaningful, but not other actions? Is only the Torah meaningful, but not other texts? Is significance inherent in certain actions, or is it bestowed through certain other factors, such as space, time, or intention? What is the significance of seemingly insignificant actions? *'Uvda* is an important term in the *Zohar*'s consideration of these questions.[197] This study can only touch upon the *Zohar*'s use of this term, specifically as it relates to the *Zohar*'s spatial orientation. To do this, I shall concentrate on one zoharic text, the first pages of the *Zohar* to *B'ha'alot'kha*.

The zoharic commentary on the portion begins with the description of the Cosmic Tree, quoted earlier,[198] compared to the menorah and to the Torah. After this, Rabbi Abba extols Israel's good portion, for through the

Torah, Israel was freed from Egyptian bondage. Here begins a detailed exposition of the Exodus story. Egypt corresponds to the Other Side, so the battle to free Israel is of cosmic significance. The Israelites help the divine forces by singing during their paschal celebration and by placing the blood of the paschal lamb and of their own circumcisions upon their doorposts.[199] The *Zohar* remarks:

> Here it is necessary to look [more deeply]. If it is the Holy Blessed One Who comes and kills in the land of Egypt, and not some other emissary, why this mark on the opening, for all is revealed to Him? And furthermore, what is "and He will not permit the Destroyer" [Exod. 12:23]? It should say, "and He will not destroy." Rather it is certainly this way, as it is written, "And God struck every first-born" [Exod. 12:29]. "And God,"—He and His Court.[200] And that Court is found here. And in all[201] it is necessary to show an action [*'uvda*] in order to be saved, just as on the altar, in order that the Destroyer should not be present.[202]

The *Zohar* teaches that God did not need a sign on the doorposts in order to know which house was an Israelite house. Rather, in order for Israel to be saved, God demanded of Israel that they perform an action.[203] Although the Torah emphasizes that God had no partners or agents in liberating Israel, the *Zohar* insists that Israel had to take part in its own redemption, making Israel God's partner. The nature of this partnership is explained by the analogy to sacrifices. Israel's action was not a signal for God, but an apotropaic act directed against the Other Side, the other force that would wish to get into the picture. The act is analogous to the paradigmatic acts of sacrifice.

The *Zohar*'s story of the extrication of Israel from Egypt is replete with references to the Shekhinah. It was together with Shekhinah that the twelve tribes went into Egyptian exile, as the *Zohar* taught at the beginning of *Sh'mot*. Now Shekhinah, especially in Her stern aspect of Judgment, is involved in getting them out. Shekhinah is the altar itself,[204] the place where all significant actions take place. The actions that Israel offers on the altar of their mundane space are verbal and physical. Their verbal act is their singing, a practice that prepares the unification of Shekhinah with the higher potencies.[205] The physical actions are the paschal offering, and more poignantly, their offering of themselves through circumcision.[206] After establishing these two types of significant action, the *Zohar* adds another example, the blowing of the shofar on the Days of Judgment. This act combines action of the mouth and the use of a physical object.[207] "We bring out with that sound Love and Judgment together." As the Masters of Judgment are broken and the forces of Love are aroused, "all supernal lamps [*butzinin 'ila'in*][208] glow from this side and from that side."[209]

This image echoes the image of the lighting of the menorah, the starting point of the discourse. But a transformation has occurred. We have moved from a daily ritual whose performance was restricted to a priest in the Tabernacle or Temple to a festival ritual performed by any Jew, anywhere. This was done by way of an analysis of a ritual act that was performed once in Jewish history and applied to the regular Jewish cycle of life. Furthermore, the kindled lights have been spiritualized. They are not the actual oil lamps of the sanctuary. They are the supernal lamps. The path of the *Zohar*'s discourse apparently turns back to sacerdotal matters once more by including one more element in the priestly ritual, an element that could have been kept separate—the incense offering:

> Come and see—at the time that the priest intends to light the lamps below, and would offer the spice incense [*qetoret*] at that moment, then the supernal lamps glow, and all is tied together [*v'itqetar*][210] and rejoices, and happiness is present in all worlds. This is what is written: "Oil and incense will gladden the heart" [Prov. 27:9], and about this [it is written], "When you light up the lamps" [Num. 8:2].[211]

But the reference to *qetoret*—incense—is not simply a return of the discussion to the Temple precincts. The institution of incense is a crucial element with which the *Zohar* struggles to effect a transition away from the literal requirements of the sacrificial system. The *Zohar* values incense above all sacrifices. "There is nothing [as] beloved before the Holy Blessed One as *qetoret*."[212] By making this claim the *Zohar* begins its process of the displacement and replacement of the sacrificial system within the space of the Temple itself. The incense is the best means to maintain the spatial integrity of the cosmos, both by keeping the *Sitra Aḥra* in place, and by inducing the flow of divine energies downward to the mundane world. Later in the discussion about the *'uvda* of the menorah,[213] the *Zohar* contrasts the outer altar, upon which the sacrifices were offered, and the inner altar, upon which the incense burned. It notes that the outer altar was openly dedicated by the twelve tribes' leaders, but the greater ritual related to the menorah and the inner altar was Aaron's province alone.[214] It is from the inner altar that all joy derives and the outer altar is sustained. The sacrifices were a public ritual, but the incense was a private ritual. Thus, to privilege incense over sacrifice is to privilege the spiritual over the material,[215] the inner realm over the outer, and the concealed over the revealed.

The Torah's texts about sacrificial laws must be read below the surface. The zoharic reading of this text makes the Temple's ritual system into a *dugma* for its own hermeneutical project. By reading below the surface, one comes to realize that the smoke and aromas of the incense, as they becloud, conceal, and overcome the ambience of the Temple, actually correspond to the revelation of the Torah on Sinai.

> Said Rabbi Abba, "When the smoke of Sinai issued forth, the fire ascended and was crowned with that smoke in the open like this cluster and ascended and descended. And all the fragrances and aromas in the Garden of Eden would ascend [in] this smoke in the appearance of white, red, and black. This is what is written: 'smelling of the burnt incense [*mequteret*] of myrrh and frankincense from all the powders of the spice merchant'" [Song of Sol. 3:6].[216]

The displacement of the sacrificial rites to the interior of the sanctuary parallels the replacement of the lost sacrificial system of rituals—through the kabbalists' deeper understanding of Torah—with those that may be realized in the contemporary, mundane world, in exile.

THE RULE OF STORIES

Precisely at this point, the *Zohar* introduces a walking story. The Companions are walking along and come to some forbidding-looking mountains. To overcome their fear they open with words of Torah:

> Rabbi Ele'azar opened: "The ark rested on the seventh month on the mountains of Ararat" [Gen. 8:4]. . . . How beloved are the words of the Torah, for there are supernal secrets in every word. And the Torah is called the supernal

> inclusive rule [*klal*].[217] And we have learned in the Torah's thirteen hermeneutical principles [*mekhilan*]: "Anything that was in the general rule and came out of the general rule to teach, comes out to teach, not about itself, but about the entire general rule." So [with] the Torah, which is the supernal inclusive rule—even if any story [*sippur*] comes out of it, it certainly did not come out to show anything about that story, but, rather, to show supernal matters and supernal secrets, and it did not come out to teach about itself, but it came out to teach about the entire inclusive rule. Because that Torah story or that action [*'uvda*], though it came from out of the Torah, doesn't come to teach about itself alone, but it came out to show something about that entire supernal inclusive rule of the Torah.[218]

The teaching of Rabbi Ele'azar has been noted by numerous scholars because of its striking message regarding the proper way to read the Torah.[219] This text and its continuation declare emphatically that the stories of the Torah must be read as other than stories. As stories they "stick out"; they go out of the general rule of the Torah. The assumption is that the Torah, as a sacred text, cannot be interested in mundane matters. What happens and what has happened in this world is of no importance unless it serves to teach about some deeper truth. As Rabbi Ele'azar asks, when the Torah tells us the ark landed on the Ararat Mountains, "what do we care whether it lands here or there?" Instead, these stories must be included in the Torah to reveal supernal matters.

This fundamental statement about the value of stories and the actions they report must be read within its zoharic context. This statement denigrating the value of stories is itself placed within a story of the walking Companions. The walking story, in turn, comes after a discourse on the Exodus from Egypt and the meaning of sacrificial acts, including the special significance of the incense. This contextualization alerts us to the need to read the story with care. It begins:

> Rabbi Ele'azar and Rabbi Yose and Rabbi Yitzḥaq were walking on the road. They came upon the mountains of Darkness/Ararat [*turei qardo*].[220] As they were walking, Rabbi Ele'azar raised his eyes and saw those tall mountains, how dark they were, and they were all afraid. Rabbi Ele'azar said, "Were Father here we would not be afraid. But since we are three and there is Torah among us, Judgment cannot be found among us."

The first impression one has upon encountering this story is that it is an interruption. The *Zohar* had proceeded until now without recourse to narratives, using the standard give-and-take between sages about the mystical exegesis of Torah verses and their theosophical and theurgical implications. The story itself seems irrelevant. In what way might this story be connected to the previous discussion? We must bear in mind that the preceding discourse was not solely a lecture on theurgic ritual. That issue is of moment particularly because the *Zohar* is concerned with the question of sacrificial displacement and the possibility of meaningful actions in this world. Its transvaluation of *qetoret* into a paradigm for the displacement and replacement of the sacrifices can serve the Companions in meeting their own personal situation.

The walking story presents the Companions in exile. They are in the vicinity of Ararat. They are displaced and disoriented. As they peer at the dark mountains they are afraid. Fear is a normal reaction to traveling on the road, since roads are dangerous places. But fear has another meaning for the *Zohar*. It is the result of alienation from God caused by sin, and the resulting sense of displacement:

> "And they heard the sound of God Almighty walking Himself (*mit'halekh*) in the garden" [Gen. 3:8]. "Walking" [*m'halekh*] is not written here, but "walking Himself."[221] Come and see—until Adam sinned he would ascend and stand in the Wisdom of the supernal light, and he would not separate from the Tree of Life. Since his desire to know and to descend below increased, he was drawn after them until he separated from the Tree of Life, and he knew evil and abandoned good. About this it is written: "For You are not a God Who desires wickedness; no evil dwells with You [*lo y'gurkha r'a*]" [Ps. 5:5].[222] Anyone who is drawn after evil has no dwelling with the Tree of Life. And until they sinned they would hear a voice from above and know the supernal Wisdom, and stand in the pillar [*qiyyuma*] of the supernal light, and they would not be afraid. Once they sinned, they could not stand before even the lower voice.[223]

The dislocation of Adam from the Tree results in his becoming afraid of God's voice. His punishment will be exile. In the same way, notes the *Zohar*, until Israel sinned at Mount Sinai, they were fearless, capable of seeing God at the Red Sea without becoming afraid, and capable of hearing

God's voice revealing the Torah. But after they sinned, they were even afraid to look at Moses' face. In their case, the response was the dislocation of the Tent of Meeting and the concealment of Moses' face. In addition, fear was not only the portion of the sinners:

> From this Anger and Ire issue forth a thousand and many tens of thousands [of forces]. And they all go out and alight upon people, those who passionately study [*de-mishtadlin*][224] Torah or passionately try to do matters of mitzvah and who walk in the path of mitzvah, so that they may be pained and not be happy in it. And it is from these two that Moses was afraid when Israel sinned and he descended from the mountain, as it is written, "For I was afraid [*yagorti*] of the Anger and the Ire" [Deut. 9:19].[225]

The Companions are fearful and bereft. Rabbi Ele'azar explains that were his father with them, they would not be afraid. It is entirely possible that this story transpires after Rashbi's death. The situation of the Companions is analogous to Israel's condition after the loss of the sacrificial rites. What can replace them or him?[226] The substitution is the three Companions themselves, as they prepare to engage in Torah.[227] On one level, their sense of security stems from the tradition that demons avoid groups of three.[228] But this idea takes on new meaning from the earlier discussion about the Exodus and sacrifices. The mixture of the paschal and covenantal bloods was brushed onto the doors in three marks. The Companions are also three. The three marks are the three letters *yud* that represent God's Name.[229] The walking of the Companions on this earth is equivalent to the marking of the altar with the blood of sacrifices. "A person who is worthy [*zaka'ah*] is himself an actual [*mamash*] sacrifice for atonement. . . . Thus the righteous person is an atonement in this world, and an actual sacrifice."[230]

Standing before the Ararat mountains, Rabbi Ele'azar begins his teaching about how to read Scripture's stories. His teaching that happenstance is not a fitting subject for Torah is prompted by the happenstance of his day's walk. He recalls that Scripture relates that the ark descended upon these very mountains. "Who cares where it landed?" he asks. But his question is provoked by his knowing the very fact that he considers immaterial. Only because he knows this seemingly meaningless fact can Rabbi Ele'azar make the connection between the biblical *'uvda* and his own. The narrative of seemingly mundane circumstance is not, as he seems to be saying, an element that can be dispensed with once its more profound meaning is apprehended.[231] The profound truth rests on the mundane, just as surely as the ark rested on the mountains.

Why, then, is this story being told by the *Zohar*? The conclusion of Rabbi Ele'azar's homily will interpret the story of the ark as a reference to the Rosh Ha-Shanah ritual that was connected to the story of the Exodus at the start of the zoharic discourse to this parashah. The *Zohar* thereby presents a well-crafted, even virtuosic text that makes far-ranging connections between various laws, customs, events, and mythic values in Jewish tradition. These connections are made through a text whose literary segments are likewise connected with great skill. So the walking story plays its part in this literary production, this *'uvda*.[232] But if we can appreciate the sophisticated use of the walking text as text, we can still ask the question that lies behind the text—why were the Companions walking on that road in the first place? We are tempted to answer, "For the sake of the text and its teaching." Such an answer would seem to be in keeping with Rabbi Ele'azar's message. The story must be coming to teach some profound truth of Torah.[233] The *Zohar* means to teach that the telling of a mere story—*ma'aseh* or *'uvda b'alma*—can also be a significant act in the world, an *'uvda ba-'alma*. But that answer misses a subtle change that Rabbi Ele'azar makes in the language of the hermeneutical rule. The original formula, first cited in Hebrew, states that an exception to the rule does not leave the general "to teach about itself, but it came out to teach about the entire general rule." However, Rabbi Ele'azar's twice-stated Aramaic adaptation of this sentence adds one word: "it did not come out to reveal something about itself *alone* [*bilvad*], but it came out to show something about that entire supernal inclusive rule of the Torah."[234] In his formulation, Rabbi Ele'azar maintains the integrity of the story as a separate element that persists beside the realm of revelations of Torah. It is not swallowed up into that all-inclusive regime. There is room for both realms, just as there is room enough for the non-divine spaces of *Sitra Aḥra* and the phenomenal world alongside God. The story must be allowed to reveal itself as itself. The Companions' walking precedes their Torah discussion both narratively and conceptually.

The distinction between walking, plain and simple, and the Companions' engagement in the realm of Torah is explicit in the continuation of the text. After the discourse reaches its conclusion by drawing the story of the ark back to the original topic of Rosh Ha-Shanah, the narrative picks up again: "They walked all that day." We are told that they come upon a cave in which they encounter wondrous personae with whom they study Torah, returning the discourse to the topic of the kindling of the lamps. But the Torah discussion does not transpire during the time the Companions were walking. The *Zohar* reports this fact without embellishment. There is a basic contrast between the duration of the action itself—"They walked all day"—and the text devoted to it, a total of four words. The Companions' walking is pure action. It is an *'uvda* that is as yet indeterminate as to its significance. Is it a mere story, a mere action, or does it hold deep, concealed significance? Such determinations can be made, if at all, only after the act is done of itself.

The zoharic discourse continues after this fragmentary walking episode. It takes place within the secure enclosure of a cave. The Companions discuss the secrets of divine union and the resultant release of divine effluence.[235] They also explore themes that concern the relationship between Torah and the mundane world, stasis and movement, and the spatial activity of Shekhinah. One theme is the model relationship enjoyed by Zebulun and Issachar. As the Deuteronomic verse is interpreted, Zebulun is a mobile traveler, while Issachar remains in the enclosed tent of Torah. Zebulun is identified with Shekhinah in Her manifestation in the realm of mundane space and action, including battles and sacrifices, while Issachar is identified with the more remote *Tiferet*, from which the blessings of Torah derive. Each depends on the other.

The union of these potencies within the Divine was interrupted by the exile. The focus of Shekhinah's attention is now diverted to caring for earthly Israel. She accomplishes this through spatial activism. The *Zohar* combines theosophical and cosmogonic linguistic traditions with its image of the protective Shekhinah in its exposition regarding the seventy-two-letter Name of God. The back-and-forth movement of the angel who guarded Israel at the Red Sea, thus establishing their secure space, is reflected in the back-and-forth movement of the letters of the verses that spell this Name, in turn paralleling the influence of the higher *sefirot* (the Patriarchs) upon the Great Sea (Shekhinah), exerted so as to produce the space needed for Israel to walk through in safety. This part of the discourse concludes: "And the Companions know how to walk in the straight path, to prepare actions as appropriate, and with this Name, the knot of the Patriarchs, paths are found for judgment and for love, for succor, for loving-kindness, for fear, for Torah, for life, for death, for good, for evil. How fortunate are the righteous who know the paths of the Torah and know how to walk in the paths of the Holy King. They are fortunate in this world and in the coming world."[236]

Thus we must maintain a clear distinction between the *Zohar*'s snippets of walking narratives and the Torah discussions in which they are embedded, but we must also maintain a clear recognition of their embeddedness. The walking of the Companions is nurtured by and influences the Torah of the Companions, just as the mundane world in which it transpires is nurtured by the divine realm and affects it, while remaining separate from it. This paradox of distinctness and embeddedness is what makes efforts to separate the narrative portions of the *Zohar* from its other portions particularly problematic. Here and there phrases and episodes may be isolated for consideration. But their resonance depends on their taking their places within the broader landscape of the entire *Zohar*.

Prior to and hidden beneath the many-layered garments of sophisticated and profound hermeneutical teachings is the truth, stripped bare (*peshat*), the truth of mundane, embodied, spatial reality. Why were the Companions walking? Because "the body wishes to walk on its way."[237]

CHAPTER 4

The Body Wishes to Walk

In the normal course of events, sooner or later, any healthy baby will one day get up and try to walk. Unlike the drives for sex, food, shelter, or power, there is no obvious, a priori purpose to this act. Yet it seems to be a basic, instinctive drive no less than the others. Right away we apply hermeneutical pressure to the toddler's act. In the beginning, we ask her to walk to someone or something. In that way, we try to endow the baby's walking with a meaning. But first we walk. Only gradually do we develop our emotional, intellectual and moral faculties. And these develop along with an ever more sophisticated orientation toward space. Gradually, our walking takes on a complex of meanings. Eventually, our act of walking becomes a metaphor for living life, for making moral choices, for pursuing relationships or adventures, for negotiating meanings, or for the human condition itself.

The *Zohar* knows how to utilize this constellation of possibilities to the fullest. Expanding upon biblical and traditional imagery, it ascribes various purposes to the act of walking and various meanings to the path upon which one walks. Paths are ways of behavior; walking them means behaving in a certain way. But walking is not only a means of traversing a path, it is also the way paths are created. There are crooked paths of evil that lead to Gehinnom and straight paths of righteousness, paths of God, paths of Torah that lead to Paradise.[1] Sometimes walking the path means acting with simple goodness to others and sometimes it is the way toward uncovering the secret of supernal Wisdom.[2] There are paths of sexual self-control and paths of casual heedlessness or abandon.[3] There are paths of divine conjunction or protection and paths of worldly experience, exile, or death.[4] Paths are also channels of communication. There are paths of solitude and paths of fellowship.[5] Walking these roads can mean speaking truthfully or in falsehood, saying helpful or destructive words,[6] sharing common knowledge or opening new paths of esoteric revelation.[7]

On the other hand, the *Zohar* also knows that a symbol that is capable of being illuminated by any number of interpretations becomes a symbol that sheds no light of its own. The motif's multiple significances serve to conceal its essential in-significance while its in-significance, made manifest, hides its many meanings. We find ourselves on one of the *Zohar*'s favorite paths, the road of revelation and concealment. But, as the *Zohar* knows, "the body wishes to walk on its way."[8] First we walk.

Pure Walking—Silence and Freedom

The *Zohar* works in various ways in order that we might understand that the Companions' walking possesses this primal quality. We have seen that there is a tradition that fuses the Companions' walking with their Torah study.[9] While a good number of walking texts are stories that do not include the Companions' studying, the overwhelming majority of zoharic walking texts are, indeed, devoted to expositions of Torah. Furthermore, many of these expositions reflect on the various meanings, noted above, that walking can have. Still, when we attend to the way the walking motif is employed within these texts, we notice the *Zohar*'s appreciation for walking as an act unto itself.

For example, the *Zohar* tells of Rabbi Ele'azar and Rabbi Yose who went out on the road. They left very early and saw the morning star. This prompts discussion about the union and separation of the divine potencies. This discussion is then interrupted by the narrator: "As they were walking, day dawned and the time for prayer arrived. Said Rabbi Ele'azar, 'Let us pray and [then] let us walk on.' They sat and prayed. Afterwards they arose and walked on."[10] The ensuing discussion, beginning with mention of the seven heavens, then develops without any reference to the Companions' walking. What need was there for this interruption? Yet it seems that the *Zohar* feels compelled to interject this small narrative fragment, although it apparently has nothing to add to the discussion.

In the following excerpt, the *Zohar* even more clearly separates the Companions' walking from their Torah study:

> Rabbi Ḥiyya and Rabbi Yose were walking [*azli*] on the road. As they were walking [*azli*], they saw Rabbi Yose the Elder [*Sabba*], who was walking [*azil*] behind them.[11] They sat down until he reached them. Once he reached them they said, "Now the road is set before us." They walked on [*azlu*]. Rabbi Ḥiyya said, "It is time to act for God."[12]

We hear about the Companions walking three times before Rabbi Ḥiyya calls the group to Torah. In addition, another sage, not a member of the Associates, happens to be walking at the same time. This isolates the act of walking from being identified exclusively with the act of discussing Torah and also from being identified too exclusively with the Companions. There is no explanation for anyone's walking. The walking is prior to the formation of the group and prior to their engagement in Torah.

Similarly, we read that these two sages were going together from Usha to Lod.[13] Rabbi Yose stops the pair because it is time to pray the afternoon prayers. The pair then resume traveling until sunset.[14] At that point Rabbi Ḥiyya asks Rabbi Yose why he is so silent. Rabbi Yose answers that he has been thinking about the relationship between the masses and their rulers.[15] Rabbi Ḥiyya takes this theme and adopts it as the subject of a Torah discussion. It is not necessary to recapitulate the rich analysis of this story offered by Mordekhai Pachter.[16] For our purposes it is important to notice the period of silent walking that precedes the expository content of the narrative.[17] It must be noted that, while the story begins by assigning terminal coordinates to the Companions' journey, implying that their travel is purposive, the story relates that they decide, because of their conversation, to change direction and seek out their master, Rashbi, who is in Tiberias, not Lod.[18] Rashbi is the Companions' ruler no less than a king rules his countrymen. He is their leader in Torah. As Pachter points out, the Companions' initial discussion is not a mystical one. That level of Torah must await their arrival before Rashbi. Pachter summarizes their journey: "The journey of Rabbi Yose and Rabbi Ḥiyya from Usha to Lod, which actually turned into a journey from night to morning, from a night of not-knowing, or limited knowing, to the morning light of perfect knowing, which only Rashbi could bestow upon them, is, therefore, a journey of redemption. A crucial role in this journey is assigned to Rashbi, whose image becomes more powerful, taking on the dimensions of a redeemer."[19] But this characterization must be modified slightly. The journey of the Companions does not begin at night. It begins in the afternoon, as a journey of silence. Their journey goes from mundane, silent movement to political musings to exoteric Torah and then to esoteric revelation.

The *Zohar* uses the walking motif before it presents a Torah discussion as a kind of "pre-amble." The first walking text in the published *Zohar* begins: "Rabbi Ḥiyya and Rabbi Yose were walking on the road. When they got to a certain field Rabbi Ḥiyya said to Rabbi Yose, 'That which you said—*bara shit* is certainly so.'"[20] Thus we should understand that the sages walked for a while before they arrived at a certain place at which they began to engage in Torah. But, since this is the beginning of the text, and the Companions are not yet located anywhere previously, is it really necessary to have them walk to the field? Why not open the story in the field itself? The use of the motif teeters awkwardly between unexceptionable convention and excusable superfluousness. At other times, the walking phrase precedes a Torah discussion, without imparting any information or context necessary to the discussion.[21] The *Zohar* certainly uses the motif of walking in its stories in order to get—the story, its characters, and the reader—places. But it often insists on inserting the motif where it plays no such role. The Torah discussions in which the Companions engage are sometimes punctuated with the remark, "They walked," with no advancement of the plot or the discussion thereby. It is as if the *Zohar* cannot let their Torah stand on its own. We are prodded to remember that the Companions, besides engaging in Torah, also walk.[22] Therefore, we also find their walking continues after they engage in Torah, as they often go their separate ways.[23] The Torah discussion is concluded and the text temporarily returns to the image of silent walking.

The walking motif displays a fragile but persistent independence that stands as a recalcitrant refusal to accept any imposed meaning. Before it means anything, walking is meaningless. Before it becomes anything else, walking is freedom. Silence is the expression of that momentary freedom. The Companions are simply free to move about. This is evident in the lack of direction that characterizes their walking. As noted, even when a destination is assigned to their travel, the text does not usually report that Companions reach their destination. Even more evocative of their unfettered mobility is the recurrent phenomenon of deflected journeys. The *Zohar* introduces the Companions en route to a particular destination, sometimes for a particularly urgent purpose, only to have them decide, on the way, to go somewhere else.[24] But the opening up of a space of pure freedom does not, itself, take place in a vacuum. As the textual fragments that convey the walking motif are embedded in the *Zohar*'s text of many-layered meanings, so the positing of such moments of freedom is embedded within a complex of moments of historical, social, political, and religious significances.

The Context of Freedom

CONTEMPORARY CONDITIONS

The *Zohar* creates its picture of unfettered movement through space for sages living in the land of Israel around the second century of the Common Era.[25] But this imaginative production took place within the Jewish reality of thirteenth-century Spain. The walking motif must be apprehended from within this context and against that background.

The world of the medieval Spanish Jew was demarcated—by the natural, religious, commercial, and political forces that acted upon him[26]—into specific spaces. His immediate and main environment was characterized by a set of enclosures. These consisted of spaces within the Jewish quarter itself—his home, synagogue or study hall, courtroom, and places of work and business—and then the spaces outside the quarter, in which the Jew had various levels of access or proprietorship. His place of business may have been located, by special grant, in a fortified bazaar, *alcaiceria*. This was a space occupied in common by Jew and non-Jew.[27] Only the few had lands outside the Jewish quarter or charters to farm taxes from outlying areas.[28] The non-Jewish world encompassed the buildings—official, commercial and residential—of royalty and nobility, Church, and general populace, with whom the Jew had complex interactions. They were surrounded by the expanses of field and wilderness that would lead to the sea or to other cities and countries, including Jerusalem and the Holy Land.

The Jewish quarter was gradually closed in with physical gates and walls, as well as with legal restrictions. This was a product of political control, but also of heightened security measures against harassment and danger.[29] This produced a general atmosphere of constriction and insecurity. One scholar writes:

> Even though the rate of growth of the Jewish population was smaller than that of the urban gentile population, the situation in the neighborhoods in the central cities was extremely difficult. The Jews had no possibility to expand, and the crowding weighed upon daily life, which was hard enough because of all the restrictions placed upon the Jews' movements. A very few were exempt from some of the limitations; it was permitted to the physicians of a number of communities, for example, to leave freely at night in order to treat their patients, and Christians were even allowed to visit them in the Jewish neighborhood.[30]

Mobility was the lot of only certain groups. Yitzhak Baer writes, "New settlements remained close to the old established centers; the Spanish Jew did not readily change his residence. Except for a certain type of indigent scholar or craftsman, the Spanish Jews were not accustomed to migrate from place to place, as their brethren in France and Germany were compelled to do by political and economic pressures."[31] As in talmudic times, travel on the open road was considered dangerous.[32] Among the actions taken by the *aljama*, the Jewish community, Rashba records that: "The *kahal* forbade, under the pain of *herem*, travel to a certain place because the roads were dangerous. This prohibition was to be in effect until the first of Nisan, with its possible extension to the first of Iyyar, depending upon the judgment of the *berurim*. If they find that conditions on the roads have improved they will permit travel, otherwise they will not."[33] It is of interest that Spanish rabbis differed from their Ashkenazic counterparts on the question of requiring the special blessing for being saved from a mortal peril—the *Gomel* blessing—after travel on the roads. Ashkenazic decisors limited the requirement to travel through a desert or other such area, while the Spanish tradition applied the blessing to all travelers, since they accepted the Palestinian Talmud's statement that "all roads are presumed dangerous."[34] Rabbi David Abudarham reports that the common Spanish practice was to recite the blessing.[35]

Unencumbered travel was the privilege of Jews who were economically and politically well-connected. The poet Todros Halevi Abulafia describes his travels with his patron, Don Isaac ben Zadok, in the entourage of Alfonso X: "And it happened in the dear and delightful days of our youth, when this noble (Don Isaac) was 'prince and commander of nations,' that we travelled through the vineyard country, boldly for all to see, accompanied by a large retinue of wealthy, worthy and wise men. We made a tour of all the Castilian ports. Time was kind to us and the days were pleasant and free from fear."[36]

On the other hand, travel was necessary for business and earning a living, and for community representatives who had to deal with official matters. Such travel was subject to the same dangers, difficulties and uncertainties noted above. One Spanish traveler wrote home: "By God, if you can avoid it, do not go abroad. If God wills, I shall set out for Marrakesh. . . . I have no other aim, by God, than saving you from trudging along the streets and traveling overland."[37] Moreover, those summoned to the court on official business were often held hostage by the officials: "They had to travel about from place to place, following the court's movements, and were persecuted if they took their leave too soon."[38] In those cases, their travel was another form of enclosure.

Among those compelled to walk the roads were also itinerant scholars who needed to find patrons and opportunities to teach and write. Such figures, as Moshe Idel has pointed out, were crucial to the dissemination of ideas and traditions, the enrichment of Jewish culture, and the founding of certain currents of thought. He writes: "This is evident in the case of Rabbi Sabbetai Donnolo, Rabbi Abraham ibn Ezra, Maimonides, Rabbi Judah he-Hasid, Sabbetai Sevi and the Baal Shem Tov. This is particularly true in the case of the founder of ecstatic kabbalah, Rabbi Abraham Abulafia, who roamed from Spain to Acre, to Greece, Italy to Catalonia and Castile in Spain, again to Greece and Italy, and finally to Sicily."[39]

Students of Torah also felt the need to travel to find the best teachers and academies.[40] Sometimes the travel was considered necessary for the distance it placed between the student and his comfortable, potentially distracting home. Nevertheless, M. Breuer writes that parental opposition was the exception. "In general sons left with their parents' permission. Furthermore, the father instigated his son's trip, determined its destination and himself prepared his son for his journey."[41] Yet it may be no accident that this period, as pointed out by Moshe Idel, sees a proliferation of creativity that breaks out of familial dynasties.[42] By and large, these were individuals pushing toward a known destination. But the pure experience of travel could not be ignored even in such a seemingly controlled system. Mordekhai Breuer cites the words of Rabbi Meir Halevi Abulafia: "The fire of wandering grew ever more powerful until it scorched the heart and bowels within me."[43] Breuer sets this passion for wandering within the context of the travel explosion of the twelfth century, but he limits its applicability regarding Jewish travelers:

> "The fire of wandering" flared up at that time with great power in the souls of the youth on the heels of the Crusades and the great movement they caused from one end of the world to the other, as well as following the rise of teaching and research centers in many countries. The roads filled with travelers and wanderers, among whom were many who circulated in the lands without a purpose or a specific destination. But there were also many who set out to learn certain subjects in a particular place and with a specific teacher. Among these last the Jewish wanderers were generally included.[44]

One way or another, Jews occupied medieval space, which, in the characterization of Henri Lefebvre, "was by definition a space of exchange and communications, and therefore of networks. What networks? In the first place, networks of overland routes: those of traders, and those of pilgrims and crusaders."[45]

CRUSADERS

The *Zohar* was written "at a time when Palestine, after the vicissitudes of the Crusades, was again in the hands of the Arabs."[46] In the *Zohar*'s words:

> And the sons of Ishmael are fated [*ve-zaminin*] to rule over the land of Israel while it is empty of everything for a long time, just as their circumcision is

> empty and incomplete. And they will prevent the Children of Israel from returning to their places until the merit of the sons of Ishmael shall be complete. And the sons of Ishmael are fated to wage fierce battles in the world, and to gather the sons of Edom against them. And they will wage war with them, one on the sea and one on land and one close to Jerusalem. And these will rule over those and the Holy Land will not be given over to the sons of Edom.[47]

The restoration of the People Israel to its Land would have to wait until the divine historical plan was fulfilled. The medieval Jew was thus challenged to develop a cogent historical and messianic theory with which he might meet the challenges of the period. As Wolfson writes:

> within the eschatologically charged milieu of Christendom in the High Middle Ages, the shaping of identity could not be isolated from the issue of messianic redemption—that is, a primary concern on the part of the religious leaders engaged in polemical confrontation with respect to the identification of the devout Jew or faithful Christian had to do with the belief in who was the true Messiah and when the Messianic Age did or would arrive. Holy crusades against infidels, forced conversions and public disputations were different ways of expressing in the social sphere the eschatological zeal and theological intolerance that prevailed in medieval Christianity.[48]

It is not the purpose of this study to explore the theosophical and historiographic repercussions of this polemical clash.[49] Rather, our focus is on the question of the *Zohar*'s spatial orientation as it developed in this period. Given that Jewish messianic anticipation and fervor could not be sustained for long periods of time, it was necessary to develop an orientation to the pre-messianic present. By the time the *Zohar* was written, the Crusades had been going on for almost two hundred years. Jews had been witnessing thousands of people walking the roads to do battle for the Holy Land. Two civilizations were engaged in a gigantic struggle over control of a space that the Jews also considered sacred, but from which they were universally and doubly exiled. Not only were the Jews displaced from their Holy Land, but they were also excluded from participation in the conflict over the land's possession. Rashi begins his classic commentary to the Torah with a reworking of midrashic materials in order to proclaim that the

Jews are, despite the world's challenges, the real owners of the Holy Land. In the north, their connection with the land could be tragically affirmed, since they, in their role as surrogates for the occupiers of the Holy Land, were sometimes massacred by the Crusaders. In countering the Christian onslaught, Jews conceived of their martyrdom in sacrificial terms. Robert Chazan shows how sacrificial imagery of the Temple became an important element in commemorative accounts of the Crusades' and the Blois massacres. He characterizes one aspect of these chronicles thus: "The sacrifice of Jesus and its emulation by his followers throughout the ages is replaced in these Jewish narratives by the Temple ritual and its reenactment by present-day Jews."[50] Aside from its polemical force in validating Jewish experience in the face of powerlessness, degradation, and death, this stance also serves to compensate for the Jews' dislocation from the contested sacred space now claimed by others. Messianic redemption is assured in the future. For now, in these texts, the Temple cultus is relocated and restored through the sacrifices that carnal Israel offers of itself.

This was not the only response possible. Various views developed regarding the role and relevance of the Temple and its service, or of the land of Israel itself, in the spiritual life of the contemporary Jew. Maimonides' choice to incorporate into his code even those laws applicable only to Temple times may be seen as a statement in defiance of his political reality.[51]

By the end of the thirteenth century, the Jews saw a dampening of Crusader fever, to be sure. Furthermore, the Spanish experience was different. Here the Crusader quest for the Holy Land was displaced into the Reconquest of Spain itself. Thus, a monk of Toledo was able to have a vow to embark on the First Crusade annulled by the pope "because of his participation in the war against the infidel in Spain."[52] The Jews in Spain were spared much of the tragedy of their Ashkenazi kin because, for Spanish Christians, the Jews were a valuable asset in their quest to take Spain away from the Muslims.[53] If anything, then, the position of the Jew was emphatically ambiguous. As his impotence with regard to the Holy Land was clearly evident, so was it also clear that his condition was one of great opportunity. This period of the eclipse of the Jewish presence in Israel coincided, as if in compensation, with a growing midrashic and kabbalistic preoccupation with the desert Tabernacle, the Temple, and its destruction.[54] The spiritualization and displacement of the sacrificial service, including the kabbalists' assumption of the sacerdotal role of the priesthood, has been noted by scholars.[55] But if the Temple cultus had disappeared, the physical land of Israel had not. Kabbalists were divided in their evaluations of the importance of that space. Could that place become a spiritualized space despite its geographical reality? Did the exilic state of the people attain such a mythic reality that it could eclipse the spiritual focus on the physical expanse of the land? Ḥaviva Pedaya suggests that these questions exemplify a more basic quandary—the problem of the relationship between the reality of this world and spiritual reality. She suggests that it is possible to see the struggle of kabbalists such as Rabbi Ezra, Rabbi Azriel, and Naḥmanides with

> the tension between the actual and the spiritual, in all its aspects, as tied to the stance of each one of the kabbalists studied with regard to their relationship to the land of Israel. This abstract problem was considered by each kabbalist according to his thought, his way of life, and his character. For Rabbi Ezra, the tension was connected to the activity of *tiqqun*, which was a dedication to spiritual action, nullifying or deflecting physical activity. For Rabbi Azriel, a similar principle obtained, but with a progressively increasing emphasis on the spiritual in itself, which was accompanied by both a disengagement from the symbols of the land of Israel, and all that was connected to it, and a lack of interest in considering questions of exile and redemption and the story of the supernal Land.[56]

Naḥmanides, on the other hand, did not allow his mystical values to cancel his appreciation for the realm of physical reality, connected to spiritual forces, yet retaining its own integrity.[57] According to Pedaya, he believed that the upper realms were not flawed, but that they were a perfect source of blessing for this world. Not accidentally, he felt duty-bound to find his way to the Holy Land to live.

> This position of Naḥmanides is not only tied to the different character of esoteric traditions that he possessed. Rather, it was in the conscious and consistent sharpening of the importance in themselves of the [realm of the] material and of actual doing, a sharpening that stands out particularly in his meta-interpretive

> positions. We have noticed that, in accord with Naḥmanides' reinforcement of the status and importance of *peshat*, he values the importance of the physical land and actual life in it. . . . He mainly drew positions, types of connections, and a general orientation from the teaching of Rabbi Yehudah Halevi, all of which he internalizes. Thus, for instance, he is influenced by Rabbi Yehudah Halevi's fundamental approach, which is expressed in the concept of act, body, experience, land, commandments, and prophecy.[58]

What is important for us is the possibility of a mystical stance that makes room for "act, body, experience" in the realm of the mundane. Our discussion has tried to show that the *Zohar* evinces its own struggle with the tension between the material and the spiritual. Its synthesis differs from the one arrived at by the kabbalists studied by Pedaya. The *Zohar* did not adopt a completely spiritualized orientation of the kind characteristic of the Geronese kabbalists, nor did it opt for real emigration to the Holy Land. Instead of going to Israel himself, the author of the *Zohar* places the Associates in that space, allowing them to traverse it freely. In so doing, the *Zohar* has relocated the Holy Land, not into the celestial spheres, but into the space of narrative action, the space of *'uvda*. The space of narrative could do double duty. In such a space, the Companions' unfettered walking could take place simultaneously in the Holy Land and in Spain.

A NARRATIVE OF SILENCE

It is important to emphasize this narrative element, lest we oversimplify the *Zohar*'s achievement. In one study, Moshe Idel analyzes the meaning of the land of Israel for the mystic. He notes the land's significance as the feminine divine potency and then writes: "Only the righteous man can settle the earth, because only he, who has entered the covenant of circumcision, inherits the land. Therefore, according to the *Zohar*, there is clear ritual meaning to the very inhabiting of the land as a geographical place, by mystical participation in intra-divine processes."[59] But the point to remember is that, while living in Israel is given theosophical and symbolic meaning, the kabbalists of the *Zohar* are really not in Israel. Real life intrudes on the mystic's symbology in various ways—through everyday life and through the dislocation of the ideal from the real in space and time—from second-century

Israel to thirteenth-century Spain. For the *Zohar*, the mediating vehicle for this dislocation is the tool of narrative.

When we realize that the *Zohar*'s narrative includes fragments of a retelling of moments of silence in action—of Companions walking in silence—we may wonder whether conceptual dualities, though of considerable heuristic power, can adequately map out the *Zohar*'s orientation to space and time. In his study on the mystic's relation to the land of Israel, Idel posits that walking on the land has a particular meaning for the mystic. Comparing the three monotheistic faiths, he writes: "In all three of them the mystical forms adopted similar approaches regarding the religious centers. A spiritualist dimension was bestowed upon the sanctified geographical centers, as identifying with spiritual processes; the earthly, horizontal journey over the land was interpreted as reflecting, esoterically, an interior journey—the ascent of the soul to its source, or an epistemological process, in the Aristotelian spirit."[60] While this interpretation certainly falls within the range of meanings to be found in the *Zohar*, our understanding is that the *Zohar* makes deliberate use of the walking narratives in order, to some extent, to forestall just such an interpretive leap. The narrative preserves that moment of silent walking that directly precedes the moment when this action will be incorporated into the mystical repertoire of significant acts. In this way the *Zohar* has achieved a different order of incorporation, for it has created a space that encompasses both a mundane and a mystical realm, without collapsing them into one, thereby preventing an act of union that would ultimately obliterate the non-mystical realm. In other words, Idel's description could very well be what the *Zohar* would reply were it compelled to directly answer the question, "What is the mystical meaning of walking on the land?" But the *Zohar*, unlike many other mystical texts, chooses another way to answer, replying, in effect, "Who says that walking on the road has only a mystical significance?"

If this is correct, then we must broaden the range of mystical responses to the mundane beyond the parameters set out by Idel in his essay. In that study he pursues his ongoing project of defining differences between the theosophical and ecstatic strands of kabbalah, here distinguishing between the two in their approaches to Eliade's concept of the Sacred Center:

> There are at least two different recognized paths to relating to the sacred center: the person's being at the center, and his being the center itself. The ritualistic viewpoint, upheld by the theosophical kabbalah, strives for the situation of "being in the center," while the mystical viewpoint, upheld by the ecstatic kabbalah and *ḥassidut*, posits that the perfected man himself is the true center.
>
> The first type concentrates mainly on the tangible, geographic axis or the axis set in space; religion is taken as a system of beliefs and ritual acts that are tied to certain ceremonial actions in the spatial axis in the tangible world. In the Jewish religion this spatial axis is organically tied to the temporal axis; and so also the eschaton, to which human history proceeds, can only be realized along this specific axis. In this religious mentality space-time pairings are only significant if there is a special religious meaning to a particular place in space, or to a particular moment in time, a significance that will be absorbed over time by the person who is able to open himself to this experience and is ready for this.[61]

The contrast Idel proposes seems to follow along the lines suggested by J. Z. Smith in his critique of Eliade's model.[62] Ritual significance is essentially rooted in connection with a sacred center that participates in cosmogonic and theosophical realities. The ecstatic kabbalah is the anthropocentric, utopian alternative to that pole. Idel continues:

> Although the religion is not limited solely to experiences relating to entities anchored in the space-time axis, nevertheless, these entities fulfill a central role in the religious activities: the qualities hidden in the sacred space and the holy place are emanated onto the believer, and from their power he is capable of reaching the perfect religious experience.
>
> Compared to the geosophic mentality, the mystical mentality sees human activity as moving along an axis of values: the stations in the mystical life are considered a ladder of religious values that go beyond space and time. This ladder of personal experiences does not depend on the other two axes: it may be apathetic to them, or it may compete purposely with them in order to take their place, or, even, according to Ramban and Rabbi Nahman of Bratslav, the ladder may benefit from the qualities hidden in the axes of time and space. In principle, however, the mystical axis is independent.[63]

This analysis leaves very little room for any other conceptual approach. Yet, the choice of the *Zohar* to speak narratively establishes the space necessary to articulate just such an alternative. At the same time that the *Zohar*, in its theosophical discourses on the *heikhalot*, can celebrate the anthropocentric, utopian mystical hero in the figure of the tzaddiq, it can also situate its mystical heroes, the Companions, in a mundane space that is as independent, in its own way, as is the "mystical axis" toward which they travel and from which they derive their identity as mystics. The *Zohar* recognizes that ritual—*'uvda*—does not mean only significant action. Rather, adopting terms of ritual theory that Smith suggests, we may say that it accepts the reality of the ordinary as the ineradicable ground upon which rituals, and all actions, are played out.[64] Eliade's concept of vertical axis is supplemented, through the *Zohar*'s walking narratives, with a more generous spatial concept.

Such a concept is generous, but it is not complacent. It includes within it enough room for the paradox of the coexistence of the mundane and the mystical in all its tension. To return to Idel's study, we note that Idel is sensitive to this struggle, but chooses to frame it in terms of competing mentalities:

> The mystical space in the thought of the Middle Ages can be mapped by means of concepts drawn from psychology or philosophy more than from concepts of topography or geography. Even when the mystical mentality developed, developing personal and experiential values, the earlier, mythical mentality, that was based on the geographical foundation, remained in force; and these differing ways of thinking brought about a struggle between differing conceptions. The early mentality is bound up with national-religious and historical experiences; the mystical mentality is tied to the experiences of the individual.[65]

This study has attempted to go in another direction. At least for the *Zohar*, concepts of topography and geography are not as irrelevant as Idel suggests. The struggle expressed by the zoharic use of a narrative of silent walking through a landscape is not simply about choosing between competing epistemic systems or mentalities, but is the struggle to do justice to the lived experience of mystics who, before and after they engage in mystical acts, thoughts or experiences, feel themselves vitally located, as embodied, grounded creatures, in a mundane world. One possible model for the *Zohar* of this contradictory combination was offered by Lefebvre's other medieval figure, the pilgrim.

PILGRIMS AND THE MUNDANE

The period of the Crusades was also a period that saw the growth of the phenomenon of pilgrimage.[66] This was due to a number of factors. One was the example offered by the crusader himself. As Jonathan Sumption puts it, "The notion of the true crusader remained inseparable from that of the pilgrim."[67] But while the crusader was supposed to be trying to reach the Holy Land, pilgrimage sites began proliferating locally. Edith and Victor Turner explain:

> When access to the Holy Places was blocked for a time by Islam, there developed a tendency to "reduplicate" the Palestinian shrines in the Christian countries of Europe, either by imitation or through claim to direct, supernatural translation of material relics from Palestine to Europe. . . . The Spanish traditions—and, indeed, traditions in England and Italy as well—express the folk belief that if Europe could not go to the Holy Places, the Holy Places, or material tokens of them, could come to Europe.[68]

The development of a culture of pilgrimage in Spain was promoted not only in opposition to Islam, but also by internal rivalries within Christendom. The Turners write: "Catholic Spain, in opposition to iconoclastic Islam, used icons and images as mobilizing points. In rivalry with Rome for the leadership of Christendom's struggle with Islam, Spain miraculously imported an apostle of her own, St. James, to counterpose SS. Peter and Paul, and in her traditions linked him with her own major Marian shrine, that of the Virgin del Pilar."[69]

The Jews could participate in this phenomenon to a limited extent by, as noted above, engaging in journeys to a certain center of learning or a particular sage. Occasionally a zoharic walking text will refer to someone who is coming to learn with Rashbi,[70] or with "the Masters of the Mishnah."[71] But this is not the case with the great majority of these texts. The wandering Associates, by and large, can be clearly distinguished from pilgrims, because the Associates' walking lacks the central defining element of pilgrimage—the intention to reach a sacred destination.[72] Breuer's contention, mentioned above, that Jewish travelers were purposive, while other travelers may have wandered aimlessly, is the very reverse of the zoharic situation. Nevertheless, studies of pilgrims and pilgrimage present various aspects of the pilgrimage experience that are relevant for understanding the phenomenon of the walking Associates. The link between pilgrimage and mysticism was most directly made by Victor Turner. He theorized that pilgrimage was an example of liminal activity. The pilgrim on the way has left behind his familiar world and has not yet arrived at the sacred theophanic shrine of his destination. Turner suggests that "we might speak of ritual liminality as an exteriorized mystical way, and the mystic's path as interiorized ritual liminality."[73] However, this is not really the common ground that connects the Companions and pilgrimage. Rather, it is the mix of the mundane and the spiritual that attends the walking itself.

Philo, commenting on the pilgrims of his day, already noticed the mixture of spiritual direction and mundane pains and pleasures that were subsequently given theoretical formulation by Turner. He explains that by mandating that Jews travel to Jerusalem to offer sacrifices, God tests Israel, for only one truly committed would "endure to quit his country, and his friends, and relations, and emigrate into a distant land."[74] But, while Philo ascribes the decision to leave home to piety, he astutely notices what is gained by the pilgrim:

> For innumerable companies of men from a countless variety of cities, some by land and some by sea, from east and from west, from the north and from the south, came to the temple at every festival, as if to find some common refuge and safe asylum from the troubles of this most busy and painful life, seeking to find tranquility, and to procure a remission of and respite from those cares by which from their earliest infancy they had been hampered and weighed down, and so, by getting breath as it were, to pass a brief time in cheerful festivities, being filled with good hopes, and enjoying the leisure of that most important and necessary vacation which consists in forming a friendship with those hitherto unknown, but now initiated by boldness and a desire to honour God, and forming a combination of actions and a union of dispositions so as to join in sacrifices and libations to the most complete confirmation of mutual good will.[75]

Philo is sensitive to the array of experiences, positive and negative, that surround pilgrimage. He understands that pilgrimage entails leaving the familiar for the sake of immersion in the unfamiliar. He assumes that no one would suffer separation from one's home and society without a genuine sense of piety. But he admits that the convivial atmosphere of strangers joined by a common purpose can be enjoyable and refreshing. Philo understood the value of pilgrimage as a vehicle for the experience Turner would call *communitas*. Although Philo describes this aspect only at the destination point, the pilgrim center, pilgrimage was inherently tied to a sense of intense fellowship, often beginning in a group that initiated the trip, or was created spontaneously along the way.[76] This sense of fellowship and shared purpose aptly characterizes the Companions of the *Zohar* as well. "Rabbi Ḥiyya said, 'Companions, when we are on the road, we should walk with one heart.'"[77]

What is not as clear in Philo, but what becomes clearer in the medieval period, is the sense of release and freedom afforded the pilgrim, not upon reaching his destination, but upon leaving his home and while on the road. The Turners' thinking about the forces motivating someone to embark on a pilgrimage moves in a direction that is the very opposite to Philo's:

> The point of it all is to get out, go forth, to a far holy place approved by all. In societies with few economic opportunities for movement away from limited circles of friends, neighbors, and local authorities, all rooted alike in the soil, the only journey possible for those not merchants, peddlers, minstrels, jugglers, tumblers, wandering friars, or outlaws, or their modern equivalents, is a holy journey, a pilgrimage or a crusade. On such a journey one gets away from the reiterated "occasions of sin" which make up so much of the human experience of social structure. If one is tied by blood or edict to a given set of people in daily intercourse over the whole gamut of human activities—domestic, economic, jural, ritual, recreational, affinal, neighborly—small grievances over trivial issues tend to accumulate through the years, until they become major disputes over property, office, or prestige which factionalize the group. One piles up a store of nagging guilts, not all of which can be relieved in the parish confessional, especially when the priest himself may be party to some of the conflicts. When such a load can no longer be borne, it is time to take the road as a pilgrim.[78]

Pilgrimage was liberating, but from what? It could, indeed, be a release from humdrum worries and responsibilities. Those who were more pietistically minded could see it as a release from the mundane world itself. Jonathan Sumption credits Irish ascetics with this view:

> Their distinctive contribution to the spiritual life of the "dark ages" was the idea of the aimless wanderer whose renunciation of the world was the most complete of which man could conceive, far more austere than the principles of Benedictine monasticism. . . . By wandering freely without destination, the Irish hermit felt that he had cut himself off from every material accessory to life. In his eighth sermon St. Columban dwells on the transitory nature of life, and declares: "I know that if this earthly tent of mine is taken down, I shall get a new home from God made by no human hands. It makes me sigh, this longing for the shelter of my heavenly habitation . . . for I know that while I am in my body I am travelling away from God." The notion of a specific destination did not enter into Columban's thinking; his only destination was the heavenly Jerusalem.[79]

But for most pilgrims the release was more likely to be from responsibilities at home, social pressures, political and even religious strictures. The extreme open-endedness of this choice made establishment figures uneasy. In their eyes it was too open to abuse through excessive, uncontrolled religiosity and superstition, on the one hand, or excessive license and worldliness, on the other. The thirteenth-century preacher Jacques de Vitry complained that pilgrimage had lost its religious meaning: "Some light-minded and inquisitive persons go on pilgrimages not out of devotion, but out of mere curiosity and love of novelty."[80] But rationalists and puritans also felt unhappy about pilgrimages, seeing them as "mere peregrinations, wasting time and energy that might be better put to the service of demonstrating, in the place where God has called one, that one has been personally 'saved,' by a thrifty, industrious, and 'pure' style of life."[81] Critics from both sides sensed, all too well, the unbridled freedom of being on the road.

In late thirteenth-century Spain, in this environment of constriction, limitation and fear, and of expanding horizons and increasing individual initiative, at a time when the known space of all of Europe and the Mediterranean world was being contested and subject to acts of possession and redefinition, the *Zohar* conceives of a band of men who travel the roads at will. The sound of their walking silently through the land conveys, as did the sound of God silently walking in the Garden, a deep sense of ownership and control. But this sense of ownership and control did not derive from heteronomous sources, whether of the prevailing non-Jewish civilization or of the *aljama*. The spatial autonomy of the Companions is a product—*'uvda*—of the zoharic narrator. The image of the wandering Companions could thus assimilate or counter crusader or pilgrimage resonances as well as those of Judean sages of rabbinic times. But it could do this because, before it meant anything else, it signified, in the most mundane terms, freedom and release.

AWKWARD SILENCES

Michel de Certeau tries to capture the subtle moment of transition in the mystic's experience when an insignificant detail fills up with meaning: "A play of light arrests the reader's attention: ecstatic instant, a spark of insignificance, this fragment of the unknown introduces a silence into the hermeneutic medley. Thus, little by little, common everyday life begins to seethe with a disturbing familiarity—a frequentation of the Other."[82]

Walking's pure state of hermeneutical emptiness cannot last for long. The empty space demands to be filled. If it is not filled with "a frequentation of the Other" Who is Holy, it may be filled, instead, with other, mundane concerns. Therefore the *Zohar* knew that, just as the pilgrims could be inspired by lofty dedication or be deflected into coarse conversation and preoccupation, so the Companions had to cope with the open-ended nature of walking. Since walking is an essentially mundane activity that is distinct from learning Torah, it may also become an impediment to Torah study. Although, in most cases in the *Zohar*, Rashbi teaches while traveling,[83] in one instance he declares: "Surely wisdom does not settle in unless one is sitting and not walking, but, rather, staying in one's place."[84] Well aware of the mundane nature of walking, Rashbi worries about the distractions that walking along may cause. In another story he admonishes a sage who has met him while the sage was riding his donkey to get off his animal. But he gives him a choice: "Cappadocian! Tie up your donkey and come down, for a Torah matter requires clarity [of mind] [*tzaḥuta*].[85] Or turn yourself around and walk after me and focus your heart."[86]

Before any of that happens, before the silence is filled one way or the other, the silent act of walking proceeds with an uneasy sense of awkwardness. "Rabbi Ḥiyya and Rabbi Yose were walking on the road. Meanwhile they saw a person coming who was wrapped in a tallit [*'itufa de-mitzvah*], with weapons tied underneath." The Companions are not sure whether they can trust this person. When they meet up, the Companions greet him but the man does not return their greeting. The Companions remain perplexed as to the nature of this silence, whether it indicates that the person is a scoundrel or not. "They walked on as one and the man did not speak to them. Afterwards Rabbi Ḥiyya and Rabbi Yose went off and engaged in Torah."[87] Only after the stranger sees the sages studying Torah does he speak to them. They realize that they had been mutually suspicious of each other, but now they can engage in Torah together.[88] The misunderstanding is cleared up. But the duration of their walking together in silent waiting and apprehension should not be forgotten. The Companions and the stranger walk together for awhile before the Companions embark on a Torah discussion. That silence is filled, not with words, but with the sound of their footsteps. During this time, waiting to see what might happen, what this all meant, they were not sure whether they all shared the same sacred devotion, but they all knew that they were walking together. Only afterwards are they able to walk together in Torah.

In another story, the sages feel compelled to postpone their Torah discussion until they are able to walk away from a place of evil:[89] "Rabbi Yose and Rabbi Ḥiyya were walking on the road. Rabbi Ḥiyya said, 'Tell us of the excellent words that your father said about the soul's delights.' He said to him, 'Let us get out of here, for these Cappadocians lack good deeds.' . . . After they left and went on the road, Rabbi Yose said, 'I will tell you a word.'"[90] We are meant to feel the tension as the sages walk on their way, waiting until it is again safe to speak choice words of esoteric Torah. It is not accidental that this narrative fragment is embedded within teachings about walking and about the watchful guardians, the *notrim* who patiently guard God's vineyard. Rabbi Yoḥanan teaches:

> Come and see how much a person must take care and check himself and his actions every day. How so? When he arises in the morning he should say, "May it be Your desire, God, My Source of Strength, that my heart be set and given to my control so that I do not forget you." When he stretches out his legs to walk, let him inspect his legs' strides so that they do not wander toward evil. If he walks to do a mitzvah let him run, as it is said, "They will go after God like a roaring lion" [Hosea 11:10]. And even on Shabbat it is a mitzvah to run. After the whole day has passed he must inspect himself as to what he did that day. And if necessary, let him repent for himself immediately before he sleeps. The rabbis taught: What is written, "There was a vineyard of Solomon's at Baal Hamon. He gave it to the guardians [*notrim*]. A man can get a thousand pieces of silver for its fruit" [Song of Sol. 8:11]? Said Rabbi Yehudah, "'There was a vineyard of Solomon's'—this is the King to Whom Peace belongs; 'in Baal Hamon'—these are the angels of Peace. 'He gave it to the guardians'—these are the guardians of the trust of the Earth [*mishmeret ha-aretz*]."[91]

The *Zohar* continues with an alternative teaching—that the *notrim* are "Israel, who are the ones who guard Her [Torah's] trust." And Rabbi Yose's precious teaching is that the vineyard is the soul, given to those who keep God's commandments. In light of this story, we understand that to keep the commandments means to choose one's manner of walking. Sometimes one will have to guard one's step and watch and wait for the proper moment to act or speak. However, there is no choice but to walk.

We understand, so far, that the meaning of the Companions' walking—conceived by the *Zohar* as an adequate response, whether participatory or defiant, to the world in which it was created—is determined by three factors: the very act of walking as an act of spatial appropriation, the focus of the hearts of the Companions as they walk—their intention and its expression, and the spaces in which the act takes place. The possibility that the Companions will succeed in bringing these factors to bear upon a space—encountering it, appropriating it and transforming it—depends on the nature of the space they enter into. Is the space totally open for appropriation or does it carry an identity of its own? What forces—by human or other means—will the space itself exert upon the Companions? If the space's nature is strongly determined, how much space will it leave the Companions? It is necessary that they travel through spaces congenial to their project. This means that their walking is not only a walking towards open spaces; it is also a walking away from spaces closed in by physical or other types of constraints.

Outside the Beit Midrash

THE SACRED CONFINES OF THE *BEIT MIDRASH*

The open space that the Companions create by their walking is literally a space in the open since their walking takes them out of the study hall. This move can be understood from a number of perspectives. These relate to the spiritual, sociopolitical, and epistemological realms identified with the study hall. In walking out of the study hall, the Companions walk away from each of these realms.

Among the ways that Judaism responded to the destruction of the Temple was to create localized sacred spaces—the *beit knesset* for prayer, and the *beit midrash* for Torah study. The sanctity of the synagogue and its appurtenances was gradually recognized. We find a somewhat back-handed treatment of this by the Mishnah, which applies to them a system of graded hierarchy reminiscent of the one applied to the sanctity of Jerusalem and the Temple. But the sanctity of the synagogue became more accepted as time went on.[92]

The Mishnah is not explicit about the sanctity of the *beit midrash* but by amoraic times it, too, was considered sacred space. This is a new concept, since, while the Torah had demanded that service to God be done in a specific place to be chosen by God, it never indicates that the study of Torah (itself an idea that is not biblically well developed) required or produced sacred space.[93] Nonetheless, the Babylonian Talmud applies Isaiah's term *miqdash me'at* (Isa. 11:16)—a small sanctuary—to both synagogues and study halls.[94]

Scholars have debated what the nature of the rabbinic study halls, whether in Palestine or Babylonia, might have been—arguing whether they were institutional settings or informal places of study.[95] Jeffrey Rubenstein suggests that the rise of the rabbinic academy as an institution goes hand in hand with the production of the dialectical literary product we recognize as our Talmud. "The transition from short, apodictic utterances of the Amoraim to the discursive, verbose, argumentative expressions of the Stammaim may reflect a larger structural change in rabbinic society such as the rise of a new type of institution," Rubenstein writes. "Production of a distinct literary stratum suggests a distinct social setting."[96] These remarks are suggestive in pointing to a link between intellectual productions and the spaces in which they are produced.[97]

The study hall was a sacred space, but it was also a space that represented an intellectual elite. David Halperin, theorizing that early medieval *Heikhalot* literature was the product of groups excluded from the rabbinic elite, felt that "the *Hekhalot* literature, with its dual emphasis on heavenly ascent and acquisition of Torah, seems to me to make sense as an effort by low-status Jews to actualize the ascension myth as it was communicated to them in Moses stories. The act of ascension mirrors their hankering for higher social status; the hostile angels they imagined waiting for them mirror the rabbinic elite who they supposed blocked their quest for this status."[98] One might add that the struggle is translated into spatial terms. The *Heikhalot* mystic is denied social status by being denied a significant place in the *beit midrash*. Instead, he yearns for entry into a more glorious, elaborate network of spaces, the very palaces of God. Concomitantly, this spatial substitution reflects a substitution for the rabbinic intellectual project of a very different concept of Torah knowledge, as expressed in the *Sar Torah* traditions. The simple space of the House of Study is the space for convoluted and strenuous intellectual discourses beyond the ken of the *Heikhalot* mystic. He hopes, instead, to negotiate the byzantine spaces of heaven—or to adjure heavenly princes to descend to his space—to arrive at a pure and simple spiritual apprehension. On the other hand, one element of the sacred character of a space is its restricted accessibility. The issue of how much the access to the *beit midrash* should be controlled is an old one, reflected in rabbinic sources.[99]

The identification of the *beit midrash* as a sacred space is given particularly powerful expression in the midrashic work, *Tanna debe Eliyahu*.[100] The entire work extols the importance and special qualities of the House of

Study. As in the *Zohar*, the collection tells many stories of its protagonist walking about. But, unlike the *Zohar*, *Tanna debe Eliyahu* does not depict this outside space in a positive way. In this midrash the world outside the House of Study is a place of ignorance, danger and oppression. The *beit midrash*, on the other hand, is the place of redemption and purification of Israel. At the end of days, the righteous will sit in God's own House of Study: "In the future the Holy Blessed One will sit in His *beit midrash* and the righteous of the world will sit before Him. And they will argue back and forth [*ve-nos'in ve-notnim*] about Scripture, Mishnah, Laws and *Aggadot*, saying about the impure 'Impure,' and about the pure, 'Pure,' about what is impure in its context and pure in its context."[101]

The Middle Ages saw a consolidation of this attitude. Maimonides codifies the sacred status of both synagogue and study hall, ranking the study hall above the house of prayer.[102] As noted, the rabbinic schools became centers drawing eager young students from far and wide. For the rabbinic elite, the study hall was home. *Tanna debe Eliyahu* asks, "What is the reason that Jacob merited a life in this world without pain and without the Evil Inclination, such as what He is to give the righteous in the Future [World] to Come? Because he was in the *beit midrash* from his youth until his old age, expert in Scripture, Mishnah, Midrash, *halakhot* and *aggadot*. As it is written, 'And Jacob was a complete man, sitting in tents' [Gen. 25:27]."[103] In a similar vein, and closer to the milieu of the *Zohar*, Rabbenu Yonah Gerondi writes, "'The righteous shall blossom like a palm tree . . . planted in the house of God' [Ps. 92:13–14], for the righteous are planted in the house of God from their youth, and they grow up in the houses of study from the time they are lads."[104]

The importance of the space of the study hall as the *Sitz im Leben* for the rise of medieval kabbalah has been stressed by Ḥaviva Pedaya.[105] The rise of kabbalah is marked by a transition from an esotericism preserved and cultivated in a murky oral ambience, to the appearance of literary works that form the foundation of all subsequent kabbalistic work. This transition, Pedaya claims, takes place within the *beit midrash*, the spatial locus for the competing intellectual and spiritual trends of medieval Jewry. She has pointed out that the spiritual and intellectual atmosphere and culture of a *beit midrash*, as well as the scholars and literary productions stemming from it, very much derive from that house of study in its concreteness as a spatial entity. Building on Elḥanan Reiner's work, she distinguishes the rabbinic response to the challenge of the Temple's destruction with that of the Karaites. The Karaites not only opposed rabbinic hermeneutical activity, they in a positive way emphasized the importance of ascetic and mourning attitudes and practices in honor of the Temple. The rabbis did not merely reject the adoption of an extreme attitude of mourning, and did not only create an ongoing interpretive tradition. They also created the House of Study as a concept and as a physical space. Pedaya writes:

> In a dialectical manner we may describe the *beit midrash* as a constructed architectonic focal point [*moqed*], where, in the consciousness of those who enter it, the way to making God present in reality is through study and not by means of the attempt to produce an ecstatic experience tied to concentration on recalling the [Temple's] destruction. If the Temple was a building that actualized ritual service within it and that tried to offer a focus for the indwelling of God and His revelation, the *beit midrash*, as a building and an institution organizing study, is, among other things, the substitute for the Temple as the institution organizing the ritual service. Study is the eternal enlivening of God's word as a constructed episteme [*ke-yeda' muvneh*], and, as a result, the experience is one of its renewed establishment in the student's consciousness at all times. In other words, the *beit midrash* represents, as well, the transition from revelation to exegesis [*derashah*]. The transition from divine inspiration [*ru'aḥ ha-qodesh*] to exegesis as a religious phenomenon is expressed on the literary plane by the transition from prophetic literary creation to sages' exegeses, and on the architectonic plane by relying on the *beit midrash* as the architectonic focus in place of the Temple.[106]

The dialectic is a complex one. The ascendancy of the study hall should not be seen as reflecting the complete vanquishing of the religious impulses treasured by the Karaites. Pedaya sees an experiential and chronological continuum between apocalyptic traditions and values, the Karaitic culture, and pietistic trends, all present within the walls of the *beit midrash* itself. She describes the Provençal *beit midrash* at the start of the thirteenth century as "a focal point of meeting for scholars from various distances and intellectual horizons. In this way the place becomes a central point, a cultural intersection, a space that brings together differing spirits of the time."[107] Possibly rubbing shoulders in the same study hall room were followers of the talmudist and halakhist RaBaD, the philosopher and translator Rabbi Yehudah ibn Tibbon, and the pure mystic Rabbi Isaac the Blind. The study they had in common was the rabbinic/talmudic curriculum. On that basis, the student would evince tendencies and talents that would encourage his teachers to induct him into other disciplines, including esoteric traditions.

Pedaya suggests that the ambience of the *beit midrash* can be appreciated through a text she places in the Provençal milieu of the early thirteenth century, *Sefer Ḥuqqei ha-Torah*.[108] Whether this document truly reflects the reality of that world or is merely a utopian projection upon it is not relevant here.[109] What is relevant is the image of the *beit midrash* that it conveys. The sacred precincts of the house of study become an all-encompassing world for *perushim*—young men dedicated to Torah study as to the priesthood. The third rule of *Sefer Ḥuqqei ha-Torah*—demanded "that the *perushim* not leave the House [of Study] for seven years, eating and drinking there and sleeping there. Nor shall they speak idle talk in the [*beit*] *midrash*. No wisdom is absorbed by a student who enters and leaves [*ha-nikhnas ve-yotze*],[110] but only by one who mortifies himself in the tent of Torah."[111] The Torah records a similar injunction prohibiting the priests from leaving the Tabernacle during the seven days in which they were ordained.[112] For *Ḥuqqei ha-Torah*, the experience of the dedicated Torah scholar is that of a much prolonged period—seven years—of sanctification and preparation. The image proffered in these regulations is of a space that is self-sufficient and all good. It claims exclusive allegiance from those who would ally themselves with Torah and holiness.[113] This is clearly the very opposite of what emerges from the *Zohar*'s picture of the walking Companions.

THE *ZOHAR* AND THE *BEIT MIDRASH*

The *Zohar* affirms the link between the Temple cultus and the alternative sacred spaces of synagogue and study hall. The coupling of these institutions together, as is common in rabbinic sources, often stems from reference to activities other than intensive Torah study such as one would expect in a rabbinical academy. The *Zohar* sometimes conceives of these places as places for textual recitation and meditation: "Said Rabbi Kruspedai, 'For one who recalls orally [*demidkar b'fumai*] in synagogues and study halls the subject of the sacrifices and their offering and meditates on them [*vi-yekhaven b'hu*], a covenant is struck so that those angels who would recall his sins to do him evil will not be able to do anything but good to him.'"[114] The text continues that in times of plague, one should enter the synagogue and study hall and recite the Torah passages about *qetoret*. The power of the space in which this recitation takes place seems to derive from its role as a liturgical and cultic center for the community, rather than as an intellectual center. Aside from the protective function of certain recitations performed in the synagogue and study hall, other texts can be read for consolation: "If not for all the good things that they wait for and see written in the Torah, they would not be able to exist and bear the exile. But they go to the houses of study and open books and see all those good things that they wait for and that they see written in the Torah, about which the Holy Blessed One promised them, and they are consoled in their exile."[115]

When the *Zohar* talks about Torah study in the *beit midrash*, it does not resort to the imagery of fierce analytical combat, as it does in other contexts.[116] But there are some instances where the *Zohar* does attribute power to the Torah study of scholars in the *beit midrash*. In discussing the meritorious power of the Temple as the place from which the Divine Presence radiates throughout the world, the *Zohar* insists that this Presence also alternatively radiates "'from the lairs of lions' [Song of Sol. 4:8] . . . Rabbi Yudan says, 'from the lairs of lions'—these are the disciples of sages who engage in Torah in 'the lairs' the houses of study and in the synagogues, who are lions and leopards in Torah."[117] The power of those engaged in deliberations in the *beit midrash* can be intimidating to younger scholars. A young man that the Companions encounter in an inn explains that he has refrained from showing his own Torah learning, much to the chagrin of his family, because "I was afraid, for the inhabitants of this land are lions in Torah."[118] In another story, the *Zohar* tells how difficult it was for Rabbi Huna to be noticed and included in a colloquy in the house of study.[119]

The *Zohar* occasionally advances the traditional image of the sage who does not leave the *beit midrash*. Thus, when it describes the relationship between Zebulon and Issachar, it is Zebulon who has "thighs," which are for moving about. He is the businessman, while his brother, the Torah scholar, is supposed to stay sedentary, in the enclosed tent, the *beit midrash*.[120] In discussing the palaces of the Other Side, the *Zohar* warns that this "Strange God"—*'el nekhar*—may wish to tempt a person to go out of the *beit midrash*. "This is the one who tempts a person who works at Torah or who is in the house of study. This powerful spirit tempts him to think various thoughts and says, 'What are you here for? It is better for you to walk in the company of those who lord it over people and those who go after beautiful women and who partake of mundane pleasures.'"[121] In this zoharic text we learn that to remain in the house of study is to remain with the Side of Holiness. The outside world and its temptations, subsumed under the activity of walking, are the subject of the *Zohar*'s social critique. Such a text leads one to expect that the *Zohar* would insist that the Companions stay within the sacred precincts of the Side of Holiness, within the *beit midrash*. It would have been easy for the *Zohar* to develop a locative orientation that privileged the *beit midrash* over the space outside it. The force that tempts the student to leave the study hall is the *'el nekhar*. Elsewhere the *Zohar* warns against pursuing a gentile woman, a *bat 'el nekhar*, "daughter of a strange god." The *Zohar* conceives of this transgression as a transgression of space, the introduction of the *brit*—the circumcised phallus—into the wrong place. This in turn causes "the Holy Blessed One to leave this world."[122] In short, it would have been easy for the *Zohar* to equate leaving the space of the *beit midrash* with causing God's Presence to leave the world. But we know that the opposite is the case. The *Zohar* does not try to emphasize the connection of the Companions to the *beit midrash*. Rarely do we find the Companions in the *beit midrash*, even when they are not specifically described as walking along.[123] And, of course, in the walking texts, their activities and their Torah take place outside and away from the House of Study, without any hint that this is not desirable.

The absence of the *beit midrash* as a significant locale for the zoharic fellowship calls into question the attempt by Israel Ta-Shma to situate the

Zohar in the world of the study halls of Naḥmanides and Rabbenu Yonah Gerondi. Ta-Shma's theory derives from his conviction, supported by many examples, that the *Zohar*, despite its Spanish origin, draws heavily from the traditions of Ashkenaz and its Pietists. He perceives the link connecting these two worlds together in the career of Rabbenu Yonah, who studied in the French yeshivah of Evraux, an academy influenced by the German Pietists.[124] Ta-Shma claims that such academies served as models for the authors of the *Zohar*. "And from what their eyes saw and their heart understood of what was accomplished and what was happening between the walls of the great academies of Naḥmanides and Rabbenu Yonah and their students in the area of exoteric Torah, the sages of the *Zohar* transferred [*he'etiqu*] to the esoteric realm."[125] Ta-Shma refers here specifically to the culture of creativity, the production of talmudic novellae—*ḥiddushim*—that characterized the Spanish academies of the period. It is not as if Ta-Shma ignores the difference between the world of the *Zohar* and the world of the *beit midrash*. He writes about this quite clearly:

> Attention should be paid to the fact that the *Zohar* turned upside-down all the fundamentals of yeshivah scholarship, establishing them as the complete reverse. Most of the novellae—and perhaps all of them—are stated "as you walk on the road" [Deut. 6:7] by a small group of two to three sages who walk together—walking on the road is considered to be the preferred opportunity to converse about Torah matters—or at night, in general near midnight, when the sages who were walking together from place to place during the day, and who were exposed to all kinds of dangers of the way, natural and unnatural, took lodging in a convenient Jewish inn, in one of the villages that were along the route of their travel, and awoke close to midnight—which is also a particularly auspicious time for this—to converse in Torah matters.[126]

He continues by pointing out that many of the new insights that the Companions hear are offered by persons who are not Torah sages from the study hall. Their subject matter is not halakhic or talmudic, but rooted in the Bible and in aggadic values. Most telling is the contrast between the dialectical method of analysis and argumentation that characterized the Spanish talmudic method, adapted from the Tosafists, and the immediate acceptance of the kabbalistic novellae on the part of the Companions. After pointing out how the *Zohar* is diametrically opposite in all these areas from the characteristics of the *beit midrash* culture, Ta-Shma concludes: "That is to say: The adoption of the creative—and authoritative, withal!—principle of *ḥiddush* that was so dominant in the world of the Spanish yeshivahs of the time, by means of a complete and diametrical reversal of all the norms of study accepted in those academies, is the precise and historical *Sitz im Leben* of the innovative project of the producers of the *Zohar*."[127] He accepts the characterizations of Jacob Katz and Moshe Idel regarding the secondary status of the zoharic authors in comparison to the primacy of the halakhic giants of the time.[128] In Ta-Shma's opinion, "the background against which the mighty spiritual construction of this secondary type [the *Zohar*] was made possible is the world of the masters of *ḥiddushim* to the Talmud from the *beit midrash* of Naḥmanides, who laid the foundations and the conceptual platform needed for the daring of the sages of the *Zohar*."[129] Ta-Shma is so convinced of this connection-by-reversal that he believes it justifies a new theory about the composition of the *Zohar*. He places the authors of the *Zohar* "in the environment of Rabbenu Yonah and his circle. Thus, one should predate the time of the *Zohar*'s composition to somewhere around the 1260s and 1270s, completely divorce the young Rabbi Moshe de Leon from any authorial status regarding the *Zohar*, and establish the place of the composition of the book—most probably—as Toledo, where Rabbenu Yonah acted as Yeshivah Head already in the 1240s . . . and perhaps even in neighboring Guadalajara, the place of Rabbi Moshe de Leon's activity."[130]

These theories have been vigorously rebutted by Yehuda Liebes.[131] After acknowledging Ta-Shma's contribution to the study of the halakhic aspects of the *Zohar*, Liebes argues that Ta-Shma has not fully appreciated the vast divide that exists between the *Zohar* and the Ramban in the realm of kabbalah and in their conceptions of *ḥiddush*. Naḥmanides was a very conservative kabbalist, opposed to the innovative and publicizing orientation of the *Zohar*.[132] The activity of *ḥiddush* was an exercise of the human intellect specific to the creation of exoteric Torah and had no place in the realm of received mysteries concerning the deeper meanings of Torah.[133] For the *Zohar*, on the other hand, the kabbalistic *ḥiddush* had less to do with intellectual prowess and everything to do with cosmic creation and renewal. These differences make it hard to imagine the study hall of Naḥmanides as the life setting of the *Zohar*.

One might add that Ta-Shma's evidence produces contradictory possibilities. The *Zohar*'s affinity with German pietistic values would lead us to expect it to be less embracing of the ideology of intellectual innovation championed by the Tosafists.[134] Furthermore, the concept of the *beit midrash* as a place of halakhic creativity certainly dates from before the time of Naḥmanides.[135] Liebes counters Ta-Shma's theory with a different explanation for the phenomenon of creativity shared by the halakhists and the *Zohar*:

> One should not make a connection between the *Zohar* and Naḥmanides' circle—neither from an objective standpoint nor according to the *Zohar*'s consciousness. The connection is only in a more general framework, in the renaissance-consciousness of the *Zohar*, that is, in the consciousness that was prevalent in those generations in Spain, of revitalizing the religion and its ancient literature. This consciousness came to expression in various fields, of which the talmudic novellae of Naḥmanides and his circle are also included, alongside the philosophical and halakhic project of Maimonides, the renewal of kabbalah, poetry, science and more.[136]

Liebes presents a picture of a culture in a period of harmonious, multifaceted vitality. Though he is conscious of the major differences between the talmudic/halakhic camps and the kabbalistic camps, he preserves harmony by keeping them separate. He does not account for interaction and tension between the groups. Ta-Shma seems to offer a clear appreciation of the differences between the camps with regard to approaching Torah study in that he admits that the *Zohar*'s approach and rhetoric is diametrically opposite to that of the reality of the *beit midrash*, but he nevertheless situates the *Zohar* in that very world. Completely absent from his study is any discussion of what it might mean to be part of a world that one is constantly busy negating.

Ta-Shma produces a powerful construction of the *beit midrash* as the space of *ḥiddush*. This is, he maintains, the *Zohar*'s *Sitz im Leben*. Does the *Zohar* convey an appreciation of such a construction? Indeed it does, but it displaces such a *beit midrash* to the heavens above.[137] The term most often used for that space is the *metivta*, the yeshivah. This space is populated by deceased sages, angelic beings, and the Holy Blessed One. Even here, the concept of *ḥiddush* is transformed. In one place the *Zohar* describes the periodic entry of the yeshivah heads into the yeshivah of Aaron, the priest: "And they are renewed [*mitḥadshan*] there from the purity of the holy dew that falls on his head. And Moses his master who pours it on him—with him they all are renewed through renewals [*ḥiddusin*] of love.[138] Here the term signifies personal purification rather than intellectual innovation. What is the significance of the *Zohar*'s adamant displacement of the spaces, activities, and personalities of the *beit midrash* from its purported life situation?

On the even more extreme move by the *Zohar* of placing the Companions out on the road, Ta-Shma's treatment is equally unsatisfactory. He simply notes that learning Torah out in the open was not unheard of in talmudic times.[139] Elsewhere I have shown that a very definite contrast exists between the talmudic picture and the zoharic walking motif.[140] But aside from this, it is clear that the *Zohar*'s conception, common to all medieval Jews, was that the Talmud was overwhelmingly a product of learning in the academies. The power of this tradition, as well as the reality of the contemporary Spanish rabbinic world, is totally negated by the *Zohar*. Though he refers to Idel's model of primary and secondary elites, Ta-Shma does not seem to see the differences between the *Zohar* and Spanish yeshivah world as making any real difference. Yet Ta-Shma describes this situation as a kind of *Sitz im Leben* by negation, without giving any analysis of this paradox, and without addressing the kinds of tension that surely must inhere in such a situation.

WALKING AS A TACTIC

It is necessary to do justice to these contradictions and tensions and to find a more adequate means of appreciating the different path taken by the *Zohar*.[141] Despite important differences and modifications, the perspective to be offered here draws confirmation from the analyses of Michel de Certeau, who discerned that the practice of walking was a notable element in some forms of mystical living and in modern, everyday life. The act of walking figures in studies by de Certeau focused on the Christian mystics of the sixteenth and seventeenth centuries and on modern urban civilization. In each context, de Certeau examined individual responses within an overarching system of religious, cultural, sociopolitical, and economic control.[142] In each context, de Certeau assumes a dominant culture—conceived along the lines of the panopticon conceptualized by Bentham and Foucault—within which and against which the everyday "consumer" acts. He explains that, relative to Foucault's, his approach

> could be inscribed as a consequence, but also as the reciprocal, of Foucault's analysis of the structures of power. He moved it in the direction of mechanisms and technical procedures, "minor instrumentalities" capable, merely by their organization of "details," of transforming a human multiplicity into a "disciplinary" society and of managing, differentiating, classifying, and hierarchizing all deviances concerning apprenticeship, health, justice, army, or work. "These often minuscule ruses of discipline," these "minor but flawless" mechanisms, draw their efficacy from the relationship between procedures and the space that they redistribute in order to make an "operator" out of it. But what *spatial practices* correspond, in the area where discipline is manipulated, to these apparatuses that produce a disciplinary space? In the present conjuncture, which is marked by a contradiction between the collective mode of administration and an individual mode of reappropriation, this question is no less important, if one admits that spatial practices in fact secretly structure the determining conditions of social life. I would like to follow out a few of these multiform, resistance, tricky and stubborn procedures that elude discipline without being outside the field in which it is exercised, and which should lead us to a theory of everyday practices, of lived space, of the disquieting familiarity of the city.[143]

While Foucault saw the need to analyze how manifold details all contribute to the creation of the all-embracing disciplinary system that is society, as he saw it, de Certeau wished to study the manifold details that operate within this controlling environment, but that nevertheless escape from society's panoptical surveillance. Moreover, his approach is divergent from Foucault's in making two other assumptions. He assumes that the totalitarian project of society may encounter periods of breakup during which the individual finds greater opportunity and impetus to cultivate independent practices—this is his view of contemporary urban civilization and of the mystics' experience in sixteenth- and seventeenth-century Christian Europe.[144] He also assumes—against Foucault[145]—that, no matter how powerful and efficient the panopticon may be, there is always room for the individual as a unique, independent actor.[146] These two assumptions make it possible to learn from his analysis of walking despite the different historical contexts of his studies. Thus, although de Certeau's walking subjects function in places, times, and cultures vastly different from thirteenth-century Spain, his assumptions about the relationship between the individual and his sociopolitical environment allow his insights to be fruitfully applied to the zoharic milieu. Furthermore, in making comparisons between de Certeau's walkers and the *Zohar*'s, we may also come to suggest certain modifications in de Certeau's paradigm.

De Certeau distinguishes between "strategies" and "tactics." The former are the province of power elites—cultural "producers." These elites are the groups who control what Henri Lefebvre calls "social space." Social space is the space created by the accumulation and intersection of "crowds, products in the markets, acts and symbols."[147] Strategies are founded on the control of social space that also authorizes its manipulation or reconfiguration. "A strategy assumes a place that can be circumscribed as *proper* (*propre*) and thus serve as the basis for generating relations with an exterior distinct from it (competitors, adversaries, 'clientèles,' 'targets,' or 'objects' of research.)"[148] A tactic, on the other hand, is the operation of the disenfranchised, the marginal, the consumer. It is a practice that takes place within social space without permanently altering that space. "Many everyday practices (talking, reading, moving about, shopping, cooking, etc.) are tactical in character. And so are, more generally, many 'ways of operating': victories of the 'weak' over the 'strong' (whether the strength be that of powerful people or the violence of things or of an imposed order, etc.), clever tricks, knowing how to get away with things, 'hunter's cunning,' maneuvers, polymorphic simulations, joyful discoveries, poetic as well as warlike."[149] When measured by the standard of spatial control, walking is a particularly poignant tactic. "To walk is to lack a place. It is the indefinite process of being absent and in search of a proper."[150]

How applicable are these characterizations to the situation of the zoharic fellowship? In what sense can their walking be seen as the tactic of a dislocated, weak group of consumers? To be sure, de Certeau also applies this analysis to the pre-capitalist environment of the post-Renaissance Christian mystics. But this sharpens the question. On the one hand, we are alerted to interrogate the position of the zoharic mystics in relation to their cultural milieu. We are pushed, thereby, to recognize aspects of disenfranchisement and marginalization that must be assessed. On the other hand, we must ask whether de Certeau's theoretical dichotomy between powerful cultural producers and marginal cultural consumers is adequate to describing the makeup of society and the dynamic operating within it.

Prodded by de Certeau's model, we should come to realize that the zoharic fellows—those in the text and those producing the text—were subject to a number of panoptical regimes. They were under the control of the non-Jewish world. Their relation to this world was a composite of shifting forces of resentment, acquiescence, envy, critique, opposition, and accommodation. Their role as Other to the non-Jewish society is obvious. Their wish to be free of non-Jewish power and surveillance can be assumed. But the *Zohar*'s kabbalists were also subject to the panopticon of traditional Judaism and traditional Jewish society. Their subjection to this system is more subtle and must be understood in light of the fact that they were active participants in this society. De Certeau describes the nature of a prevailing social system in harsh terms. It is a "system that saturates places with signification and indeed so reduces them to this signification that it is 'impossible to breath in them.'"[151] This seems to assume a high degree of alienation from the system on the part of its consumers. Would that fairly characterize the kabbalists' relationship to traditional Judaism?

Here the oversimplification of de Certeau's schema must be faced. His binary opposition between the powerful and the weak, the cultural producer and the consumer must be modified in a number of ways. First, it should be accepted that this opposition can exist within the self-same person or group. Even the most powerful cultural elites themselves operate within a system. As such, they are consumers of the system, subject to its definitions, whether conceptual, spiritual, or behavioral. As they exercise their power to create a system that is increasingly adequate to their own world of experience, they progressively deprive themselves of a space of their own. And yet each individual must make his way and find his place. Every thought, experience, or act, no matter how much in consonance with the system's requirements, is the product of individual choice and adjustment. Each individual's participation in the system is, for however brief a moment and however much it is concealed, an instantiation of freedom. Second, de Certeau describes totalitarian situations, controlled by one elite, without allowing for competing social elites of equal or varying levels of power.

Keeping these modifications in mind, we may appreciate that the zoharic kabbalists were indeed subject to the Jewish panopticon on a few levels. On the simplest level, they were no different from every other Jew who was, automatically, as we have just argued, subject to it. In addition, as M. Idel has pointed out, these kabbalists, while they were learned and pious, were not the only elite group, nor did they even belong to the first level of Jewish elites. There were economic and political elites as well as intellectual and spiritual elites, the latter divided among those who concentrated on halakhic, philosophical, or kabbalistic concerns. Ta-Shma describes the Spanish yeshivah in terms we can understand as pertaining to a "proper." We can equally understand the *Zohar*'s move outside the *beit midrash* as, not a simple negation, but, a resistance.

This conception of resistance can be helpful in framing the ongoing question of the possible antinomianism of the *Zohar*.[152] In general there is a sense that the *Zohar*'s rebellion was implicit, reaching the surface in the later strata of the *Ra'aya Meheimna* and the *Tiqqunim*.[153] Arguing against Ta-Shma, Liebes insists:

> Nonetheless, the anti-halakhic potential (I intend by this term to refer to halakhic figures and not to opposition to care in observing the commandments) exists in all parts of the *Zohar*, though in varying measures of consciousness and sharpness. Only thus is it possible to explain the background for the anti-halakhic eruption of the authors of the *Tiqqunei Zohar*. Though, indeed, his style is his personality, nevertheless, since he was a direct continuator of the zoharic fellowship, one should not assume that he would have de-

> veloped such an extreme anti-halakhic stance had the circle of the *Zohar* seen itself as part of the halakhic establishment, according to Ta-Shma's theory.[154]

But this statement unnecessarily limits the question to one of social position. To conceive of the production of social spaces and the success or problems anyone may have in inhabiting that space solely in terms of power relations between competing groups is to be overly reductive. Social spaces are indeed formed, deformed, and reformed or dissolved through the push and pull of what Lefebvre calls "commands" and "demands." That is, the active forces that produce any space do so in anticipation of or in response to pressing needs. These forces and needs may exist in harmony or tension, be recognized or concealed. Any space emerges from the interplay of these forces and needs through a creative process that cannot be reduced or assigned to only one force or element of the social world in which it took place:

> Rather, the creative capacity in question here is invariably that of a community or collectivity, of a group, of a faction of a class in action, or of an "agent" (i.e. "one who acts"). Even though "commanding" and "demanding" may be the functions of distinct groups, no individual or entity may be considered ultimately responsible for production itself: such responsibility may be attributed only to a social reality capable of investing a space—capable, given the resources (productive forces, technology and knowledge, means of labor, etc.), of producing that space.[155]

The complexity of this process is well expressed. The production of a space is often experienced as the collective accomplishment of many groups, each contributing energies deriving from divergent sources. Furthermore, the power of knowledge and spiritual values cannot be ignored as a constitutive factor in the production of a space.

Social space is the product and producer of intellectual and spiritual values. The constraints experienced in relation to any spatial complex are not to be seen merely in terms of political power relations. The spiritual density of spaces constructed within a religious system is aptly described by Henri Lefebvre in his concept of "absolute space." He writes: "Later, absolute space—the space of religion—introduced the highly pertinent distinctions between speech and writing, between the prescribed and the forbidden, between accessible and reserved spaces, and between full and empty. Thus certain spaces were carved out of nature and made complete by being filled to saturation point with beings and symbols, while other spaces were withdrawn from nature only to be kept empty as a way of symbolizing a transcendent reality at once absent and present. The paradigm became more complex as new contrasts came into play: within/without, open/closed, movable/fixed."[156]

To take these factors seriously is to acknowledge that each person and group, no matter how invested in a particular system and its spatial world, or, perhaps, precisely as a result of that intense investment, may simultaneously feel the pressure, the "demand" of a need or value incongruous to their presently constituted spatial world, heretofore conceived as a total environment.

It is in this sense that the *Zohar* may be seen as antinomian. No matter how loyal to the halakhic universe, the *Zohar* dares to conceive of a space outside its walls. The denial of the total adequacy of the halakhic space, though it is made in terms of traditional piety, is a challenge to the halakhic system insofar as the halakhah makes a claim of total adequacy. We may draw an analogy from the extravagant project for the construction of a church embarked upon by Antonio Gaudi, as described by Lefebvre. Lefebvre points out that Gaudi's program is ostensibly orthodox, but that in the way Gaudi felt compelled to pursue his plan, he made the construction of this church a challenge, in effect, to the authority of the Church as the Sacred Center:

> He pushed the Baroque as far as it would go, but he did not do so on the basis of accepted doctrines or categorizations. As locus of a risible consecration, one which makes a mockery of the sacred, the [Church of the] Sagrada Familia causes modern space and the archaic space of nature to corrupt one another. The flouting of established spatial codes and the eruption of a natural and cosmic fertility generate an extraordinary and dizzying "infinitization" of meaning. Somewhere short of accepted symbolisms, but beyond everyday meanings, a sanctifying power comes into play which is neither that of the state, nor that of the Church, nor that of the artist, nor that of theological divinity, but rather that of naturalness boldly identified with divine transcendence.[157]

Gaudi stepped out of accepted architectural conventions, although he was supposedly following them.[158] He attempted to retrieve an expression more attuned to nature as he pushed architecture to extremes. In pursuit of the same confluence of the mundane and the transcendent, the kabbalists could not redesign the *beit midrash*, since it was, unlike the synagogue, a space with no architectural identity. They could not reconfigure its motifs to include nature, since it had none. Instead, they had to leave the *beit midrash* and, as we shall see, enter the natural world.

The argument being advanced is not a naïve denial of the reality of social conflict and group competition and resentments. It is simply a claim that struggle takes place, not only between groups as political entities, but also deeply within groups and individuals as they define, balance, and express their spiritual values. It is a claim that such struggle is itself real and not a mere cover for sociopolitical power conflicts. The discomfort of the *Zohar* with the halakhic space of the *beit midrash* does not have to be conceived in terms of a rejection of halakhah, but, more literally and more aptly, as a sense that there was no room for the *Zohar*'s "demands" in that space. The exit from the *beit midrash* is not simply an expression of conflict between mystics and ruling, normative elites. It is, rather, a search for the answer to a new demand. The nature of that felt demand differentiated kabbalists, not only from halakhists and talmudists, but also from others among the kabbalists themselves, who fell into various groups. Their differences were determined by geography, but, more pertinently, by their affinity for a more conservative or, in the case of the *Zohar*, more innovative kabbalah.[159] That is, the kabbalists themselves, in demanding a different kind of space, an open rather than enclosed space, felt different "demands" with regard to the need for freedom and innovation. This study seeks to point out that, for the *Zohar*, an expression of that very demand for innovation is to be found, aside from in its purely kabbalistic discourses, in its narrative use of the walking motif.

With these adjustments in mind, it is possible to embrace certain fundamental insights about the walking motif as seen through de Certeau's lens. We recognize, in de Certeau's idea of the tactic, that moment of freedom and resistance to system that we have been exploring so far. As a mundane act, walking joins other quotidian moments "of meetings or daily tasks. What is of fundamental importance is inseparable from the insignificant.

This is what makes the anodyne stand out in bold relief. Something stirs within the everyday."[160]

But this means that the hermeneutical silence of the Companions' walking has already been broken. Indeed, de Certeau insists that, despite its silence, or, rather, by virtue of its silence, walking should be seen as a type of speech act. That is, it is inherently expressive in being a tactic—in being enacted in a way that is not dictated by any firm, determinative rules that are not themselves subject to individual application—the arbitrary uniqueness of which produces a style—that is, a unique example of a way to communicate within the language. For de Certeau walking is expressive in the urban setting because, in the most basic way,

> It has a triple "enunciative" function: it is a process of *appropriation* of the topographical system on the part of the pedestrian (just as the speaker appropriates and takes on language); it is a spatial acting-out of the place (just as the speech act is an acoustic acting out of language); and it implies *relations* among differentiated positions, that is, among pragmatic "contracts" in the form of movements (just as verbal enunciation is an "allocution," "posits another opposite" the speaker and puts contracts between interlocutors into action). It thus seems possible to give a preliminary definition of walking as a space of enunciation.[161]

But de Certeau claims that this was sensed in earlier epochs and cultures as well, including those closer to the zoharic period. He writes of the pure walking of Saint Francis of Assisi: "It was a Franciscan dream: that a body might preach without speaking, and that in walking around it might make visible what lives within."[162] As such, walking is aligned with another aspect of resistance to the panopticon, evincing resistance not only to behavioral directives but also to the systematic organization of thought and knowledge. De Certeau aligns the panoptical intellectual project with writing. Walking is conceived to be a kind of speech act in its resistance to this writing. In his study of post-Renaissance Christian mysticism, de Certeau detects a move away from "the hierarchical organization of knowledge and the validity of statements," which he equates with writing, to "a way of inquiring we can recognize today as being that of the speech act."[163] The speech act is reduced to texts, but texts that lack the authority of scholarly writing. They are fables about experiences and encounters brought about by walking along. "Down the paths or ways of which so many mystic texts speak goes the itinerant walker, *Wandersmann*."[164] These narrative texts are not taken as seriously as more normative intellectual or religious works, except by the mystics themselves.

The parallel to the zoharic fellowship is striking. The walking motif reports a tactic of resistance through the textual form of narrative, a literary choice that is, itself, a tactic that seeks to make room for itself alongside more intellectually respectable systems of halakhic and philosophical discourse. But, even more, the silent walking of the Companions should be seen as a momentary resistance against every system of signification imposed upon or adopted by the kabbalists—from the oppression of the non-Jewish environment, to the systematized way of life of traditional Judaism, and even including the *corpus symbolicum* of kabbalah itself. Just as these walking texts take their place outside the major esoteric texts of the *Zohar*, so they do so outside of what we would consider mystical experience.[165] If the kabbalist's quest is for the most intense spiritual experience, if the kabbalistic enterprise is a total dedication to a sacred erotics, then the *Zohar*'s recurrent motif of mundane travel insists on contextualizing that enterprise within a space that refuses to remain charged. The totalizing impulse of the kabbalistic hermeneutic itself—the attempt to map out the entire universe within assigned territories of good and evil, sacred and profane, integrated or disunited, giving and taking, male and female—requires the taking of a stand upon which to survey the universe and categorize it. But the walking motif repeatedly shows that there is always a moment prior to the taking of that position, and that the taking of that position already presupposes the movement toward that position from a prior place or state that does not yet have these categories applied to it. For how could that place be given a name before one is positioned to give names? To get to that place, one must walk. From this we conclude that walking in silence is already a walking toward speech.

These miniature narratives of walking create temporary free zones within the totalizing systems that surrounded the kabbalists. By opening those spaces, repeatedly, but fleetingly, the *Zohar* signals that there is something else—or someone else—not included in the given panopticon. Otherness suffuses the walking motif in every way. It is a tactic that declares the obdurate otherness of the actor who, in resisting the overarching spatial control of the panopticon, opens a space for otherness—other words, other objects, other places, and other people.

But the question must still be asked: Why was the creative symbiosis of the Provençal *beit midrash*, as described by Pedaya, not sustained? What was at issue for the *Zohar* that compelled its imagining a walk away from the *beit midrash* when, before, the kabbalists, philosophers, and talmudists were able to share that space together? One could legitimately point to the ascendancy of the circle of Naḥmanides as communal leaders as the development that disturbed the previous balance between the groups.[166] The focus here will be, instead, on the concurrent and related cultural struggle concerning the question of textuality and orality, writing and speech, in some of its many forms.

Textuality and Orality as Spatial Practices

WRITTEN AND ORAL TORAH IN THE *BEIT MIDRASH*

The thirteenth century saw the appearance of written kabbalistic works to an unprecedented degree. There is a manifest shift from orality to textuality in the kabbalistic community. Scholars have recently considered this development from a number of perspectives.[167] It is also the period in which the divisions between the intellectual and spiritual camps of halakhah, kabbalah and philosophy became more pronounced. Ḥaviva Pedaya has linked these phenomena to the struggle between various groups over their differing attitudes toward tradition and knowledge and to the breakdown of the *beit midrash* as the "architectonic focus" of the creative energies of the Jewish religious community. Pedaya describes how the desire for intense interaction between varied and differing systems of knowledge in the *beit midrash* was the necessary basis that ensured that the study hall serve as such a focal space. However, she writes that

> there is a correlation between the crumbling and disintegration of this life situation and the unequivocal transition to the pursuit of open knowledge and closed knowledge as "independent" processes, separate from each other,

a transition to defined structures of thought that isolate themselves in their structures. The body of esoteric knowledge seemingly detached itself from the soil of its birth and tried to live its life separate from the broad knowledge system in which it had been rooted as an immanent part of the reality of the *beit midrash*. . . .

It appears that there is a connection between the decline of the *beit midrash* as this [kind of space] and between different forms of alienation and tension between the two circles of knowledge and between, in actuality, the start of the rise of esoteric societies whose connective focus was a written esoteric teaching; this is a type of detachment from the model and structure of transmitting knowledge orally, in which there is a basic connection between one who addresses, the addressee, and the message just from their being found together under one roof.[168]

Pedaya charts a parallel development for the knowledge systems of Talmud/halakhah, philosophy, and kabbalah. They all undergo a shift from an oral to a textual culture. The free interchange between them is prevented by the isolation of each field within its own written texts. This encourages the development of communities that will concentrate on those texts to the exclusion of the others. Considering the kabbalists, we see them detach from the *beit midrash* as the space uniting the community. Their virtual *beit midrash* is displaced to their kabbalistic texts. Pedaya then goes on to reexamine the struggle over orality and textuality within the kabbalistic groups, rereading the famous letter of Rabbi Isaac the Blind for further insights into this matter.

Before pursuing that line of research, though, it is necessary to give a bit more attention to the question of the fate of the *beit midrash* for the kabbalists. In effect, Pedaya's theory of the *Sitz im Leben* of the kabbalists' literary creations is the opposite of Ta-Shma's construction. For Ta-Shma, the *Zohar* stems—by negation, to be sure—from the *beit midrash* of talmudic innovation. For Pedaya the kabbalistic literary project stems from a *beit midrash* that has a more heterogeneous identity. The hegemony of the talmudic/halakhic dialectic within the *beit midrash*, forming it into the space we know, only occurs after the abandonment of the *beit midrash* by the kabbalists. The innovative spirit that drove both camps to literary creativity was the common force that drove them apart.

But the question then arises: Why did the *beit midrash*, as it lost its identity as the common focal space of all spiritual communities, specifically become the exclusive space of the talmudic/halakhic community? Why did the kabbalists not fight for that space? Why did they not try to appropriate the *beit midrash* for themselves? Or, alternatively, why did they not develop another, even competing, set of spaces to serve as their own *battei midrash*? Understanding the concepts of social spaces and practices discussed above should help in seeing this issue more clearly. Certainly part of the dynamic at play here is connected to the kabbalists' devotion to esotericism. The *beit midrash* was a public space, not conducive to the maintenance of secrecy. Even when kabbalah had a place in the *beit midrash*, the exchange of esoteric learning took place under the cover of the din and activity of other forms of Torah learning. A public place devoted to esoteric Torah, a kabbalistic *beit midrash*, would be a contradiction in terms. But this cannot be the whole answer, since the kabbalists were engaging in an effort to publicize their teachings at this very moment, and using the methods—written texts and public teaching—that precisely signaled their detachment from the *beit midrash*.

We must recall de Certeau's concept of *proper* to more fully appreciate the kabbalists' detachment from the *beit midrash*. That space was not simply a public space, for so were the streets and marketplaces in which some of the more adventurous disciples of Rabbi Isaac the Blind found themselves. It was, more important, a *proper*, a space occupied, charged and invested with the community's values and symbol system. It participated in the absolute space of the community as it constituted itself traditionally as well as socially and politically. Precisely because the kabbalists submitted to the halakhic and talmudic panopticon, they were forced toward a spatial tactic if they were going to express anything of their own. They were forced to walk out of the *beit midrash*.

WRITING AND SPEAKING

Thus, the transition from orality to textuality entailed a transition in spatial practices. It should not be surprising, therefore, that this second transition is as problematic as the first. The kabbalists themselves struggled with these two issues simultaneously. This is evident in the famous letter of Rabbi Isaac the Blind protesting the revelation of Torah secrets. This epistle has been cited as evidence of his opposition to the writing down of kabbalistic doctrines. Rabbi Isaac writes:

> For I was filled with great concern when I saw scholars, men of understanding and Hasidim, engaging in long discourses and presuming in their books and letters to write about great and sublime matters [of kabbalah]. But what is written cannot be kept in the closet; often these things are lost or the owners die and the writings fall into the hands of fools and scoffers, and the name of heaven is thus profaned.[169]

Rabbi Isaac opposes the abrogation of the requirement that the transmission of esoteric wisdom be done orally. It may be that there is also a protest against losing the authority that is granted to the sage who is the oral transmitter of such teachings.[170] Rabbi Isaac objects that the written text cannot be controlled. But we cannot simply posit a correspondence between esotericism and orality based on his opposition to kabbalistic writings, for, as Pedaya points out,[171] Rabbi Isaac also explicitly and more vehemently attacks another practice. He writes in the same letter, "I have also heard from the regions where you dwell and concerning the men of Burgos that they openly hold forth on these matters, in the marketplaces and in the streets in confused and hasty discourses, and from their words it is clearly perceptible that their heart has been turned from the All-highest and they cause devastations of the plants."[172] The publication of kabbalistic matters in writing defiles these matters by exposing them to the public. Rabbi Isaac seems to accuse those disciples who discourse in public of the same violation. His accusation characterizes their sin in the severest terms of heresy. Is it possible that he actually suspected these kabbalists of such a transgression of the faith? The polemical force of his words may convey a different concern, just as serious. Conceivably, in his view, while writing violated the esoteric content of kabbalistic gnosis, the use of public speeches to disseminate kabbalah defiled the sacred method of its transmission, a method that had its own value as a sacred praxis.[173]

Whatever Rabbi Isaac may have felt, he could not stem the tide of the proliferation of kabbalistic literary productions and kabbalistic discourses. Yet, even as the kabbalists wrote more works, they continued to present orality as an important value. This means that orality was not the exclusive concern of the more conservative mystics, but was espoused by the innovators as well. Yaakov Elman and Israel Gershoni have pointed out the basic difference in this regard between rabbinic and kabbalistic texts. The former were produced in an oral context and betray their oral background in their textual characteristics. "These have not been shown to be characteristic of orally transmitted kabbalistic esoterica. Orality in the later period is thus a *claim* rather than reflecting an organized practice for the transmission and dissemination of a large body of esoteric material. The kabbalists of the thirteenth century committed their teachings to writing; they composed and disseminated volumes of kabbalistic teachings, even while insisting on the essential oral modes of transmission by which these teachings reached them."[174] What is the function of such a claim? Elliot Wolfson explains that the appeal to orality in medieval kabbalah, as in the earlier rabbinic tradition, is not a symptom of conservatism but that, "[o]n the contrary, oral tradition has functioned as a means of fostering new ideas or interpretations of traditional texts as well as instituting new rituals. The claim to orality, therefore, is a means to legitimate and contextualize innovations as authoritative tradition."[175] This is important, because in dealing with the *Zohar* one deals with the most innovative of kabbalistic texts.[176]

Wolfson reminds us that "there is no orality that does not presuppose textuality."[177] His own attention has focused on the hermeneutic implications of this presupposition. This study cannot consider the full range of issues implied in the interplay between orality and textuality in the *Zohar*, but attempts to explore what insights may be gleaned from looking at the these questions from the aspect of spatial orientations. From that perspective it must be pointed out that one of the salient innovations of the *Zohar* is its presentation of the teachings of its mystic fellowship in the context of narrative, a narrative that presents the Companions engaged in speaking while walking. This means that, as a written text, the *Zohar* chooses to present itself as a special case. It further means that by placing the Companions outside the *beit midrash*, the *Zohar* has distanced them as much as possible from the traditional space of textual study.[178] While Wolfson is correct to point out that kabbalah, and the

Zohar in particular, is intensely concerned with textual exegesis, the scenario the *Zohar* invents for the Companions—walking on the road and discoursing—compels the Companions and their other interlocutors to engage in exegeses of a text that exists only as an oral performance. While the *Zohar* may occasionally appeal to a special library of books,[179] it also tells of the frustrating experiences of Associates who gain possession of celestial books, only to have them disappear with their wisdom.[180] Books are not the operative source of their learning and teaching. That source resides in speech acts.[181]

In discussing walking as a tactic, I referred above to de Certeau's concept of walking as a speech act. Further developing the Saussureian duality of speech (*parole*) and language (*langue*), he advances an additional distinction between writing and speech, aligning writing with systematized knowledge, organized by society, while speech is representative of instantaneous, relational, communicative behavior. In de Certeau's study of post-medieval Christian mystics, writing is knowledge and speech is love.[182] In the urban civilization of today, writing is a strategy of the panopticon and speech is a marginal tactic.[183] De Certeau presents his distinction between speech and writing as being between horizontal communication and hierarchical knowledge. The kabbalists make a corresponding distinction between Oral Torah and Written Torah, in that the Oral Torah is the province of *Malkhut* while the Written is above, at *Tiferet*. Generally, in rabbinic tradition, the Oral becomes the Written because it takes place in the study hall. But the push of the *Zohar* is to insist that the Oral Torah of the Associates take place outside the *beit midrash*. It takes place not under the watchful supervision of the panoptical tradition, but out in the open, not in a static place but in motion.[184] Since the effect of *nomos* (*din*) is to define space conclusively, the *Zohar*, by setting the Companions on their way into undefined space may be fairly said to be antinomian.

This distinction between speech and writing is echoed, as well, in the thinking of Henri Lefebvre. He links speech with the initial "biomorphic and anthropological" experience of social space. The multiple residues of these immediate experiences endure and accrue.

> Space so conceived might be called "organic." In the immediacy of the links between groups, between members of groups, and between "society"

> and nature, occupied space gives direct expression—"on the ground," so to speak—to the relationships upon which social organization is founded. Abstraction has very little place in these relationships, which remain on the level of sex, age, blood, and, mentally, on that of images without concepts (i.e. the level of *speech*).[185]

To this more primary level of producing space, Lefebvre counterposes "abstract space," a space that has gradually undergone a process whereby it has been taken over "by a part of that space endowed with an illusory special status—namely, the part which is concerned with writing and imagery, underpinned by the written text (journalism, literature), and broadcast by the media; a part, in short, that amounts to abstraction wielding awesome reductionist force vis-à-vis 'lived' experience."[186] The production of this level of abstraction serves the purpose of suppressing the singular into the general. "Here rhythms, bodies and words are subordinated to principles of coexistence dictated from above, and indeed, often written down."[187] Walking is a tactic in that it leads away from the proper of writing and toward embodied speech. "The restoration of the body means, first and foremost, the restoration of the sensory-sensual—of speech, of the voice, of smell, of hearing," Lefebvre writes.[188] From this perspective, leaving the space of the written for the space of speech is a reassertion of the singular individual as an embodied being.

CHAPTER 5

The Broad Dissemination of Torah

"The Torah is not the heritage of only one place"

The complex interplay between space, writing and speech, tradition and innovation, society and body is exemplified and localized in the multiple meanings of the rite of circumcision.[1] The *Zohar* has extensive and multilayered expositions of the significance of the rite of circumcision, especially at the end of its treatment of the Torah portion, *Lekh L'kha*. Examination of all these teachings is beyond the purview of this study. But the preceding discussion leads to certain understandings of the significance of *brit milah*. The innovation of the *Zohar* is to have the Companions seek to retrieve their own bodily experience in speech by walking into nature and away from the enclosed textual space of the *beit midrash*. Out in the open, their purely oral Torah, created without resort to a written text in hand, is recorded in the zoharic text. Yet, in retrieving their bodies, the Companions also retrieve a divine text, since their bodies are inscribed with God's Name.[2] The opening of circumcision is through the localization of God's word in the physical body of the Jewish male rather than in any particular geographical place.[3] This entails the broad geographic dissemination of Torah rather than its local concentration. "The Torah is not the heritage of only one place," the *Zohar* tells us. In Jonathan Smith's terms, the locative has been displaced by the anthropomorphic.[4]

To Walk or Not to Walk

Confirmation of this connection may be found in the *Zohar*'s extended treatment of the theme of circumcision within an important narrative about Rabbi Abba.[5] It is a remarkable text in that it is both a walking story and an anti-walking story. It contains indications that the notion of the wandering Companions, whether regarding their preeminent status or regarding the value of their walking about, was open to question and challenge. It begins:

> Rabbi Abba was coming from Tiberias to his father-in-law's *bei teronya*[6] and Rabbi Ya'aqov, his son, was with him. They came upon Kfar Tarsha.[7] When they wished to lie down to sleep Rabbi Abba said to the owner of the house, "Is there a rooster here?" The owner of the house said to him, "Why?" Said he, "Because I am to rise at midnight exactly." He said, "There is no need, for I have a signal in my house in that scale in front of my bed which I fill with water. And it keeps dripping, 'Drip, drip.' And at exactly midnight it runs out of water and this attachment [*qitfa*][8] rolls over and sounds, and its sound is heard throughout the house, and it is then midnight exactly.[9] And I had an old man, who would get up every midnight to exert himself in Torah [*ve'ishtadel be'oraita*],[10] who made it for this." Said Rabbi Abba, "Blessed be the Merciful One Who sent me here."

Rabbi Abba and his son are on the road to visit Rabbi Abba's father-in-law.[11] They have obtained lodging in an inn or house. They are conscious of their special standing as men whose devotion to learning Torah is so strong that they rise at midnight for study.[12] They assume that they will have to make special arrangements for this. But the householder is not particularly impressed. He is used to this practice already, and, in fact, has a new invention, unknown to the sages, whose purpose is to serve as an alarm clock for a resident Torah scholar. The story continues that when midnight comes Rabbi Abba and son are awoken by the clock, as is the old scholar with his (not one but) two sons. Listening to their study in fellowship, "Rabbi Abba said to Rabbi Ya'aqov, 'Surely we should partner with Shekhinah and join as one.'" As we have seen, joining with Shekhinah through Torah study can be done without walking on the road.

He finds out, to his surprise, that there is a tradition of Torah scholarship here, as the old man relates that he has learned the teachings from his own grandfather. Rabbi Abba bestows a kiss upon the man and says, "Yes, that is the way it really is. Blessed is the Merciful One Who sent me here." We have seen that when a Companion uses this gesture, it contains ambivalent elements. It is an expression of admiration, but also of a reassertion of the Comrade's premier position, conveying that the teaching, though not issuing from him, still requires his stamp of validation.[13]

Now Rabbi Abba joins the session. He relates a teaching, claiming for it the pedigree of his own teacher, Rashbi. But he is challenged by the old man's young son (*yenuqa*), who says he has another explanation. Rabbi Abba invites him to say it: "Rabbi Abba said to him, 'Say, my good son, and may your mouth's word be the voice of a lamp [*qala d'butzina*].'" This may simply mean that he wishes for the child's words to be enlightening. But the term *butzina*—lamp—is a term applied within the Companions' fellowship. It often refers to divine forces or sparks of new Torah learning. By extension, Rashbi applies it to his disciples and they call him "The Holy Lamp." Given that Rashbi's teaching has just been pushed aside by the child, Rabbi Abba's invitation may be a form of defense as well.[14] After hearing the wise words of the child, Rabbi Abba blesses him. He exclaims, "I had actually thought that wisdom is only found among the righteous who have acquired it. Now I see that even the children of Rabbi Shim'on's generation have acquired supernal wisdom. How fortunate are you, Rabbi Shim'on. Woe to the generation from whom you will depart."

Rabbi Abba's words express mixed emotions of surprise, joy, pride, and sadness. He acknowledges that the Companions do not have a monopoly on true understanding of Torah. He then reasserts Rashbi's primacy by declaring that anyone's Torah knowledge ultimately derives from Rashbi's merit, all words of Torah being an echo of Rashbi's voice, "the voice of the lamp." But then he realizes that one day, the generation will be bereft of this source of Torah. The grim deduction that should follow is that there will be no new Torah insights after Rashbi's death.[15]

The group continues to learn through the night, expounding the secrets of *brit*—circumcision.

> Meanwhile daylight had arrived, and they had been speaking words of Torah. They got up to go. The man said to them, "You should complete what you were dealing with during the night." They said, "What is that?" He told them, "Tomorrow you should see the face of the master of the covenant [*mareih d'qayama*],[16] for my wife has made this request of you, and the *brit milah* [*g'zar qayama*] of the son just born to me will be celebrated tomorrow." Rabbi Abba said, "This is a request for a mitzvah, and in order to behold the face of Shekhinah, we shall stay."[17] They waited all that day. That night the

> man gathered all his friends and they passionately studied [*'ishtadlu*] Torah all that night. No one slept.[18]

Because the wife's request is that he perform a mitzvah, Rabbi Abba must accede to it.[19] His intention to continue on his way must be deferred—for the sake of attending the *brit* ceremony and in order to behold the face of Shekhinah.[20] This consideration somehow outweighs the choice to travel on and join with Shekhinah while on the road. The contrast is developed as the story continues. The group takes turns teaching new insights into the meaning of circumcision. It is this rite that sustains the world and sustains Israel. It is a rite centered in the body, demanding vigilant protection. The Israelites cannot move on into the Promised Land unless they perform circumcision. Moses cannot continue on his way to Egypt to liberate his people unless he performs this act. The nature of *brit*, in this context, is to demand self-limitation, exemplified by control of mobility and concern for proper sexual relations.[21] The final teaching of this first series strongly emphasizes the localizing, limiting nature of *brit*. The anonymous friend declares:

> And if he merits and guards it, Shekhinah will not separate from him. When does She [Shekhinah] remain fixed in him? When he marries and that sign enters its proper place. When they partner as one to be called one name, then supernal *Ḥesed* dwells upon them. In which place does it dwell? On the male side. And who is *Ḥesed*? The *Ḥesed* of *'El*, who comes out of the supernal Wisdom and is crowned in the male, by which the female is perfumed. We have further learned: *'Eloah* is this—*'El*, the light of Wisdom; *Vav* [*o*] is male; *Heh* [*ah*] is female. When they partner together as one, they are called *'Eloah*, and the holy soul is unified from that place, and all depend on that sign. Thus it is written, "*And from my flesh I will behold God*." [Job 19:26] That is the completion of all—*from my flesh*—tangibly [*mamash*]! From that sign—tangibly! That is why holy Israel merit to conjoin with the Holy Blessed One. They are of merit in this world and the coming world. Concerning them it is written: "*And you who cleave to God*," . . . for that "*you are all alive today*" [Deut. 4:4].[22]

In emphasizing the importance of circumcision, the speaker repeatedly concerns himself with issues of place and locale. Shekhinah will stay with a man—and not go somewhere else—only if the man finds a wife who becomes the proper place for his sign. The grace they enjoy must be located by the speaker, and its place of origin denominated. The localized sign is a focal point calling together sexual and divine forces. The human/divine conjunction is emphatically localized and delimited: "*from my flesh*—tangibly! From that sign—tangibly!"

Rabbi Abba is taken by the power and sophistication of the teachings he has heard. But he still does not understand how these Torah scholars can be satisfied to remain in a restricted space. He asks, "What is this, your being such sages and yet you sit here?" He cannot understand why they do not want to move about, as he does. He has only temporarily quashed his desire to move on, while they seem to have no such desire at all. Their answer to him is an ardent declaration of attachment to their place:

If birds are expelled from their place,
  they do not know whither to fly.
This is what is written,
  "*As a bird wandering from her nest,*
Is a man who wanders from his place" [Prov. 27:8].[23]
  And this place acquired us for Torah.
So this is our way: every night—
  half we sleep, and half—
We study Torah.

And when we arise in the morning,
  smells of the field and the water streams
illuminate[24] Torah for us,
  and it settles in our hearts.[25]

Well, this place—They judged it once
  on high. So many Guard Commanders[26]
Were taken away in that judgment,
  as a punishment for the Torah.

So our efforts, night and day,
  are in Torah.
And this place,
  it helps us.
So anyone who leaves
  this place
Is as one who leaves
  eternal life.[27]

For this group of sages, there is no question about going on the road. "This is our way—*orḥa*," they explain, using the term that, as in English, can refer to a path, a road, or a way of doing things. They use it to refer to their devotion to remaining in their place. It is a place that nourishes them, but also a place that needs their devotion for its own repair and redemption. These sages remain in Kfar Tarsha to make up for the time when local Torah sages sinned against the Torah.[28] They and the place were judged and punished. But now the sages and the place live in harmony, mutually sustaining each other in Torah. To abandon this place would be to abandon life itself.

Rabbi Abba cannot help but be moved by this devotion. But, as a Companion committed to walking on the road, this cathectic bond to a static place is strange and antithetical and, indeed, threatening:

> Rabbi Abba raised his hands and blessed them. They sat until daybreak. After day dawned, they told the children who were before them, "Go out and see if the day has dawned,[29] and let each one say a new word of Torah to this great man." They went out and saw that day had dawned. One of them said, "A fire from above is in store for today." "And in this house," said another. Another one said, "There is one old man here who is going to be burned by this fire." "May the Merciful One save us!" said Rabbi Abba. He was astounded and could not speak. He said, "the Knot of Will[30] has been caught on Earth."[31]

Rabbi Abba is overwhelmed by the fearsome prospect of divine revelation so confidently predicted by the local children. He had already praised the precocious abilities of the children, but has now witnessed their uncanny attunement to the divine dynamic. But if their words prophesying the descent of a divine fire sounded frightening, the awesome reality that ensued was, instead, a source of ecstasy and joy. The text continues:

> And so it was. For on that day the comrades saw the face of Shekhinah and were surrounded by fire. And Rabbi Abba's face glowed like a flame from the joy of Torah. It is taught—they did not leave the house that whole day. And the house was surrounded by a ring [*itqattar be-qitra*][32] and the words were joyous among them as if they had received the Torah from Mount Sinai that very day.[33]

Rabbi Abba sees the face of Shekhinah without having to go on the road. In fact, the narrator emphasizes, the group did not leave the house all day. The house is encircled with the fragrant protection of the Divine Presence.[34] The experience is disorienting. After the children leave, the group "did not know whether it was day or night." Rabbi Abba invites the remaining adults each to say a Torah teaching. Each person contributes a teaching dedicated to the circumcision, including the elucidation of the biblical story of Abraham's circumcision and its spiritual effects. Rabbi Abba is delighted and praises them, and participates as well.[35] He concludes by blessing them and the newborn child, after which they escort him some distance out of the village. They explain that the father's good fortune is due to his having performed the mitzvah of levirate marriage, so that the child will be called after the deceased husband of his mother. The meaning of *yibbum*—levirate marriage—is not dealt with in this fleeting reference. This revelation is done with so quickly that its significance is hard to register.[36] It is only faintly sensed that there may be a parallel between the act of the father who takes the place of his deceased brother and the dedication of the sages of this town, who take the place of their deceased predecessors. Just as the father makes up for the failure of his brother to have a son by taking his place, so these sages whom Rabbi Abba has met make up for the failure of the previous generation to create Torah by literally taking and holding their place.[37]

It is time for the conclusion of the story:

> Rabbi Abba blessed them and went on his way. When he arrived he set forth these things before Rabbi Ele'azar,[38] but was afraid to tell Rabbi Shim'on. One day he was before Rabbi Shim'on and Rabbi Shim'on said, "What is it that is written, 'And Abram fell on his face and the Almighty spoke to him, saying—I present my covenant with you [Gen. 17:3–4]?' It seems that until he was circumcised he would fall on his face and speak with Him, but that after he was circumcised he stood upright [*qa'em be-qiyumeih*] and was not afraid. 'I present my covenant with you'—that he found himself circumcised." Rabbi Abba said to him, "Would it be agreeable before the Master to say some of the superior words that I heard about this?"

Rabbi Abba has returned home, to his teacher, Rashbi. But he has not revealed to Rashbi the story of his experience in Kfar Tarsha, nor has he shared the words of Torah that he heard there. On the other hand, he felt safe to recount all this to Rashbi's son, Rabbi Ele'azar. The reasons for his fear and his choices to conceal or reveal are not explained. Whatever they may have been, Rabbi Abba recalls his stay at Kfar Tarsha after he hears his master teach about circumcision. At this point he decides to break his silence, explaining why he has waited until now:

> He said to him, "I was afraid lest they be punished on my account." He said to him, "Heaven forbid! 'He fears not from any evil tidings. His heart is prepared, trusting in God' [Ps. 112:7]." So he told him the story and set forth all the teachings before him.[39] Said he to him, "If you had all these superior teachings hidden with you, why didn't you say them? I decree [*gozarna*][40] against you that these next thirty days you will study but forget. Does it not state, 'Do not withhold goodness from its owners if you are capable of doing so' [Prov. 3:27]?" And so it was.

Rabbi Abba has explained that he was afraid for the sages of Kfar Tarsha. He worried that by revealing what had happened, he would bring a punishment upon them, but he does not say why he had such a fear. Rashbi reassures Rabbi Abba that his fears are unfounded, but once Rabbi Abba reveals both the story and the teachings, Rashbi becomes upset. Unexpectedly, it is Rabbi Abba himself who is first punished, sentenced to a month of frustrated study. All he learns he will immediately forget; anything revealed to him will be immediately concealed again.[41] But Rashbi is not finished reacting:

> He said, "I decree that for this Torah they will be exiled to Babylonia [*de bid'oraita da yiglun le-bavel*] among Companions."[42]
>
> Rabbi Abba was dispirited. One day Rabbi Shim'on saw him. He said to him, "The state of your heart [*tufsera* (*tufsa*)[43] *de-libakh*] is evident in your face." He said to him, "It is not about me, but about them." He said to him, "Heaven forbid that they were punished. Rather, because these things were so exposed among them, they should be exiled among the Companions and learn these ways, so that these things will be hidden among them. For these matters should not be revealed except among us. The Holy Blessed One having thus concluded with us. And it is through us that matters will be revealed."
>
> Rabbi Yose said, "'Then your light will break forth like morning' [Isa. 58:8]. . . . The Holy Blessed One is prepared to make a declaration concerning His children, and say, 'Then your light will break forth like morning,[44] and

your healing will soon sprout. Your righteousness will walk before you and the Glory of God will gather you in.'"

Rabbi Abba bears his suffering visibly, but selflessly. His concern, the story repeats, is only with the others in that village. Rashbi seeks to reassure him, but what he has done and why remains unclear. This ambiguity may reflect an ambivalence in the narrative. Have the sages of Kfar Tarsha been punished by exile? Have their teachings been taken from them and revealed to others, or have measures been taken to ensure their concealment? Despite Rashbi's disclaimer, it is clear that the utopian reality of Kfar Tarsha has been destroyed, forever transformed into "Mata Meḥasya," a Babylonian center of exoteric learning. Rashbi has an agreement with God that gives him exclusive control over the revelation of Torah secrets.[45]

Rabbi Abba understood that this was Rashbi's conviction, hence his fear was well-founded. By keeping the truth from his master for as long as he did, he had engaged in an unauthorized act of concealment, an act that aided and abetted the ongoing project of the sages of Kfar Tarsha who were revealing more and more Torah secrets. What had made Rabbi Abba withhold this information from his teacher? It seems that he had been deeply moved by the beauty of that community, a community that, in actuality, was far more concealed in its activities than Rashbi and his disciples. That group was committed to remaining in its own place. No matter how much Torah they revealed, they revealed it to themselves alone, only sharing their secrets with an occasional distinguished visitor[46] who happened to come by. In contrast, the Associates were engaged in Torah study on the road, everywhere and with everyone. Rabbi Abba had repeatedly expressed his admiration, devotion and loyalty to Rashbi and the Companions while he was visiting the village, but his loyalty is tested when he returns to Rashbi. While his bond to Rashbi ultimately holds, the competing bond that Rashbi wants him to forget, as he decrees that he will forget his learning, will not be easily discarded. Perhaps the *Zohar* attempts, through the soothing coda supplied by Rabbi Yose, to ameliorate the unsettling ending of this story by joining images of the righteous walking and divine embrace.

The Nest

A theme that runs through this narrative is the theme of filiation in its many varieties and complexities. It is a story of filiations realized and unfulfilled. The story begins with father (*abba*) and son en route to visiting the father's father-in-law. That destination is never reached. The father-in-law never appears in the story. The figure of Rabbi Ya'aqov, Rabbi Abba's son, also eventually drops out of the story. Instead, Rabbi Abba and son happen upon a place saturated with manifestations of filial devotion. An old man rises at midnight to learn Torah with his sons in a house that is about to celebrate the *brit* of the owner's son.[47] Yet, the son is not really a son, since he is the issue of a levirate union. His father is dead. Nonetheless, the dead fathers of the town are ever present for its inhabitants. The devotion of the living to the dead binds them to this place, as they engage in Torah study in their memory and faithfully follow their ceremonial customs.[48] The children of the place are gifted with prophecy, a gift that is frightening, but is the source of supreme joy as well. While the role of the children is to be sources of delight and paragons of devotion, the duty of the father is to sacrifice his son, a duty fulfilled through the act of circumcision. This is the lesson Rabbi Abba will learn when he finally comes before his master. The murky role of Rashbi's real son, Rabbi Ele'azar, is eclipsed by the drama of the struggle between spiritual father and son, Rashbi and Rabbi Abba. Rabbi Abba does not fully meet the test of devotion. He is not the completely faithful son. In his struggle, he is drawn to try to become the sacrificial son of the village. He is overcome with worry and fear. But Rashbi teaches that Abraham was able to overcome his fear though the act of *milah*. When Rabbi Abba can no longer contain himself, it is to admit this fear. But Rashbi is insistent. He quotes the Psalmist's idealized picture of the righteous father who has no fear. Ironically, Rabbi Abba's fear places him in the realm, not of Abraham, the father, but of Isaac, the son.[49] But he is an imperfect, not fully compliant son. Rashbi must sacrifice his son, Rabbi Abba, as a father circumcises his son (*gozarna 'alakh*). Rabbi Yose concludes the section with the teaching that the reconciliation of fathers and sons will have to await the end time, as prophesied by Isaiah.[50]

Having seen that Rabbi Abba is torn by competing loyalties, we must try to clarify the source of his conflict within himself, and determine what demand it was that he understood Rashbi to be making of him and that was so difficult to honor. The conflict revolves around two related epicenters. One is a question that has merited much attention by contemporary scholars. That is the issue of the proper approach—conceptual, practical, and hermeneutic—to revealing and concealing esoteric truths of Torah. This problem is essential and constant for the mystical tradition. Liebes, Matt, and Wolfson have offered extensive and profound treatments of this issue as it was handled by the *Zohar*.

Less attention has been paid to the second issue around which this text constantly revolves. This is the issue of determining and maintaining a proper orientation to space. This question seems extremely pertinent when we read the text with the traditional commentators. It seems that the crux of the conflict for Rashbi is not so much about whether to reveal or conceal these secrets as about who will have the power to make decisions about it. The narrative ends with Rashbi's retaking control over the dissemination of Torah secrets. He will decide when—and *where*—the Torah will be revealed. Thus, the competition between two mystical communities is expressed in a dispute, not about the desirability of revealing esoteric truths, but about one's attitude toward particular spaces. In the most general terms, the contrast is made between a localized spatial adherence, as exemplified by the villagers of Kfar Tarsha, and an unfettered, free-ranging spatial practice, lived out by the wandering Associates. The pertinence of this issue for our text is evident in numerous ways. The explicit expression of the villagers' attachment to their home, and Rabbi Abba's questioning of it has been indicated above. The free-floating quality of Rabbi Abba's experience is also expressed in the previously noted fact that he never arrives at his father-in-law's home. Moreover, the displacement that causes this failure is tellingly expressed in a simple way. Rabbi Abba is introduced as one who is walking from one named place to another. His route is first deflected toward another place, a place of extraordinary attractive power. His abandoning of that place, after some delay and ambivalence, results in his coming before his master, Rashbi—who inhabits no named place at all.[51]

It is fitting that this question of competing spatial orientations be conjoined with the issue of filiation, mentioned above. The issue of spatial production is integrally tied to the question of how we occupy our bodies and, more poignantly, how and what we produce with our bodies. "For it is by means of the body that space is perceived, lived—and produced."[52] The body may produce many things along with space. But its ultimate concern is to produce and reproduce itself. Lefebvre points out that the body's first spatial production is itself.[53] Biological reproduction is also the production of other spatial beings, who will themselves produce space. These concerns cannot be separated. Lefebvre writes: "Theoretical and practical questions relating to space . . . tend to resituate concepts and problems having to do with biological reproduction, and with the production both of the means of production themselves and consumer goods."[54] From this perspective, it may be said that as an attempt to create a nurturing and protective environment for oneself and one's offspring—one's productions and re-productions—all spatial production is a kind of nesting.

The *Zohar* indeed applies the image of the nest to this world. In this story, the villagers of Kfar Tarsha explain that they do not wish to leave their homes because a wanderer is like a bird separated from her nest.[55] This verse from Proverbs recalls the biblical law of sending away the mother bird when wishing to take her chicks or eggs from her nest.[56] The rationale of that law was the subject of continual speculation.[57] While the *Bahir* applied the verse to conceiving of the hierarchy of divine potencies,[58] the *Zohar* related it to the relationship between God and Shekhinah as effected by this-worldly Israel.[59] At the start of the collection of stories about the wandering sage, Rabbi Bun, the *Zohar* explains the significance of sending away the mother bird. Rabbi Bun, while he sleeps, hears a voice explicating the verses about sending away the mother. The voice analyzes the verse's terms to apply them to the divine realm pulled asunder by the exile of Shekhinah when the Temples were destroyed, leaving Israel in the lower world abandoned as well. By making the Torah's scenario a history-making drama, with God as the protagonist, the question arises as to what the proper response must be to this situation, and whether the simple meaning of the verse offers instruction for this. The voice that Rabbi Bun hears seems to express a struggle with this question, apparently offering a degree of protest against the demands of this law in the name of the tragic state in which Shekhinah is found. The voice seems to suggest that the mitzvah of sending away the mother bird should not be performed, for "one who has mercy leaves the mother and her children and walks away."[60] Shekhinah is imagined keening for Her children, echoing words found in a talmudic story that has God "moaning like a dove" for exiling Israel, "Woe is Me that I have destroyed my house and burnt My palace and exiled My children among the nations."[61] Only in this way can God's mercy be aroused, as the *Zohar* repeatedly states, "for the Merciful One can only be found thus."

This interpretation is followed by a statement that initially seems unrelated to the topic: "When the Holy Blessed One created the world, He created it with three knots [*qitrin*], and they are Wisdom, Understanding and Knowledge. . . . And all these knots are found in the human being, and the knot of faith[62] that came out of them emanated into the other creatures, so that there is wisdom in all of them, each in their own way."[63] After this enigmatic statement about creation and emanation, the *Zohar* returns to the subject of the mother bird:

> This bird, when she flies from her chicks and is chased away from her children, keeps chirping and does not know where to go, vowing to put an end to herself. The Holy Blessed One, of Whom it is written, "And His mercies are upon all His creatures" [Ps. 145:9] even upon any small fly, His love is upon all.[64] The one appointed over the birds is bestirred toward the Holy Blessed One. And the Holy Blessed One is bestirred over His children. Then a voice issues from Him and says, "As a bird wandering from her nest, is a man who wanders from his place" [Prov. 27:8]. Then He is aroused with love upon all those who wander from place to place, and from one station to another, brokenhearted, broken in strength, and love is aroused over all the worlds and He has mercy on them and lets go of the sins of those wandering from their places, and He has mercy on them and on the whole world. Therefore did the Holy Blessed One say to make the bird dwell away, so that she should arouse love upon the whole world. Who is the one who caused

> [Him] to have mercy on the world and to arouse love upon them? It is that person who sent away that bird to afflict her in two ways. Thus the Holy Blessed One is bestirred and is filled with love for all those masters of sorrow and all those who wander from their places. And therefore the reward for that person, what does it say about it? "so that He will be good to you and you will live long" [Deut. 22:7].[65]

Here the *Zohar* has offered a very different explanation of the commandment to send away the mother bird. The focus is back on the person who must perform this mitzvah. Furthermore, the focus is no longer upon the suffering caused by the destruction of the Temple and the exile of the Shekhinah.[66] The theme of wandering has been expanded to refer to all wanderers. This explains the teaching immediately preceding this new reading of the mitzvah. The *Zohar* reaches back to the creation of the world, pointing out that prior to the exile of Shekhinah from the Temple, there was a fundamental alienation of Shekhinah in Her being the Mother of the mundane world, in Her leaving the knot of faith so that all creatures could be endowed with wisdom—the stuff of creation—in their own way.[67] The difference between the orientations of the villagers of Kfar Tarsha and of the Companions of the *Zohar* is brought home in the difference between the different ways the two groups read the same verse from Proverbs. It is quoted by the villagers of Kfar Tarsha when they justify their staying put. They are keenly aware of the pain that wandering can bring. They know the pain of the wandering bird and want no part of it, so they will choose to stay home, leaving their nest undisturbed. The *Zohar* recognizes the pain of the wanderer, too, but it formulates a different, activist response. For the *Zohar*, it is incumbent upon all to be cruel and cause a mother bird the anguish of being expelled from her nest, away from her chicks, so that her cries will start a chain reaction that will lead to the amelioration of the world's pain and to the final redemption.[68] If wandering is ever to cease, it must first be increased.

The Tower of Babel

That the two groups are divided over the issue of spatial orientation is reflected in Rashbi's reaction. Rashbi's opposition to this competing group is not expressed through condemnation or by a discourse on revelation and concealment. He thwarts the group by exiling them from their place and by dispersing them among Companions. He thwarts their attempt to remain in one place and forces dislocation upon them. When he sends them to Bavel, his act recalls, not only the Babylonian exile that ended the era of the First Temple, but more precisely, the first instance when Babylonia is mentioned by the Torah, in the story of the Tower in Genesis 11.[69] The Torah tells of a group who wished to build a tower "whose top would be in the heavens."[70] There, too, God was concerned with the declaration of the inhabitants of the place that they wished to remain concentrated in that one place alone. Rashbi follows God's model by decreeing that the group endure exile and dispersion. The parallels notwithstanding, it is surprising to think that the villagers of Kfar Tarsha, pious and devoted to Torah learning, could be compared to the Generation of Division—*Dor ha-P'lagah*. On the other hand, bearing these parallels in mind, Rashbi's insistence that his action is not meant to be a punishment raises the question of how God's actions at the Tower should be seen.

That episode occupies an important place in the historiography of the medieval kabbalists. Aside from its inherent interest as an etiological myth about the proliferation of nations and languages,[71] it was compelling to kabbalists in the way it brings the vertical and horizontal axes into conflict. The Bible portrays the attempt of a group to ascend to heaven. For some reason this provokes God's descent from above and His drastic response of dispersing the population and assuring their continued separation. The kabbalists, along with all serious readers of the text, had to decide what the nature of the Tower project was—praiseworthy, misguided, or sinful[72]—and, correspondingly, the nature of God's response—corrective, protective, or punitive? Naḥmanides, in his brief treatment of the biblical story, rejects the explanation of the "masters of *peshat*," who explain that the biblical text allows us to conclude that the builders of the Tower were concerned only "that they should remain together."[73] Ramban cannot believe that the builders could be such "fools." By looking more deeply into their declared desire to make a "name" for themselves, he deduces that they had a more insidious agenda in mind:

> But one who knows the meaning of "name" will understand their intention, by their saying, "Let us make for ourselves a name" [v. 4], and will understand

> the measure of what they conspired to do by making the tower, and will understand the whole matter—that they conceived an evil thought, and the punishment that came upon them to separate them by languages and lands was measure for measure. For they were cutting the plantings [*qotzetzim ba-neti'ot*]. Now their sin is similar to the sin of their father, so that perhaps because of this they explicated "that the sons of Adam built" [v. 5] [thus]: "Said Rabbi Berakhyah, 'What, were they sons of asses, sons of camels? But they were the sons of Primal Adam. . . .'" Observe that in the entire context of the Flood "Elohim" is mentioned, while in the context of the Division the Unique Name was mentioned, because the Flood was in order to destroy the world, but the dispersion was because they cut the plantings, so they are punished through His Great Name. This is also the meaning of the descent, as in the measure [meted out] for Sodom. And the enlightened will understand.[74]

Ramban explains that the sin of this group was the same sin as that of First Adam, the "cutting of the plantings." This signifies the separation of the divine powers, and the exclusive attention to the lowest one, *Malkhut*. He also points out that the name of God used in the text signifies the supernal, united nature of God, the appropriate agent to punish those who wished to create separation in the divine pleroma.

Naḥmanides' teaching was adopted by other kabbalists, such as Giqatilla,[75] Todros Abulafia,[76] Menaḥem Reqanati,[77] Baḥya,[78] and the *Ma'arekhet ha-Elohut*.[79] Such an understanding of the sin of the Tower would seem totally inapplicable to the case of Kfar Tarsha. But Naḥmanides' approach was not always adopted in a simple way. For instance, the author of *Ma'arekhet ha-Elohut* was still bothered by the use of the Tetragrammaton as the description of God Who metes out what is apparently a punishment. He suggests this answer:

> However, it should be known that the intention of the men of the Generation of Division was from one aspect good. For when they saw the reign of the angels and the power of the arrangement of the stars and constellations over the lands, they tried to extricate themselves from their rule and to seek shelter beneath the wings of the Shekhinah, the place of union. And they thought that by making the building of a city, as they planned, which is a prophetic vision, as will be explained in the Corner on Adam,[80] the Shekhinah would dwell upon them immediately, and they would not be divided among the countries under the Princes apportioned to the earth's

> climates, as will also be explained in the Corner on Adam, and they would apprehend through that vision everything they desired, as it says, "and now all that they planned to do will not be withheld from them" [Gen. 11:6]. And their general thought was that the Unity, which is the Almighty of Almighties and the Lord of Lords, would rule over them so that they would not be dispersed, and the Holy Spirit would dwell upon them. So this thought was good. But the sin was in their saying, "and let us make a name for ourselves" [v. 4], as we mentioned. And our rabbis of blessed memory already mentioned, concerning "with its head in the heavens" [v. 4], that they put up an idol and put a sword in its hand. Indeed the Name of Mercy is mentioned in the context of their punishment, as in "And YHVH descended" [v. 5], as well as in "Let us descend" [v. 7]. For the matter of descent is in including Mercy in its Judgment, so as not to harm, as I hinted in the Corners of the Reason, on the subject of sacrifices.[81] And the reason that there is Mercy upon them, so as not to destroy them, is as we mentioned, because they wished to take shelter under the wings of the Shekhinah and they did not intend to destroy anything of the Leader's creation. Therefore He reserved life for them, for them to have a portion in the Coming World should they return and repent.[82]

The approach of the *Ma'arekhet* considerably sweetens the judgment advocated by Naḥmanides. God's actions cannot be considered pure judgment or punishment, but also include an aspect of mercy, as indicated by the use of the Tetragrammaton. This is because that generation really had a positive motivation for building the Tower. Contrary to Naḥmanides' total condemnation of their theosophy, the *Ma'arekhet* allows that the Generation had a proper apprehension of the complete divine structure and desired to establish an intimate, unmediated relationship with God. Their sin was that, in giving corporeal expression to their devotion, they passed into idolatry.[83]

While the explanations of the *Ma'arekhet* have certain features that bring the analogy between the *Dor ha-P'lagah* and the inhabitants of Kfar Tarsha a bit closer, the idolatrous nature of the sin of the *Dor ha-P'lagah* in his version is still far from anything we might ascribe to those pious, scholarly villagers.

Isaac of Acre also struggled with Naḥmanides' theory. After quoting other kabbalists, he explains that the "city and tower" that the Generation of Division wished to build indeed referred to the *Shi'ur Qomah*, the divine anthropomorphic structure of potencies. *'Atarah* is hinted at by "city," while *Tiferet* is hinted at by "tower" Unlike the *Ma'arekhet*, he accepts that the

Tower generation offered exclusive devotion to *'Atarah*, thus being guilty of "cutting the plantings." But then Isaac of Acre asks,

> But weren't they specifically building the tower? For were they building only the city, which hints at the *'Atarah*, there would have been "cutting." But now that they built a city as against the *'Atarah* and the tower, corresponding to *Tiferet*, wasn't there a perfect unification [*yiḥud shalem*]? It is possible to answer that their actions were good, for the act hints at unification. But their intent was evil in saying, after building the city and tower, "Let us make a name for ourselves" [Gen. 11:4], which is as if to say, 'Let us build us in the lower regions a building modeled like the upper structure, and then we shall not have to take anything into account except the *'Atarah*, which is called "name."[84]

So for Isaac of Acre the answer is the reverse of the one given by the *Ma'arekhet*. While he also splits the generation's actions from its intentions, he ascribes goodness to the actions, but evil to the intentions. Still, his explanation is not Naḥmanides' straightforward charge. The evil intention of the Generation does not arise immediately. First there is an act of symbolic unification—the building of city with tower. It is only the subsequent intention to allow such an act to suffice for the purposes of unification, thereafter allowing the Generation to concentrate solely on the *'Atarah*, that is, evil.

But however much Isaac of Acre's explanation makes our picture of the religious psychology of that generation more nuanced, it does not seem to offer an adequate description of the failings of the villagers of Kfar Tarsha. It would seem that both their actions and intentions were good, inasmuch as they devoted themselves to Torah study with the express purpose of effecting divine unification thereby. Nevertheless, Isaac of Acre's model may be helpful. His interpretation asks us to look at more than one stage of intention. The completion of an action with proper intention merely creates a new stage of required action and intention in its wake. One may succeed at the first stage, only to fail at the second. If we apply that model to the residents of Kfar Tarsha, we might speculate that, while their first level of actions and intentions was praiseworthy, their second-level intention was not. Just as the Generation of Division sinned in falling away from the continued requirements of their first successful level of unification, thereby subverting their initial accomplishment, so the villagers could be accused of failing to continue with the implications of their project of revelation and unification. Their failure is manifest in their desire to stay put and not to leave their place. The *Zohar* returns the accusation of Rabbi Isaac the Blind, who accused those disciples who took to the streets of cutting the plantings, and applies it to this sedentary group. Their devotion to staying in place was a "cutting of the plantings," because, though it was an act of devotion to God's Presence, it nonetheless thwarted the fulfillment of the next, necessary step of the process, the requirement to take to the road.[85]

This interpretation is borne out by a reading of the zoharic treatment of the Tower of Babel narrative:

> Mishnah: "And all the land was one language and single matters" [Gen. 11:1]. Rabbi Shim'on opened—"And the house in its building itself [*be-hibanoto*] was a complete stone, built by a journey, and hammers and axes, any metal tools, were not heard in the house as it built itself" [1 Kings 6:7]. "And the house in its building itself," but didn't Solomon build it, with all the artisans who were there? What is "in its building itself"? Rather, it is just as it is written, "The menorah shall be made of itself [*te'aseh*] of one piece" [Exod. 25:31]. If it is made of a piece, what is meant by "made of itself"? Rather, it was certainly all done of itself by sign and miracle. Once they started to work, the working [*'avid'ta*] taught the artisans how to work with it, something they did not know before this. Why? Because the blessing of the Holy Blessed One rested on their hands. Therefore it is written "in its building itself." It was built of itself.[86]

In contemplating the building of the Tower of Babel, Rashbi first thinks of another grandiose building project, Solomon's construction of the First Temple. Despite the scriptural evidence, he explains that the Temple was built, not by artisans, but by itself, as an expression of God's blessing.[87] Further exegesis clarifies that Shekhinah built the Temple. Shekhinah is the house, Solomon's rock, and also "*masa'*—a journey—for She took Herself and came and dwelled upon them and the work was done."[88] This journey is further explicated by Rashbi as he describes the emanative process of creation. The process involves a gradual revelation of speech, developing from the hidden Divine Will to Thought, from the Emanative Will that animates Thought. From the vocal box of the throat emerges the mixture of Fire, Breath, and Water that together produce Voice. When the Voice emerges outward through the lips, it turns to Speech—*dibbur*—another term for Shekhinah. It is this emanative voyage that gives Shekhinah the name "*masa'*—journey—for She goes out from inside and goes down and moves to the outside, leaving from above and going down and traveling below." But if this emanative process effects the emergence of speech, why does the verse say that no sound was heard from the implements—the lower forces of this world—during the building of the Temple? The *Zohar* explains that this silence obtains during the state of union between Shekhinah and the upper potencies. "When She [Shekhinah] suckles, all exist in joy and they suckle and are filled with blessing, and then all the worlds together exist in one mystery, in one union, and there are no worlds of separation in any of them."

When the divine pleroma is unified, the cosmos is in a state analogous to the silent contentment of a suckling baby. The Tower of Babel story is seen as the stage in cosmic history when separation occurred. "Come, see: 'And all the land was one language.' . . . Afterwards, what is written? 'And it was when they traveled from the Earliest [*mi-qedem*],'—from the Primal One [God] of the world,[89] 'that they found a valley in the land of Shinar' [Gen. 11:2], for it is from there that they split off to all those sides, and it is the Head of the Kingdom for Dispersion."[90] However, the negative valence apparent in this exegesis is puzzling. The *Zohar* uses a phrase from the midrash that accuses the builders of the Tower of abandoning God. Yet it is describing the creation of the lower worlds, specifically, the mundane world of differentiation—*'alma de-peruda*[91]—the result of a dynamic within the Divine. The *Zohar* itself immediately asks why this dispersion should be described in this negative way, since separation is inherent in the process of emanation from the highest level, signified by the image of the four rivers that flow from Eden. It responds that the earlier differentiation did not preclude subsequent union, whereas in this case, dispersion was explicitly chosen.

It is evident that there is an uneasy coexistence of readings here, in which a theory of divine cosmogonic actions is overlaid upon the ascription of sin and evil, more appropriate, perhaps, to the biblical story as written. The *Zohar* continues with the standard approach that sees the builders as idolaters and rebels against God.[92] The harmonious state of divine union is shattered through the decision of Nimrod, ruler of Babylonia,[93] and his followers to travel away "from this primordial union of cosmic faith—*mi-qadma'a 'iqara de-'alma meheimnuta de-kola*— . . . to leave from the Upper Realm to the Other Realm."[94] The decision to rebel against God is tied to the desire for movement. The destabilization of the static perfection of divine union is conceived in terms of spatial activity, inherent in the nature of the Other Side. Thus their travel is condemned, characterized as "drunken" and "crooked," terms that describe the way of the Serpent. This interpretation sees the real root of the builders' sin as deriving from their lack of spatial discipline, their uncontrolled movement, rather than in their desire to stay in one place. It is their desire to break through boundaries that leads, inevitably to their idolatrous construction of Tower and City. Such a drive toward spatial instability infects their speech, as well. Rabbi Ḥiyya applies to them the verse "And the wicked are like a driven sea, unable to be still, and its waters send forth mud and muck" (Isa. 57:20). Because these travelers could not abide the tranquility of divine union, they embarked on a journey of chaos, like one who embarks into a stormy sea on a boat without a captain. Just as such a sea will spew forth mud and muck, so did their lips.[95]

But then the *Zohar* shifts the focus to the upper world, for "when the Holy Blessed One looks into rendering judgment, first He looks into the upper grade."[96] Rashbi, based on Ezekiel's vision of the future Temple, whose inner gate would be locked except on the Sabbath, introduces a discussion of the divine potencies as the Days of the Week. Six days are mundane, and the Sabbath (and the New Moon) is holy, since it is the day of divine union. But the other six days are separated and closed off from Shabbat, "because it is during these six days of the mundane that the lower world is nourished."[97] These days are based in Babylonia, and they have no control over the land of Israel. Holy space is nourished through the holy temporal potency of Shabbat (and New Moon).[98] This holy nourishment is what allows the rest of the world to be sustained through the rest of the week. Rashbi explains that when God descended to view the Tower of Babel, He "descended from holiness to the mundane" to inspect what had been built in the mundane world and to frighten the lower forces. The *Zohar* continues:

> Rabbi Yitzḥaq was sitting before Rabbi Shim'on. He said to him, "What did these people see to make them do such foolishness, to rebel against the Holy Blessed One, and to all stand together of one mind about this?" He said to him, "This is spoken of, for it is written, 'And it was when they traveled from the Earliest,' they moved from above to below; they moved from the land of Israel to Babylonia. They said, 'Here is the place to cleave [*le-midbaq*]—"And we will make a name for us" [Gen. 11:4] . . . —and the support from below will cleave in this place, because when Judgment comes to descend on the world, this place faces it, and from here the world will benefit and be nourished. For it is too crowded above for the world to be nourished from it. And not only that, but we will go up to heaven and engage it in battle, so that the flood shall not come down upon the world as formerly.'"[99]

While its scenario somewhat recalls the ancient myth of the rebellious, fallen angels,[100] the *Zohar* nevertheless portrays the rebellion in noble terms. Rashbi imagines the motivation of the lower six divine forces to have been their commitment to protecting the lower realms from divine judgment. The imagery is confusing in that the division between the six potencies and the seventh would usually refer to the middle *sefirot* and Shekhinah. But how could the middle *sefirot* be depicted as rebelling against God? The *Zohar*, as it proceeds, makes it clearer that these forces are of a lower rank than the middle *sefirot*. But they are parallel to them. Thus, when God intervenes to prevent these forces from consolidating at the Tower, God adopts an indirect strategy: "Therefore, let the grades above be separated to every side and therefore all these below will be dispersed."[101] God disperses the forces below by dispersing those above.

The drama that the *Zohar* depicts is the crisis of separation within the divine necessitated by the creation of a mundane world. The Divine is conflicted between the desire and need for union and the competing demand of the lower world. The rebellion of the forces charged with nourishing the mundane world is an expression of anxiety about the relationship between upper and lower realms. If the upper realm is too unified, the lower realms fear that it will be "too crowded"—too preoccupied with itself—to care for the world below. The suspicion of the lower forces regarding the upper world translates into a fear that the upper world will attack the mundane world again, as it did with the Flood. Entrusted with the charge to nourish the world, these forces decide to band together so as to prevent judgment's wrath from descending upon the world. If this is a rebellion, it is conceived in a very morally complex fashion. These forces cannot be treated simply as evil. In order to ensure the proper development of the lower world, divine concessions are in order. Thus, divine union is denied to the middle *sefirot* in order to ensure the proper operation of the world below. Such a union is the necessary prelude to the union of all the upper *sefirot* with Shekhinah. Thus the attempted rebellion of the lower forces is the internal rebellion of the Shekhinah, Who, for the sake of the world, is deprived of unification with the middle and upper *sefirot* except on Shabbat. Divine union is still the ideal and the ultimate source of all nourishment, even down below, but practically speaking, Shekhinah must forego Her feminine desire for the male potencies above Her.[102]

The *Zohar* has turned the concept of rebellion against God around, depriving it of its conventional valence of wickedness. It continues by actually blaming God for causing such rebelliousness, "for it is because the Holy Blessed One lowered the secrets of wisdom to the world that people were ruined by it, and they desired to challenge Him."[103] In this way the *Zohar* has forged a link between sinful spatial practices and the improper relationship to esoteric knowledge. It catalogues the biblical greats—Adam, Noah, Abraham, Isaac, Jacob, and Solomon—generation after generation, who failed God in different ways after being vouchsafed this divine wisdom. Only Moses was able to remain faithful. Reverting to the human actors of the Tower of Babel story, the *Zohar* concludes: "Come, see—because of a little wisdom that they found from the wisdom of the ancients [*ḥokhmah de-qadma'i*], they challenged the Holy Blessed One and built a tower and did all that they did, until they were dispersed from the face of the earth and no wisdom remained with them to do anything."[104]

The last elements of correspondence to the villagers of Kfar Tarsha are supplied with this observation. Like the villagers, the builders of the Tower of Babel were inadequate custodians of esoteric wisdom. Moreover, they were led astray precisely in their attempt to follow the wisdom they inherited from their forebears—*ḥokhmah de-qadma'i*—just as the villagers tried to maintain their town in fidelity to their ancestors. Were the builders of the Tower conscious of the history of failure that is chronicled by the *Zohar*? If they were, then they would possibly have paralleled yet another feature of the Kfar Tarsha filial culture—its desire to make up for the sin of their fathers. This supposition is strengthened through the way the *Zohar* describes the sin of the early generation of the village. They "were taken up by that judgment regarding the punishment of the Torah *'onsha de-orayta*."[105] This has usually been understood to refer to the former sages' failure to study Torah as assiduously as necessary. But another interpretation is now possible. The provocative idea advanced in the *Zohar* regarding the failure of the generations to serve God is that it is really God's fault, for giving humans His esoteric Wisdom. In that sense, the very gift of that Torah was itself also a kind of "punishment of the Torah." Perhaps the sin of the earlier generation was not that of neglect of Torah study, but rather of some unspecified failure with regard to the study and teaching of esoteric Torah. It is in reaction to that sin that the villagers have determined to confine their Torah to that one place.

Walking and Ecstasy

Indeed, the difficulty in carrying forth esoteric traditions was recognized by Rashbi and the Companions. To misunderstand such Torah, or to disseminate it improperly was considered a serious sin, as Yehuda Liebes has shown with regard to the *Idra* gathering.[106] His comments could serve as an accurate expression of the beliefs of the villagers of Kfar Tarsha:

> The translation of the expression *ne'eman ruah* as *ruha de-kiyyuma* is based on an understanding of the word *ne'eman*, "faithful," as meaning "fixed firmly in place," as in the verse, "I will fasten him as a peg in a firm place (*makom ne'eman*)" (Isa. 22:23). The spirit of the guardian of the secret is fixed and remains in its place, as opposed to the spirit of one who tends to disclose secrets, which swirls around "like bran in water" (an expression derived from *Bava Metzi'a* 60b) and has no rest until it goes out. He who stays firmly in

> place is like a pillar and an everlasting foundation: it is he who is "Righteous, foundation of the world," whose trait is to guard the secret without disclosing it.[107]

But if this adequately expresses the locative concerns of the villagers, and they are equally shared by Rashbi, why does he wish to punish them and uproot them from their home? While the sole authority of Rashbi as the Moses of his generation is unquestioned by the *Zohar*,[108] it is insufficient to see the cause of Rashbi's displeasure in the fact that the villagers have not derived their Torah from him.[109] The Companions affirm their dependence on Rashbi, declaring that "when we stand before Rashbi all the springs of our hearts open to every side and all is revealed; when we separate, we know nothing and all springs are blocked."[110] All their Torah derives from Rashbi's inspiration. But the inhabitants of Kfar Tarsha feel no such connection or dependency. Yet, if theirs is the sin of violating Rashbi's sole proprietary authority over the teaching of esoteric Torah then we must convict all the other personalities who, encountered by the Companions in their journeys, teach them new insights of Torah and are praised for it. In such circumstances the Companions are usually content to affirm Rashbi's authority by ascribing to his merit the ability of others in his generation to create new Torah insights.[111] In that way, even though the new Torah insights seem to be coming from other sources, they can be traced back to Rashbi himself. Indeed, Rabbi Abba applies this approach when he hears the youth of Kfar Tarsha expound their Torah as "the voice of the lamp." But this approach is apparently not adequate to assuage Rashbi's displeasure. In what way, then, were the actions of the villagers more serious?

Since it is apparent that the bone of contention in this conflict is somehow connected to the adoption or rejection of the spatial practice of walking on the road, it is possible that when we recall some of the characteristics, positive and negative, peculiar to the walking texts, we may be able to see why the Kfar Tarsha case was different. Analysis of the distribution of these texts in the zoharic corpus has shown that they are absent from some of the most esoteric portions of the *Zohar*.[112] The *Idrot*, for example, at which Rashbi makes the personal and locative demands just cited above, do not partake of the walking motif. Furthermore, within the walking texts themselves there is a definite absence of reports of ecstatic experiences or heavenly ascents. The heavenly *beit midrash* may be visited by Rashbi and select students, but they do not do so typically as part of a walking text,[113] whose essence, as noted, is to walk away from the earthly *beit midrash* into the mundane world. In a number of cases we find Companions engaged in profound, ecstatic mystical experiences, signified by their being surrounded by a ring of fire or losing track of time. Yet this does not occur in a walking text. On the contrary, in one case the Companions, feeling overwhelmed by their mystical experience flee from it by choosing to discuss Torah as they go walking.[114] Yet it is precisely such an experience that was created by the villagers of Kfar Tarsha, as demonstrated by the ring of fire that enveloped them with Rabbi Abba, along with their loss of time-awareness. And it was precisely such an activity that Rashbi would not tolerate.

A clear distinction emerges between the mystical experiences the Companions may have had with Rashbi, or with his son, Rabbi Ele'azar,[115] within an intimate enclosure[116] and the experiences of adventure or Torah discourse that they had while walking on the road.[117] This distinction parallels the distinction made by the *Zohar* between the outward-looking, nurturing state of Shekhinah during the six mundane days, and Her unitive state on Shabbat. The unitive experiences on Shabbat make the disjuncture and mundane preoccupation of Shekhinah possible, but that unitive experience is precluded during the week. So too, Rashbi's esoteric Torah in its most profound level was engaged in unitive theurgy, and thus demanded strict limitations regarding its imbibing and dissemination. But there was an equally compelling need for engagement in Torah that went outside these boundaries. It seems, however, that it was not intended to effect the same kind of unification.

This requires a reexamination of the recurrent motif—found in so many walking texts—of uniting with Shekhinah. Indeed, the zoharic discussion about the Tower of Babel that serves as a basis for much of the above, continues with a walking text, cited earlier in this study.[118] Rabbi Yose and Rabbi Ḥiyya walk on the road and discuss the benefit of saying words of Torah while walking along. Understood in the context just developed, the disjuncture noted earlier in analyzing that text, the disjuncture between the already established presence of Shekhinah for all travelers, and the Companions' desire to engage Shekhinah through Torah, takes on a new possible meaning. In this understanding, the desire of the Companions—while walking—may not be to actually effect divine union of the kind that will restore Shekhinah to the male upper realm. Their desire is, rather, to unite with Shekhinah on Her mundane mission of nourishing the material world.

Rejoicing on the Margins

This interpretation may seem identical to Rabbi Moshe Cordovero's theory of *gerushin*. However, as noted above,[119] RaMaK's understanding places a heavy emphasis on the suffering and exile of Shekhinah as a result of Israel's sins. The *gerushin* support and accompany Shekhinah as a form of penance and atonement. While the *Zohar*'s consciousness of the painful alienation of Shekhinah is fundamental to its commitment to walking, its sense is not as mournful as RaMaK's.[120] The Companions' walking is not in mourning, but in joy.[121] The vitality and excitement of the zoharic adventures bespeaks a different attitude, perhaps more accurately exemplified in J. Z. Smith's coupling of the fundamental religious value of ritual with the seemingly antithetical value of humor. As mentioned,[122] Smith sees ritual as an enactment of the gnosis that includes an awareness of what-should-be alongside the awareness that what-is-in-reality is far different. The positive acceptance of this state of difference is evinced in a humorous, joking attitude. The opportunity to walk with Shekhinah is greeted with joy and delight in an overwhelming number of texts. The Companions walk along in cheerful affirmation, not in penance.

Important observations about these elements of joy and humor in the *Zohar* have been made by Yehuda Liebes. He connects them to the *Zohar*'s erotic drive for creativity and innovation and points to examples of its ludic and even mischievous delight or "glow"—*Zohar*. "Just as the God of the *Zohar* creates His world through play [*sha'ashu'a*],[123] so the kabbalist authors of the *Zohar* created the *Zohar* and its world," Liebes writes. "And, indeed, the book of the *Zohar* is full of play and humor. One can find the basis of this play, irony, and masquerade in the pseudepigraphic form in which the book was written as well (so that the author gained great freedom to express his innovative ideas)."[124] Liebes suggests that this attitude even affects the seriousness with which the *Zohar* takes its own theosophical teachings and that this can be found in some of the theosophical puns and riddles found in some places in the *Zohar*. The interrelationship between nonsense and profundity is expressed, for example, in the identification of *hevel*—futility—with the divine breath that created the universe. Similarly, the term "emptiness—*reiqanaya*, which is the Aramaic Targum [translation] of *bohu* in Genesis 1:2, is also capable of describing the vapor [*hevel*] upon which, according to the *Zohar*, the world rests. . . . If so, there is no limit to the importance of these words of 'nonsense' (real nonsense!)."[125]

These observations can be further supported by the findings of this study. As Smith has shown, ironic humor and ritual are related in that they show the way to affirm the commanding truth of the ideal while acknowledging the unavoidable vitality of the real: "One day Rabbi Ḥizqiyah found Rabbi Yose when he was poking a skewer [*de-hava mistamit safsina*][126] into the coals of the fire and a cloud of smoke went up. He said to him, 'If the cloud of smoke of the sacrifices were always to have ascended upon the altar in this manner, there would have been no anger in the world and Israel would not have been exiled from the land."[127] The smoky barbecue of one of the Companions has become the occasion for a comparison to the world sustaining and atoning ritual of the sacrifices. The comparison has nothing to recommend it except for the ridiculous similarity that exists between this mundane cloud of smoke and the holy smoke of the Temple. To recognize the comparison despite their divergent levels of significance, and to recognize that on the physical, mundane level, their correspondence is exact, requires a sharp sense of irony and a high tolerance for cosmic jokes.

If the walking texts are seen as a tactic, in the sense put forth by de Certeau, we can better appreciate the playful function they perform in the zoharic arsenal of spiritual, as well as spatial, practices. They give voice to the recognition that there is a real gap between aspiration and fulfillment, between theory and practice:

> It is taught: One day Rabbi Shim'on was coming from Qapotqiya to Lod and with him were Rabbi Abba and Rabbi Yehudah. Rabbi Abba was tired and was running after Rabbi Shim'on, who was riding. Said Rabbi Abba, "This is surely [*vadai*] 'They will go after God like a roaring lion' [Hosea 11:10]."[128] Rabbi Shim'on dismounted. He said to him, "Surely [*vadai*] it is written, 'And I sat on the mountain forty days and forty nights' [Deut. 9:9]. Surely Wisdom does not settle in except when a person sits and does not walk about, but stays in his place. For we established these matters on what is written, 'And I sat.' Now the matter depends on rest." They sat down.[129]

The humor operates on the level of the narrator, but is also a conscious component of the give-and-take between master and disciple. The ideal demand, as Rabbi Abba quotes the verse, is for the student to follow his master with the ferocious strength of a lion. But the reality is that Rabbi Abba is worn out from running after Rashbi. He quotes the verse in rueful recognition that he cannot keep up, expressed through the common zoharic term, *vadai*, a term often used to affirm the mystic reality inhering in the exoteric level of things and verses. Rashbi sees his student's physical exhaustion. Out of consideration, he descends from his animal—he has not had to exert himself at all—and finds a verse to permit the group to sit and rest. Ironically, the prooftext he musters meant, in context, to celebrate Moses' transcendence of physical and bodily limits while he was learning Torah on Mount Sinai. But, to accommodate his student's physical weakness, Rashbi carefully edits the verse to emphasize only its first words, *va-eshev*—"and I sat"—and eliminates its contradictory conclusion. And he also emphasizes his cognizance of this trick with a literary wink—he claims that this is "*vadai*—surely" what is required in this case.[130] Here Rashbi has playfully reinterpreted Torah in order to make room for the mundane reality of a weary student.

The disparity between what the *Zohar* teaches and what the Companions actually feel they can do is discernible in another walking text, cited earlier.[131] The narrative tells of Rabbi Ele'azar and Rabbi Yose who embark on a journey. As dawn breaks they stop to pray. Then they continue walking. Rabbi Ele'azar begins a Torah discourse. The superfluous nature of this narrative has been noted. But if we look for disparity rather than continuity in the discourse that follows, we may detect an element of irony in this text. The first ironic aspect to be noticed lies in the fact that there is any continuation of the story at all. If we take seriously the zoharic teachings about the power of the unificatory prayer of the righteous, as celebrated, for example, in the *Heikhalot* section,[132] we might watch a bit bemused as these righteous Companions engage in such a theurgic act, only to then proceed along their way as if nothing has happened. Indeed, the teaching that Rabbi Ele'azar proceeds to impart concerns the prodigious power possessed by the righteous. But he refers to the righteous who are taken from this world early, before they have time to sin. Thus the *Zohar* simultaneously juggles images of extreme spiritual puissance with an acceptance of impotence in the mundane sphere of reality. Moreover, here, too, the important and ambivalent concept of *hevel*—creative breath and futility—is the basis for this teaching.

We have observed the *Zohar* play with issues of mystical power and human weakness in another case cited above,[133] when the Companions flee an ecstatic experience for the freedom of discoursing about the power of Torah while walking along. Thus, to walk along the road is to walk away from the full burden of the mystical panopticon, no less than from the halakhic/talmudic one. One of the best jokes of the kabbalists is the identification of humor with the divine aspect of Judgment. Liebes points out that the *Zohar* calls the Levites, otherwise identified with the side of Judgment, "the King's jesters."[134] The patriarch identified with this potency (Judgment) is Isaac [lit., "he will laugh"], a figure so named out of the biblical appreciation for the seemingly absurd and unpredictable manifestations of potency or impotence in this world:

> Come, see: Even though it is written regarding Abraham, "And Avram kept traveling to the South" [Gen. 12:9],[135] and all his travels were toward the South, to which he was attached, he did not ascend to his place as appropriate until Isaac was born. Once Isaac was born, he rose to his place, and he was included with him, and they were bound to one another. Therefore it is he, and not another, who called him Isaac, so as to combine water with fire, as it

is written, "And Abraham called by name the son born to him, whom Sarah bore him, 'Isaac'" [Gen. 21:3]. What is "born to him"?—Fire from water.[136]

Apparently Abraham could not fully attain his rightful place as the embodiment of Love (- water) until he was able to cheerfully proclaim that, as unlikely and absurd as it may seem, it was really he who fathered this son (- fire), the embodiment of the very antithesis of his own nature.

This is ironic because the jester, as Liebes points out, is usually conceived of as a marginal figure, one who works as a humorously impotent, though protected, counterweight to the serious powers in charge. This characteristic of humor is well exemplified in the textual phenomenon of marginalia. In medieval works, these markings, doodles, illuminations, or written glosses often expressed independent, humorous, and even transgressive feelings and thoughts in relation to the central text. Here is Meyer Schapiro's reaction to viewing them:

> The margins of books committed to a most disciplined spirituality were open to primitive impulses and feelings, and in a context of exquisite writing these miniatures, which are whimsical and often gross in idea, compete for the reader's attention. Though scattered capriciously on the margins, they are done with the same precision of detail and calligraphic finesse as the richly framed religious imagery on the same page. They are a convincing evidence of the artist's liberty, his unconstrained possession of the space, which confounds the view of medieval art as a model of order and piety.[137]

James F. Burke elaborates on this idea. He applies to these expressions the term *barbarolexis*, coined by Alexandre Leupin to refer to "the process whereby the individual, as a result of the Fall and the Tower of Babel, escapes from the positive normative and creates a language that corresponds to and answers personal need."[138] Burke suggests that the surprising coexistence of these two streams of discourse on the same page reflects antithesis but also completeness, as comprehended by the medieval episteme of total accommodation. Such a model was seen as an ideal, but it was a risky ideal to put into practice:

> Official culture in the Middle Ages, then, not only tolerated the carnivalesque but doubtless also understood it as beneficial in many ways. The world was composed of both the high and the low, the sacred and the pro-

> fane, the serious and the comic. The negative had to be accommodated, used, and controlled along with the positive.
>
> But this reverse side of culture could not be completely controlled. The activities associated with it, the concepts and ideas produced by it, could take on a significance far beyond what could be approved by official discourse. A *barbarolexis* could evolve, a language of desire shaped by the themes and imagery of the carnivalesque, through which individuals and groups could express yearnings, needs and fantasies that the ecclesiastical and legal realms would surely regard only as the result of the fallen condition of the human being.[139]

The challenge is to find a place for that which refuses to stay inside, in place. The issue of humor is the issue of the exile and dispersion from the Tower of Babel and it is the issue of the ability—the potency or impotence of the system itself—to maintain control over, though not to obliterate, the Other (Side).[140] The *Zohar* presents an ideal of unification and incorporation of all potencies and of the left into the right. Yet it also recognized the disparity between that ideal and the necessity of spatial accommodation in the world of separation. The *Zohar* accomplished this accommodation through the tactic of walking on the road, into that marginal, mundane space.

CHAPTER 6

Zoharic Geographics

From Kfar Tarsha to Babylonia

The *Zohar*'s sense of the world is centered around the land of Israel, and its orientation to that center has been studied extensively.[1] The walking texts purport to take place in this zoharic holy land for the most part. However, it is not always clear whether the *Zohar*'s geographic sense is secure enough to trust in this regard.[2] For the *Zohar*, the antipodal land to Israel is Babylonia. This is the place to which Rashbi decides to exile the villagers of Kfar Tarsha. To further understand his decision, it is necessary to examine the *Zohar*'s geographics a bit more extensively.

The *Zohar*'s view of Babylonia was conditioned by that place's role in biblical and Jewish history. It is the scene of the episode of the Tower of Babel. It is the home of the power that exiled Israel and destroyed the First Temple.[3] As such it is identified as a place of the forces of separation and evil.[4] The exile of the Jews to Babylonia brought about the sinful contamination of the community through the taking of gentile wives.[5] In the zoharic view, as we have seen, to take a gentile wife is both a leaving of one's proper place and entry into an evil place.[6] Thus Babylonia is very much the Other Side of the Land of Israel. It is a place infected with the evil impulse to enter inappropriate places, breaking boundaries, leaving the Primal One, and causing exile.

But it is also the place that became the second home of the Jewish people, in which, benefiting from the faithful presence of Shekhinah,[7] they produced a community of Torah scholars who created the greatest work of Oral Torah, the Babylonian Talmud.[8] On this level, Babylonia is no longer a geographical entity. Rather, it stands for a community and a text that rivals the zoharic fellowship and its literary project.[9] To counter this community's claim to primacy, the *Zohar* sometimes shows that it knows something the Babylonians do not know. Thus, with regard to the important *'uvda*—meaningful action—of blowing shofar on Rosh Ha-Shanah,[10] the *Zohar* sharply declares: "But about these two days of Rosh Ha-Shanah—why are there two days? Because they are two courts that join together, Higher Justice, which is harsh, with Lower Justice, which is gentle, and both are together. About this, these Babylonians don't know the secret of sobbing and wailing, and don't know that both are required."[11] It has been pointed out that this statement refers to a Palestinian position recorded in the Talmud, and not a Babylonian position.[12] However, if we understand the appellation to have polemical, rather than geographical significance, there is no difficulty. In disparaging the Babylonians, the *Zohar* is really arguing against a group that engages in halakhic analysis but does not appreciate kabbalistic interpretations of halakhah.

But the *Zohar* also refers to students of esoteric Torah by this name. Rashbi expresses his extreme displeasure and frustration with Babylonians:

> Rabbi Shim'on said: When I am among the fellowship[13] of Babylonians gathered around me, and I teach matters in the open, they place a strong iron seal on them from all sides. How many times have I taught them the ways of the King's garden, the ways of the King? How many times have I taught them all those levels of the righteous in that world? And they all are afraid to say these words. Rather they belabor them in stammerings. That is why they are called stammerers, like a stutterer who stammers with his mouth. But I judge them favorably because they are afraid, for the holy atmosphere and holy spirit abandoned them, and they suckle from the atmosphere and spirit of the Other Realm.[14]

These are harsh words. Even when Rashbi wishes to "judge them favorably" he denies them a portion in the realm of holiness, the realm of the land of Israel, and uses the term "Babylonians" to mean that they occupy the mythic region of evil. Boaz Huss has forcefully argued that this text is one expression of the *Zohar*'s polemic against conservative kabbalists of the school of Naḥmanides.[15] Recalling Rashbi's anger at the villagers of Kfar Tarsha, we note that his words, there, betrayed the same combination of a severe reaction coupled with a statement that he was really being magnanimous. Rashbi is explicit here in the reason for his wrath. The Babylonians refuse to learn from him—not the content of his esoteric teachings, but the lesson that these teachings must be promulgated openly, without fear.[16]

Significantly, the issue is also manifested in terms of spatial practice—the displacement and exposure of the Torah during times of trouble, such as lack of rain. This practice is mentioned in the Mishnah: "What is the program [*seder*] for fasts? They take out the ark into the plaza of the city, and they place burnt ashes upon the ark."[17] The dislodging of the Torah ark and its public exposure and degradation are drastic actions that, accompanied with public chastisements and prayers, are meant to inspire public repentance. The drastic nature of these actions was explained in two ways by the Talmuds.[18] Either the main point was to enact a ritual of exile or it was to indulge in public exposure and degradation. The Babylonian Talmud asks what the difference is between the two explanations, answering that going from synagogue to synagogue would satisfy the requirement for an exile ritual, but only the plaza would satisfy the requirement for public exposure and degradation.

The *Zohar* combines both these ideas, playing on the dual meaning of the root *glh*—signifying both exile and revelation. Rashbi, along with complaining that the Babylonians are fearful and reticent, adds that they are also unappreciative of the fact that he is the one protector of the world. What will happen after he is gone?[19] Rashbi explains that only the uncovering and promulgation of a perfect Torah can help the world. When the Torah is uncovered this will prompt outpourings of prayer and penitence. The living will rouse the dead and all will elicit mercy from the Holy Blessed One.

> And this is from the exile of the *Sefer Torah* from its place. And the living come to plead for mercy on the graves of the dead. Woe to the generation if it needs the *Sefer Torah* to be exiled from place to place, even from one synagogue to another, for there are none to be found among them able to watch over them. And this is something not all people know. For the Shekhinah, when She was exiled in the last exile, until She ascends above, what is written [about Her]? "Would that someone would place Me in a visitors' inn while in the wilderness" [Jer. 9:1]. Afterwards, in a time when trouble is

more common in the world, there She is found, and in the exile of the *Sefer Torah*—there She is. And all are aroused over Her, above and below.[20]

The Torah must be taken outside. It must be exiled/uncovered. The revelation and dissemination of Torah is the only way to spread the presence of Shekhinah in this unredeemed world, especially after Rashbi is gone. The dynamic is similar to that of sending away the mother bird from the nest. The pressure caused by this dislocation and exposure will arouse the divine mercies. This is made explicit in a parallel zoharic passage that compares the exile of the Shekhinah to the exposure of the Torah scroll, "at first from synagogue to synagogue; afterwards, to the street; after that 'in a visitors' inn while in the wilderness,' said Rabbi Yehudah. 'Babylonians are fearful, and they do not do this even from one synagogue to [another] synagogue, let alone this.'"[21]

The "foolish" Babylonians refuse to move the Torah from its place, even from one synagogue to another, let alone to bring it out into the open. Rashbi complains that their fears are rooted in their lack of appreciation for the legacy of Rav Hamnuna Sabba. Rav Hamnuna taught about the role of the Patriarchs in helping the world. But he taught more than that. "And this is what Rav Hamnuna revealed and said, that they had shown him that Rachel, by staying at the crossroads for any time that the world may need [her], did more than all of them. And the secret of the matter is that the ark, cover and cherubs were in Benjamin's portion, for he was born on the road, and the Shekhinah is over all."[22]

The Babylonians—those whose place is Babylonia, who "suckle from the Other Realm"—exhibit their derivation from the Other Side in a paradoxical way. The Other Side is characterized by a strong desire to break through boundaries. The Babylonians, however, are fearful of leaving their place as they are fearful of revealing esoteric Torah. But this locative fearfulness is precisely condemned by the *Zohar* because it signifies that, in keeping with the rebellious drive of the Other Side, the Babylonians refuse to be where they should be or go where they should go, or—by extension—speak what they should speak. In a sense, the Babylonians condemned by Rashbi are trying to make up for the sin of Babylonia, only to repeat it.

So too, perhaps, the Kfar Tarsha villagers, to make up for the sin of their ancestors, only end up repeating it.[23]

The villagers of Kfar Tarsha share this locative timidity with the Babylonian fellowship. In that sense, they are already Babylonians themselves, and Rashbi is justified in reassuring Rabbi Abba that he is not really punishing them. He has not exiled them to Babylonia, for, in their refusal to take their Torah on the road, they are already there.[24]

In contemplating the nature of Babylonia, the *Zohar* itself takes on an aspect of anxiety. Integral to its discussions about Babylonia are issues of mortality and fear. The world is likened to a desert, in which the homeless Shekhinah pleads for temporary lodging. In this discourse, the *Zohar* justifies its spatial activism out of a sense of crisis and tragedy. We have seen, though, that an important element in the Companions' walking is their joy and sense of life. In part, this positive attitude must be fought for. The Companions must face up to the reality of death, overcome their own fearfulness, and face whatever the mundane wilderness will bring them. These are crucial elements of the *Zohar*'s spatial orientation.

From Love to Death

Rooted in their holy place, the land of Israel, the Companions are prepared to wander. Because they refuse to move about, the Kfar Tarshans are sent into exile, to the land of dispersion and wandering. Thus the many-layered conflict between Rashbi and his disciples, on the one side, and the inhabitants of Kfar Trasha, on the other, is expressed not only in the difference between their respective spatial practices but, also, in the difference between the two places they are destined to inhabit, Israel and Babylonia. Babylonia is a synecdoche for the entire geographical area outside the Land. The antipodal relation between the land of Israel and the area outside it, exemplified by Babylonia, is not only relevant to this small group of individuals. The difference between the two places carries fundamental significance. The *Zohar* distinguishes between those who die in the Holy Land and those who die outside it. Only those who die outside of Israel convey the corpse impurity decreed by the Torah. This is because it is only outside of Israel that death is caused by the Angel of Death, and corpse impurity derives from that angel. Those who die in Israel, on the other hand, are taken by the Angels of Love:

> And of this it is written, "Your dead will live; my corpses [*n'velati*] will arise. Wake up and sing you who lie in the dust" [Isa. 26:19]. . . . "Your dead will live," these are the ones who die in the Holy Land, for they are His dead, and not from the Other, for the Other Side does not rule there at all, and therefore it is written "Your dead." "My corpses [*n'velati*] will arise," these are the ones who die in a strange land at the hands of that destroyer. And therefore they are called *n'velah*. Just as a *n'velah* causes impurity [*metam'ah*] as a load, so do these dead outside of the Holy Land cause impurity as a load, and therefore they are called *n'velah*. And this is the secret of "He is as his name" he is *Naval* and "Naval is his name and wickedness [*n'valah*] is with him" [1 Sam. 25:25]. And therefore, in every place he dwells it is called *n'velah*. This disgusting one [*menuval*] only dwells in an inappropriate [*p'silu*] place, and therefore any disqualified slaughter is his and is called by his name.[25]

The *Zohar* applies the concept of impure carrion—*n'velah*—to all who die outside Israel, in the realm of the Other Side. That is, it explains the laws of impurity in terms of spatial practice and propriety. Impurity derives, not so much from death, as from being in the wrong place.[26] Babylonia has been explicitly identified as the realm of the Other Side. This text, while not mentioning Babylonia by name, may be making a subtle allusion to it in that when God descends to confound the language of the builders of the Tower of Babel, the verse reads: "Let Us descend and there We will mix up—*ve-navlah*—their language" (Gen. 11:7). Thus Babylonia is identified as the place of *navlah/n'velah*.

Following this zoharic discussion we would expect to find that the opposite of Babylonia, as a place and an orientation, is identified with the land of Israel itself. But the *Zohar* does not proceed in such a simple manner. Developing biblical and post-biblical traditions, it finds the radical opposite to Babylonia in a place called Luz.

The name Luz is mentioned in a few biblical contexts. It is the place where Jacob slept and dreamt his ladder. As such, later traditions more or less connected it to the location of the Holy of Holies of the Temple. However, other biblical references and rabbinic traditions make this identification uncertain.[27] A midrash tells that "Luz is Luz where they make the *tekhelet* dye.

This is Luz where Sennacherib [king of Assyria, d. 681 B.C.E.] attacked and Nebuchadnezzar [king of Babylon, d. 562 B.C.E.] did not unsettle it [*ve-lo bilbelah*] nor destroy it. This is Luz where the Angel of Death did not ever rule. The elders within it, what do they do to them? Once they become very old they take them out past the wall and they die."[28] These traditional elements allow the *Zohar* to create a more complex antithesis. The midrash has established Luz as the place over which neither Babylonia[29] nor the Angel of Death has sway. It is also, apparently, not identical to Jerusalem, since Nebuchadnezzar is said not to have succeeded against Luz. The *Zohar* redraws the picture of Luz in this way:

> There is a place in civilization [*be-yishuva*] in which the Destroyer does not rule and into which he has no permission to enter. And all those who live there do not die until they leave to go out of the city. There are none among all the inhabitants there who do not die. And all of them die like other people, but not in the place [*mata*].[30] Why? Because they cannot live in the place all the time. Rather, these go and these enter, and therefore, they all die. Why does the Destroying Angel not rule there? If you should say that it is not in his realm, but the entire Holy Land is not in the Other realm, yet they die. Why don't they die in that place? If you say it is because of sanctity, there is no place of holiness in all civilization like the land of Israel. And if you say it is because of that man who built it, there are many people whose merits are greater than his.[31]

This special place is not identical to the land of Israel, since those who dwell in Israel eventually die, while those who inhabit this place do not die, except in that they leave it. Here the *Zohar* has subtly changed the midrash. The midrash explains that when, because of their great age, these old people are ready to die, they must be taken out of the city of Luz so as to make their demise possible. But the *Zohar* turns this situation around. In its scenario, the reason people who inhabit this place die is because they find it impossible to stay in one place. They naturally must come and go and that brings about their deaths. The *Zohar* ties death to the natural desire of the body to walk.

The *Zohar* then asks what the source of this place's special power is. The *Zohar* is convinced that the place cannot lay claim to any special holiness or any special merit of its founder.[32] "Rabbi Yitzḥaq said, 'I have not heard and

I cannot say.' They went to ask Rabbi Shim'on."[33] Before we hear Rashbi's answer, we might want to ask the other side of the question: What place is it that people cannot remain in, despite the advantage of immortality that it affords? Rabbi Yitzḥaq's refusal to attempt an answer and the report that "they went to ask Rashbi" reminds us that this text is part of a longer discussion introduced a few pages earlier, recording a study session involving Rabbi Yitzḥaq, Rabbi Yose and Rabbi Ḥizqiyah, and revolving around the construction of the Tabernacle and its use of *tekhelet*—the royal blue coloring used, as well, for ritual tassels. Rabbi Yitzḥaq's reluctance to speculate about the reason for Luz's special status has drawn notice from Daniel Matt. He writes: "This conservative attitude contrasts with the *Zohar*'s frequent emphasis on innovation."[34] But Rabbi Yitzḥaq's attitude is of a piece with the statements uttered by Rabbi Yose at the beginning of their study session. After Rabbi Yitzḥaq bemoans the fact that there is a paucity of mystical explication of the building of the Tabernacle on the part of the Companions, Rabbi Yose suggests that it is best to leave these matters to Rashbi, the Holy Lamp, for his teachings are incomparably sweet and nourishing, leaving no room for "anyone to cast any salt into them."[35] The discussion proceeds to extol the special status of Rashbi's generation, surpassing even the generation of Solomon. But, underlying this sense of privilege is also a sense of anxiety caused by knowing that Rashbi must, someday, die.[36] If Rashbi is the exclusive source for the revelation of the hidden truths of the Torah, as Rabbi Yose and Rabbi Yitzḥaq imply, how can the Companions leave his side? The question echoes the mystery of Luz, and the problem of Kfar Tarsha, joining the problem of spatial mobility with the threat of death.

It falls to Rashbi to offer an answer. He refers to the myth of the world's creation through the alphabet:

> The letters revolved and circulated throughout the world in inscriptions [*be-gilufei*] and when the world was revealed and extended [*ve'itpashat*] and was created and the letters were going around to create, the Holy Blessed One said that it should stop with *yud*. The letter *tet* was left at this place hovering over it in the air. Once the Holy Blessed One said, "Enough. It shall conclude with *yud*," the letter *tet* was left by itself hanging in the air over this place. *Tet* is the sign of the living lights.[37]

The *Zohar* returns to the topic of the Tabernacle and Temple, another source of life for the world. It juxtaposes the Luz myth with the myth of the creation of the Foundation Stone, the center of the world, the place of the Temple. God threw the stone down into the watery depths, engraved with the seventy-two-letter Name. "From there that stone started to walk, not finding a place to stay in, except for the Holy Land. And the waters were following after it until the stone arrived beneath the altar and there it sank in and the world was established."[38] The *Zohar* differentiates between the place of the altar and Luz (despite the strong midrashic tradition that links this very myth to the stone that Jacob chose at Bethel/Luz) in that Luz derives its power from only one letter, while the altar has all the divine letters collected there.[39] Although Luz has a quality lacking even in the Temple, the Temple surpasses Luz in its sacred power. The letter *tet* indeed starts the word *tov*—good—the characteristic that marks the world at creation, but its power is limited to its own place. Once someone leaves that place, the Other Side has the authority to visit upon him destruction and death. The life-giving power of the hovering *tet* is infinite in time, but limited in space, and that limitation makes it less worthy than the life-giving power of the Temple, whose power is limited temporally (since it does not negate mortality), but whose extension is global. The Luz myth leaves the letter *tet* in a permanently stationary position, hovering over one place. But the Foundation Stone myth incorporates movement—the stone walks!—before it reaches repose.[40] Another difference that might be noticed is that the power of Luz derives from an entity that hovers over the place but does not touch it, while the power of the Altar derives from an entity that has sunk down and embedded itself deep beneath the soil of the place.

Rashbi's explanation of the special quality of Luz raises more questions than it answers. He arrests the letter *tet*, leaving it hovering over one small location. Yet he also declares that "The letter *tet* settles well in any place, and it is prepared to settle properly."[41] In the guise of settling questions, it leaves the basic issues unsettled. We experience a struggle with conceptions of goodness and life as realized in this world.[42] The sacred center must surely be conceived as wholly good, but the *Zohar* cannot refrain from fragmenting that concept and undermining it, just as the residents of Luz cannot refrain from leaving their perfectly secure place. Midrashically, Luz is aligned with the Temple Mount and the Foundation Stone under the altar. But the *Zohar* seeks to displace it from that spot. Its attitude toward Luz is ambivalent. It speaks of it as being more special than all Israel, but then it delimits its power until it is almost turned into a negative quality.

This teaching remains obscure and it may relate to other obscure teachings. It shares with the "alphabet of creation" myth, at the beginning of the Introduction to the *Zohar*,[43] the notion that this letter was held back from use in creating the world. The Introduction text ascribes this to the exceeding goodness—*tov*—that the letter signifies, a goodness too great for this world. Both discussions are aware of the unfortunate juxtaposition of the letter *het* to *tet*, thereby associating *tet* with the notion of sin.[44] And both discussions recall a moment at which the Temple foundation or structure sank into the earth. In the Luz text, the primordial sinking of the Foundation Stone—the Temple's beginning—is recalled. In the Introduction text, the gates of the Temple sink into the good earth at the end of its history, when the Temple is destroyed. The tenuous nature of goodness and life is thus given spatial imagery. The Luz text identifies goodness with a place that no one can stay in for long, abutted by forces of sin and death. The Introduction text adds that goodness must be identified with *'eretz*—the land. When God denies *tet* the role of creation, He says: "And also, because your goodness is concealed, the gates of the Temple [*de-heikhala*] will sink within you. This is what is written, 'Her gates sank into the earth' [Lam. 2:9]."[45] Thus we have a discourse struggling with images of the Divine Presence in Her relation to this world. The hovering *tet* lives in tension with the sunken Stone and the sunken Temple gates. It alludes to the ninth divine potency,[46] ever seeking loving union with Shekhinah. Indeed, this is the divine aspect that the *Zohar* associates with Rashbi himself.[47] Thus Rashbi's explanation of the special power of Luz and its limitations is also a warning to the Companions to avoid restricting their spatial activity in their desire to maintain their connection with him.[48] He cannot forever hover over them. The letter *tet*, hovering over Luz, exhibits a paradoxical mixture of puissance and impotence. "The Holy Blessed One does not wish for any person to ever die in that place."[49] Yet the result of that loving desire is to create a place whose inhabitants will all feel compelled to leave in order to live mortal lives, in order to die.

The Place of Fear

The hovering *tet* signifies goodness, but it cannot be isolated from its neighbors; it cannot be separated from sin. The Other Side crouches right outside Luz's gates. Indeed, while, in the earlier part of the discourse, the *Zohar* declares that "One who sees *tet* in his dream—it is a good sign for him and life is prepared for him," it later, on the same page, referring to the *tekhelet* dye produced in Luz, says, "All colors are good for a dream except *tekhelet*, as it was said, because it is the seat for judging and punishing souls."[50]

The *Zohar*'s ambivalence causes it to shift back and forth in evaluating Luz and its role. After moving from a positive description to a negative one by focusing on the identity of *tekhelet* and Judgment, the *Zohar* shifts again. Looking at *tekhelet* (a biblical command, after all)[51] is good because it strikes fear into people, so that they will keep the commandments. The *Zohar* compares this to the case of the Brazen Serpent: "When they would look at it they would be afraid [*daḥlei*] before the Holy Blessed One and would guard themselves from all sins. At the time of that fear of the Holy Blessed One coming over them they immediately would be healed. Who caused them to have fear before the Holy Blessed One? That Serpent, that strap that they were looking at."[52]

The *Zohar* has taken the rabbinic teaching about the Brazen Serpent and turned it around the way a person twists and turns a strap. The Mishnah had wondered about the miraculous cure effected by the Serpent. It argued, "Could it be that a snake can cause death or restore life? Rather, as long as Israel look heavenward and submit their hearts to their Father in Heaven, they are healed. And if not, they are wiped out."[53] The Mishnah does its best to deflect the gaze of the Israelites (and the reader of the biblical text) away from the Serpent itself. But the *Zohar* redirects that gaze, turning it back to the Serpent. It is specifically the Serpent that is the object of Israel's gaze, their object of fear—*daḥala*. This turn mirrors the turning, shifting quality of *tekhelet*. Through the *tzitzit* [ritual tassels comprised of one string of tekhelet and three white strings], its color turns from dark judgment to loving white. "And thus, with the turning of colors it turns from Judgment to Love, and so from Love to Judgment, all by the turning of the colors."[54]

Thus, after the *Zohar* had established that there was no place for *tet* in the Temple, it could now find room for *tekhelet* in the Tabernacle. In this way the *Zohar* teaches that fear, from the side of *Din* or from the Other Side, is beneficial if it leads people to keep the Torah. But the wrong kind of fear is the idolatrous fear of the Babylonians: "'And we will make a name for us' [Gen. 11:4], 'This place will be a fearsome god [*daḥala*] for us, and none other. And we will build a city and tower for this place. Why should we ascend upward whence we will not be able to derive any benefit?' 'And we will make a name for ourselves,' an object of fear [*daḥala*] to worship there, 'lest we be dispersed' (ibid.), and we will be separated to the corners [*le-sitrei*] of the world."[55] Such a fear seeks to preclude movement from place to place. The Companions' commitment to walking on the road means that they will engage this issue frequently.[56] Rashbi, in the conclusion of the Kfar Tarsha episode, challenges the fearful Rabbi Abba with the ideal of the righteous person as one who has no fear. The walking narratives often tell of the mundane struggle to reach this ideal.[57]

The zoharic passage discussed above explained that immortality is a feature of a mythical place, Luz, in which humans can never remain settled. The impossibility of defeating death and attaining immortality is explained in another passage, linked to the experience of the Israelites at Mount Sinai. The reaction of Israel to the powerful divine revelation was to shrink back in fear. They appealed to Moses to serve as their intermediary:

> "Rather, you [*ve'at*] should speak to us" [Deut. 5:24]. We do not desire the supernal power from above. Rather, [we desire it] from the place of the female and no more—"Rather you[58] should speak to us." Moses said, "Surely you have weakened my strength and you have weakened the strength of the Other."[59] For had Israel not distanced themselves, but had listened to that Word as at the beginning, the world would not be able to be desolate afterwards, and they would have lived for generations. For at the first hour they

> died. Why? Because this was necessary, for the Tree of Death brought this about. Afterwards, when they lived and were established and multiplied, and the Holy Blessed One wished to raise them to the Tree of Life that stands over that Tree of Death, so that they should live forever, they distanced themselves and did not wish it. Then Moses' power over them was weakened and the power of the Other was weakened. Said the Holy Blessed One, "I wanted to set you in a supernal place and to attach you to Life. But you wished for the place where the feminine dwells. Therefore, 'Walk, tell them' [Deut. 5:27], etc. Each one should walk to his female and unite with her."[60]

Israel's fearful response precluded their attaining immortality. But, more than that, it was an expression of desire for existence in the lower realm of the mundane world, ruled by the feminine aspect of God. Once more God's desire has been thwarted. Just as God's wish that no one die in Luz is defeated by the yearning of its inhabitants to leave, so is God's plan to set them in a "supernal place and attach you (them) to Life," ruined because of their fearful choice to abide "where the feminine dwells."[61] By so choosing, Israel has weakened the power of the divine potencies to unite together. Instead, they have chosen a lower form of union, a union that entails the obligation to walk. The *Zohar* continues by advising people on the proper way to walk on the road. The rabbinic tradition instructs that one be prepared for prayer, ingratiation, and struggle.[62] The *Zohar* adds that the most important is prayer and then it continues: "But even though prayer is more [important], above them all is [to have] two or three friends who study words of Torah, for then they will not be afraid, because the Shekhinah will join together with them."[63]

By walking on the road, the Companions force themselves to encounter places, circumstances, personalities, and creatures that can cause fear. These include mountains, caves, and deserts and dangerous people or snakes.[64] Despite Rashbi's assurances to Rabbi Abba that the righteous do not feel fear, the Companions often become fearful. But they endeavor to overcome their fears.

Some of the challenges and orientations of the Companions are expressed in the following walking story. The text follows a teaching by Rabbi Yehudah concerning the verse, "Do not fear you worm of Jacob" (Isa. 41:14). Rabbi Yehudah explains why Israel is called a worm. But his teaching omits any discussion about fear. This is the context for this walking text placed right after his homily:

> Rabbi Ele'azar and Rabbi Yitzḥaq were walking on the road and the time for reciting *Sh'ma* arrived. So immediately [*ve-qam*] Rabbi Ele'azar recited the *Sh'ma* and prayed his prayer. Afterwards Rabbi Yitzḥaq said to him, "Didn't we learn that before one leaves on the road one should ask permission from his Master and offer his prayers?"[65] He said to him, "It is because when I set out it was not the time for reciting prayers and the time for recitation of *Sh'ma* had not arrived. Now that the sun is shining I have prayed. But before I left I petitioned Him and asked permission of Him. But this prayer I did not pray because I was passionately studying Torah from midnight, and when morning came it was not then time to pray because that time of the morning darkness is when the Woman is found talking with Her Husband. And They are intimately united for She must walk to Her dwelling place in Her concealment, where They live. And therefore a person should not interrupt Their words that are joining together and to put in another word between Them.[66]

The connection to the theme of fear is not yet clear. But we already sense it in the background. The obligation to pray before embarking on a journey is for fear of encountering dangers on the road. Rabbi Yitzḥaq takes this fear seriously. In addition, he is afraid that his comrade has not sufficiently observed this requirement before leaving for their trip. Rabbi Ele'azar is more sure of himself and reassures his comrade. He has, indeed, taken the necessary precautions before leaving on the road. But he is aware of other dynamics which he must respect as well. He is more aware than Rabbi Yitzḥaq of the temporal and spatial coordinates of his world. He will not intrude upon the early morning intimacy of the divine potencies by interposing his own words, though they are prayers. Rabbi Ele'azar is secure in his sense of respectful distance from the divine unificatory dynamic of which he is not a part. He knows his place. After some further explanation of this idea the text engages the problem of fear explicitly:

> They walked. When they got to a field they sat. They lifted their eyes and a mountain appeared, with strange creatures climbing its peak. Rabbi Yitzḥaq was afraid. Rabbi Ele'azar said to him, "Why are you frightened?" He said, "I saw that that mountain is mighty and I saw some creatures that are strange and I was frightened that they might kill us." He said to him, "[Only] one who

is afraid of the sins he has should be fearful. Come, see—aren't these some of the mighty creatures who were found among the mountains?" He opened and said: "'And these are the sons of Tziv'on—and 'Ayah and 'Anah. . . . This is 'Anah who found the *yemim* [in the desert]' [*Gen.* 36:24]. . . . They were strange creatures who, when Cain was exiled from the face of the earth . . . come from his children's children, on the side of spirits and whirlwinds and demons."[67]

Rabbi Yitzḥaq is frightened by the sight of a tall mountain with strange beings scaling its heights. He is afraid they will leave the mountain and come to kill the two rabbis. But Rabbi Ele'azar seeks to reassure his friend, as he had reassured him before about his religious observance. Only sinners need to fear. By implication, the Companions will not come to harm because they are righteous. Then Rabbi Ele'azar explains what they saw. These creatures are strange-looking, but they are not unknown to those who are familiar with the stories of the Torah. They are *yemim*—desert creatures who are the offspring of Cain after he was exiled from living in any permanent home. They are thus the children of sin and dislocation. Rabbi Ele'azar elaborates regarding their unstable nature:

For, when the Sabbath day was about to begin, spirits were created from that side, naked, without a body. And they are not from the Sabbath day nor from Friday, and both those days remain in doubt in them, and therefore they do not exist either in this one or that. . . . And they appear to people and he ['Anah] found them and they taught him to bring *mamzerim* into the world. And they go among the mountains and they live in a body once a day and afterwards they remove themselves from it. . . . And come, see—these are them. And many others that come from these all come from that side and walk in the desert and appear there because there is a desolate place in the wilderness and that is their dwelling place. But nevertheless, all people who walk in the ways of the Holy Blessed One and who fear the Holy Blessed One are not afraid of them.

They walked on and climbed the mountain. Said Rabbi Yitzḥaq, "Is this the way all those desolate mountains are, their dwelling place?" He said to him, "That is so. And for all those who passionately study Torah it is written, 'God will protect you from all evil, protect your soul. God will guard you going out and your coming in from now and forever' [Ps. 121:7–8]."[68]

This text, through exegesis, exhortation, and narrative, combines teachings about the nature of biblical creatures, the *yemim*, the nature of evil, and human religious psychology. It also subtly depicts the interaction between two specific personalities. The *yemim* derive from evil in that they lack a sure sense of place. They come from uncertain regions of space and time. Moreover, they exemplify the boundary-crossing drive of the Other Side in their attempts to encourage humans to transgress sexual boundaries so as to produce *mamzerim*, beings who will share their dislocated nature. The *Zohar* understands that encounters are fraught with danger and call for delicacy. The meeting of night and day requires that Rabbi Ele'azar display great sensitivity rather than upset the meeting of the divine potencies appropriate for that time. The *yemim* are the product of an uncertain meeting of day and night, the liminal zone of Sabbath eve, between profane and holy. The encounter between 'Anah and these creatures had terrible results.

But not all encounters are unfortunate and not all dangers are realized. Looking back at the start of this narrative, at the first part of the discussion of the two comrades, we come to recognize that Rabbi Yitzḥaq and Rabbi Ele'azar, walking together on the road, may not have embarked on that day's journey together. It is only some time into their trip, after the sun rises and Rabbi Ele'azar prays, that Rabbi Yitzḥaq, who apparently prayed before leaving for the road, understands that Rabbi Ele'azar must have set out without praying. Apparently, these friends have left separately and met on the road. This is a common trope in zoharic walking texts.[69] Their meeting was worthwhile. This is because Rabbi Ele'azar can teach Rabbi Yitzḥaq that he may go out on the road without fear. Rabbi Ele'azar's teaching reassures Rabbi Yitzḥaq, so that he is willing to climb the mighty mountain inhabited by frightening creatures. Here the *Zohar* adds a final piece of artful narrative. As they climb, Rabbi Yitzḥaq hesitatingly turns to his teacher for one more reassurance. Rabbi Ele'azar cites the appropriate verse to give him confidence. The righteous can come and go freely, without fear, because God protects them.

The role of Rabbi Ele'azar in this story bears further attention. The son of Rashbi instructs his fellow sage so as to calm his anxieties and fears. This is the role of the truly righteous. Not only is the righteous person one who has no reason to fear, as we have seen above, but the righteous person teaches others not to fear. The *Zohar* identifies the righteous of the generation with the trees that must not be destroyed in times of siege. They study Torah and nourish the world with their creative productivity.

> "For man [*adam*] is the tree of the field" [Deut. 20:19]. The one who is known above and below is called *adam*. "Tree of the field,"—the great and mighty tree of that "field blessed by God" [Gen. 27:27]. Related to it is the tree known to that field always. "To come from before you in a siege"—this matter returns to the beginning of the verse where it is written, "You shall not destroy her tree [*'etzah*],"—the one who gives them advice[70] and who prepares the city "to come from before you in a siege"—he gives them advice to prepare themselves and return in repentance. And he prepares weaponry and trumpets and shofars. "To come from before you,"—what is [the meaning of] "to come from before you"? To come before Me and to come in "from you"—from your fear.[71]

The righteous are engaged constantly in study of the Oral Torah, in constant connection with the Field, Shekhinah. Their productive presence is nourishing, like a fruitful tree. But their ability to convey comfort, reassurance and advice (*'etzah*) is also analogous to the shade offered by a verdant tree.[72] The tree protects a person from the too-fierce rays of the sun.[73] Similarly, the righteous are like the cosmic Tree that creates shade for the lower potencies and allows for the development of the mundane world.[74] Such protection allows the person who wishes to come under the tree's shade to overcome their own fears and, thereby, get out of themselves.[75]

The Companions are, from this perspective, righteous persons in training. They go out on the road and conquer their fears through their encounters. But, beyond that, they also occasionally succeed in moving to the next level, helping others dispel their own fears. Most especially, they help others overcome their fear of saying words of Torah. This follows from the zoharic myth of the Sinaitic revelation. For the *Zohar*, as we have seen, the fear of encounter, of going outside oneself, is at the root of the Israelites' flight from God and their appeal to Moses to be their intermediary. Eventually, they became afraid of Moses as well.[76] Thus, ultimately, Moses' role was not simply to accept the Torah and teach it to Israel. It was also to strengthen the people so that they themselves would not be afraid to engage in Torah.

In one extended walking text,[77] the *Zohar* traces the steps of Rabbi Ḥiyya and Rabbi Yose. At one point on their journey they run into a cave after escaping from robbers. Rabbi Ḥiyya opens with the verse, "And you, fear not, my servant Jacob . . . for I am ready to save you from afar" (Jer. 30:10). The discussion between the two sages revolves around the themes of fear, distance from God, traveling and returning to God. The discussion is interrupted by the appearance of two traveling merchants, who literally come close to them from afar. The *Zohar* repeats the message it taught regarding the righteous, protective tree of the field: The truly fearless person is the one who draws close to God by returning to God in repentance. The rabbis and the merchants join together. The merchants, however, are not as capable in discussing Torah. Struggling to understand a verse, one of the merchants regrets that he has spent so much time doing business and neglecting his studies. They appeal to the rabbis for help in deciphering Psalms 52:11, "I will thank You forever [*le'olam*] for what You have done, and I will hope in Your Name, for the good before Your pious ones." They wonder, what has God done and isn't God good even with regard to those who are not pious?

> Said Rabbi Ḥiyya, "for what You have done,"—Surely. And what did You do? *Le-'olam*—for the world. Because it is on account of this world, that God made and prepared, that a person should thank the Holy Blessed One every day. "And I will hope in Your Name, for the good before Your pious ones."—This is surely the way it is. The Name of the Holy Blessed One is good vis-à-vis the meritorious ones, but not vis-à-vis the sinners who treat Him with disrespect every day and do not passionately study Torah.
>
> He [the merchant] said to him: "This is fitting. But I heard a word from behind the wall and I am afraid to reveal it."
>
> Rabbi Ḥiyya and Rabbi Yose said to him, "Say your word, for the Torah is not an inheritance for only one place."[78]

The hesitant merchant is thus persuaded to overcome his fear, and he reveals an elaborate Torah discourse. He admits, at the end of it, that he has spoken the words, but that he really does not understand the meaning. Nevertheless, the rabbis approach him and kiss him on the head. The merchant has revealed to them Torah that they could not have come to know on their own. But it is thanks to their righteous, fearless encouragement.[79]

The Way of the Serpent

Because they are still only "righteous-in-training," the Companions' encounters do not always proceed so clearly. In one instance,[80] these same rabbis, "as they were walking," meet a man standing under the shade of a tree. He is suffering from terrible facial sores. They decide that the man must be a wicked sinner if he suffers from such obvious leprosy. Loving punishment or admonishment is done in a concealed manner. Only a recalcitrant sinner merits punishment that is visible to all. The man is indignant and admonishes them: "You have come at me bound in one counsel [*'itah*].[81] You are certainly none other than some of those whose dwelling is in Rashbi's house, who are not afraid of anything. Woe to you when my sons who come after me will accuse you for how you spoke your words in the open."[82] The man attacks the Companions by caricaturing their values. Their fearlessness is apparently well-known.[83] But it is not a positive quality in the man's eyes. Playing on the word counsel/tree, the man implicitly accuses them of failing to live up to their calling. They are not acting like a righteous, nourishing tree. But Rabbi Ḥiyya is not cowed. He responds, "This is the way the Torah is. As it is written, 'She shall call out at the top of bustling streets, at the openings of the gates. She shall say her statements in [the midst of] the city' [Prov. 1:21]. Imagine, if we were to be afraid of you regarding Torah matters, we would be left in shame[84] before the Holy Blessed One. And, furthermore, the Torah requires clarity [*tzaḥuta*]."[85] Meanwhile the man's sons arrive. The youngest son begins with a homily about the difficulties of the righteous in this world of darkness and evil. In such a world it is indeed hard to see clearly. It emerges that his father was very much the opposite of the Companions. He was so concerned not to embarrass anyone that he refused to admonish sinners publicly or privately and prevented his sons from doing so. It is for this sin of excessive reticence and concealment of his righteousness that he is punished.

Another son speaks and, instead of exonerating his father, he builds a case against him. The great quality of the human being is his ability to speak. Of all creatures, only the human being can stand and speak before the Holy King.[86] All depends on how a person uses this gift. When he speaks evil

> these words ascend upward and, as they ascend, all announce and say, "Get away from being around so-and-so's evil word. Make a place for the path of the mighty Serpent." Then the holy soul goes away from him and leaves and cannot speak, as it is said, "I have been made dumb in silence, I have kept quiet from the good" [Ps. 39:3]. And this soul departs in shame in the pain of all and they do not give her a place, as before. And about this it is written, "One who guards his mouth and tongue guards his soul from troubles" [Prov. 21:23]. "His soul," to be sure! She who was speaking was made mute because of evil speech. And then the mighty Serpent is involved, for everything returns to its place.[87]

The son first describes the direct abuse of the gift of speech through gossip and other forms of prohibited speech. Uttering such words causes one's fully developed soul to flee in shame. A spatial vacuum is created, filled by the Serpent. The evil spirit that takes the soul's place causes impurity and the need for containment and enclosure, as mandated by the Torah laws on leprosy. Speech and spatial production and practice are aligned again.

Significantly, the son has turned his father's most important concern back against him.[88] The father had desired that no one be embarrassed or shamed. But the son argues that by misusing one's power of speech, one shames oneself. He finally extends this sin to explicitly include his father's behavior: "Just as this person is punished for evil speech, so is his punishment when an opportunity to say good speech comes to him, but he does not speak. For then he wounds that speaking spirit that is prepared to speak above and below, all in holiness. How much more so if the people walk in a crooked path and he can speak to them to admonish them, but he is silent and does not speak." In the case of the Companions, silence leads to speech. But in the case of evil speech, speech brings silence. In effect, the son has condemned the father for not understanding that the battle against evil cannot be fought through silence. It requires open speech. When people adopt the ways of the Serpent, crooked paths, the only way to counter this is to speak goodness plainly and in a straightforward fashion. As the *Zohar* points out explicitly,[89] "leprosy" is called *segiru*—"confinement, closure"—in the Targum. The way to combat evil is to combat evil speech through open spatial production—by means of fearlessly speaking Torah in the open.[90] As "righteous in training," the Companions embody the Righteous One, the divine potency that must combat the Serpent most directly. And if confinement is the proper spatial attribute of the feminine,[91] who is vulnerable to the Serpent's manipulative exploitation of fear, then the righteous and the righteous in training must fearlessly go forth into the open, onto the road.

The arena in which this battle takes place is the mundane world. The Serpent of the Other Side yearns to take over this realm. This is so fundamental a fact of the cosmos that the entire mundane world—and not only Babylonia or the lands outside of Israel—is often called by the *Zohar* the "realm of the Other Side."[92] But this does not mean that the Serpent has indeed succeeded in realizing his desire to take over the entire mundane world. The struggle between Good and Evil forces is continuous; the battle lines—within individuals, among peoples and over spaces—are shifting constantly. Sometimes one side gains territory and sometimes the Other. In general, however, the *Zohar* concedes that the Serpent has greater power in some regions than in others.

Since the Serpent caused the first humans to sin by misleading them with his speech, any evil speech grants additional power to him, who was once deprived of his legs. In describing the evil palaces, the *Zohar* says:

> Come, see—When that stimulus of evil speech is aroused below, then the "Devious Serpent [Leviathan]" [Isa. 27:1] raises his scales and sets them rising, and is aroused from his head to his feet. And when his scales are raised and aroused then his whole body is aroused. These scales of his that are outside are all the patrolling forces that monitor behavior. And all of them are aroused and take hold of that evil word and are aroused toward that "Rod-like Serpent" [Isa. 27:1]. Then the entire evil body is aroused from his head to his feet in all those places, as we said.[93]

It seems that evil speech bestows new legs upon the Snake, so that he can invade new territories.

Rabbi Joseph Angelino, in a sermon he gave in about 1320, clearly draws these lessons from the *Zohar*. He emphasizes the imperative need to publicly rebuke wrongdoers and specifically condemns them in terms of evil speech:

> For truth has failed in the street with the fall of supporters of Torah, who give legs and thighs to falsehood, to the Serpent, who has no legs. And the Holy Blessed One cut off his legs and his voice went from one end of the world to the other, as it says, "*Her voice shall go like a snake*" [Jer. 46:22]. The Serpent came to teach about Egypt's standing and became an object lesson, that when the Holy Blessed One said to him, "*You shall go on your belly*" [Gen. 3:14], and angels came and cut off his legs, his voice left. And this is a precious secret, that the level of falsehood, of a person's foolishness in his lying, has no legs. But truth has legs. And the sins of Israel strengthened and gave thighs and support with their money, the legs of falsehood.[94]

Angelino denounces the corruption of the Jewish community, a corruption that he considers the cause for the continued exile of the people. As he accuses the community of dishonesty and refusal to support Torah, he echoes themes found in the *Zohar*, allusively connecting the concepts of voice and legs, of talking and walking, and, specifically, of speaking the truth and walking. To tell the truth is equivalent to the ability to walk about. The Serpent, because it lied, was deprived of its legs, and thus, of its voice. Only humans can give legs to the Serpent by telling lies or engaging in deceit. The most complete opposite of this would be the speaking of truth (Torah) while walking. The connection between truth speech and walking about is an organic, necessary connection, while the connection between telling lies and walking is parasitic. But why must truth be spoken in this manner. Why not speak the truth from a delimited place of truth, a place of holiness or a house of study? The myth of the alphabet of Creation was one way of saying that the world was created through speech—*dibbur*—a name for Shekhinah. All reality in its spatial existence is the manifestation of divine speech. It follows from this that speech is simultaneously the source of truth and of space. Speech and space are coextensive. The connection to the dread of the first humans when they hear "the *voice* of Almighty God *walking* in the Garden" (Gen. 3:8) becomes explicit. At that moment, they give up the idea of occupying space, of "filling the world and conquering it" (Gen. 1:28), and wish that space would swallow them up; they hide. But, instead, space spits them out, and they are expelled from the Garden.

The Wilderness

Expelled from the Garden, they are sentenced to struggle for sustenance in a world of "thorns and thistles" (Gen. 3:18), in constant conflict with the Serpent (v. 15). In light of this it is understandable that, in certain texts, the *Zohar* should locate the realm of the Serpent in the desolate wilderness.[95] The connection is reinforced for the *Zohar* because the word for wilderness—*midbar*—has the root *dbr*—meaning "speech." Thus the *yenuqa* asks the Companions why the daughters of Zelophehad said that "our father died in the wilderness [*ba-midbar*]," when so many thousands of Israelites died there? He interprets the verse to mean that he died "by the speech of his mouth."[96] And he explains further that when they say that their father died "for his sin," they mean that their father died of the same sin as the Serpent: "What is the meaning of 'by his sin'? By the Serpent's sin. And what is that? The speech of his mouth."[97] But this teaching implies the intimate struggle between the Serpent and the Shekhinah, since She, too, is denominated by the term *dibbur* [*speech*]. Indeed, the *Zohar* reads the verse, "Who is that who comes up from the desert?" (Song of Sol. 3:6) to refer to Shekhinah: "'Comes up from the desert,' 'from the desert,' certainly! From that word of mouth She ascends and enters among the wings of Mother, and afterwards, through speech She descends and settles over the heads of the holy nation."[98]

There are some heroic individuals who fight the Serpent by going into the wilderness to dedicate themselves to Torah study there.[99] In one text, Rashbi, his son, and some Companions meet an old man, a *Sabba*, who has come from a group of desert hermits (*parishei midbara*) who have been intensely studying Torah. He has returned to civilization (*yishuva*) "so as to sit in the shade of the Holy Blessed One during these days of the Seventh Month."[100] He explains why he and his associates go to the desert to learn Torah. They are following what God did after the Exodus.

God led the Israelites into the wilderness because He wanted to break the power of the Serpent in the Serpent's own territory. By walking in the desert, Israel was to crush the Serpent's head. They almost succeeded, but finally the Serpent bit them in the heel and they all died of their sins in the desert.

> And we, in the same way, have separated ourselves from civilization to [go to] the powerful [*taqifa*][101] desert in order to study Torah deeply there so as to subdue that Side. And also, there is no other place but there where the words of Torah are reconciled [*mityashvan*], for there is no light except for that which comes out of darkness. For when that Side is subdued, the Holy Blessed One ascends upward and is glorified in His Glory. And there is no service to God except through darkness. And there is no goodness except through evil. And when a person enters an evil path and leaves it, then the Holy Blessed One ascends in His Glory, and this is the perfection of all, good and evil as one, and to ascend finally in goodness. And there is no good except that which comes out of evil. And in that good His Glory ascends and that is perfect service. And we, until now, were living [*yativna*] there all the days of the year in order to subdue that Side [while] in the desert. Now that the time has arrived for the holy service of the Holy Side, we have returned to civilization, for that is where its service is. And furthermore, now, at Rosh Ha-Shanah, the time has come for that Serpent to demand Judgment before the Holy Blessed One. And since he rules there, therefore we have left there and have come to civilization.[102]

The old man incorporates a sense of Israel's sacred history with a theory of personal spatial practice and divine service. The Israelite trek through the wilderness was meant to be the means of defeating the Serpent, already weakened by God's victory over Egypt. But Israel failed at that time. Now it is up to him and his group. He divides the world into two regions—settled and desolate. Further in his discourse he states that the Other Side is the center of the region of destruction and desolation, while the Holy Side is the central point of all settled areas of civilization.[103] It is significant that this central point has an identifiable, named place—Jerusalem, while the center of the desolate realms is anonymous and lacking in real geographic specificity. From the sacred central point the vertical axis of the Holy ascends, connecting the lower and upper realms. The vertical, sacred axis is thus opposed to an inchoate region with no delineated places.

The hermits have chosen to invade the space of the Serpent and engage in Torah study there, so as to subdue the Other Side. This act is justified by a theory of worship that demands the emergence of goodness from out of evil. The old man gives the example of the repentant sinner, valorized in classical rabbinic literature as the supreme exemplar of the divine servant. But he also seems to conceive of this idea in literally spatial terms. Apparently, the Torah study of the group, emerging as it does from deep in the desert, the realm of evil, has greater potency than it would were it to come out of the less evil region of civilization. But there is a paradox here, for precisely as the Days of Awe approach, he chooses to leave the desert so as to engage in service to God in holiness, untainted by the proximity to evil. Does he mean to say that his worship on these holy days will be more powerful because he has literally come to it from out of the realm of evil? This notion is undermined, however, by his admission that another reason for his leaving is that the Serpent is simply too powerful on his own turf for the old man during this season.

In a way, then, the *Sabba* virtually admits that he has failed in his mission to subdue the Snake, since he must get out of the desert on Rosh Ha-Shanah when the Snake is too powerful. This is crucial, for, despite the evident respect that Rashbi accords him and his compatriots, the old man's way is not a way that Rashbi and his disciples seek to emulate. The *Sabba* went into the desert to break evil. His way is not the path chosen by the Associates, who stay close to civilization and are often frightened of getting too close to the wilderness or mountains. They prefer roads or fields—domesticated nature. Similarly, their enterprise may not have been conceived of in the same extreme terms. They are not out to confront and subdue, but to encounter and assimilate. Or, more accurately, their concept of what might count as a defeat of the Serpent is different.[104]

Their approaches can be distinguished by the different means of spatial practice they employ. The speech of the old hermit is full of usages of the root *ysv* (Aram., *ytv*), meaning "to sit, to settle." The hermits seek to impose upon the desert the mode of habitation of civilization—*yishuva*. Thus, they set up camp (*yativna*) in the desert for the entire year. There they learn

Torah. In this way they seek to break the Serpent's power. But this can be accomplished, in the hermit's view, only through a certain type of Torah learning. He seeks to apprehend words of Torah that are settled (*mityashvan*). Only in this way can God's Glory ascend. But the Companions exemplify another way. They are not settled and do not try to establish outposts in the face of the Other Side. Their way is fluid and transient. Their Torah, also, is the product of unceasing new-old words and insights.

The Companions are not militant crusaders seeking to create beachheads in alien territory. Their mission is far less dramatically charged, as is their field of operations.[105] The Companions sometimes enter places where the Serpent's power is to be feared or reckoned with. These places include the mountains and deserts that they sometimes enter or walk through. The caves they find may also be included in this category. The cave has a special resonance for the *Zohar*, since it is such an important element in the myth of Rashbi's esoteric education. In the talmudic story, the cave is a place of hiding, refuge, and security, in which the purity of nature coheres with the spiritual pursuit of Torah.[106] The biblical Cave of the Makhpelah is also such a place of special holiness[107] Thus for the *Zohar*, a cave is sometimes a place of shade and safety, a place to rest and relate Torah insights.[108] But the cave is also a place engendering fear and uneasiness. The cave of Rashbi's refuge, an unspecified location in the Talmud, is, in the zoharic version, located in the desert, as are other caves in other stories.[109] The cave is also associated with fearsome mountains and with the snake.[110] This association is to be expected, since snakes dwell in dark places and crevices.[111] This means that the encounter with caves may become an encounter with the Other Side. But it may not. So the Companions overcome their fears and enter those caves, sit in them and say words of Torah, and then move on.[112]

More frequently, the Companions find themselves in fields.[113] In this setting, associated with the Shekhinah, the Companions are usually more at ease. "Rabbi Yehudah and Rabbi Yitzḥaq were walking on the road. Said Rabbi Yehudah to Rabbi Yitzḥaq, 'Let us walk in that field, for it is a straighter path.' They went."[114] There is less of a sense of danger or risk.[115]

Indeed, as they relax under the shade of a tree, the Companions often enjoy the scents and scenes of nature, stimuli that can inspire them to meditate aloud on their deeper significance. While Rashbi may be called upon to confront evil and annul divine decrees,[116] the Companions often express their preference to avoid trouble and evil people. They don't want to confront evil aggressively if they can help it. Still, it is also not their desire to find a safe, sheltered space in which to avoid the world.

The hermit's dichotomous geography figures in another text as well. Rabbi Ḥiyya and Rabbi Yose encounter a donkey driver on the road. He also teaches that the earth is divided into the settled realm of civilization and the desolate realm of the Other Side, centered in the great desert through which Israel walked. The two discourses have much in common. But there are differences in the donkey driver's teaching. He agrees that the Israelites failed to completely stamp out the evil Serpent. But he maintains that they succeeded partially. "The Other Side rules in that desert, and Israel walked over it against his will and broke his power for forty years."[117] This accomplishment was permanent. It is because Israel succeeded as well as it did that there is no need to send the scapegoat for the Other Side into that desert. "Since Israel had already walked in it for forty years, his power was broken. And his power is [only] strengthened in a place where no one has ever passed by."[118] In the view of this traveling laborer, the evil is defeated by walking about, by the mere assertion of human presence in space. The scapegoat is sent out to a place that is not humanly habitable. There the Serpent can rule undisturbed, and there it must be appeased. But wherever people have been, the Serpent's power is forever weakened. The donkey driver can therefore be sure that the beneficent power of the Temple still operates in the world of human settlement, just as Israel's walking in the desert so long ago is still effective.

The Israelites lived in the Great Desert for forty years. But their habitation was one of temporary encampments and much walking. There is an identification of *yishuva*—settlement—with traveling about, with spatial activity. This is another fundamental difference between the hermit's approach and the driver's. For the donkey driver attributes the defeat of the Other Side to the mere act of human walking, without requiring the intensive engagement in Torah study that is the hallmark of the hermit's project. The driver's theory is more in keeping with the practice of the zoharic fellowship. Although their devotion to Torah study is inarguable, we must recognize that by their simply moving about, by their pure act of walking, they contribute to *yishuvo shel 'olam*—the settling of the world. And we must appreciate that such a settled world is not limited to the vertical axis of holiness that reaches from the Temple to heaven. It is true that by walking the Companions make sure that the Side of Holiness controls ever-widening spheres of influence, while the Serpent will be kept in his place. But this is so because the sphere of influence of the Side of Holiness has been defined negatively and minimalistically. It is any region that is not desolate. It is the entire, humanly inhabited, mundane world.

Conclusion

The Quotidian Utopia of the Zohar

"[They] were walking on the road." "They walked on." There is a great temptation to read the flittering phrases describing the Companions' perambulations as conveyors—if not as conveyors *of* meaning, then as conveyors *toward* meaning. The wondrous nature of many of the Companions' encounters while on their journeys has strengthened the tendency among the *Zohar*'s readers to see the Companions' walking itself as equally wondrous. But if we allow these phrases to speak for themselves we can begin to discern the special space they produce. It is the mundane space of the road, which is to say, nowhere in particular.[1] This utopian quality—this being nowhere—is exquisitely elusive. Because the walking itself lacks the defining coordinates of "from" and "to" in any serious way,[2] the temptation is to impose such a directionality upon the act, anyway. But this denies the walking act a reality of its own in any sense that does not make it point to something other than itself. Thus Naomi Tene concludes her analysis of one walking text:

> The journey of the fellowship in search of the hidden meaning of the verse from the Torah is also a journey in search of the God hiding behind His Word. Walking on the road invites the holy event of revelation, for its walkers have their ears primed for the song of the souls and angels praising the Holy Blessed One; their eyes are sharpened for the birds who tell what was decreed in the Court above; their hearts are full of the sweetness of the Torah's secrets, and their fellowship is the fellowship of friends and lovers.[3]

Toward the beginning of his study of zoharic texts, most of them walking stories, Nathan Wolski writes even more explicitly about the heightened mystical awareness that he is convinced is exemplified by the Companions' walking:

> Whatever the origins of this literary motif, it is, as Melila Hellner-Eshed has so beautifully observed, the consciousness of the way that is decisive. Accord-

> ing to the *Zohar*, the world is best experienced from the changing vantages of a wanderer. Only the traveler has the fresh eyes, the unique perspective, from which the deepest dimensions of reality and Torah can be fathomed. One must know how to read the Torah *be-orḥa keshot*, according to the true way, and to do so, one must *azil be-orḥa* walk on the way.[4]

Much later in his study, Wolski adds: "'Walking on the way' also demands a special state of consciousness, and the Companions are able to both notice and then decipher seemingly innocuous signs and symbols. In this heightened mystical-poetic state everything is meaningful, with all of reality grasped as a semantic field where everything is a sign pointing beyond itself."[5]

These characterizations are beautiful but inaccurate. They betray a desire to imagine the Companions exclusively as enjoying a continuous state of mystical elevation. But in acceding to that desire they let go too quickly of the actuality of the walking itself, however fleeting or insubstantial it may be, for the sake of other elements that may or may not attend the act in any given example. To understand the walking of the Associates as a spatial practice is to recover the reality of the act itself and the very space in which it is performed and which it concurrently produces. Tene portrays the Companions walking toward revelatory encounters. But, by the end of each narrative, they just as surely walk away from them. Just as surely as the Companions, by walking on the road, are walking away from the *beit midrash*, just as surely are they walking away from the *yenuqa* or the donkey driver or the hermit. They are just as surely walking away from any innovative insights into Torah. If these are the experiences and encounters from which and to which they walk, then where are they when they are in between? What calculus is possible for plotting their location if the coordinate axes are missing? Scholars agree that it is pointless to try to use zoharic statements such as "Rabbi A and Rabbi B were going from *x* to *y*" for establishing the spatial coordinates of their journey. But this is because their spatial coordinates are already known. The "to" and "fro" that bound their space are the "to" and "fro" of the mundane world. We need not ask where the Companions are because their quotidian utopia is here.

After Adam and Eve heard God walking in the Garden in the breeze of the [waning] day, they ran to hide. "And God Almighty called out to Adam and said to him, 'Where are you?' And he said, 'I heard Your Voice in the Garden, and I became afraid because I am naked, and I hid'" (Gen, 3:9–10). God asks Adam where he is, but Adam never answers. The spatial question, unanswered, remains, for Adam was afraid to answer, "Here."

The "here-ness" of the Companions' space is a key to its elusive, hidden, even invisible quality. Space tends to be seen as what is "out there." This apprehension arouses the fear of or the desire for the Other, or the Other Side. The road can be that space of desire/fear if it is infused with that drive to go elsewhere. But by equally moving toward encounters and also leaving them, the Companions accept and co-opt their desire and fear. The paradoxical richness of the zoharic motif includes this paradox as well: that the constant insistence of the Companions on going outside is an expression of appreciation that it is not necessary to go anywhere else but here in order to find space. It is the reclamation of space, if only for a moment, without a sense of tragedy or exile. It is the reclamation of the toddler's delight in pure walking, before "to" and "fro" become determinative of its meaning.

The extraordinary feature of the walking texts in the *Zohar*, its literary uniqueness, cannot be reduced to an explanation that does not do justice to how extraordinary and unique this feature is. It is extraordinary that a kabbalistic work should take real notice of the non-mystical realms of human experience in any other than a dismissive manner. The tendency of profound religious thinkers and mystics might be to narrow their focus to include only the realm of the numinous or to expansively define all aspects of reality as partaking of the numinous. The almost impossible task that the *Zohar* undertook was to make room in its all-encompassing Secret of Faith for that which is mundane as such, for that which is outside the realm of the Divine—to incorporate it without obliterating it.

There is no intention here to downplay the theosophical and esoteric concerns of the *Zohar* in any way. But this study proposes that the *Zohar* gives expression to another, seemingly unrelated context, within which the kabbalists' mystical practices and theories developed—the context of the everyday. This context may be thought of as the very antithesis of that mystical world, as an obstacle to it, or, at best, as an irrelevancy. Yet every mystic knows that, until the final mystical conjunction, the context of the everyday is fundamental and inescapable. It is the thesis of this study that the *Zohar* developed a unique approach to formulating that statement, an approach that was developed in order to incorporate this seemingly irrelevant context within the *Zohar*'s project of accounting for all of reality.

The unique approach adopted by the *Zohar* was to couch its mystical midrash within a quasi-narrative. Its teachings are conveyed as mystical soliloquies, dialogues, and conversations occurring among sages, along with others whom they meet, as they travel through a landscape. This movement through space is usually left unexplained, unjustified in the text. Only sometimes is a destination or a purpose given for the trips the Associates take. Most of the time, though, their perambulations and journeys are seemingly aimless. While other kabbalistic works may employ the midrashic form or use parables and stories, no other work has maintained this narrative framework. And while older stories of the Sages in the talmudic and midrashic collections sometimes portray them as travelers on a road, and while these stories surely served as models for the *Zohar*, only the *Zohar* utilizes this motif with such regularity and such apparent arbitrariness.

Scholars have increasingly turned their attention to the stories of the *Zohar*, but have not systematically considered the significance of this feature. The results of this study show that the walking motif can be understood by seeing it in multiple contexts. The abundance and regularity of the walking motif apparently counters the tendency developing in the best contemporary scholarship[6] that increasingly sees the *Zohar* as a collection of free-standing texts. The recurrent motif of walking on the road suggests that there is some thread tying these disparate texts together. If the *Zohar* is not a "book," it may perhaps be considered a literary project. The maturation of the motif from its early use in the *Midrash ha-Ne'elam* into its many enunciations in the body of the *Zohar* speaks of a concerted commitment to its integral role in these various textual units. The literary zoharic context indicates that the motif functions only in certain sections, those that are not emphatically dedicated to the most esoteric concerns of the *Zohar*. By placing these texts within the historical, social, and cultural context of late thirteenth-century Spain, it becomes possible to read them as statements, reactions, and gestures relevant to their time and place. This was a time of conflict over geographic spaces and cultural values. The *Zohar* engages in its own acts of spatial appropriation through the use of walking texts, in conversation and in polemic with the surrounding non-Jewish culture.

The motif can also be understood in the context of the ferment evident within the Jewish religious and cultural elites of the time. The relationship between the talmudic/halakhic enterprise and the kabbalistic project was under negotiation. As the *Zohar* was being composed, the theosophical concepts of the kabbalists were undergoing increasing systemization. Kabbalistic works such as *Sha'arei Orah* and *Ma'arekhet ha-Elohut* are evidence of that tendency. Such systemization afforded the kabbalists great power in promoting and explaining both exoteric and esoteric traditions and behaviors. The *Zohar*, however, went a different way. Its use of the motif of aimless walking through a landscape introduces an entirely different context to these charged mystical practices. Here the *Zohar* introduces the aspect of the unintentional, the undirected, the fortuitous and the meandering. This is done only with some effort. Theosophical and cosmogonic conceptions were not easily reconciled to spatial concerns, however insistent they might be. Furthermore, the *Zohar* shows that it knows this choice to be controversial. The walking texts evince an effort to take a position that is independent of both contemporary halakhic/talmudic trends and other kabbalistic outlooks.

The Sacred Center (whatever the adequacy of Eliade's concept for the general phenomenology of religions) seems an overwhelming concern for the mystic. Yet the thesis of this work is that the inescapable and unique element of the walking texts in this mystical classic is its acknowledgment that to establish a center, one must acknowledge a periphery. In order to establish the boundaries of sacred space, one must test those boundaries. As the *Zohar* constructs its vertical, theurgical-visionary system, it also sends its heroes into the landscape to test the boundaries of happenstance and order, of land and sea, mountain and cave. These friends and disciples are tested as well, as any mystic well might be, by the challenge of walking through the mundane world with delight.

The advantage of this thesis is that it allows for a fuller appreciation of the zoharic walking texts without seeking to impose a theosophical system of symbolism upon them. The strange and anomalous character of the walking motif is understood in terms of a strange and anomalous project undertaken by the *Zohar*'s authors. By accepting the strangeness of the *Zohar*'s turn to the mundane, the history of the neglect or inadequate treatment of this motif is better understood. In the general field of the study of religion, formulating the question of the walking motif in terms that go beyond the issue of narrative to include spatial practice and production opens up the question of spatial orientations in religions for further consideration. Utilizing that framework reopens, as well, the question of understanding mystical practices and beliefs themselves, and in relation to the religious traditions of which they are a part. But the greatest benefit that this study could bring is to open more possibilities for the *Sefer ha-Zohar* to continue teaching and inspiring its readers in new-old ways.

. . .

> "If you walk in My statutes . . . I will walk along among you and I will be your Almighty" [Lev. 26:3, 12]: They told a parable. To what can this be compared? A king went out to stroll with his tenant in the orchard. The tenant would hide from him. Said the king to that tenant: Why are you hiding from me? I am just like you! . . . Could it be that My reverence would not be upon you? The verse teaches: And I will be your Almighty.
>
> What does the strolling mean? And what does "I am like you" mean? And what does "My reverence upon you" mean? This is not the place to explain it, for they are cosmic secrets. But the enlightened will understand and will shine like the splendor of the firmament.
>
> Rabbi Yitzḥaq Eisaac Yehudah Yeḥiel Safrin of Komarno
> *'Asirit Ha-Efah, Torat Kohanim B'ḥuqqotai 3:3*

REFERENCE MATTER

APPENDIX I

The Walking Motif in the Zohar: *A Listing of Texts*

The following is a listing of the texts that portray the personae of the *Zohar*—Rabbi Shim'on bar Yoḥai (Rashbi) and his Associates—traveling on the road. The list first examines the literary unit called *guf ha-Zohar*—the main body of the *Zohar*. It then lists texts found in other strata and units, including texts in *Midrash ha-Ne'elam* (*MH*), *Zohar Ḥadash* (*ZH*), and then in *Tosefta* and *Sitrei Torah* (*ST*) (cited as printed in the contemporary standard editions from Mossad Ha-Rav Kook, edited by R. Reuven Margaliot). In the main body of the *Zohar*, the divisions according to weekly Torah readings are noted, as are other important sections or components of the *Zohar*, though they may contain no "walking" texts. The designations of strata follow the indications of the printed text, though modern scholarship has assigned some pages of the main text to other strata. These assignments are noted. Gershom Scholem's analysis of the literary strata or components of the zoharic corpus, as set forth in his collection of articles *Kabbalah*, 214–219, is utilized for this purpose. Sections outside the main body of the *Zohar* are not noted if they do not contain texts for this list. This study does not include the *Tiqqunei Zohar* or *Ra' aya Meheimna* sections, inasmuch as these are viewed by modern scholarship (and by some others) as later than the *Zohar* proper.

Each text is listed with a beginning and ending, though making such determinations is often problematic. Scriptural citations are shown in italics to distinguish them from the text of the *Zohar* proper.

For appendices 2, 3, and 4 to this book, see www.sup.org/roadstoutopia

Guf ha-Zohar: *The Main Body of the* Zohar

1:1a–14b: *Haqdamat ha-Zohar*

(1) 1:3b—R. Ḥiyya and R. Yose were walking on the road)—4b—*and I shall fill their storehouses*

(2) 1:5a—R. Ele'azar was going to see—7b—*face to face*

1:15a–(38a)–59a—*Bereshit*

Tiqqunei Zohar—22a–29a; *Heikhalot*—38a–45b

(3) 1:49b—*Therefore shall a man leave . . .* R. Shim'on was walking—51a—R. Shim'on and the Associates returned

(4) 1:57b—R. Shim'on was walking—*remove dross from silver*, etc.

(5) 1:58b—R. Shim'on was walking on the road—59a—*Amen and amen*

1:59b–76b—*Noaḥ*

(6) 1:62a—R. Ḥiyya and R. Yose were walking—and they fall to the ground and die

(7) 1:63a—R. Ḥiyya and R. Yose were walking—64b—he said he certainly said well

(8) 1:65b—R. Ḥiyya and R. Yose were walking—66a—*to one who yearns for Him*

(9) 1:69b—R. Ḥizqiyyah was walking—70b—that the Holy Blessed One hid in the Act of Creation

(10) 1:76a—R. Yose and R. Ḥiyya were walking—76b—*Amen and amen*

1:76b–96b—*Lekh Lekha*

(11) 1:83a—R. Shim'on was walking on the road—84b—*you are all alive today*

(12) 1:86b—R. Ele'azar was walking—88a—*and you shall rejoice in God in holiness*, etc.

(13) 1:92b—R. Abba was coming from Tiberias—96b—*and God's Glory will take you in*

1:97a–120b—*Vayera*

(14) 1:107b—R. Yitzḥaq and R. Yehudah were walking . . .—108a—and in The Coming World

(15) 1:115b—R. Yehudah and R. Yose were walking—118b—engendering fire from water

1:121a–134a—*Ḥayyei Sarah*

(16) 1:125b—R. Yitzḥaq and R. Yose were walking . . .—127a—remove from the earth

(17) 1:132a—R. Shim'on was coming to Tiberias—133a—that I merited to hear it

1:134a–146b—*Toldot*

(18) 1:145a—R. Ḥiyya and R. Yose were walking—146b—*Blessed be God forever*, etc.

1:146b–165b—*Vayetze*

(19) 1:148a—R. Yitzḥaq was sitting—150b—and all are stamped with the secret of Wisdom

(20) 1:155b—R. Shim'on left for business—156a—how much more so

(21) 1:157a—R. Ḥiyya and R. Yose were walking—157b—therefore, *Halleluyah*

(22) 1:160a—R. Yehudah and R. Ḥizqiah were walking . . .—160b—and to dwell with him

(23) 1:164a—R. Yitzḥaq and R. Yeisa were walking—164b—*to be enhanced by the work of My hands*

1:165b–179a—*Vayishlaḥ*

(24) 1:173a—R. Yehudah and R. Ḥizqiyah were walking . . .—173a befouled abomination

(25) 1:173b—R. Ele'azar and R. Yose were walking—174a—*in red-stained garments from Batzrah*

(26) 1:178a—R. Ele'azar and R. Yitzḥaq were walking . . .—178b—[*I will satisfy him with*] *length of days*, etc.

1:179a–193a—*Vayeshev*

(27) 1:186a—R. Ele'azar and R. Yose and R. Ḥiyya were walking . . . —186b—to your brother's wife. . . .

(28) 1:192b—R. Ele'azar and R. Yose were walking—193a—*Amen and amen*

1:193a–205a—*Miqetz*

(29) 1:195a—R. Ḥiyya and R. Yose were walking . . . —195b—and in a true path.

(30) 1:197b (see 2:31a–b—more extensive and with some small changes [no. 53])

(31) 1:204b—R. Ḥiyya and R. Yose were walking—205a—*Amen and amen*

1:205a–211b—*Vayiggash*

No walking stories.

1:211b–251a—*Vayeḥi*

Editor's note at start: fols. 211b–216a are not *Zohar* (see Scholem, 217—some editions label these pages *MH*, but they are probably a later text).

(32) 1:213a—It was taught: R. Hamnuna Sabba went—the coming world

1:214b—R. Abba was walking (see note at no. 97)

(33) 1:219a—R. Yose was walking—219b—*and I shall tell God's works*

(34) 1:223a—It was taught—One day R. Shim'on—223b—it is above the sun

(35) 1:229b—R. Ḥizqiyah and R. Yose and R. Yehudah—233a—to learn Torah

(36) 1:235b—R. Yose and R. Yesa were walking—it would have been good for us.

(37) 1:237a—R. Yehudah and R. Yitzḥaq were walking—237b—and not other nations

(38) 1:238b—R. Yehudah and R. Yitzḥaq were walking—240b—*My spirit that is upon you*

(39) 1:242b—R. Shim'on, R. Yose, and R. Ḥiyya were going—243a—to overcome all

(40) 1:243b—R. Yose and R. Ḥizqiya were walking—244b—tied in one place

(41) 1:244b—R. Eleazar and R. Abba escaped into a cave—251a—*Amen and amen*

2:1a–22a—*Sh'mot*

MH—4a-5b—possibly (see Scholem, 217).

(42) 2:4a—*And these are the names*. R. Ele'azar and R. Yose were walking—*Each came with their household*

(43) 2:5a—R. Ḥiyya was walking from Usha to Lod—*with Jacob*

(44) 2:7a—R. Ele'azar, R. Abba and R. Yose were walking)—8a—paths of Torah

(45) 2:10a—R. Ele'azar and R. Yose were walking—11a—(*David's fallen sukkah*)

(46) 2:12b—R. Yose and R. Yitzḥaq were walking—that Jacob and Moses saw

(47) 2:13a—R. Ele'azar and R. Abba were walking—14a—and went along

MH—14a–22a (Scholem, 217)

(48) 2:16a—R. Yehudah bar Shalom was walking . . . —16b—tribes went up, etc.

(49) 2:17a—R. Yehoshu'a went up—swallowed up in their places

(50) 2:17b—R. Yose set out—even one moment

(51) 2:20a—R. Abba was walking—20b—those who learn Torah

2:22a–32a—*Va'era*

(52) 2:30b—R. Yehudah and R. Ḥiyya were walking—31a—and inherited it

(53) 2:31a—R. Yeisa and R. Ḥizqiyah were walking—32a—to know the secret of Wisdom

See also no. 30 above.

(54) 2:32a—R. Yose and R. Ḥiyya were walking on the road—*Amen and amen*

2:32b–43b—*Bo*

Scholem, 217—*MH* 35b–40b—possibly

(55) 2:36b—R. Ḥiyya and R. Yose were going from Usha to Lod—38b—and they sat before him

2:44a–67a—*Beshalaḥ*

(56) 2:45b—R. Yitzḥaq and R. Yehudah were going—46a—from the land of Egypt

(57) 2:47b—R. Yose and R. Yehudah were walking—*Jacob is His given portion*

(58) 2:49a—R. Ḥiyya and R. Yose were walking in the desert—50a—*for them*, precisely.

2:67a–94a—*Yitro*

(59) 2:68b—Thus, one time R. Ele'azar was walking—to shine

Raza de Razin—2:70a–75a and 70a–78a

(60) 2:80a—It is taught, R. Yose—bless the Merciful One Who saved you

(61) 2:80b—R. Ele'azar was walking—like a human form on it from above

(62) 2:86a—R. Yehudah was walking—87a—for that is His Faith

(63) 2:87b—R. Ele'azar was walking—*that I be enhanced through you*

(64) 2:89a—R. Yudai asked R. Shim'on—89b—for that which requires intention

RM—2:91b–94a

2:94a–126a—*Mishpatim*

Saba de Mishpatim—2:94b–114a

(65) 2:121b—R. Abba was walking—122a—*all who devour him shall be culpable*, etc.

2:127a–179a—*Terumah*

Idra de Vei Mashkena—2:127a–146b

(66) 2:138b—At that time R. Shim'on rose—147a—and in the Coming World

(67) 2:149a—Said R. Yitzḥaq: Surely this is so—through him

(68) 2:152b—R. Ḥiyya was walking—155a—as we said

(69) 2:155b—R. Yose and R. Ḥiyya were going—157b—how fortunate his portion

(70) 2:160b—R. Ḥiyya and R. Yose were walking—162b—*like Your people, like Israel*, etc.

(71) 2:163b—R. Yose, R. Yehudah and R. Ḥiyya were going—164a—*may your parent rejoice*

Sifra de Tzeni'uta—2:176b–179a

2:179b–187b—*Tetzaveh*

(72) 2:183b—R. Shim'on and R. Ele'azar his son—187b—so as not to appear

2:187b–194b—*Ki Tissa*

(73)2:188a—R. Yose and R. Ḥiyya were walking—190a—to never leave me

194b–220a—*Yayaqhel*

(74) 2:198a—R. Ḥiyya, R. Yitzḥaq and R. Yose—217b—and your image perfect

2:220a–269a—*Pequdei*

(75) 2:223a—R. Yose and R. Yitzḥaq were walking—223b—the deed of the Calf

(76) 2:225a—R. Abba, R. Aḥa, and R. Yose—226b—but in the Upper World

(77) 2:232b—R. Ele'azar, R. Yitzḥaq, and R. Yehudah—235a—*I shall be filled, the ruin*

Heikhalot—2:244b–262b; *Heikhalot de Rashbi*—2:262b–268b

3:2a–26a—*Vayiqra*

(78) 3:6a—R. Aḥa was going—8b—*that I be enhanced through you*

(79) 3:15a—Such as R. Shimon ben Yoḥai—15b—turn compassion to judgment

(80) 3:20a—R Ḥiyya and R. Yose were walking—23a—Amen, may it be so desired

(81) 3:25b—R. Aḥa was walking 26a—*their prayers*, etc.

3:26a–35b—*Tzav*

(82) 3:31a—R. Ḥiyya and R. Yose were going—32a—*I spoke and I acted*

(83) 3:35a—R. Ele'azar was going—35b—*Amen and amen*

3:35b–42a—*Shemini*

(84) 3:36a—R. Ele'azar was going—37b—on that day for them

(85) 3:39a—R. Yehudah and R. Yitzḥaq were going—41a—*I knew you in the womb*

3:42a–52a—*Tazri'a*

(86) 3:42b—R. Abba was walking—42b—were said concerning *Knesset Yisra'el*

(87) 3:45b—R. Ḥiyya and R. Yose were going—47a—*until the day is set*

(88) 3:51a—R. Yitzḥaq and R. Yehudah were walking—*in you and your seed*

(89) 3:51a—R. Yitzḥaq was walking—51b—*like a glowing light*, etc.

(90) 3:52a—R. Ele'azar was walking—*Amen and amen*

3:52b–56a—*Metzor'a*

(91) 3:53b—R. Yehudah and R. Yitzḥaq were walking—54a—*to near and far*, etc.

(92) 3:54a—R. Ḥizqiyah was sitting—56a—*Amen and amen*

3:56a–80a—*Aḥarei Mot*

(93) 3:56b—R. Ḥiyya said, "One day . . . "—like them in Israel

(94) 3:59b—It is taught: R. Yose said—64b—*I drew you close in love*

(95) 3:69a—It is taught, one day—69b—*pure waters*, etc.

(96) 3:71a—It is taught: R. Yehudah said—71b—in the Bundle of Life

(97) 3:75b—R. Abba was walking—76b—*and all that is yours is whole*

(a fragment of the beginning of this is found at 1:214b)

3:80a–88a—*Qedoshim*

(98) 3:80b—R. Yose was going on the road—81a—*for I, God, am holy*

(99) 3:84b—R. Ele'azar was going—88a—*Amen and amen*

3:88a–107b—*Emor*

(100) 3:90a—R. Shim'on was walking—90b—*and will be compassionate to you*
(101) 3:97a—R. Abba and R. Ḥiyya were walking—98b—*I will rescue and honor him*
(102) 3:105a—R. Yose and R. Yitzḥaq were walking—105b—*He was a Savior for them*
(103) 3:106b—R. Shim'on was walking on the road—107a—*all your deeds*

3:107b–112a—*Behar*

(104) 3:110b—R. Ḥiyya and R. Yose were walking—111a—and this has been said

3:112a–115b—*B'ḥuqotai*

(105) 3:115a—R. Ḥiyya and R. Yose were going- 115b—*seed blessed by God*

3:117a–121a—*Bemidbar*

No walking stories.

3:121a–148b—*Naso*

(106) 3:122a—R. Yitzḥaq and R. Yehudah were going—122b—*in God's expansiveness*

Idra Rabba—3:127b–145a

(107) 3:148a—R. Abba was going to Lod—*Who dwells in Jerusalem*

3:148b–156b—*Beha'alotekha*

(108) 3:149a—R. Ele'azar, R. Yose, and R. Yitzḥaq—151a—and in the coming world

3:156b–176a—*Sh'laḥ Lekha*

(109) 3:157a—R. Ḥizqiyah and R. Yeisa were going—158a—of a faithful agent
(110) 3:159a—R. Yehudah was walking on the road—159b—and I apprehended them

Rav Metivta—3:161b–174a

3:176a–179b—*Qoraḥ*

No walking stories.

3:179b–184b—*Ḥuqqat*

No walking stories.

3:184b–212b—*Balaq*

Yenuqa—3:186a–192a

(111) 3:186a—R. Yitzḥaq and R. Yehudah were going—188a—among the Associates
(112) 3:188a—R. Ele'azar wished to see—192a—and so it was
(113) 3:193a—R. Ele'azar and R. Abba were walking—193b—of faith
(114) 3:200b—R. Pinḥas was walking—203b—for the holy nation
(115) 3:204a—R. Ele'azar was going—206b—this has been said (a *Yenuqa* story)

3:213a—259b—*Pinḥas*

(116) 3:214a—R. Ele'azar, R. Yose and R. Ḥiyya—214b—*to the Lord, your God*, etc.
(117) 3:217b—R. Abba and R. Yose arose—219a—to learn this
(118) 3:221b—R. Shim'on was going—233a—until here is the path of R. Pinḥas

Ra'aya Meheimna—3:222a–239a

(119) 3:233a—R. Shim'on went—233b—to walk on our way

(120) 3:240a—R. Yitzḥaq and R. Yehudah—*from which you were gouged*

(121) 3:241b—R. Shim'on was going to Tiberias—242a—*is Awe of the Almighty*

Ra'aya Meheimna—3:242a–258a

3:259b—*Mattot*

No walking stories.

Mas'ei

Devarim

3:260a–270b—*Va'et'ḥanan*

(122) 3:261b—that R. Ele'azar and R. Ḥiyya were—262a—*and I shall rescue him*

(123) 3:265b—R. Abba was coming from seeing—267a—*inherit the land*, etc.

(124) 3:268a—After daylight they rose and went—270b—*with Your Presence*

3:270b–274a—'*Eqev*

Ra'aya Meheimna—271b–283a

No walking stories.

3:274b–275b—*Shoftim* (*Ra'aya Meheimna*)

No walking stories.

3:275b–283a—*Ki Tetze* (*RM*)

No walking stories.

3:283a–286a—*Vayelekh*

No walking stories.

3:286a–299b—*Ha'azinu*

Idra Zuta—3:287b–296b

(125) 3:298a—R. Yitzḥaq was going—298b—*from God*, etc.

Midrash ha-Ne'elam

MH in *ZH*

Bereshit

(1) 5d—R. Yoḥanan was walking—*Mine is Might*

(2) 6a—R. Ḥizqiyah was walking on the road—*and You girded me with joy*

(3) 7a—R. Dosta'i asked—of schoolchildren

(4) 7d—R. Ele'azar b. R. Shim'on went to see—rejoice at that time

(5) 9d—R. Ḥiyya bar Abba was walking—couldn't drink from them

(6) 10a—The Rabbis taught: Once R. Yoḥanan was walking—10b—shall you be in your generation

(7) 11b—R. Zera said—once—what can I do?

(8) 11b—The Rabbis taught—R. Yose ben Pazi said—One time—11c—and I told him this

(9) 12d—R. Yitzḥaq asked—13a—*all that He made*

(10) 13d—R. Yitzḥaq went to visit R. Zera—*that it was good*
(11) 14c—The Rabbis taught: Once he was walking—15a—*taught of God*
(12) 15b—R. Abahu, R. Ḥiyya, and R. Natan were walking—15d—*joy to those with honest hearts*
(13) 16c—R. Ele'azar and R. 'Aqiva were walking—16d—*God rejoice in His works*
(14) 18b—R. Ḥiyya and R. Yose were walking—another world, the Coming World
(15) 20d—R. Ele'azar and his father-in-law R. Yose—*in all your ways*
(16) 21c—Said R. Yehoshua b. Levi—and I was saved
(17) 22a—R. Yose and R. Ḥiyya were walking—that the Holy Blessed One desires

Lekh Lekha

(18) 25c—The Rabbis taught: Once R. Dostai was going—26a—*we shall rejoice and be happy in You*

MH in Main Body of *Zohar*

Vayera

(19) 1:100b—Said R. Pinḥas: One time I was walking—that death be annulled from them

Toldot

(20) 1:138a—R. Yitzḥaq bR. Yose was coming from Qapotqia—the essence of all
See also nos. 41, 42, 47–51, and 55 above.

Zohar Ḥadash

Balaq

(21) 53c—Said R. Abba: One day—53d—*You will hear my voice,* etc.
(22) 54a—The Associates walked—together

Midrash Rut

(23) 76c—R. Nehorai and R. Yitzḥaq rose—76d—with other nations
(24) 77b—*And it was in the days;* All his days R. Bun—77d—to hear your word
(25) 77d—R. Bun was walking—78a—*with few people in it*
(26) 78a—R. Bun was carrying/guiding—*the judges judged*
(27) 82a—R. Ḥidqa and R. Shim'on bar Yose were walking—and does not receive a reward
(28) 83a—R. 'Azaryah and R. Ḥizqiyah were going up—83d—Torah and *mitzvot* like a pomegranate
(29) 84b—R. Zemira'ah left for the Oni farm—84c—happened to R. 'Aqiva
(30) 86c—R. Bun and R. Yose ben R. Ḥanina—87d—and made him head of them all
(31) 90a—One day he was walking in a field—91b—I found up to here

Tosefta *and* Sitrei Torah

(32) 1:89a—R. Ḥiyya was walking—90a—*happy is the man whose strength is in You—ST*
(33) 3:55b—R. Ele'azar and R. Yose his brother-in-law—*was for me—Tosefta*

Notes

Abbreviations

BT	Babylonian Talmud
M	Mishnah
MH	*Midrash ha-Ne'elam*
MTJM	Scholem, *Major Trends in Jewish Mysticism*
OH	*Oraḥ Ḥayyim*
PT	Palestinian Talmud
SA	Shulḥan 'Arukh
ST	Sitrei Torah
T	Tosefta
TDE	Tanna debe Eliyahu
Tur	Yaakov ben Asher, *Arba'ah Turim* (ca. 1270–1340 C.E.)
ZH	*Zohar Ḥadash*

Two Introductions

1. *MTJM*, 156. On the history of the reception of the *Zohar*, see Huss, "*Sefer ha-Zohar*," which includes references to the relevant works of other scholars, including Isaiah Tishby, Yehuda Liebes, Moshe Idel, Roland Goetschel, Israel Ta-Shma, Elliot Wolfson, and Daniel Abrams.

On the difficult question of the *Zohar*'s coherence as a "book," see Huss's relevant works listed in the Bibliography (collected in his book *K'Zohar ha-raqi'a*). See also Wolfson, "Anonymous Chapters." The most far-reaching questioning of this concept has been advanced over the years by Daniel Abrams, culminating in his massive *Kabbalistic Manuscripts and Textual Theory*, §4 of which expands upon his previous essays on the *Zohar*. Abrams sees no basis for considering it as a book in the modern sense. He thus rejects both major theories of zoharic authorship currently held by scholars, maintaining that the *Zohar* is not a book intentionally created as such. He therefore questions the legitimacy of thematic studies that read across zoharic texts. Within this group, he cites the works of Joel Hecker, Hartley Lachter, and myself, but without discussing them. Abrams's strictures are based on solid scholarship and serious analysis of the zoharic corpus through the lens of current textual theory. *Roads to Utopia* seeks to avoid the most egregious errors that Abrams bemoans. Nevertheless, I remain convinced that the "walking story" data I have assembled are a strong indicator of the connected nature of the group of texts traditionally identified as *guf ha-Zohar*—the (main) body of the *Zohar*.

2. See Meroz, *Ḥiddushei Zohar*, "Introduction," 11–12.

3. These stories will be called "walking" stories, although the method of travel is not always explicitly described. Sometimes one person is said to ride, while another walks along beside him. As noted later, this ambiguity is found in Christian pilgrimage narratives as well. On the adequacy of the term "story," see further discussion.

4. De Modena, *Ari nohem*, chap. 22, as quoted in Hillel Zeitlin, *Be-Fardes ha-ḥassidut ve-ha-qabbalah* (Tel Aviv: Yavneh, 1960), 112–113. For a slightly different text, see Yehudah Aryeh of Modena, *Leqet ketavim*, ed. Peninah Naveh (Jerusalem: Bialik, 1968), 228. On Modena as an early critic of the *Zohar*, see Tishby, *Mishnat*, 1:49–50.

5. This question is touched upon at the conclusion of this study.

6. This applies as well to the treatments of M. Hellner-Eshed and N. Wolski. Wolski's book *A Journey into the Zohar* concerns itself with a selection of mostly walking stories, but he does not focus on that aspect of the stories. See my Conclusion above at n. 4 and ff.

7. E.g., 2:14a: "R. Ḥiyya Rabba was going to the Masters of the Mishnah to learn from them. He went to R. Shim'on ben Yoḥai and saw. . . . " See chap. 2, n. 11, below.

8. If the motif occurs in this manner in sufficient quantity, it may also cause us to reevaluate its use in the unproblematic cases. I have not dealt with this possibility.

9. Stith Thompson, *The Folktale* (New York: Dryden Press, 1946), 415–416.

10. Thompson in *Standard Dictionary of Folklore, Mythology and Legend*, ed. Maria Leach (New York: Funk & Wagnalls, 1972), 753.

11. In his commentary to the verse "And a man from the house of Levi went . . ." (Exod. 2:1), Naḥmanides is bothered by such a question. See his comment, s.v. *Vayelekh ish mi-beit levi*.

12. For a basic listing of the sections, see *MTJM*, 159–163. For a comparison between that listing and Scholem's revised list, see Abrams, *Kabbalistic Manuscripts*, 289–290. For earlier listings, see ibid., 267, 271. And see n. 1 above.

13. It should be noted that the *Sabba* section begins right after the Companions have finished walking for the day, arriving at the Tower of Tyre to spend the night. In the section itself, the term *orḥa*—"path"—is used repeatedly in all its permutations. The Sabba also reports that he would undertake to follow sages when they went out walking on the road (2:95a).

14. Liebes has placed great emphasis on the *Idrot* in developing his readings of the *Zohar*. He has also measured the adequacy of the readings of Cordovero and Luria against their appreciation of the place the *Idrot* occupy in the zoharic corpus. Farber-Ginat, "'Iqvotav shel sefer ha-Zohar bekitvei Rabbi Yosef Giqatilla," *'Alei Sefer* 9 (1981): 70–83, has argued that Giqatilla was strongly influenced by the *Idrot*, as well as by zoharic Merkavah texts and, especially, the *Heikhalot*. Giller's study, *Reading the Zohar*, concentrates on the *Idrot*, *Sabba*, *Sifra deTzeni'uta*, and other texts, from which the walking motif is absent. However, as noted above, Abrams questions the notion that such a cross-textual connection should be made.

15. On this itinerant scholar, see Huss, "NiSAN"; Fishbane, *As Light Before Dawn*.

16. Quoted in Matt, *Zohar: The Book of Enlightenment*, 4. Discussions of this report as it may shed light on the question of the *Zohar*'s authorship can be found in *MTJM*, 190–192, and Tishby, *Mishnat*, 1: 28–32.

17. See Matt, *Zohar: The Book of Enlightenment*, 25–28, who speculates about auto-

matic writing. This technique is discussed with regard to *Tiqqunei ha-Zohar* by A. Goldreich, "Berurim bir'iyyato ha-'atzmit shel ba'al Tiqqunei ha-*Zohar*," in *Massu'ot*, ed. Oron and Goldreich, 483–491. Accepting Goldreich's findings regarding the *Tiqqunim*, Liebes, "Ha-*Zohar* v'ha-Tiqqunim," 269, rejects the idea that automatic writing produced the *Zohar*. C. Mopsik writes that the *Zohar* "could be the product of prophetic experience of thirteenth century kabbalists . . . most prominently, R. Moses de Leon" (*Sefer sheqel ha-qodesh*, "Introduction," 5–6, cited in Abrams, *Kabbalistic Manuscripts*, 321). See Goldreich's full-length study *Shem ha-kotev u-kh'tivah otomatit b-sifrut ha-Zohar u-va-modernizm* (Los Angeles: Cherub Press, 2010), 43–53, where he revisits this issue, specifically with regard to the *Zohar* proper.

18. In *Studies in the Zohar*, 72, Liebes speculates as to the quality of de Leon's sexual relationship with his wife. Rather than speculating about any crisis or dysfunction, I seek more broadly to point out the necessary fact of a humdrum domestic milieu. See also chap. 1.

19. By the phrase "religious and mystical cultures," I mean to refer to groups of people who explicitly identify with a set of religious beliefs, values, and practices and whose cultural productions—inherited and newly created—are expressions of such beliefs, values, and practices.

20. Eliade, *The Sacred and the Profane*, 21.

21. Ibid., 23–24.

22. Ibid., 17.

23. Ibid., 28–29.

24. Smith, *Map Is Not Territory*, "The Wobbling Pivot," 100–101.

25. Smith, *Imagining Religion*, "The Bare Facts of Ritual," 63.

26. Ibid., 65.

27. Ibid., 63.

28. Ibid.

29. E.g., Liebes, *Studies in the Zohar*, "The Messiah of the *Zohar*" and "How the *Zohar* Was Written."

30. E.g., Wolfson, *Through a Speculum*, "Forms of Visionary Ascent" and "Hermeneutics of Visionary Experience."

31. E.g., Hellner-Eshed, *River Issues Forth* (in Hebrew; trans. Wolski as *River Flows from Eden*).

32. E.g., Hecker, *Mystical Bodies, Mystical Meals*, and his previous studies cited therein.

33. Tene, "Darkhei," 185–186.

Chapter 1. The Dregs of Tar

1. 1:49b. Where there is no possibility of ambiguity, the *Zohar* is cited by volume and page as shown here. Translations from it are mine, following the standard printed Aramaic text and, where possible, compared with the text edited by Daniel C. Matt, www.sup.org/zohar.

2. Two clarifications are needed here, regarding the numbering of the story and the term I use to describe this and other stories like it:

(a) Most scholars accept that the *guf ha-Zohar*, the main body of the *Zohar*, which is the primary focus of this study, was roughly organized according to the weekly Sabbath Torah readings, beginning with Genesis 1. But Abrams, *Kabbalistic Manuscripts*, posits that there is no evidence for this organizing principle until the early sixteenth century (see "Two Introductions," n. 1, above). Thus, according to Abrams, since we do not know how the texts of what later became known as the *Zohar* first made their appearance, one cannot call any text the "first" of its type in the *Zohar*. Furthermore, while there are two walking stories that precede this story in the *Zohar* as it is presently published, the other two stories are found in the text known as *Haqdamat ha-Zohar*—"Introduction to the *Zohar*." Yet, despite its traditional title, that section does not really function as an introduction, being neither a statement of authorial intention nor identification. As Abrams has shown (in his "Ematai ḥubrah ha-Haqdamah le-Sefer ha-*Zohar*?"), it is doubtful that this section was really intended to serve as the start of the *Zohar*. Nevertheless, there is early evidence for the recognition of a collection of texts as comprising "the wondrous *Zohar*," to borrow R. Menaḥem Recanati's phrase from the early fourteenth century, referring to the *guf ha-Zohar* and to *Midrash ha-Ne' elam* (see Idel, *R. Menahem Recanati ha-m'qubbal*, 103–104, cited in Abrams, *Kabbalistic Manuscripts*, 260) Thus, encountering the *Zohar* as it is presently constituted, this is one of the first walking stories.

(b) As noted ("Two Introductions," n. 3), all these stories will be called "walking" stories, though the method of travel is not always explicitly described. In this particular story, it would appear that R. Shim'on and the others are riding along and then dismount in order to sit under a tree (Matt translates "came down" as "dismounts"). On this ambiguity, see chap. 2, n. 10, below.

3. Acknowledging that the present arrangement of the *Zohar* cannot be taken as the expression of an original compositional intention, it is still possible to use these first pages as exemplars of the options available and used in the *Zohar* proper (*guf ha-Zohar*). While the story is found on p. 49b, the preceding pages belong to various literary sections of the zoharic library of texts. The body of the *Zohar* (*guf ha-Zohar*) begins on page 15a, after the Introduction (see previous note). This text is interrupted by the *Tiqqunei Zohar* section, which comprises 22a–29a. It then resumes through to 38a, at which point there is an extensive separate section, called *Heikhalot* (38a–45b). It then resumes through 59a. See Oron, "Sh'loshah perushim l'Ma'aseh B'reshit," who discerns three somewhat independent sections of commentary to Genesis. She cites evidence that they may have appeared as independent works, since some early authors seem not to have knowledge of all three. She also speculates that the third commentary, in which our walking text appears, seems to be building on the other two. This implies that the narrative strategies utilized by the earlier sections were available as models to this section's author. The three sections comprise approximately seventeen pages of *guf ha-Zohar* that have preceded this story, with the immediately preceding four pages acknowledged as part of this textual unit. Based on the comprehensive listing appended to this study, the average spacing in the *guf ha-Zohar* between walking stories (from the end of one story to the start of another) is approximately five pages. Moreover, if we eliminate the esoteric sections that punctuate the *Zohar*, which, as mentioned elsewhere, have no walking stories, and thus account for many of the larger gaps, we arrive

at an average of approximately three and a half pages between walking texts. These data point to two aspects of the collection of texts comprising *guf ha-Zohar*: it is entirely possible for the *Zohar* to proceed for many pages without a walking story; nonetheless, the *Zohar* repeatedly couches its teachings in walking stories.

4. On the *ḥevrayya*, the fellowship of Rashbi and his disciples, see Hellner-Eshed, *River Issues Forth*, chap. 2, "Rashbi's Fellowship and Its Self-Image," 77–104 (in Hebrew; in the English translation, "The Companions of Rabbi Shim'on in Their Own Eyes," 62–84), and passim. It was noticed early that just as there are ten *s'firot*, so, too, there were altogether ten members of this circle—Rashbi and nine disciples (ibid., 20; Eng., 11). See introductory remarks to Azulai, *Or ha-Ḥamah*. In his Introduction to Matt, *Zohar*, Pritzker ed., 1: lxv, Arthur Green also counts ten, but in his *Guide to the Zohar*, 71, he reduces the number to nine—Rashbi and eight disciples. Tishby, *Mishnat*, 1:71–72 (trans. Goldstein, 1:58–59), mentions the eight Companions, excluding Rashbi and R. Eleazar. See also Liebes, *Studies in the Zohar*, 20.

5. R. Pinḥas is not one of those disciples. He is identified by the *Zohar*, in other places, as Rashbi's father-in-law, although in earlier rabbinic literature, he is identified as Rashbi's son-in-law. See MTJM, 169, Tishby, Mishnat, and Matt, *Zohar: The Book of Enlightenment*, 290–291.

6. On the scriptural hermeneutics of the *Zohar*, see Wolfson, "Beautiful Maiden without Eyes" and *Through a Speculum*, chap. 7, 326–392. See also Hellner-Eshed, *River Issues Forth*, pt. 3, chap. 2, 222–236 (in Hebrew; Eng., 189–203), and 258n129 (Eng., 411n42), where Hellner-Eshed refers to the work of Moshe Idel and to the question of whether the *Zohar* saw itself or can be seen as engaging in "aggressive hermeneutics." She posits that the *Zohar* did not see itself as such. However, our discussion will suggest that the tension created by the *Zohar*'s reading is not inconsiderable.

7. 1:49b.

8. Traditional commentators assume that this refers particularly to the Traveler's Prayer, *T'filat ha-Derekh*. See Matt, *Zohar*, Pritzker ed., 1:275n1292, and Judah ben Samuel, *Sefer Ḥasidim*, ¶257 (Bologna) and ¶480 (Parma). And see *Zohar* 1:178a (#26), where the prayers recited before the journey are the statutory prayers of *Sh'ma* and the morning *'Amidah*; also 2:130b, where a person who wishes to embark on the road is told to rise when it is still dark, contemplate the stars, seeing them as letters associated with God's forty-two-letter Name and with the Priestly Blessing, and then offer his prayers and start his journey.

9. 1:50a.

10. See BT *Berakhot* 31a, *Shabbat* 30b, *Pesahim* 117a. As noted by R. Moshe Cordovero, *Pardes Rimmonim* 2:29b, the term "mitzvah" here alludes to the union of Shekhinah with Her male Partner. See 1:157a (#21).

11. See *Zohar* 1:83a, and see Rashi to both these verses.

12. See 1:115b–116a (#15).

13. See the commentary of Naḥmanides on this episode.

14. Since Abraham's denial of his own "coupling"—of his being "male and female" together—jeopardizes the Divine coupling itself, God's intervention is warranted on that count as well.

15. Gen. 12:17. This is how the *Zohar* reads the words *'al d'var* in that verse—as indicating Divine communication (*dibbur*) with Pharaoh. See 1:83a.

16. 1:50a.

17. Or "praiseworthy," or, as Matt translates, "admirable," or, most simply, "better."

18. On the erotic associations linked to the "road," see chap. 3, 76–80.

19. 1:49b–50a.

20. See Cordovero's comment to this text, as recorded in Azulai, *Or ha-Ḥamah*, 1:46a, s.v. *'ad*: "However, if he does not then pray *T'filat ha-Derekh*—for Shekhinah is called '*sh'mirat ha-derekh*,' . . ." and his subsequent comments. And see chap. 2, 39–41.

21. 1:50a. As R. Moshe Cordovero explains, here the terms "Upper and lower" are relative to one another, and do not refer to two Divine potencies, such as Binah and Shekhinah. Rather, the contrast is between Shekhinah as the "Upper Mother" and the earthly female, the wife.

22. The term *l'it'atra* conveys the meaning of being crowned, adorned, and encircled. It is also associated with Shekhinah.

23. 1:50a.

24. See, e.g., 1:115b–116a (#15). And see the discussion regarding Sarah above.

25. 1:50a.

26. Instead, they accord R. Pinḥas the honor of escorting him quite a distance and then return to resume their discussions (1:51a) In another walking story concerned with a meeting between R. Pinḥas and Rashbi (#114), the *Zohar* beautifully conveys the difference between R. Pinḥas's gentle piety and Rashbi's more forceful and questing spiritual stature.

27. Matt, *Zohar*, Pritzker ed., 1:278n1315. The phrase *la pathi pitra qamakh* conveys the idea that "none can open [*pathi*] a conclusive or dismissive argument [*pitra*] before you." R. Moshe Cordovero explains that *pitra* means "to have a chance to say [*pithon peh*] something regarding the Torah" (see Azulai, *Or ha-Ḥamah*, and *Nitzotzei Orot* in *Sefer ha-Zohar*, ed. Margaliot, ad loc.). The term *pitra* can be associated with the root *ptr*, meaning (womb) opening, dismissal, conclusion, exclamation.

28. 2:34b, as quoted by Liebes, *Studies in the Zohar*, 16, who paraphrases Rashbi's opening statement at the *Idra* in his essay "The Messiah of the *Zohar*" (ibid., 12).

29. Ibid., 72. Liebes also insightfully speculates there that this portrayal of Rashbi may take support from the second-hand information we have about R. Moshe de Leon's domestic life given to us by R. Isaac of Acre. See "Two Introductions" above and n. 38 below.

30. See chap. 2.

31. Indeed, a number of the Companions figure in a greater number of walking stories than Rashbi does. See online Appendix 2.

32. Matt's Aramaic text differs somewhat from the printed text. His translation reads: "We have already aroused our awareness of the mystery of the left and right, corresponding to the good impulse and the evil impulse" (Matt, *Zohar*, Pritzker ed., 1:274).

33. See Hellner-Eshed's discussion about words with the root *'vr* having associations with arousal, awakening, and insightful comment, *River Issues Forth*, pt. 3, chap. 3, 99, 237–267 (in Hebrew; Eng., 80–81, 204–228), and passim.

34. On the connection between the inappropriate revealing of the Torah's secrets and the prohibition against sexual immorality, see Liebes, Studies in the *Zohar*, 23–26ff.

35. Matt, *Zohar*, Pritzker ed. Matt's translation is according to his Aramaic text, corrected from among variants. It follows Tishby's reading in *Mishnat*, as he notes. Nevertheless, I believe that the punctuation of the phrase *'ad kan*—"to here"—is open to discussion. Matt reads it as the last words of a sentence. I suggest that it be detached from Rashbi's statement and read as the beginning of a demarcating note.

36. The "Introduction to the *Zohar*" is here disregarded, as explained above, n. 2. R. Eleazar is the first of the Companions mentioned, at 31a. See Matt, *Zohar*, Pritzker ed., 1:188n660.

37. Of these ten sages, R. Aḥa is missing from the ten who were present at the *Idra Rabbah*, and R. Yose b. Ya'aqov, who is listed as present at the *Idra*, is missing here.

38. Lavi, *Ketem Paz*, 129d. It is startling to read an allusion to forgery in this comment. The well-known story of Moses de Leon's acrimonious exchanges with his wife fed assertions that the *Zohar* was actually a forgery produced by de Leon. Liebes had already speculated that de Leon's domestic troubles are transposed to Rashbi's biography (see n. 29 above). Is it, perhaps, also the backdrop for this text that implicitly accepts the necessity of leaving home, despite the ideal image it offers of domestic and spiritual bliss?

39. See Rashi's comment, based on BT *Sotah* 12a, regarding the clay and tar coating of the basket in which the baby Moses' mother placed him to float on the Nile. Rashi remarks: "Tar on the outside and mud on the inside, so that such a righteous one should not smell the bad odor of the tar" (cf. Exod. 2:3).

40. See *Zohar* 2:11b–12, 3:174a, and *Zohar Ḥadash* 35a, where the double coating of Moses' ark is seen as a symbol of the dual nature of Torah, with positive and negative commandments, or of Grace and Rigor. The ark itself is also a common reference to Shekhinah as container or protector. This biblical story, which tells of the marriage of Moses' righteous parents and his subsequent conception, is also tied to God's defeat of the evil Leviathan by depriving him of his female mate. The double coating of white and black is a protection "against those sea fish who swim in the Great Sea" (3:174a).

41. See Hellner-Eshed, *River Issues Forth*, pt. 3, chap. 3, 78–83 (in Hebrew; Eng., 63–67).

Chapter 2. Walking with God

1. Eliade, *History of Religious Ideas*, 1:3.

2. 1:158a. This is based on BT *Berakhot* 13b. See Matt's note for additional citations. See also in Gruenwald, "Some Critical Notes," *Sefer Yetzirah* 1:7 (493–494), and 1:15 (509–510). The *Zohar* doubles these six directions by linking the spatial nature of this world with the Upper World's, for an additional six directions. These twelve directions are reflected in Jacob's twelve sons and in the two sentences that begin the *Sh'ma*, each comprised of six words. Deut. 6:4, "Listen, Israel . . . ," refers to the Upper World. The rabbinically ordained phrase "Blessed is the Name . . ." refers to the Lower World. In doing this, the *Zohar* establishes a vertical pole that overrides the original picture of the horizontal nature of the four-directional spread of the world. See chap. 3.

3. It is interesting that Michel de Certeau, *Mystic Fable*, 81, in discussing the difference between the Jewish tradition, "anchored in their biological and social reality," and the Christian tradition, "founded on *the loss of a body*—the loss of the body of Jesus Christ, compounded with the loss of the 'body' of Israel, of a 'nation' and its genealogy," reads this verse from a Christian perspective as referring, not to bodily displacement, but to disappearance of the body.

4. Rashi ad loc., based on *Sifra*, *B'ḥuqqotai*, 3:3.

5. Joseph of Hamadan, *Sefer Tashak*, ed. Zwelling, 452. While Joseph of Hamadan does not include walking texts of the *Zohar*, still, in a different way, walking is very significant for him. He gives extensive attention to the theme of the legs, shoes, and movement of the divine pleroma. See from 328 to the end of the book. In his striking exposition (412–413), it is the movement of the Chariot creatures that causes the movement of human beings on earth. This is in keeping with his pantheistic orientation. Any mention of human walking is secondary to his concentration on the supernal. See 208–209, 408. On the relation of this work to the *Zohar*, see the editor's introduction, and see Liebes, *Studies in the Zohar*, 103ff.

6. Noah—Gen. 6:9; Abraham—17:1, 24:40, and 48:15; Isaac—48:15; Enoch—5:22, 24.

7. Ps. 116:9.

8. Deut. 6:7.

9. Tene, "Darkhei," 10–11.

10. As Wolfson notes in his essay on Hasidic walking practices, "Walking as a Sacred Duty," in his *Along the Path*, 224n3, also included in the anthology *Hasidism Reappraised*, ed. Ada Rapoport-Albert (London: Littman Library of Jewish Civilization, 1997), 180–207, the Aramaic term *'azl*, like the Hebrew term *hlk*, can mean "walk," "go," "ride," "travel," etc. These terms are used interchangeably in this study unless there is a clear indication of which means of locomotion is intended by the text. This ambiguity is not limited to this literature alone. It has been remarked that it is not always clear from pilgrim accounts whether their journey was by foot or by conveyance. See also Pachter, "Bein laylah le-voqer," 314n13; Debra J. Birch, *Pilgrimage to Rome in the Middle Ages: Continuity and Change* (Rochester, NY: Boydell Press, 1998), 58–60; Sumption, *Pilgrimage*, 127.

11. So also, e.g., 2:14a: "R. Ḥiyya Rabba was going to the Masters of the Mishnah to learn from them. He went to R. Shim'on ben Yoḥai and saw . . ." (A parallel text was published by M. Idel, "Qeta' lo noda' mi-Midrash ha-Ne'elam," 79ff. in Dan, ed., *Meḥqerei Yerushalayim be-maḥshevet yisra'el*.) For a discussion of this text, see E. Fishbane, "Tears of Disclosure," esp. 35ff.

12. Meroz, "Path of Silence," has found at least one more walking story that was not included in the *Zohar* as we have it.

13. The total number of texts emerges from the enumeration of the texts listed in Appendix 1, from which the data cited in the following discussion are culled. To get an idea of how abundantly this walking motif is used, consider that in all of the standard rabbinic literature (Mishnah, Tosefta, the two Talmuds, and halakhic and aggadic midrashim), a literature many, many times vaster than the *Zohar*, there are, by my count, about 124 texts with comparable literary elements. Thus, the *Zohar* has as many walking stories as all rabbinic literature combined. For a more thorough discussion of the

relationship between the *Zohar* and these rabbinic precedents, see Greenstein, "Aimless Pilgrimage," 182–189 and Appendix VII, 591–615. On the question of the midrash *Tanna debe Eliyahu*, see ibid., Appendix VII.F, 616–621.

14. In the *Zohar* proper, there are twenty-one texts stating "R. A was going from place *x* to place *y*." There are another eight texts that tell us that the rabbi was traveling "to place *x*," without saying where he was coming from. In *MH*, there are two "from *x* to *y*" texts and two "to *x*" texts. There is one "from *x* to *y*" text in *Tosefta*. See online Appendix 3, A.9 and B.11.

15. Four in *MH*; one in *Tosefta*. Scholem, "She'elot be-viqoret," 44, notes that stories about going to visit someone are "very common in the *Zohar*, but are always referring to distances that are not too great."

16. In the *Zohar*, ##58, 116, 117. In *MH*, ##5, 7, 9. In *ZH*, #21. All text numbers are from Appendix 1. See also online Appendix 3, A.10.e. and B.12.e.

17. 3:39a (#85). On the various places mentioned in the *Zohar*, see the lists compiled by Scholem in "She'elot be-viqoret."

18. 2:86a (text #62). Margaliot assumes that Lod was Rashbi's place (see *Nitzotzei Zohar* in *Sefer ha-Zohar*, ed. Margaliot, at 1:69b, n. *heh*), so that when texts tell of sages traveling to Lod, we are to understand that they are traveling to visit Rashbi. Of course, the *Zohar* also places Rashbi in other locales, such as Tiberias. (See Meroz, "R'qimato," 188n81, and her distinction between "Tiberias stories" and "Qapotqiya stories.") On the location of these places, real or imaginary, see Scholem, "She'elot be-viqoret" and Margaliot's counterarguments in his essay of the same title. Scholem's rejoinder to Margaliot is found in *MTJM*, 389n64. Tishby summarizes the discussion in *Mishnat*, 1:75–76. See also Matt, *Zohar*, Pritzker ed., 1:409n508.

19. Sages reach their friends or teachers in six out of fifteen cases, while in one case, #115, the successful completion of the journey is not found in the *Zohar*, but in its continuation in *ZH* (#22). Online Appendix 2a.

20. In one story (*MH* #4), R. Ele'azar goes to visit his father-in-law, R. Yose b. R. Shim'on Laqonya, but when he arrives, his father-in-law is not there. Soon, however, R. Yose comes home. The story has a playful quality, utilizing teasing, coincidence, and a closing message extolling the need to rejoice. On playfulness and humor in the *Zohar*, see 181–186. And see the discussion in chap. 5 of a story in which R. Abba does not reach his destination (#13).

21. Writing about one elaborate walking story, #115, Tene, "Darkhei," 152, observes:

> At first sight it would seem that the case of walking is a case of progression in motion: being between the point of departure and the point of arrival. But this, it seems, is not "actual" movement in the geographical sense, since it lacks clear parameters of space and time. The locational definition loses its force in the absence of a point of departure or a defined goal. Though originally there is a purpose to the walking (to visit R. Eleazar's father-in-law), already in the first narrative section . . . they veer away from the original goal and reach another place, the *yenuqa*'s house. Furthermore, the overall story concludes without their arriving at any set place, for after the visit with the *yenuqa* the Companions once again go out on the road—"they kissed that *yenuqa*, blessed him and went."

22. See the listing in online Appendix 3.

23. 1:5b (#2). See online Appendix 2a. The phrase *le'itat'qena*, which I have translated as "set ourselves," is a form of the term *tiqqun*, an important term in the extended zoharic literature. Drawing on earlier usages, the zoharic authors endowed the term with various related meanings. The basic meanings include "make straight, firm, right, to mend or put in order, or prepare" (Jastrow, *Dictionary*, 2: 1691–1692). It can refer to the preparations of a woman or bride to meet her partner. Thus *Targum Sheni* renders the Hebrew phrase *u-vetamruqei ha-nashim* in Esther 2:12, translated by JPS as "women's cosmetics," as *u-vetiqqunei neshaya*. These meanings were applied by the zoharic authors to the Shekhinah, to all the *sefirot*, and to the ways the Associates could relate to them, influence them, or even embody them. See Liebes, "Peraḳim be-milon," 197–198, 238, and "Messiah of the *Zohar*," in his *Studies in the Zohar*; Wolfson, *Circle*, 68, 164, and passim; Giller, *Enlightened*, 130n6, and *Reading the Zohar*, 92–95.

24. 1:58b (#5).

25. Lavi, *Ketem Paz* 1:145b, s.v. *Sham, R. Shim'on*.

26. See Appendix 1. In two of those texts—4 and 121—he travels alone.

27. Lavi, *Ketem Paz* 1:171c, on *Zohar* 1:69b (#9), s.v. *Sham verso, R. Ḥizqiyah*.

28. For lists of zoharic texts that have one rabbi traveling, see online Appendices 2a and 2b. In some zoharic texts that have one rabbi traveling, he continues alone, but in others he meets another sage, who joins him.

29. See Meroz, "R'qimato," 187–193, for a characterization of "Qapotqiya stories."

30. Margaliot, *Nitzotzei Zohar*, in *Sefer ha-Zohar*, ed. id., n. 7, ad loc., cites two talmudic parallels, but neither says what R. Yeisa says. The text in BT *Eruvin* 54a is a suggestion that if one has no company to offer protection, one should learn Torah. It is contradicted by the implication of the text at *Ta'anit* 10b, which says that only when traveling with a companion must one study Torah. The inference to be drawn is that a lone person is not so obligated.

31. 1:69b (#9).

32. Lavi, *Ketem Paz* 1:171c.

33. This is missing in the parallel to this story, *ZH* 77d (*Rut*) (#25). On the playful element in the *Zohar*, see citations in n. 20 above and Liebes, "*Zohar* ve-eros," 80–85.

34. 1:70a. The gesture of bestowing a kiss on a younger person for relating a teaching is found at the end of *Exodus Rabbah* 52 (and *Song Rabbah* 3:21), where R. Shim'on bar Yoḥai kisses the son of R. Yose ha-G'lili for saying a teaching of his father's. (Rashbi's exclamation, "Had I not come except to hear this explanation, it would have sufficed," is found occasionally in rabbinic texts—see BT *Berakhot* 16a and parallels cited there—and is echoed frequently in zoharic stories. Of course, in that case, Rashbi knows that he is asking for the teaching of a great authority, and there is no element of surprise or competition.) These sages also occasionally kiss each other after one of them delivers a discourse. See Tene, "Darkhei," 150–151. This motif of kissing is to be distinguished from the mystical motif, discussed by Hellner-Eshed, *River Issues Forth*, 352–357 (in Hebrew; Eng., 296–300). See also Hecker, "Kissing Kabbalists," for an extensive discussion.

35. This is the first place in the story where the youth is referred to as *yenuqa*. There are a number of *yenuqa* stories in the *Zohar*, including one section bearing that title. See

MTJM, 161 and notes, and Matt, *Zohar: The Book of Enlightenment*, 286. They do not include this text in their list of sources. However, it exhibits, in a mild form, the ironic element present in the other texts. See Liebes, "*Zohar* ve-eros," 89, n. 144. For an extended treatment of *yenuqa* stories, see M. Oron, "The Motif of the Yanuqa ('The Child') in the *Zohar*," in *Ḥiddushei Zohar*, ed. Meroz, 129–164. She discusses this story on 135–137. And see Jonatan Benarroch, "'Yanuqa' and 'Sabba'—Two That Are One: Allegory, Symbol and Myth in Zoharic Literature" (diss., Hebrew University, 2011; in Hebrew).

36. On the nature of Shekhinah's accompaniment, see the discussion in chap. 1 above.

37. *Malkhut* or Shekhinah. See 1:52a.

38. The phrase "and God"—*va-YHVH*—signifies "He and His Court" (= Shekhinah). See 2:37b, 3:149a. (Margaliot, *Nitzotzei Zohar*, in *Sefer ha-Zohar*, ed. id., ad loc., cites *Exodus Rabbah* 12:4 as a parallel. But this is already preceded by *Bereshit Rabbah* 51:2. See Theodor's citations, ad loc., for other sources. And see Wolfson, "Left Contained in the Right," 38n54.) The term thus indicates that two aspects of God are working together. The other aspect is signified by the Tetragrammaton, signifying *Tiferet*. The union of these two grades is explained in the notes of *Nitzozei Orot* to mean that the female is incorporated into the male when they are united (a major subject in the studies of E. R. Wolfson). On the involvement of *Tiferet*, rather than Shekhinah, in the act of walking, see 41, 44.

39. *Tzedeq*. This term is usually taken to refer to Shekhinah. See 3:65a.

40. 1:76a (#10). For a list of walking stories that open with an invitation to Torah study, see online Appendix 3, A.5.

41. See 2:17b (#50), and see also 44–55, "The Case of R. Yose."

42. Lavi, *Ketem Paz* 1:190b–c, s.v. *Daf 76a R. Yose*.

43. See chap. 6, 205–214.

44. R. Yose's statement is somewhat ambiguous. He first refers to any person—whether righteous or not—who walks on the road, and then mentions a righteous person. However, since, as he continues, one's righteousness is defined here in negative terms, as refraining from *'ervat davar*—one is presumably righteous until proven otherwise. Compare PT *Qiddushin* 1:10 (61d): "Said R. Mana, 'Fortunate are the innocent of the road . . .'" (Ps. 119:1).

45. Shekhinah is associated with "speech." See, e.g., *Zohar* 1:25a. See *ZH* 41b–c and Wolfson's discussion of this text, "Erasing the Erasure," in id., *Circle*, 72–74, concerning the priority of the visual over the auditory.

46. See Wolfson, *Through a Speculum*, 274, n. 14, 357–368; id., "Eunuchs," 166–167; id., "The Image of Jacob," esp. 57, in *Along the Path*, "Coronation of the Sabbath Bride." Wolfson's approach has met with some resistance. See, e.g., M. Idel, *Absorbing Perfections: Kabbalah and Interpretation* (New Haven, CT: Yale University Press, 2002), 580n135. Arthur Green's *Keter: The Crown of God in Early Jewish Mysticism* (Princeton, NJ: Princeton University Press, 1997) can be read as an attempt to present an alternate understanding of this image, purged of the erotic charge that Wolfson has shown to be so significant.

47. Wolfson, "Eunuchs," 166–167.

48. But see 1:58b–59a (#5), a closely parallel teaching. There the attention is given

to the person who refuses to follow this regimen. He is a *sakhal*—a fool—who denies the meaning of the Torah's teachings and rites, such as circumcision. Such a person "even on the road, when he travels, will not study words of Torah, so that, as a result, his heart is empty and he does not walk with his Master and is not found on His path." Apparently, the lack of Torah study is indicative of this person's wickedness. Moreover, he is foolhardy to neglect Torah study on the road, the most dangerous time for a person without merit. In this text, Torah study is conceived of as a prophylactic and an indicator of character. But this is not the expression of a fundamental imperative relating to walking on the road. See also 3:80a.

49. 2:232b (#77).

50. See n. 75 below.

51. See 3:81a: "Come and see. One who wishes to be sanctified as his Master desires should not engage in intercourse except from midnight on. . . . This is for all other people, but for students of sages, who know the paths of Torah, midnight is their time to rise and study Torah, to couple with *Knesset Yisra'el*, to praise the Holy Name of the Holy King." See Wolfson, "Eunuchs."

52. Wolfson, *Through a Speculum*, 374, and "Forms of Visionary Ascent," 227ff.

53. Cordovero, *Zohar 'im Perush Or Yaqar*, 5: 29a, s.v. *bekhol zimna*, commenting on *Zohar* 1:157a (#21). See also his *Tomer Devorah* (Jerusalem, 1969), chap. 9, where he identifies Shekhinah with *sh'mirat ha-derekh*.

54. Cordovero, *Zohar 'im Perush Or Yaqar*, 6: 39a, s.v. *u-vegin kakh*, on *Zohar* 1:178a (#26).

55. On this detail, see chap. 3.

56. 2:155b (#69).

57. Azulai, *Or ha-Ḥamah* 2:192b, s.v. *R. Yose ve-R. Ḥiyya*.

58. See Sack, *B'sha'arei ha-qabbalah shel R. Moshe Qordovero*, 17–21, 217–220, 226–227, 264–266. See also Fine, "Contemplative Practice," 82, who connects Cordovero's *gerushin* to the zoharic stories of visiting graves, rather than to the walking motif. See also Giller, "Recovering the Sanctity," 156–159.

59. Wolfson, "Walking as a Sacred Duty: Theological Transformation of Social Reality in Early Hasidism," in his *Along the Path*, 91. This essay explicates the significance of walking as an act and as an image in early Hasidism.

60. Sack, *B'sha'arei ha-qabbalah*, 217, 246.

61. Liebes deals with this aspect of *zohar* in his "*Zohar* ve-eros."

62. See Sack, *B'sha'arei ha-qabbalah*, 18–20.

63. See, e.g., ##18, 21, 22, 23, 25, 35, 38, 40, etc.

64. Lit., "to the villages." This translation is based on Azulai, *Or ha-Ḥamah*, citing Rashi to BT *Berakhot* and *Pesaḥim*. See Matt, *Zohar*, Pritzker ed., 2: 368n391.

65. Tishby, *Mishnat*, 1:3, adopts this translation. Matt, *Zohar*, Pritzker ed., prefers "They sat for three days." The printed text offers both variants.

66. 1:155b (#20).

67. Lavi, *Ketem Paz* 2:312b, s.v. *R. Shim'on*.

68. The relation between the walking motif and the *beit midrash* is explored in chap. 4.

69. Engaging the presence of Shekhinah or discussing Her actions and manifesta-

tions occupies over half of the walking texts in the *guf ha-Zohar*. Sometimes reference is to *Qudesha Berikh Hu* and not Shekhinah. See Meroz, "Path of Silence," 330–331. See online Appendix 3, A.8, and for the other strata, ibid., B.10. And see also n. 38 above.

70. See 37 above.

71. 2:17b (*MH*) (#50).

72. This is in keeping with its provenance in the *Midrash ha-Ne'elam*, a relatively early and more straightforward zoharic text.

73. Meroz, "Path of Silence," 323, erroneously states that the snake really bit R. Yose. This is not in the text. Her reading misses the story's ironic humor.

74. E.g., 2:6b.

75. 1:117b–118a.

76. See also 3:6b–7a, where R. Yose takes a pratfall into some water. Emerging, he angrily curses the water, only to be admonished by Rashbi that he must learn to honor every aspect of God's creation. See also 1:176b, as discussed in chap. 5, 182.

77. 2:198a–217b (#74).

78. Similarly, R. Ele'azar greets the three Companions he meets on the road by saying, "Indeed, I see the Face of Shekhinah" (2:163b). See Wolfson, *Through a Speculum*, 368–372, for a discussion of "The Mystical Fellowship as Constitution of the Divine Face." The Companions also identify Rashbi with the Face of Shekhinah. See 3:79b (cited in Wolfson, *Through a Speculum*, 372n157). See also 1:223a (#34). It is noteworthy that the verse from Hosea is the prooftext for the talmudic homilies on *imitatio dei* when quoted in the *She'iltot* (3 vols.; Jerusalem: Kook, 1969), nos. 3, 34, 104. The unease about the *Zohar*'s explicit identification of the sage with the Divine was forcefully expressed by R. Jacob Emden. See Pachter, "Bein laylah le-voqer," 339, and his references to R. Margaliot and Y. Liebes. See also E. Fishbane, "Scent," 332–334. It may be that the celebration of the Companions' appearance in terms of the Face of the Divine Presence, found explicitly in 2:163b and 2:198a, depends on the coming together of four sages. In each of these cases, three sages meet up with a fourth, at which point the celebration is expressed. Perhaps the four sages constitute a chariot upon which the Shekhinah may rest.

79. R. Abba discusses the relationship between cities and their leaders. The righteous are willing to be broken in suffering for God's sake. He applies this teaching to the Companions and extols them, "you supernal holy ones, who suffer physical breakdown going from place to place for the sake of the Holy Blessed One, how much more so do you deserve that miracles and salvation be performed for you, and that you may merit life in the Coming World."

80. R. Abba again praises the Companions for their exceptional spiritual powers, discussing the institution of gifts to the Tabernacle (*t'rumah*).

81. R. Abba discusses the ordering of subsequent history as programmed in the original six days of Creation. This includes the story of Jonah and the Great Fish (199a): "Here we have some support for the actions of people in this world." There follows an elaborate homily on Jonah as a symbol for the human soul. He ends with emphasizing the importance of repentance before death. For a translation and commentary on this section, see Wineman, *Mystic Tales*, 107–125.

82. On the motif of the Companions' kissing, see n. 34 above.

83. This reading is to be distinguished from Joel Hecker's discussions of the theurgic significance of embodiment in the *Zohar* in "Mystical Eating and Food Practices," in *Judaism in Practice*, ed. Fine, 353. He writes that, "mundane realities have an immediate effect upon and relationship to the divine realms. Ultimately the mundane serves as an entryway or portal to these supernal reaches." While this may be true concerning certain mystical practices, his description does not fit our scenario. Here the mundane is not a gateway, but a divergence, a turn away from ascent toward the celebration of the capacities of the Companions to attain such theosophical insight and power.

84. [200a] He returns to the subject of *t'rumah*. The Torah is God's supernal Palace. Torah study is the means to be saved from all suffering, whether in this world or the next. He then moves into more esoteric, theosophical realms. *T'rumah* signifies the uplifting of the lower Divine realms towards the higher realms.

[200b] He proceeds to discuss the order and meaning of the traditional morning prayers, crediting "the Holy Lamp," Rashbi. "I was not given permission to reveal this, except to you, supernal pious ones."

85. R. Abba voices a similar concern at 2:23b and see the references collected by R. Margaliot in *Nitzotzei Zohar*, in *Sefer ha-Zohar*, ed. id., ad loc., n. 3. See chap. 3, at n. 224, and chap. 5, at n. 15 and references there.

86. Men who are "wise of heart" (Exod. 35:10) are rare. Service of the heart is greater than any service of the body. The secrets of inner spiritual service, of the 13 inner organs of the spirit, has been taught by Rashbi and "are known among the Companions. How fortunate is their portion!" [201b] Israel's words of prayer, fittingly offered, ascend and are kissed by the celestial officials, who occupy the four directions of heaven. They, in turn, praise Israel.

[202a] The prayers ascend to the 13 gates. They rise through each heaven and the celestial hosts bow in reverence before them, including those forces that opposed the granting of the Torah to humans, below. [202b] For the prayers to ascend through the 7 Palaces, a person must be aware of the various commanded purposes of each section of the service. The ultimate commandment is to be willing to give up one's life to God.

87. It will have to suffice merely to note that the teaching dealing with the subjugation of the Other Side during Shabbat also employs much spatial imagery. Other *Heikhalot*-related teachings included in this string of discourses also encompass much spatial description and action.

88. [204a] On Shabbat eve a person must wash himself off from all mundane usage. The six profane days belong to the other nations, but the six days, when connected to Shabbat, belong to Israel.

[204b] The spiritual gift of an extra soul enables Israel to endow its material and physical enjoyments on Shabbat—its eating and drinking, etc.—with theurgic power.

[205a] A special type of extra soul is granted to the "wise ones who know the mysteries of Wisdom." They know that the union to be effected on Shabbat night is preferable because it is more inclusive than that of other evenings of the week. The evening of Shabbat is also endowed with a special quality of Divine protection. Nevertheless, in practical terms, a person should not go out alone on either Wednesday night or Friday

night. On Wednesday night the danger of lurking evil forces is too great. On Friday night, even though there is an overall "Sukkah of Peace" protecting Israel, an individual person who does not take care to maintain that Divine Crown may be unlucky and be assaulted by evil forces. The day of Shabbat is a day of spiritual joy, a day of the soul, not the body.

[205b] It is given over to songs and praises of God. Anyone who engages in mundane matters [*milin de'alma*] on Shabbat is guilty of desecrating Shabbat and has no portion in the people of Israel or the Holy Blessed One. The morning prayers of Nishmat and 'El 'Adon are explicated in terms of their theurgic effect. The higher celestial letters are more spacious than their counterparts below. The rest of the prayers are mentioned and the Torah service presents the opportunity to expound upon the meaning of the Torah. This continues to 207a. Then the discourse returns to matters of Sabbath observance and the transition from Shabbat back into the mundane week.

[207a] "No person may leave his place on the Seventh day" (Exod. 16:29). "Place" alludes to Shekhinah. One who walks away from God desecrates the Sabbath.

[208ab] The ritual of Havdalah is discussed. The "outer" fingernails designate the outer forces that derive benefit from the lower lights. But the "inner" fingers derive benefit from the supernal source of light.

89. On this theme, see chap. 3.

90. Cf. *Avot* 3:14.

91. On the motif of weeping in the *Zohar*, see Fishbane, "Tears of Disclosure," who studies examples of weeping by personae who reveal mystical teachings, such as Rashbi and the Sabba de Mishpatim. He ties the act of weeping to the emotional stress inherent in the tension between the imperatives of revelation and concealment that characterizes the *Zohar*'s project. But our case involves those who hear these teachings, not those who reveal them.

92. The title "Master of the Countenance" is associated with various angelic beings. See *Nitzotzei Zohar*, in *Sefer ha-Zohar*, ed. Margaliot, ad loc. The Aramaic term used here, *'anpin*, means "face." But the Hebrew word for face, *panim*, can also be read *p'nim*—"inside"—making the angel the "Prince of the Interior."

93. A long discourse follows, continuing to page 214a. It deals with the various heavens and their relation to the lower world, moving to the topic of the righteous in the Garden of Eden who are rewarded for their good deeds and Torah study. Others are punished. The Messiah bears the suffering of the righteous and the sinful. Only the select few who "enter and exit" comprehend the mystical truths and means of Divine union. During nocturnal sleep, the soul ascends and enters into a supernal process of renewal. By morning, it is reborn.

94. On the phrase "enter and exit," see Hellner-Eshed, *River Issues Forth*, pt. 3, chap. 3, 78–83 (in Hebrew; Eng., 63–67).

95. Although the Companions have already explained the meaning of the Ark (*'aron*) of the Covenant (Shekhinah) in "the Holy Idra," there is more to say. The ark, to contain the Torah, must have six sides. The place of the ark, where the Binding of Isaac happened, had to change hands, moving out of the Other Side, in order for King David to repossess it for sacred purposes. A coffin (*'aron*) is only to be used for righteous people.

96. The recording of this outburst momentarily interrupts the discourse and heightens its pathos. Here the person weeping is, indeed, the person teaching, and not the listener. Yet it is questionable whether the context justifies seeing this as an example of the cases discussed by Fishbane, cited above, n. 91.

97. This refers to circumcision and proper sexual thoughts and behavior as a prerequisite for a relationship with the Divine. See Wolfson's numerous studies. Only the supernal Pietists ascend with both soul and body. Only they may see Shekhinah, for they did not sin against the Covenant.

98. There has been no prior indication that they were traveling to their teacher.

99. On the expression *sidru milin*, see chap. 5, n. 38, below.

100. Rashbi discourses on the theme of roads and pathways: "'The path of the righteous' is the path of truth, the path that the Holy Blessed One delights in, the path along which the righteous proceed, with the Almighty, as it were, leading the way, whilst all the heavenly legions come down to listen to their expositions and teachings; 'as the light of dawn', that is, as a light that continues without ever darkening, as opposed to the way of sinners, whose way always darkens, as it says, 'The way of the wicked is like the darkness,' etc."

He then distinguishes between a "road" (*derekh*), which is the way of popular convention, and a "way" (*oraḥ*), which is the newly opened way of innovation trod by the righteous. For a similar teaching, see chap. 3, "The Spatial Orientation of the Zohar," at nn. 109, 125. See also Hellner-Eshed, *River Issues Forth*, 146–148, 235–236 (in Hebrew; Eng., 118–120, 202–203).

101. See the beginning of chap. 4.

102. A discourse about Moses as the Sun (Divine Masculine) and Joshua as the Moon (Divine Feminine) and their eventual unification, as indicated by Joshua's ordination by Moses. This process entails spatial construction and expansion.

103. R. Shim'on's teachings continue for a couple of pages. He offers a discourse on the necessity for prayer before eating anything in the morning. The spiritual must preempt the physical. Rashbi praises "you supernal holy ones" for understanding and practicing this and for understanding the inner intention of the morning prayers.

[216a] "How fortunate is my portion with you in this world and in the world to come. The commandments of the Torah regarding prayer are certainly the way you said." The discourse moves to consider fear and love of God.

[216b] A discourse on the proper mystical recitation of Sh'ma, credited to Elijah and to Rav Hamnuna Sabba. The intent must be to unify the six spatial directions. This unification is not final, since Shekhinah is in exile. She is not divorced from God, only sent to accompany Israel.

[217a] Rashbi explains the intentions of the liturgy leading to the Amidah prayer and the Qedushah prayers. He again extols the Companions: "The secret of handing over one's soul to one's Master is well said by you, Friends. How fortunate is your portion and how fortunate are my eyes who saw thus. For I have merited in my life that these words are aroused in this world and all are written above before the Holy King." Rashbi pictures the delight that the King takes in these words. This description applies "in the Lower Firmament, as you said, Companions. How fortunate is my portion and

how fortunate is your portion." The words of the mystics arise to create an image "in the likeness of Adam."

[217b] This image is the image of the righteous who adorn themselves with these words.

104. On physiognomy in the *Zohar*, see Ron Margolin, "Physiognomy and Chiromancy: From Prediction and Diagnosis to Healing and Human Correction" (*Zohar* 2, 70a–78a; *Tiqqunei Zohar, Tiqqun* 70) (in Hebrew), in *Ḥiddushei Zohar*, ed. Meroz, 199–249. His study does not discuss this text.

105. The text that follows is merely tangential to this story, explaining Rashbi's special powers of observation, illustrated by our episode.

106. BT *Ḥaggigah* 14b. See n. 94 regarding the phrase "enter and exit."

Chapter 3. The Spatial Orientation of the Zohar

1. On the *Zohar*'s pantheistic tendency, see Scholem, *Kabbalah*, 144ff., esp. 147–148. And see J. Ben-Shlomo, "Gershom Scholem on Pantheism in the Kabbala," 56–72, in *Gershom Scholem: The Man and His Work*, ed. Paul Mendes-Flohr (Albany: State University of New York Press; Jerusalem: Israel Academy of Sciences and Humanities, 1994). For an expanded Hebrew version, see id., "On Pantheism in Jewish Mysticism According to Gershom Scholem and His Critics," *Da'at* 50–52 (2003): 461–481.

2. For a discussion of the *Zohar*'s elaborate system of "palaces" (*heikhalot*) that serve as buffer zones between the divine and the mundane worlds, see Greenstein, "Aimless Pilgrimage," 209–229.

3. For treatments of the spatial orientations of the biblical, rabbinic, and German pietistic periods, see ibid., chap. 1, 33–100.

4. Notice that it has already become impossible to avoid spatial terms and images.

5. Tishby, *Mishnat*, 1:381. Tishby's entire section 3 is devoted to various aspects of the zoharic teachings about the world below the deity.

6. Ibid., 390.

7. Gottlieb, "Litfisat beri'at ha- 'olam be-torat ha-qabbalah," in *Meḥqarim*, 18. The essay goes on to discuss the lengths to which kabbalists such as R. 'Azriel and, following him, R. Moshe ibn Gabbai, went to deny that any reality could exist outside of God. For a comparative analysis of various kabbalists' understandings of *Ma'aseh Bereshit*, and specifically considering the question of the relation between God and the mundane world, see Michal Kushnir-Oron, "Ha-'Peli'ah' ve-ha-'Qanah'—yesodot ha-qabbalah she-bahem, 'emdatam ha-datit ḥevratit ve-derekh 'itzuvam ha-sifrutit" (diss., Hebrew University of Jerusalem, 1980), chap. 3, 116–229.

8. 1 Kings 8:27–53.

9. For Maimonides' attempts to interpret spatial terms as applied to God, see *Guide for the Perplexed*, bk. 1, chaps. 8–13, 15, 17–28. For a clear exposition of how embodiment and spatiality imply each other, see Jung, "Feminism and Spatiality."

10. See, e. g., John 14:2. BT *Ḥaggigah* 5b. In "Religious Authority and Mysticism," in his *On the Kabbalah and Its Symbolism*, 12, Scholem cites an image transmitted by Origen of "Talmudic mystics" comparing the Torah to a house with many, many rooms. On the phrase *ḥadrei ha-merkavah*—the rooms of the Chariot, see J. Dan, "Ḥadrei

Ha-Merkavah," *Tarbiz* 47 (1978): 49–55. Pedaya, "Divinity as Place and Time," discusses images and ideas from the apocalyptic and Merkavah literatures, and formulates a variety of approaches adopted for seeing God in space or as space, including considerations of kabbalistic and later Jewish mystical thought. In discussing kabbalistic approaches, however, she explicitly refrains from discussing the *Zohar.*

11. E.g., Ps. 5:8. 26:8. The traditional prayer book calls for these verses to be recited upon entering the synagogue.

12. On the relation, or lack thereof, between apocalypticism and Merkavah mysticism, see, among others, Ithamar Gruenwald, *From Apocalypticism to Gnosticism: Studies in Apocalypticism, Merkavah Mysticism and Gnosticism* (New York: Peter Lang, 1988); Halperin, *Faces of the Chariot*, 63–114; Martha Himmelfarb, "Heavenly Ascent and the Relationship of the Apocalypses and the *Hekhalot* Literature," *Hebrew Union College Annual* 59 (1998):73–100; Peter Schäfer, "The Aim and Purpose of Early Jewish Mysticism," in his *Hekhalot-Studien* (Tubingen: Mohr, 1988), 289–295.

13. See sources cited in the preceding note, as well as, among others, Scholem, *Jewish Gnosticism*; Y. Liebes, "de Natura Dei—'al ha-mitos ha-yehudi ve-gilgulo," in *Massu'ot*, ed. Oron and Goldreich, 243–297; Wolfson, *Through a Speculum*, chaps. 1 and 3; C. R. A. Morrey-Jones, "Transformational Mysticism in the Apocalyptic-Merkabah Tradition," *Journal of Jewish Studies* 43, no. 1 (Spring 1992): 1–31; A. Goshen Gottstein, "Is *Ma'aseh Bereshit* Part of Jewish Mysticism?" *Journal of Jewish Thought and Philosophy* 4 (1995):185–204. This last study includes an interesting instance of the erasure of spatial terminology through reinterpretation. Gottstein shows how the terms "what is above and what is below, etc." in M*Ḥaggigah* 2:1 have been read as anthropomorphic or temporal terms, rather than as spatial terms.

14. For a discussion of the religious culture of the German Pietists as a precursor of the *Zohar*, and of the Pietists' approach to spatiality, see Greenstein, "Aimless Pilgrimage," 74–96.

15. Quoted in Wolfson, *Through a Speculum*, 59. Wolfson's work establishes the strong role of vision in the predominantly kataphatic Jewish mystical tradition. This approach entails some kind of recognition of spatiality as a fundamental category—not only of expression, but of being. See Greenstein, "Aimless Pilgrimage," chap. 1, 78–79n166.

16. For a discussion of the fundamentally kataphatic nature of early kabbalah, see Wolfson, "Negative Theology and Positive Assertion."

17. Tishby, *Mishnat*, 1:416.

18. See, e.g., M. Idel, "Ha-Sefirot she-me'al ha-sefirot," *Tarbiz* 51 (1982): 239–280.

19. 1:15a. Translated by D. Matt in his *Zohar: The Book of Enlightenment*, 49, and see his notes on the text for the sefirotic symbolism. The more recent translation of Matt, *Zohar*, Pritzker ed. (1: 109–110), is substantially the same. For another text that describes creation in terms of the *butzina* going forth, making pathways and roads and eventually constructing a house, see 1:172a. On the notion of the house as a place whose very spatiality is secure, see the *Zohar*'s discussion below on the difference between the Tabernacle and the Temple. And see discussion of the imperative to stay home rather than go out on the road, *Zohar* 1:49b–51a (#3) in chap. 1 above.

20. On this image in the *Bahir*, see Scholem, *Origins*, 68–80, and Wolfson, "The Tree

That Is All: Jewish-Christian Roots of a Kabbalistic Symbol in *Sefer ha-Bahir*," in his *Along the Path*, 63–88,187–223.

21. The term *aḥid* plays on the connotations of the Hebrew word *eḥad* ("oneness") and the Aramaic term *aḥad*, "taking hold, joining together."

22. 3:148b.

23. As Altmann, in distinguishing the philosophical idea of emanation from the kabbalistic idea of the *sefirot*, has pointed out: "Reality is not seen as unidimensional, but in perspective. Hence the phenomenon of emanation in Jewish mysticism does not have the character of a series or succession but of space, of multidimensionality. Seen from this perspective, it becomes possible to understand the symbol of the sefirotic tree and the odd localization of the principles in space" (Altmann, "Maimonides's Attitude toward Jewish Mysticism," 213). In other words, it is not enough to say that God is present in the dimensional world He created. Nor is it enough to say that God is the space in which creation exists. But, by saying that God's attributes exist in spatial relation, the mystic posits an essential spatiality to a Creator God.

24. See Wolfson, "Left Contained in the Right."

25. See the discussion and sources cited at the beginning of this chapter.

26. On the various meanings of this term, see the summary by Tishby, *Mishnat*, 1:387–388. Scholars have noted that the kabbalists inverted the meaning of this term from its original philosophical denotation, so that, for the kabbalists, it signaled the separation of that world from the Godhead.

27. On the subject of the *Sitra Aḥra*, see ibid., 285–377; Scholem, "*Sitra Aḥra*: Good and Evil in the Kabbalah," 56–87, in his *On the Mystical Shape*; J. Dan, "Samael, Lilith, and the Concept of Evil in Early Kabbalah," *AJS Review* 5 (1980):19–40 (reprinted in *Essential Papers on Kabbalah*, ed. Fine, 154–178); Wolfson, "Left Contained in the Right"; M. Idel, "'Ha-Maḥashavah ha-Ra'ah' shel Ha-'El," *Tarbiz* 46 (1980): 356–384. Sometimes the *Sitra Aḥra* is, indeed, depicted as being below the Divine *sefirot*—see, e.g., *Zohar* 3:70a.

28. 2:247a. This text combines the gnostic view typical of the Cohen brothers, Moses of Burgos, et al., expressed in the beginning of the text, with the neo-Platonic view of R. Ezra and R. Azriel of Gerona. See Tishby, *Mishnat*, 1:286–288. On the mystery of the coexistence of an evil inclination with the good inclination, see Scholem, *Qabbalot*, 259–260.

29. See discussion and references in Wolfson, "Left Contained in the Right," 28n7 and 29nn9, 12–13.

30. Tishby, *Mishnat*, 1:288.

31. Ibid., 289.

32. 2:244a–b.

33. At other times human imagery is applied to *Sitra Aḥra* as well. Sama'el and Lilith are human figures. And animal imagery is fundamental to the Chariot Work. Still, in general, the term *adam* is not applied to the Other Side. See Liebes, "*Zohar* ve-eros," 87n126; Wolfson, "Occultation," 131n56. Aside from its ontological significance, the distinction here must be granted its emotive and rhetorical weight. See also Matt, *Zohar*, Pritzker ed., 6:413n449.

34. See, e.g., 1:154a. 241a–b.

35. This image works on two levels. One is the positive value given to the inside as opposed to the outside. We see the privileging of the inside over the outside in the descriptions of the *heikhalot*. (See also 2:208a–b—the discussion of opening and closing one's fingers during the *havdalah* ceremony, with the fingernails labeled "hindquarters" (*aḥorayyim*); and see 2:251a: the seventy lights that are on the right—for good—are more inside than the ones that are on the left—for judgment.) The second level is, in a sense, the reverse, but is not contradictory. The oxen are oriented so that they face outward and their rear quarters are hidden from view. This is a more appropriate orientation for a holy vessel. The Other Side, however, violates propriety by exposing its rear to the outside. In addition, the implication is that its face must, therefore, be turned to the inside, but this is an improper intrusion for that Side. See 70, 80–87.

36. 2:241a.

37. "The Point" is a term for Shekhinah. See 81 above.

38. 2:242a. See also 2:152a, discussed in chap. 6 at n. 41.

39. 2:242b.

40. Ibid.

41. Apparently the elbow. See 1:154a. But Matt, *Zohar*, Pritzker ed., 6:410n440, identifies it with the entire lower right arm.

42. 2:243b.

43. See Scholem, *Qabbalot*, and "Le-ḥeqer qabbalat R. Yitzḥaq ben Ya'aqov Ha-Kohen," published serially in *Tarbiz* nos. 2–5 (1931–34). Scholem, *Qabbalot*, 195–196, cites these zoharic pages as specifically deriving from R. Yitzḥaq's teachings. See also Abulafia, *Sha'ar ha-Razim*, ed. Kushnir-Oron, 24–29; Liebes, *Studies in the Zohar*, 16–18; Tishby, *Mishnat*, 1:287–288.

44. Scholem, *Qabbalot*, 251. It is a nice touch by R. Isaac to refrain here from giving an explanation that would not be in its proper place!

45. Ibid., n. 1.

46. Ibid., 249.

47. This idea harks back to ancient myths about the fallen angels, as found in Gen. 6:1–4 and in the apocalyptic literature. See, e.g., Giqatilla's *Sod ha-Naḥash*, quoted below. See *Zohar* 3:308a.

48. Scholem, *Qabbalot*, 251.

49. 2:248a.

50. 2:248b.

51. 2:249b. Anger is a fundamental aspect of the Other Side. See the text quoted above from 2:243a–b. (And see 102 on Moses' fear.) On the subject of the earthly realm as the battleground between God and the Other Side, see Tishby, *Mishnat*, 1:476–477.

52. 2:251b.

53. 2:251b–252a.

54. 2:253a.

55. 2:254b.

56. Here is a deep paradox. Usually, the forces of the Other Side are considered related to the forces of Judgment and are seen as occupying the Left, as does *Din*. But

from the perspective of spatial practice, *Din* is fundamentally a force of limitation. The drive of *Sitra Aḥra* to break boundaries is more analogous to the force of *Ḥesed* or *Ahavah*. From this angle, *Sitra Aḥra* could even be considered a corrective to the restrictive nature of Shekhinah. The paradoxical nature of the uncontrollable energy of *Sitra Aḥra* is particularly evident in that it creates its own counterforce, *Nesir"a*, who breaks away from it and whose forces "do evil to their Side in order to work miracles for those who are on the Side of Holiness" (2:268a).

57. Since it is a higher palace, this reading makes more sense than "to take" (*le-natla*).

58. 2:254a. This recalls Jacob's analogous behavior in adopting Esau's traits in order to thwart him, as explained at 1:138b, 139ab, 160a. See also R. Moshe de Leon, "She'elot u-Teshuvot," 45–46.

59. Scholem, *Qabbalot*, 251.

60. Ibid., 252. As Dan ("Samael, Lilith, and the Concept of Evil," n. 7) has noted, Gamali"el and Nahashi"el are equivalent, the former name referring to the Serpent's camel-like appearance before it lost its legs in punishment for instigating Adam and Eve's sin. In n. 1, Dan refers to Scholem, who cites other, similar traditions and points out the correspondence between the Snake and *Yesod*.

61. Gen. 3:1–15.

62. *Bereshit Rabbah* 19:1, ed. J. Theodor and Chanoch Albeck (Jerusalem: Wahrmann Books, 1965), 171, and see notes for other sources.

63. Ibid., 20:5, ed. Theodor and Albeck, 186.

64. BT *Sotah* 9b.

65. Abulafia, *Sha'ar ha-Razim*, ed. Kushnir-Oron, 51b–52a, 66, and see her notes.

66. *Teli*, mentioned in *Sefer Yetzirah* 6:1.

67. R. Yosef Giqatilla, "The Secret of the Serpent and Its Sentence [Destiny]," cited and translated in Scholem, "*Sitra Aḥra*," 79. Scholem published the Hebrew text in *MTJM*, 405n113. See now Raphael Kohen's annotated edition, *Sod ha-Naḥash u-Mishpato*, 4–5 and Introduction, 3.

68. R. Isaac uses the term *pargod* differently. See Scholem, *Qabbalot*, 277 and his n. 4. (Kohen, in his Introduction, 5, is imprecise when he writes that R. Isaac also uses the term *pargod* in that he quotes a text about *masakh* but not *pargod*.) The *Qav ha-Middah* (*ZH* 58d) ends by saying: "Worthy is the portion, in this world and the coming world, of one who knows and perceives. Through this rule a person will set his feet to enter the *pargod* and to walk in a straight path. He is fortunate in this world and in the coming world." See also *Sefer Sheqel ha-Qodesh*, ed. Mopsik, 86. For earlier uses of the term *pargod*, see sources quoted in Peter Schäfer, *The Hidden and Manifest God: Some Major Themes in Early Jewish Mysticism* (Albany: State University of New York Press Press, 1992), 64, 135.

69. A continuation of the text cited in n. 70 below. On the significance of this posture, see the discussion above concerning the *Zohar*'s contrast between the oxen and the *Sitra Aḥra*.

70. Ibid. This translation is my own since the one included in Scholem, "*Sitra Aḥra*," 80, is clumsy and inaccurate. Note the term "shrewd," associated in Genesis with the Serpent and used in Proverbs in a positive sense.

71. Scholem, *Qabbalot*, 251n1, points out that R. Isaac, the *Zohar*, and R. Yosef Giqatilla share this concept. In his "*Sitra Aḥra*," Scholem chose to highlight the contrasting, opposing aspects of their theories. Also see Wolfson, "Re/membering," 237–238n47. And see Benjamin Ish-Shalom, "Tannin, Leviathan, Naḥash—On the Meaning of a Legendary Motif" (in Hebrew), *Da'at* 19 (Summer 1987): 79–101.

72. Giqatilla, *Sod ha-Naḥash*, 8.

73. See the text from *Sod ha-Naḥash*, quoted at length below at n. 115.

74. Ibid., 9.

75. See Scholem, *Qabbalot*, 273.

76. "She'elot u-Teshuvot 'al Ya'aqov Rivqah ve-ha-duda'im," in Kohen's edition of *Sod Ha-Naḥash*, 10. The same point is made, but not as directly, in the version published by Tishby, "She'elot u-Teshuvot le-R. Moshe di Leon be'inyanei qabbalah," in his *Ḥiqrei qabbalah u-sheluḥoteha*, 47.

77. De Leon plays with Joseph's taunting of his brothers when he claims to have caught them as thieves (Gen. 44:15). The double meaning of the term *naḥash*, which signifies both "magic" and "snake," is often referred to in the literature. This is additionally appropriate here because Joseph is identified with *Yesod*, while the Serpent is his evil counterpart.

78. Giqatilla, *Sod ha-Naḥash*, 11. These lines are missing from Tishby's version.

79. See Wolfson, "Re/membering"; Oded Yisraeli, "The Suppressed Cry of Esau: From Early Midrash to Late Zoharic Text" (in Hebrew) in *Ḥiddushei Zohar*, ed. Meroz, 165–198. And see M. Fishbane, "Primordial Serpent," for an extensive discussion of another zoharic text dealing with these themes.

80. 1:146a. The images of their parallel unions differ in this particular respect. Esau rides a mobile serpent, while Jacob rides (sits upon) a stationary Throne (1:137b). See Wolfson, "Re/membering," 218–219 and notes, for citations of these and other places in the *Zohar*.

81. 1:146a. The state of the moon's darkness and Jacob's aloneness is the state of separation of *Tiferet*/*Yesod* from *Malkhut* (see 1:166a). The attack on Jacob's thigh is an attempt to prevent their union. The connection between the Snake and the defective spelling of the word *me'orot* has been made in the zoharic text mentioned above (2:35b). See Wolfson, "Re/membering," 239n64. On the connection between the sun and defective moon and Jacob's conflict with Esau, see *ZH* 14ab and Scholem, "Parashah Ḥadashah," 430–433. Wolfson, "Face of Jacob in the Moon," treats these motifs extensively; see esp. 267n59. See further on the meaning of the diminution of the moon, 94–96 above.

82. 1:241b. The phrase *le-nafqa u-leme'al*, which is particularly applied to the Companions, connotes motion, sexual activity, and deep study of Torah. For sources and studies, see Wolfson, "Forms of Visionary Ascent," 211 and notes there. For other instances, see chap. 1, n. 41, and chap. 2 at nn. 94 and 106, above.

83. Wolfson, "Images of God's Feet," 164, 168, points out that in the *Zohar*, the legs can signify both the male and female sex organs, and both male and female sex roles.

84. 2:257b.

85. Ibid.

86. This echoes Rashbi's exclamation at the beginning of the *Idra Rabba*, 3:127b.

87. 2:258a.

88. Ibid. See Wolfson, "Images of God's Feet," 170, for a slightly different translation. See also Wolfson, "Woman," 182.

89. The term *ve-itgalu* signifies both exile and revelation.

90. See Wolfson, *Circle*, 180–181, for a number of possible associations for this and similar terms—*hut ha-mishqal/qav ha-mishor/qav ha-yosher*, including measurement, the phallic axis, and "that which gives shape and boundary to the divine light." See Liebes, "Peraḳim be-milon," 146–147, and below.

91. 2:258a. These images have multiple meanings and associations. The phrase *bim'shikhu de-raglin* is ambiguous. It could mean either "the drawing out"—extension—of the legs (so translated in Wolfson, "Images of God's Feet," 170) or, as I have translated here, "the drawing in/withdrawal" of the legs. This may be related to the biblical image of Jacob withdrawing his feet onto the bed, taken by the *Zohar* to signify his union with Shekhinah (see ibid., 165). The prooftext here is in the verse's phrase *v'amdu*—"the legs will stand/stop." I take this to mean that walking will cease, that the legs will stop functioning. However, other meanings are possible. Wolfson (ibid., 163) cites other places where the *Zohar* quotes this verse. It is related to the ultimate execution of divine judgment, using the term "standing" as a reference to the "standing" angels (as in Zech. 3:7). Or it could refer to the erect phallus, ready for coitus. As Wolfson suggests (ibid., 171), the image of the redemption is one of divine union. This state would culminate, according to my translation, in the withdrawal of the feet of the female, i.e., the incorporation of the female into the male, the desired ultimate consummation, as explicated by Wolfson in numerous studies.

92. On the Shekhinah as God's "Great Hand" and the containing of the left hand in the right hand, see Wolfson, "Left Contained in the Right," 42–45.

93. Based on *Sifre Ki Tetze* 257, ed. Finkelstein (New York: Jewish Theological Seminary, 1993), 281.

94. 2:260b.

95. Azulai, *Or ha-Ḥamah*, 2: 269a, s.v. *ta ḥazei*.

96. The *Zohar*'s opening image of the hand holding the cup for kiddush (1:1a) can be understood in this light. The Shekhinah, as the ingathering receptacle, is analogous to the cup and the act of unification effected through the recitation of kiddush is reinforced through the use of one hand cradling the cup.

97. See Gen. 18:9. Rashi cites BT *Bava Metzi'a* 87a. See also Gen. 24:67, for which Rashi cites *Bereshit Rabbah* 6:16.

98. See Gen. 34:1, to which Rashi quotes *Bereshit Rabbah* 80:1.

99. Thus the verse about Sarah (Gen. 18:9), among others (such as Ps. 45:14), is used to support the law that Moabite women should not be barred from entry into the Israelite community, since they must surely have stayed in their tents and cannot be punished for failing to go out to help Israel (BT *'Avodah Zarah* 76b–77a).

100. M *Yoma* 1:1.

101. See Wolfson, "Occultation," 145–146.

102. *Song of Sol.* 4:12. See *Pirqei de R. Eli'ezer* (Jerusalem, 1990), chap. 21. The word

na'ul—locked—may also be related to the word for shoe or sandal—*na'al*. On the sandal as a zoharic symbol for Shekhinah, see Wolfson, "Images of God's Feet," 167.

103. E.g., 1:32b and 2:4a. See Wolfson, "Occultation," 138–141.

104. 2:4a. See also Wolfson, "Crossing Gender Boundaries," in id., *Circle*, esp. 98–105 and notes.

105. 2:258a.

106. 2:259a.

107. *Perush ha-aggadot le-R. 'Azriel* , ed. Isaiah Tishby, (Jerusalem: Magnes Press, 1983), 3. *Teshuvah* refers to the *sefirah* of *Binah*, the source of power for the lower *sefirot*. See Tishby's notes and variant readings. This description of the nature of a path is found also in *Liqqutei shikh'ḥah u-fe'ah* (reprint, New York, 1978), 1b.

108. Later in the discussion, at 4, R. 'Azriel relates the last term of the verse—*mussar*—to the notion of receptivity.

109. This concept should be traced back to the medieval understanding of the terms found in *Sefer Yetzirah*—*netivot, sh'vilin*. See also the Introduction to *Sefer Yetzirah* of R. Yosef b. Shalom Ashkenazi (attributed to RaBaD), 21 in traditional editions, where he sets out seven names for the creative pathways. And see also M*Pe'ah* 2:1 on the terms *derekh* and *sh'vil*.

110. Trans. Verman, *Books of Contemplation*, 56; see Verman's discussion, 152–153. As he points out, the very word *derekh* is grammatically either masculine or feminine (on the ambi-gendered meaning of *derekh* in zoharic texts, see 78–79 above). Verman notes that a different translation of this text by R. Keiner is included in *The Early Kabbalah*, ed. J. Dan (Mahwah, NJ: Paulist Press, 1986), 50. On the question of the relation between the *'Iyyun* Circle and R. 'Azriel, see Verman, 194–199. For further distinctions among terms for roads, see 79 above at n. 125.

111. The Hebrew text reads *roshi* instead of the correct word—*rosh*.

112. Alluding to Balaam (Num. 24:4). Scholem. "*Sitra Aḥra*," 71, points out that magical practices were viewed by the *Zohar* as attempts to override the boundaries of nature set by God. This attitude was not limited to the *Zohar*. See the popular exposition of this view in *Sefer ha-Ḥinnukh*, ed. Chavel, mitzvah 62, 113. Chavel notes that this is already expressed by Naḥmanides in his Torah commentary, at Lev. 19:19. The more apt reference is to Naḥmanides at Deut. 18:12. On the link between evil and magic, see Wolfson, "Left Contained in the Right," 33–37.

113. Giqatilla later links this to the word for accidental seminal emission, *qeri*.

114. Balaam's acts of bestiality are another example, for the *Zohar* 1:125b (#17), of the desire of magicians to transgress boundaries. See Wolfson, "Re/membering," 236n36. This act is also alluded to in the *Zohar*'s image of the *Sitra Aḥra* exposing its rear quarters (2:244b), cited above. Balaam's magical practice (1:125b–126a) is a direct application of the various mythical elements collected by Giqatilla.

115. Giqatilla, *Sod ha-Naḥash*, 3.

116. Regarding the thigh, see 72 above.

117. 1:237a (#37), 243b; 2:137a; 3:171b.

118. See 1:48b and 2:51a. Actually, this ambiguity derives from the ambi-gendered nature of Shekhinah, as the texts bear out. See 81–87 above.

119. See *MTJM*, 165, 388 n. 46. Matt, *Zohar: The Book of Enlightenment*, 250. The meaning here does not seem to be "donkey driver," since the caravan is of camels. Jastrow, *Dictionary*, 1:531, s.v., translates the term—as "traveller, esp. Arabian caravan merchant."

120. Matt, *Zohar*, Pritzker ed., 4:212, translates: "burdens wrapped in their blankets." See his n. 45.

121. 2:45b (#56). For another mention of the term *bat 'el nekhar*, see chap. 4, at n. 122. And see also chap. 6, at n. 78.

122. Ibid. This walking story ends with the comment that once the "mixed multitude" joined the Israelites, Israel lost its distinctive name: "Once they [the mixed multitude] joined up with them they [Israel] were called *'am* [and not Israel]." R. Avraham Galante, in Azulai, *Or ha-Ḥamah*, 2:55b, s.v. *keyvan*, perceptively notes: "The way to read [*shi'ur*] the verse is thus: Now, after they went out and distanced themselves from the city, and were traveling around [*mesab'vim*], which is when the mixed multitude mixed with them, then they were called *'am*." In other words, the other peoples were able to infiltrate Israel's camp only after Israel left the enclosed space of the city and began to wander on the "wilderness road [*derekh ha-midbar*]" (Exod. 13:18).

123. On the polemical use of the term "mixed multitude" against ruling elites by later strata of the *Zohar*, see Baer, *History*, 1:272–277. And see Liebes, "Ha-*Zohar* v'ha-Tiqqunim," 271–272.

124. The next verse refers to the "road of the wicked" (*derekh resha'im*).

125. 3:88a (#99). See also 2:215a (#74). In another walking text, 2:31ab (#53), there is a somewhat different interpretation of *derekh*, apparently relating the term to exoteric Torah, available to all, while the *nativ* is more special. See also chap. 2, n. 100. Deriving from the Coming World, its attribute is *Shalom*, a uniquely phallic signifier. And see 78 above at n. 118.

126. Hanawalt and Kobialka, eds., *Medieval Practices of Space*, Introduction, x.

127. Michael Camille, "Signs of the City: Place, Power and Public Fantasy in Medieval Paris," in *Medieval Practices of Space*, ed. Hanawalt and Kobialka, 1–36, at 27 (relevant studies cited in notes, ibid.).

128. See, e.g., Metropolitan Museum of Art, *The Secular Spirit: Life and Art at the End of the Middle Ages*, (New York: Dutton, 1975), 26–27.

129. See chap. 5, nn. 36, 95.

130. 1:38b, discussed in Greenstein, "Aimless Pilgrimage," 212n29.

131. See 1:49b–50a (#3), discussed in chap. 1 above.

132. For some important treatments of the *sefirah* of Shekhinah, see Tishby, *Mishnat*, 1:219–63; Scholem, "*Shekhinah*: The Feminine Element in Divinity," in his *On the Mystical Shape*, 140–196, 293–300; Wolfson, *Circle*, index, s.v. *Shekhinah*.

133. For a summary, see Tishby, *Mishnat*, 1:381–390.

134. Ibid., 385.

135. There are other possibilities. See Wolfson, *Circle*, for discussion of texts that combine the linguistic approach with emanation or that also involve Shekhinah.

136. 2:222a. This is part of a larger excerpt in Tishby, *Mishnat*, 1:398–399.

137. For an elaboration on this image, see Giqatilla, *Sha'arei Orah*, Gate I, ed. Ben-Shelomo, 63–64. And see chap. 5, at n. 87, and chap. 6, at n. 14, above.

138. See Wolfson, "Occultation," 143.

139. A similar action is reported in *Bereshit Rabbah* 8:5, ed. Theodor and Albeck, 60, regarding the debate between God and the angels over creating the world. The angels objected to creation because of human mendacity. To overcome this, "what did the Holy Blessed One do? He took Truth and cast it to the earth." The image conveys an act of determined rejection of the claims of the entity being cast down.

140. See Wolfson, "Occultation," 151–152, endnotes 4–5.

141. The appearance of this verse at the start of the printed *Zohar*'s discussions of both Genesis and Exodus is not an indication that earlier collections of zoharic material followed this same compositional layout. See Oron, "Sh'loshah Perushim," esp. 184.

142. The image of tribes, however necessary for the story (see 83, 97 above), seems out of place in the description of the Tree. Commentators refer to the twelve diagonal spatial directions given cosmogonic significance in *Sefer Yetzirah* 5:1 (Gruenwald ed., para. 47). See also *Bahir* §§82–83 (Abrams ed.; Margaliot ed., §§113–114), and the zoharic parallels cited by Margaliot. In this context, perhaps there is also a connection to light imagery—either through the association of *shevet* with "striking" or with "comet."

143. 2:2a.

144. See Liebes, "*Zohar* Ve-eros," 74–75. On the significance of this verse, see the references in Matt, *Zohar*, Pritzker ed., 1:109n14 and 4:1n1.

145. This is paralleled in the earlier "*zohar*" text (1:15b) by assigning the light to the enlightened themselves, for without their own light "they are not able to look into and contemplate that palanquin as much as is needed." The Companions sometimes sit under the shade of a tree to study Torah. See, e.g., ##3, 55, 114, 116, 117, 118, 123, *ZH* #5 (*MH*), *ZH* #22. Their teacher, Rashbi, is the Great Tree under whose shade they sit. (See Pachter, "Beyn laylah le-voqer," 344n74.) In another text (3:204b [#115]), the *Zohar* explains that Shekhinah's light is like a shade that mitigates the too extreme brightness of the higher *sefirot*. (The reading advanced here is not consonant with the readings of RaMaK or R. Abraham Galante, who conflate the firmament with the Tree. See Azulai, *Or ha-Ḥamah*, 2:1a, 1d–2a.)

146. Elsewhere, the *Zohar* has the twelve tribes support the Shekhinah below, as the twelve oxen supported the Sea of Solomon (1:240b–241a). They are the lower Chariot (3:118b). They are her adornments (1:158a, 159b, 246b).

147. The seal—*ḥotam*—is an important cosmogonic tool in Jewish traditions. It carries the sense of identity and authorization (God's seal) as well as closure. See, e.g., *Synopse* §§318–321, 430, *Ottiyot deR. 'Aqiva*, in *Batei Midrashot*, ed. Wertheimer, 2:363, *Sefer Yetzirah* 1:13 (Gruenwald ed., para. 15), *Sefer ha-Bahir* §21 (Abrams ed., §30 in Margaliot ed.). Conversely, the use of seals by the mystic adept allows him to penetrate Divine space, as in *Synopse* §219ff. The seal is also associated with the act of inscription. See Wolfson, "Erasing the Erasure," in id., *Circle*, 49 and notes. (As such, it can refer to circumcision. See Wolfson's studies on circumcision listed in the Bibliography.)

148. 1:53b, 237a.

149. See, e.g., Wolfson, "Occultation," 147, 153–154 (endnote 6), "Crossing Gender Boundaries," in id., *Circle*, 98ff. For another approach to the *Zohar*'s treatment of the drama of birth, the role of woman, the hind, and of the Serpent, see Carmeli, "'Mah

'osot ha-'ayalot ba-laylah?'" who also cites the gender theories of Wolfson, Abrams, and others.

150. 2:219b.

151. 3:249ab. For treatments of this text, see M. Oron, "Me-Omanut ha-derush shel ba'al ha-*Zohar*," in *Meḥqere Yerushalyim be-maḥashevet Yisra'el*, ed. J. Dan, 8 (1989): 299–310; Y. Liebes, "'Treyn Orzilin de-'ayalata: derashato ha-sodit shel ha-'Ari lifnei moto," in *Meḥqerei Yerushalyim be-maḥashevet Yisra'el*, ed. Y. Liebes and R. Elior, 10 (1992), 113–169. See also Tene, "Darkhei," 109–119.

152. See Wolfson, "Woman—The Feminine as Other," 188. "Coronation of the Sabbath Bride," 330.

153. The analogy is drawn to the episode of Moses hitting the rock twice. This recalls the teaching of R. Isaac Ha-Kohen regarding the redemption, in which he draws a connection between the transformation of the Snake and the rod of Moses that, in the guise of a snake, swallowed all Egypt's snakes.

154. Here we find an example of the Serpent's nature as spatial activist performing a corrective function with regard to Shekhinah's withholding nature, as suggested above.

155. 3:249b. See the additional application of this verse to Shekhinah at 2:63b–64a, regarding the prohibition on leaving one's place on Shabbat. And see 2:207a and chap. 2, n. 88 above, from 1:207a.

156. De Leon, *Sheqel ha-Qodesh*, ed. Mopsik, 72; ed. Greenup, 91–92.

157. Ibid., ed. Mopsik, 73–74; ed. Greenup, 93.

158. 1:155b.

159. See 1:160b. God says to Jacob, "Until now Rachel was with you, the head of your household [*'aqara de-beita*]. From now on I shall be with you and take the house with you through twelve tribes."

160. De Leon, "She'elot u-Teshuvot," 41. See also R. Moshe de Leon, *Book of the Pomegranate,* ed. Wolfson, 97; *Sheqel ha-Qodesh*, ed. Mopsik, 66.

161. 1:223a.

162. See G. Scholem, "The Name of God and the Linguistic Theory of the Kabbala," *Diogenes* 79 (1972): 59–81 and 80 (1972): 164–194; Wolfson, "Letter Symbolism"; id., "Dimmui Antropomorfi."

163. See the sources cited in the note above and Wolfson, "Erasing the Erasure," in id., *Circle*; Verman, *Books of Contemplation*, 121–163; M. Idel, "Reification of Language in Jewish Mysticism," in *Mysticism and Language*, ed. Katz, 42–79.

164. Wolfson, "Erasing the Erasure," in id., *Circle*, 62, while discussing the phallic nature of this activity, also notes that this act "signifies in the most elemental sense the process of forming or giving shape by digging out space from slabs of matter." The act of creating space is gendered as a male act. See 75–87 above.

165. This image comes from *Merkavah* imagery. On the letters as a chariot, see n. 169 below.

166. 2:234a–b (#77). This text is part of a larger selection included in Tishby, *Mishnat*, 1:391.

167. 2:130b, as translated in Wolfson, "Letter Symbolism," 217. The phrase *b'istakluta le-fum sha'ata* may mean that one should take only a quick glance. (Matt, *Zohar*, Pritzker

ed., 5:216, translates as "gaze momentarily.") This would enhance the impression of the movement of the stars as they dart up and down and into each other. Wolfson points out the sexual character of the stars' movements. As noted above, this discussion aims to highlight the spatial character of their activity as well. From this perspective it is significant that the *Zohar* specifically speaks here to one who is about to go out on the road. See 107 above. Cf. also *ZH* 76c (*MH*) (#23).

168. 3:2a. See Wolfson's discussion, "Letter Symbolism," 219–220.

169. The *Zohar* plays on the word *merkavah*, relating its meaning "chariot" to the associated word meaning "combination" (see Wolfson, ibid., 221). With the understanding of the letters as being space creators through their spatial movements, it may be conjectured that the creative power of combinations of letters derives not only from the creative power of the letters themselves, but also from the act of moving them around while making the various word permutations. These combinations can be imagined in terms of their spatial manipulation, moving them from one position to another relative to the other letters, as further described by the *Zohar* (1:2b–3a). Such manipulation repeats the letters' original primordial creative movements.

170. 2:130b.

171. See above, at n. 82 ff.

172. 1:9a. See Liebes, *Studies in the Zohar*, 57–60, for a slightly different translation and for commentary.

173. See chap. 2, n. 45, above, and chap. 4.

174. The term *dugma* is often used by R. Moshe de Leon in his Hebrew writings: e.g., for the Garden of Eden ("Shushan 'Edut," in "Shenei quntresim," ed. Scholem, 350, 363), human behavior (ibid., 354), human image (ibid., 355), the Matriarchs ("She'elot u-Teshuvot," 40), Esau (ibid., 45), Isaac (ibid., 47), Jacob (ibid., 52), the events and actions of this world (ibid., 56), the Patriarchs (ibid.), human skin, flesh, bones, sinews (ibid., 59), the revealed world (*'olam ha-nigleh*) (R. Moshe de Leon, *Book of the Pomegranate,* ed. Wolfson, 8–9, 23), humans (ibid., 27), washing hands (ibid., 57), this world (*ha-'olam ha-zeh*) (ibid., 97), or the entire chain of emanation down to the Lower World (*Ha-'Olam ha-Shafel*) (ibid., 243), Torah (ibid., 327), *brit* (*Sheqel ha-Qodesh*, ed. Mopsik, 51), the Tree in the Garden, this world (ibid., 80), the four elements (ibid., 95). The *Zohar* applies the term to Noah (1:48a), Jacob (1:35b), Joseph (1:251a), Jacob's blessings (3:62a), Shabbat (1:1a.48a), *Shemittah* and *Yovel* (1:48a), *tefillin* (1:129b *MH*), circumcision (1:186b), "anything Israel does below" (3:40a), the Companions (2:190b), everything below (1:156b). See Matt, *Zohar*, Pritzker ed., 2:370n414. The *Zohar* can reverse the relationship and call the upper form the *dugma* of what is below, as at 1:1a (*the Rose*). A more complicated case is found in a text collected in the supplements to the *Zohar* (3:303a, *Siman* 9). Here the subject is the biblical injunction to the priests to lift the Levites at their installation service (Num. 8:11). First, an exemplary action is adduced—that of lifting a crying baby to appease her. Then the analogy is made from this to the raising of the *sefirah* of Judgment in order to mitigate it. Finally, the explanation is brought back to Aaron's act of raising the Levites. (On the significance of the term *dugma* for the *Zohar*'s historiography, see Wolfson, "Re/membering.")

175. The most extensive discussion is Brody's "Human Hands." See also Wolfson, "Mystical-Theurgical Dimensions."

176. See Tishby, *Mishnat*, 1:290–291, 341–342, and 2:206–209. Tishby (1:290) points out that this rationale was applied to other practices, such as the quasi-sacrificial *'eglah 'arufah*, the visible hairs from the *tefillin*, and the custom of washing hands after eating.

177. See, e.g., 1:64b (#7). The *Zohar* (1:143a) sees the same strategy employed when Esau is sent out to hunt, enabling Jacob to be blessed, undisturbed.

178. See 2:242b.

179. 2:62b–63a. 1:64a (#7). See also Naḥmanides on Lev. 16:8.

180. See, e.g., 2:262b:

> The whole sacrifice—to this Side, the portion of holiness and the will of holiness. And to this Side, that portion that is the sins and transgressions that are given by confession upon the meat of the sacrifice, as it is written, "If your enemy is hungry, feed him bread . . . for you are raking coals on his head . . ." [Prov. 25:21–22]. And a [memory] device for you: "Let the King and Haman come to the feast" [Esther 5:8]. How fortunate the one who knows his path to walk in the path of truth.

See also Tishby's discussions, mentioned above, and see his comment on 2:244b, id., *Mishnat*, 1:315, s.v. *ve-ha-qorban*.

181. See 2:238b. See Matt, *Zohar*, Pritzker ed., 6:380–381nn 348–349.

182. See 2:255b, and Wolfson, "Circumcision and the Divine Name," 99–100 (esp. n. 69), and "Circumcision, Vision of God and Textual Interpretation," in id., *Circle*, 33, at n. 26).

183. See Tishby, *Mishnat*, 2:208–9.

184. Ibid., 203, based on *Zohar* 3:34b–35a.

185. Brody, "Human Hands," 209. And see 629.

186. As translated by Brody, ibid., 227, from *Rabbenu Baḥya 'al ha-Torah*, ed. Chavel, 2:556.

187. Brody, "Human Hands," 228.

188. Ibid., 235.

189. Wolfson, "Coronation," 302, describes the dynamic relation between these two poles as "sacramental": "By participating in the rite with the proper mystical intentionality, the individual not only connects with God, but acts upon God. At the same time, however, the one who performs the rite symbolically embodies, or better signifies, the sacred secret of the divine power operating in the world. Sacramentality thus entails the mutual empowerment of God and human as the one is manifest through the other by virtue of the symbolizing function of the ritual."

190. 1:70b.

191. 1:71a.

192. Ibid.

193. This subject is discussed by Brody, "Human Hands," 620–631. However, his focus is upon the intentional/theurgical aspects of sacrifices. Our focus on the problem of spatiality is meant to add another layer of meaning.

194. *ZH* 14a (also found in the supplemental 1:252a). By the way it continues the story, the *Zohar* seems to indicate that there is more to this teaching than what it writes.

R. Ya'aqov says that he has heard this explanation numerous times, but that it does not sit well with him. R. Naḥman is not forthcoming in explaining it. Then R. Yehudah rebukes R. Ya'aqov, "Do you wish to transgress your colleagues' words?" This concern is repeated later by R. Yose b. R. Shim'on Laqonya. I have found no other place in the *Zohar* where this phrase is used, but it appears in the Babylonian Talmud (*Shabbat* 134a), where a rabbi personally complies with the decision of his fellows despite his conviction that the halakhah is otherwise. Yet the Talmud indicates that he continued to rule against them in public. The point seems to be that he feels a collegial bond that he does not wish to betray. The analogy would be that in persisting in his efforts to understand this teaching, R. Ya'aqov is violating the Companions' implicit pact to refrain from revealing anything more about it. See also BT *Ketubot* 39b, 98b; *Bava Metzi'a* 78a; *Zevaḥim* 34a.

195. R. Moshe de Leon, *Book of the Pomegranate,* ed. Wolfson, 189. The translation offered here is meant to correct the somewhat misleading translation given by Brody, "Human Hands," 624–625.

196. Brody, "Human Hands," 628. De Leon elsewhere makes the connection between the New Moon offering and the Yom Kippur scapegoat (R. Moshe de Leon, *Book of the Pomegranate*, ed. Wolfson, 370). See also 1:64a, 3:79b; Wolfson, "Mystical Rationalization," 245–246.

197. See, e.g., 1:195ab (#29).

198. See 61 above at n. 22.

199. This element is not part of the biblical narrative. The *Zohar* draws on a number of midrashic sources. On the need for mitzvot as a precondition for redemption, see *Mekhilta, Pisḥa* 5, ed. Horovitz and Rabin (Jerusalem, 1998), 14. This source mentions both the paschal lamb and circumcision. Later midrashim speak of the blood of both mixing together. See *Exodus Rabbah* 19:5. This midrash is also quoted by Maimonides. See *Epistles of Maimonides*, ed. A. S. Halkin (Philadelphia: Jewish Publication Society, 1993), "Epistle on Martyrdom," 18. On the additional element of their application together onto the doorways, see *Targum Yonatan* (attrib.) to Exod. 12:13; *Pirqei de R. Eli'ezer* 29; *Ber. Rabbati* to Gen. 17:4; *Bereshit Rabbah*, ed. Theodor and Albeck, 78.

200. The aspect of Shekhinah that judges and punishes. See Wolfson, "Left Contained in the Right," 38–39, and chap. 2, n. 38, above.

201. An allusion to Shekhinah. See, e.g., 1:219a.

202. 3:149a.

203. See the parallel text, 2:35b: "When an action is done then the supernal providence is aroused. Therefore [in] everything, whether for good or for evil, the matter depends on an action."

204. See 2:138b. See also 1:49a and the comments there of Lavi, *Ketem Paz*, 128c, and in Azulai, *Or ha-Ḥamah*, s.v. *l'qabal hahu atar*. And see 195 above.

205. See 2:131b–132a. Cf. Wolfson, "Mystical-Theurgical Dimensions," 56. See also Wolfson, "Left Contained in the Right," 37ff., on the elements necessary to effect the redemption from Egypt. On music as a theurgic or mystical tool, see M. Idel, "Music," in *Contemporary Jewish Religious Thought*, ed. A. A. Cohen and P. Mendes-Flohr (New York: Scribner's, 1987), 635–642.

206. The acts of marking the doorways and of circumcision are acts of inscription as well. See Wolfson, "Erasing the Erasure," in id., *Circle*, 49–78, 155–195.

207. See 3:18ab. See also de Leon, "Sod 'eser sefirot belimah," 374 (shofar = *Binah*), 382–383 (shofar sounds in *Malkhut*), in id., "Shenei quntresim," ed. Scholem.

208. On this term, see Liebes, "Peraḳim be-milon," 136–167, who notes that besides referring to the Divine potencies, it is often linked to the mouth; he suggests (157, #89) that *butzina* may also occasionally mean a shofar.

209. 3:149a.

210. See *Zohar* 2:218b–219b, trans. in Tishby, *Mishnat*, 2:239–243, which points out that the incense is effective as an act of tying together of the *sefirot*, as well as protective against evil and plague. See Brody's discussion, "Human Hands," 612–614. And see 160 above.

211. 3:149a.

212. 2:218b.

213. This is a translation of the multivalent term *ma'aseh ha-menorah* in this Torah portion (Exod. 8:4).

214. This is the *Zohar*'s development of the *Midrash Tanḥuma, B'ha'alotekha* 5, which explains that the menorah *ritus* was given to Aaron to console him after he saw the leaders' dedication of the Tabernacle (see Rashi and Ramban to Num. 8:2). Its approach shifts the focus from the menorah to the incense. Regarding whether lighting the menorah is the exclusive right of the priests, see Maimonides, *Hil. Bi'at Miqdash* 9:7 and Rabad's gloss there.

215. See Tishby, *Mishnat*, 2:213.

216. 2:84a.

217. Shekhinah is identified with the Oral Torah, the Torah manifest in this world, and is also the inclusive *sefirah*. But in "Shushan 'edut," in "Shenei quntresim," ed. Scholem, 335, 368–369, de Leon identifies *Tiferet*/Torah with *klal* and *Malkhut*/Oral Torah with *prat*.

218. 3:149a–b. For an extensive treatment of this text, see Wolski, *Journey*, 23–46.

219. It is often coupled with two other texts—Rashbi's teaching of a few pages later, 152a (denigrating those who do not understand the fourfold nature of the Torah, and who, instead, take the Torah's stories at face value), and the parable of the maiden in the tower by the *Sabba* (2:99ab). See Tishby, *Mishnat*, 2:368–369, 400–403; Matt, *Zohar: The Book of Enlightenment*, 31–32, 43–45, 123–125 and notes; F. Talmage, "Apples of Gold: The Inner Meaning of Sacred Texts in Medieval Judaism," in *Jewish Spirituality*, ed. Green, 1:313–355; Wolfson, "Beautiful Maiden," esp. 167ff.

220. 3:149a (#108). On the name of the mountains, see Scholem, "She'elot be-viqoret ha-*Zohar*," 50, no. 14. At *ZH* 113c (*Tiqqunim*), reading "Ararat" as deriving from *arah*—to curse, they are called "accursed mountains, to execute Judgment upon them, for they are *turei qadro* [*qardo*], dark mountains in the exile, cursed in the exile." Wolski, *Journey*, 23, translates as "mountains of Kurdistan."

221. See also 1:76a (#10), discussed in chap. 2, at n. 40. As noted there, Lavi, commenting on that text, brings up the notion of the Companions' fear.

222. The word *y'gurkha* can be taken as deriving from the word meaning "dwelling" or it can be derived from the word meaning "to have fear."

223. 1:52ab. As explained in 1:76a, *mit'halekh* refers to Shekhinah, the "lower voice."

224. On this term, see chap. 5, n. 10.

225. 2:264b. See the parallel text, 2:249b, quoted above in the discussion on the *Sitra Aḥra*, at n. 51.

226. On this issue, see above, chap. 2, n. 85, and chap. 5, n. 15.

227. See 3:26a: "Anyone who passionately studies Torah is not afraid of supernal or lower [forces], and is not afraid of bad happenings of the world, for he holds fast to the Tree of Life and eats from it every day. For the Torah teaches people how to walk in the path of truth." See above, chap. 6 at n. 38.

228. See 1:230a (#36). But, as that text wryly continues, the more mundane fear of wild beasts is not obviated by this consideration.

229. See 2:35b. The marking of the Divine sign of *yud* characterizes circumcision. The three circumcised Companions walk together and will begin discussing Torah. The letter *shin* is also a Divine sign, composed of three marks, associated with circumcision and with mezuzah. See Wolfson's studies on this topic cited in chap. 4 and his "Coronation," 314ff.

230. 2:269a.

231. This argument supports, but is somewhat different from, Wolfson's argument in "Beautiful Maiden." His focus is on the hermeneutical unity between *peshat* and *sod*. The discussion here attempts to locate the shared space between hermeneutics and mundane activity.

232. For we have been alerted by R. Ele'azar that the production of the Torah text is also a type of action: "For if you think that the supernal Holy King, Blessed is He, did not have holy matters to write and from which to make [*u-leme'ebad*] Torah, but rather He collected all mundane matters . . . and all other stories that are written, and made [*ve-'avad*] from them the Torah" (3:149b). (Can this concept of textual composition shed light on the composition of the *Zohar* itself?)

233. This would appear to be the approach of de Leon in his responsum on Jacob, "She'elot u-Teshuvot," 55–57. But his discussion in "Shushan 'edut," in "Shenei quntresim," ed. Scholem, 362–363, is more in line with the argument developed here.

234. 3:149b. He adds the word *bilvad*—"alone."

235. We are told that they sat and studied together with the two men they encountered in the cave, but these men vanish from the text.

236. 3:251a.

237. 1:158a (see chap. 4, n. 8); and see 1:154a. Cf. 3:175b: "[A person] gets up in the morning and sets his legs to walking."

Chapter 4. The Body Wishes to Walk

1. See, e.g., #5, #6, #8, #11, 1:134a, 1:144b, #18, 1:152b, 1:153a, #21, 1:174b, #26, #29, 1:221a, #44, 2:8a, 2:29a, #53, 2:32b, #55, 2:49a, #58, 2:57b, 2:62ab, #60, 2:124a, #66, #71, #77, 2:262b, 3:5b, #78, #80, #87, #89, #97, 3:77b, 3:79b, #99, #101, 3:101a, 3:121b, #107, #108, 3:159b, 3:194b, #114, #125, *ZH* 18c (*MH*), *ZH* 45a, 47c, #21, #26, #31.

2. See, e.g., 1:67a, 1:108a, 1:201b, #53, #89, #114, #121, *ZH* #31.

3. See, e.g., 1:57a, 1:188a, 1:198a, #34, #56, #97, 2:84a, *ZH* #17 (*MH*), *ZH* 31d, 49b.

4. See, e.g., #3, #11,#12, #15, 1:135a, #19, #21, 1:173b, 1:178b, 1:221a, 2:63b, 2:84b, 2:124b, #69, #73, #74, #85, #92,#101, 3:126a, #110, #112, 3:260a, #122, #123, #124, *ZH* 4b (*MH*), *ZH* 17c (*MH*), *ZH* 21d (*MH*), *ZH* 47a, #24, 84d, (Tos.) #33.

5. See, e.g., #9, #10, #22, 1:168a, 1:169b, #38, #52, #58, #64, #74, #85, #92, 3:72b, 3:80a, #109, 3:196a, 3:261b, *ZH* #25.

6. See, e.g., #10, 1:108b, 1:243b, #60, 2:82b, #64, 2:245a, #87, 3:52b, #94, #99, #102, #114, #115.

7. See, e.g., #15, #38, #53, #74, #99, #107, #109, #114, *ZH* #12 (*MH*), *ZH*16a (*MH*), *ZH*19c (*MH*), (Tos.) #32.

8. 1:158a. The printed Aramaic text reads: *ba'a gufa l'meihakh l'orḥei*. However, in his Aramaic text, Matt erases the word *gufa* and translates: "[Once Jacob saw the body completed,] he wanted to go on his way" (Matt, *Zohar*, Pritzker ed., 2:379–380).

9. See the beginning of chap. 2 above.

10. 2:10ab (#45). See also *ZH* #23.

11. There is a subtle irony here. In rabbinic tradition, walking behind a sage was usually the practice of a student who followed his master (see my discussion of walking stories in rabbinic sources in Greenstein, "Aimless Pilgrimage," 182–189). R. Yose Sabba is considered a master who is able to teach the Companions. Yet the story opens by portraying him as walking behind the younger Companions. This reinforces the message that we are hearing about a fortuitous happenstance and not a planned practice.

12. 1:145a (#18).

13. 2:36b (#55). Pachter, "Beyn laylah le-voqer," 314n13, points out that R. Ḥiyya rides while R. Yose walks.

14. Compare this beginning to #91.

15. The subject of leaders and the populace is also the concern R. Abba at 1:198a. See above, chap. 2 at n. 79.

16. Pachter, "Beyn laylah le-voqer."

17. See also #50—R. Aha and R. Yose set out together, each thinking his own thoughts; #54—R. Yose asks R. Hiyya why he is walking in silence; #109—R. Hizqiyah and R. Yeisa walk together. Seeing his friend's facial expression, R. Yeisa asks R. Hizqiyah what he is thinking about. Naomi Tene notices that walking precedes the "content" of a zoharic text in another walking text (#115), but describes the terse usage of this narrative fragment as "the extreme relinquishing of any detail that does not serve the mystical purpose of the author of the *Zohar*" (Tene, "Darkhei," 142). For a text that goes in a different direction, privileging silence as a mystical path, see Meroz, "Path of Silence."

18. On the recurrent tendency for the Companions to change course in their travels, see citations at n. 24 below. For an analysis of one such case (#115), see Tene, "Darkhei," 150–156.

19. Pachter, "Beyn laylah le-voqer," 346.

20. 1:3b (#1).

21. See #3, 11, 14, 16, 22, 27, 38, 42, 46, 48, 57, 61, 65, 68, 75, 77, 80, 82, 86, 88, 90, 95, 100, 101, 103, 106, 110, 121, *ZH* #9, 13, 14, 23, 27.

22. See, e.g., # 1, 2, 3, 7, 15, 17, 18, 25, 58, 61, 73, 74, 76, 91, 94, 99, 115, 118, 125, *ZH* #23.

23. See #3, 71, 72, 79, 80, 109, 118, 119, *ZH* #11, 12, 22.

24. See #12, 36, 55, 84, 112, 114, 115, 123, 125.

25. Whether intentionally or not, the *Zohar* does not present a coherent chronological setting for its protagonists. See Scholem, *Kabbalah*, 221–222; Matt, *Zohar: The Book of Enlightenment*, 30, 290.

26. For the purposes of this subject, all generalized references will be to males.

27. See Baer, *History*, 1:83, 203.

28. Ibid., 201.

29. Ibid., 142–143. Yom Tov Asis, "Ha-Yehudim be-malkhut Aragoniah u-v'ezorei ḥasutah," in *Moreshet Sefarad*, ed. Beinart, 36–80, esp. 50.

30. Asis, ibid., 55.

31. Baer, *History*, 1:196.

32. See Sumption, *Pilgrimage*, 175–184.

33. *She'elot u-Teshuvot ha-Rashba* 5:235, cited in Baer, *History*, 1:430–431.

34. See Ramban, *Torat ha-Adam*, ed. Chavel, *Kitve ha-Ramban*, 2:49; *Tur OḤ* 219–end (see commentators there on the Rambam's opinion); *SA OḤ* 219:7.

35. *Sefer Abudarham ha-shalem, Hil. berakhot, ha-sha'ar ha-shemini* (Jerusalem, 1995), 386.

36. Baer, *History*, 1:125. On travels of Jewish courtiers and intellectuals, see his comment on 123.

37. In *Letters of Medieval Jewish Traders*, trans. from the Arabic and ed. S. D. Goitein (Princeton, NJ: Princeton University Press, 1973), 53–54. The letter is from the twelfth century, about a trip to North Africa. But there is no reason to doubt that these conditions and sentiments remained constant.

38. Ibid., 175.

39. Idel, "On Mobility, Individuals and Groups," 146, and see his "Ḥalon ha-hizdamnuyot," 28–30. See also Huss, "NiSAN," esp. 171–172.

40. See Breuer, "Nedudei talmidim va-ḥakhamim," and Ashtor, *Jews of Moslem Spain*, 3:98–99.

41. Ibid., 448.

42. See Idel, "'Ḥalon ha-hizdamnuyot,'" 8–11. On creativity, travel, and filiation, see below and the next chapter.

43. Ibid.

44. Breuer, "Nedudei talmidim va-ḥakhamim," 449.

45. Lefebvre, *Production of Space*, 266.

46. *MTJM*, 186.

47. 2:32a (#54), noted by Scholem. And cited by Tishby, *Mishnat*, 1:82.

48. Wolfson, "Re/membering," 214–215. Liebes, *Studies in the Zohar*, 67, speculates that the defeat of the Crusaders at Acre in 1291 may have influenced the messianic composition of the *Idra Rabba*.

49. See Wolfson, "Re/membering"; Baer, *History*, 1:65ff. And see discussion of the possible influence of the Crusades on the thought of R. Isaac the Blind in Pedaya, *Ha-Shem ve-ha-miqdash*, 288–291 (an earlier version is found in her "Pegam ve-tiqqun," 271–274).

50. Chazan, "Timebound and the Timeless," 28.

51. Idel, "Land of Israel in Medieval Kabbalah," 185n48, makes a similar point about Naḥmanides' pronouncements about the centrality of the land of Israel. See 116–117 above.

52. Baer, *History*, 1:49.

53. See ibid., 46ff.

54. See Pedaya, *Ha-Shem ve-ha-miqdash*, chap. 3, 148ff., and 192n49.

55. See ibid. and chap. 3 above.

56. Pedaya, *Ha-Shem ve-ha-miqdash*, 282–283. Pedaya does not include Idel's discussion of this issue in his essay "Land of Israel in Medieval Kabbalah" among her sources.

57. Pedaya, *Ha-Shem ve-ha-miqdash*, 278, and see 282ff.

58. Ibid., 283.

59. Idel, "'Al eretz Yisra'el ba-maḥashavah ha-yehudit ha-mistit," 207.

60. Ibid., 211.

61. Ibid.

62. See also Idel, "Land of Israel in Medieval Kabbalah," 180–181.

63. Ibid., 211–212.

64. See "Two Introductions" above at n. 25 and ff.

65. Idel, "Land of Israel in Medieval Kabbalah," 213–214.

66. Pierre Andre Sigal, "Roman Catholic Pilgrimage in Europe," in *The Encyclopedia of Religion*, ed. Mircea Eliade (New York: Macmillan, 1987), 11:331.

67. Sumption, *Pilgrimage*, 138.

68. Turner and Turner, *Image and Pilgrimage*, 168–170.

69. Ibid., 170.

70. See online Appendix 3, A.9.b., and see #17.

71. See 2:14a. This text has not been included in the listing of walking texts, as explained and noted above in "Two Introductions" at n. 6.

72. In all the zoharic walking texts, there is one anachronistic reference to some sages making a festival pilgrimage—*ZH* 83a (#28).

73. V. Turner, *Blazing the Trail*, 32.

74. Philo, *The Special Laws*, 1:68, 540, in *The Works of Philo*, trans. C. D. Yonge (Peabody, MA: Hendricksen, 1993). Thus every true pilgrim is another Abraham.

75. Ibid. 1:69–70.

76. See, e.g., V. Turner, *Dramas, Fields, and Metaphors*, 190, 219; Sumption, *Pilgrimage*, 196–198. Turner and Turner, *Image and Pilgrimage*, 37, note that this aspect was expressed well by Chaucer.

77. 2:3b–31a (#52). See other examples listed in this chapter, n. 5 above.

78. Turner and Turner, *Image and Pilgrimage*, 7. Sumption, *Pilgrimage*, 13, writes: "The popularity of the mendicant friars and of the local holy hermits, was undoubtedly due in part to the fact that they offered an escape from the stifling framework of parish life. Pilgrimage offered another escape."

79. Sumption, *Pilgrimage*, 95–96.

80. Ibid., 257.

81. V. Turner, *Dramas, Fields, and Metaphors*, 188.

82. De Certeau, *Mystic Fable*, 10.

83. See texts 5, 11, 17, 39, 41, 64, 66, 67, 94, 95, 100, 103, 117, 118. Rashbi seems to make a point of sitting for the sake of teaching Torah in texts 3, 17, 20, 72, 114.

84. 1:223a (#34). But see chap. 5 at n. 129.

85. On this use of the word, see *MTJM* 165n49; Liebes, "Peraḳim be-milon," 157, #87. Interestingly, in *ZH* 13d (*MH*) (#10), R. Zeira is upbraided by R. Yitzḥaq for walking in his garden and not studying Torah. He replies that he is walking in order to gain the necessary clarity of mind—*tzaḥuta*—so that he may study.

86. 1:89a (#64). We may infer from his response that R. Yudai will follow behind Rashbi.

87. 1:204b–205a (#31). See also #124.

88. This is an example of reversal of expectations and perspectives common in the *Zohar.* The story begins with the Companions, whose righteousness is obvious, having doubts about a stranger. But it turns out that it is they, rather than the stranger, who are forced to prove themselves worthy by revealing what kind of people they are.

89. See also 2:49b (#58).

90. *ZH* 22a (*MH*) (#17).

91. *ZH* 21d–22a (*MH*).

92. *M Megillah* 3:1. For a discussion of the move toward seeing the synagogue as a holy place, echoing the Temple, rather than as a social space, and the reasons for it, see Lee I. Levine, *The Ancient Synagogue: The First Thousand Years* (New Haven, CT: Yale University Press, 2000), 182–190, 229. See also Steven Fine, "From Meeting House to Sacred Realm: Holiness and the Ancient Synagogue," in *The Sacred Realm: The Emergence of the Synagogue in the Ancient World*, ed. Fine (New York: Oxford University Press and Yeshiva University Museum, 1996), 21–47. For a discussion, regarding synagogues, of the problems of access such a designation could engender if applied very strictly, see Ta-Shma, "'Miqdash me'at'."

93. It should be noted that Mount Sinai was only temporarily sanctified when it served as the place of the giving of the Torah.

94. BT *Megillah* 29a, cited by Levine, *Ancient Synagogue*, and *Sacred Realm*, ed. Fine. On the relative sanctity of the synagogue as compared to the study hall, see Levine, *Ancient Synagogue*, 449–451.

95. See Rubenstein, *Talmudic Stories*, 21–22, 270–272, and references, for a summary of the views of David Goodblatt and Isaiah Gafni (and others) and an updating of their debate.

96. Ibid., 22.

97. In the story of the Oven of Akhnai (BT *Bava Metzi'a* 59a–b), the argumentation of the sages literally (de)forms the walls of the study hall. See Rubenstein, *Talmudic Stories*, 42. Pedaya, *Ha-Shem ve-ha-miqdash*, 13n53, sees this more exclusively as the work of the *bat qol.*

98. Halperin, "Ascension or Invasion," 57.

99. See, e.g., the controversy over Rabban Gamaliel's restrictive policy, BT *Berakhot* 28a (cf. Maimonides, *Hil. Talmud Torah*, 4:1). On 28b the mishnah records the prayers of R. Nehuniah ben Ha-Qanah that mark the entry into and exit from the space of the *beit midrash.* The story of Hillel's poverty in BT *Yoma* 35b assumes that access was controlled by charging admission.

100. This comparison between *Tanna debe Eliyahu* (TDE) and the *Zohar* is based on the more extensive discussion in Greenstein, "Aimless Pilgrimage," Appendix VII.

101. *TDE*, ed. Friedmann, chap. 3, 15. It might be noted that R. Sherira Gaon (in

what seems to have been a fund-raising letter meant to exalt the status of his academy in the eyes of his addressee) mentions the talmudic statement that the Shekhinah has left Israel to reside in the synagogues of Babylonia (BT *Megillah* 29a) and continues, "and these places are our study hall [*midrashenu*] in which the yeshivah is established to support the *Shekhinah*" (first published in S. Schechter, *Saadyana* [Cambridge: Deighton & Bell, 1902], 123, as reconstructed by B. M. Lewin, *Rav Sherira Gaon* [Jaffa, 1917], 6; see also Lewin's *Otzar ha-Geonim*, vol. 4, *Ḥagigah* [Jerusalem: Wagshal, 1984], 21n7).

102. Maimonides, *Hil. Talmud Torah* 4:9; *Hil. Tefillah* 8:3. In the latter law, Maimonides requires a quorum in the *beit midrash* for scholars to remain there for prayer. But some Ashkenazic authorities privileged the study hall so much that they felt that solitary prayer there was preferable to prayer with a minyan in a synagogue. There is some discussion regarding the type of study hall implied. Was only a public hall of greater sanctity, or even a private study hall? See authorities cited in *Beit Yosef* to *Tur OḤ 151*. Although the study hall was of greater sanctity, it appeared to many that behavioral restrictions were less stringent there, since it was a place that was used in a less formally ritualized way and was, as noted below, a place where scholars may have lived. But *Nimmuqei Yosef* (early fifteenth century) to BT *Megillah* 28b (ed. Blau [New York, 1960], 54–55), s.v. *ve-eyn ne'otin*, tries to explain Maimonides' more stringent approach in this regard by suggesting that perhaps Maimonides differentiated between the talmudic cases and "the study halls here, which are similar to synagogues." This indicates that *beit midrash* does not always refer to a space functioning as a rabbinic academy, but sometimes also to the space of public lectures and sermons. See also Ta-Shma's observation, "'Miqdash me'at,'" 352, that in the popular consciousness the synagogue, not the *beit midrash*, was the exemplary sacred space.

103. *TDE*, ed. Friedmann chap. (5) 6, 29.

104. Rabbenu Yonah Gerondi in *Sha'arei Teshuvah, Sha'ar sheni, ha-derekh ha-sheni'ah* (Jerusalem: Lewin-Epstein, 1966), 36.

105. Pedaya, *Ha-Shem ve-ha-miqdash*, particularly the Introduction, 1–72.

106. Ibid., 13.

107. Ibid., 16.

108. See ibid., 21–22, for Pedaya's arguments with reference to Guedemann, Assaf, Scholem, Dinur, Kanarfogel, and others.

109. See Salo W. Baron, *A Social and Religious History of the Jews* (New York: Columbia University Press; Philadelphia: Jewish Publication Society, 1958), 6:140–141.

110. Here, ironically, a student not abiding by this rule is called one "who enters and leaves"—a common term for a kabbalistic adept. See also chap. 3, n. 82, and chap. 2, at n. 41, above.

111. Pedaya, *Ha-Shem ve-ha-miqdash*, 24n99. Also in Guedemann, *Ha-Torah*, 74. There are two such seven-year periods, one for children and one starting from age sixteen (see Guedemann, 80).

112. Lev. 8:33.

113. Another rule decrees that "when the *Rosh ha-Yeshivah* leaves the synagogue in the morning, he should enter the *beit midrash* without an interruption [*hefseq*], meaning, that he should not speak meanwhile" (Guedemann, *Ha-Torah*, 77).

114. 1:100a (*MH*).

115. 2:188b (#73). Later R. Yose makes the same point, referring to synagogues along with study halls, apparently in the context of readings from Scripture or public sermons.

116. See chap. 5, 159 at n. 26.

117. 2:5b (*MH*).

118. 2:168a.

119. 2:174b.

120. 1:240b–241b. See above, chap. 3, from n. 235.

121. 2:265b.

122. 2:3b. The term *bat 'el nekhar* can be found at 2:45b. See above, chap. 3, at n. 121.

123. See 3:41a (#85). Meroz, "Zoharic Narratives," 13, sees a reference to Rashbi's *beit midrash* at 2:36b–39b (#55). But this is questionable. See Lavi's comment, cited in chap. 2 at n. 64.

124. See Ta-Shma, "Hasidut Ashkenaz biSefarad: Rabbenu Yonah Girondi" and "Rabbi Yonah Girondi: Spirituality and Leadership," in *Jewish Mystical Leaders and Leadership*, ed. Idel and Ostow, 155–177. He has added material to *Ha-Nigleh she-ba-nistar*, his study of the *Zohar*, in "More on the Ashkenazic Origins to the *Zohar*," *Kabbalah* 3 (1998): 259–264, and "Additional Inquiries into the Problems of Ashkenazic Sources to the *Zohar*—II," *Kabbalah* 5 (2000): 353–358 (both in Hebrew).

125. Ta-Shma, *Ha-Nigleh she-ba-nstar*, 38.

126. Ibid., 39.

127. Ibid., 39–40.

128. See the citations of Katz in Ta-Shma, *Ha-Nigleh she-ba-nistar*, 40 and passim. Moshe Idel has written about this, inter alia, in "Kabbalah and Elites in Thirteenth-Century Spain," *Mediterranean Historical Review* 9 (1994): 5–19; "Nahmanides: Kabbalah, Halakhah, and Spiritual Leadership," 15–96, esp. 84–96; *Absorbing Perfections: Kabbalah and Interpretation* (New Haven, CT: Yale University Press, 2002), 397, 401–402, 434–435, and passim. On the opposition of Naḥmanides, Rabbenu Yonah, and other kabbalists to Jewish economic and political elites of the time, see, e.g., Septimus, "Piety and Power in Thirteenth-Century Catalonia"; Baer, *History*, 1:243–305.

129. Ta-Shma, *Ha-Nigleh she-ba-nistar*, 40.

130. Ibid., 52.

131. Yehuda Liebes, "Ha-*Zohar* ke-sefer halakhah," *Tarbiz* 64, no. 4 (1995): 581–605.

132. See Idel, "'We Have No Kabbalistic Tradition On This'"; id., "Nahmanides: Kabbalah, Halakhah, and Spiritual Leadership" (Hebrew version in *Tarbiz* 64, no. 4 [1995]: 535–580). Wolfson credits Naḥmanides with a more developed hermeneutic and with the desire to publicize it. See his "By Way of Truth: Aspects of Naḥmanides' Kabbalistic Hermeneutic."

133. See, e.g., Naḥmanides' Introduction to his Torah commentary and his comments on Gen. 1:1. On the influence of this stance on later kabbalists, see Wolfson, "Beyond the Spoken Word," 181–182.

134. On the displacement of the pietist elite by the Tosafists, see Soloveitchik, "Three Themes," 351ff. Ephraim Kanarfogel, in "*Peering through the Lattices*": *Mystical, Magical, and Pietistic Dimensions in the Tosafist Period* (Detroit: Wayne State University

Press, 2000) and *Intellectual History and Rabbinic Culture in Medieval Ashkenaz* (Detroit: Wayne State University Press, 2012), has done important work in expanding and enriching our appreciation of the spiritual life and concerns of the Tosafists, showing that the line between the Pietists and the Tosafists is not as clear-cut as previously supposed. Nevertheless, I believe that the fundamental point made by Soloveitchik still stands. The ascendance of the Tosafists, with the prioritizing of talmudic dialectics over mystical and pietistic concerns, is a fact of sociological and intellectual Jewish history.

135. See, e.g., M *Yadayim* 4:3. T *Yadayim* 2:7 and the parallel at BT *Ḥaggigah* 3b.

136. Liebes, "Ha-*Zohar* ke-sefer halakhah," 599. See also his "Ha-*Zohar* ke-renesans."

137. See the extensive but fragmentary section 3:161a–186a. And see Liebes, "Ha-*Zohar* ke-sefer halakhah," 588–597, on the relation between the lower heavenly yeshivah of the sages and the higher rank for the yeshivah of the children. See, too, Megged's chapter "Ha-tiyyul ha-misti b'yeshivot shel ma'alah," in id., *Ha-Or sheneḥeshakh*, 24–36. Megged, in his own way, touches on many of the issues dealt with here. Zeev Gries, in his review of Megged, *Kiryat Sefer* 55, no. 2 (April 1980):373–378, denies that there is any conflict between the image of the *talmid ḥakham* and the mystic, whether in the *Heikhalot* literature or in the *Zohar*. See also Wolski and Carmeli, "Those Who Know Have Wings."

138. 3:163a.

139. Ta-Shma, *Ha-Nigleh she-ba-Nistar*, 104n103.

140. See Greenstein, "Aimless Pilgrimage," chap. 2.C.c., 182–189, and Appendix VII, 591–615.

141. Hellner-Eshed has a short discussion of this issue in her chapter on the walking motif in *River Issues Forth*, pt. 2, chap. 2, 138–148, esp. 141–144 (in Hebrew; Eng., 111–120). Her treatment is essentially an appreciation of the motif rather than an investigation of it. (And see 147 above at n. 165.)

142. De Certeau sought, as well, to develop the possibility of a method of study that would not itself become an intellectual model of such control. See 146–147 above.

143. De Certeau, *Practice of Everyday Life*, 96. Earlier on the same page, he calls these practices "surreptitious creativities."

144. In *Mystic Fable*, 21–22, de Certeau writes: "In the sixteenth and seventeenth centuries, the mystics most often belonged to the regions and social categories that were going into a socioeconomic recession, were disfavored by change, pushed aside by progress, or financially ruined by the wars. That impoverishment developed the memory of a lost past; it clung to models deprived of efficacy and available for an 'other world.' It redirected toward the spaces of utopia, of dreamy imaginings and writings, aspirations before which the doors of social responsibilities were closed." See also, ibid., 6, where he states that the mystics operated "within a world that was 'passing away.'"

145. Buchanan, "Extraordinary Spaces," writes: "A genealogy is, in Foucault's own words, 'a form of history which can account for the constitution of knowledge, discourses, domains of objects, etc., without having to make reference to a subject . . .' While Foucault offers a powerful critique of regimes of domination and marginalization, his theorization of the marginalized offers no avenue for meaningful change. In the last instance the system will assimilate and accommodate all attempts at change, rendering revolutions meaningless."

146. This is so despite de Certeau's disclaimer at the very start of *Practice of Everyday Life* (xi) : "The examination of such practices does not imply a return to individuality." I understand this denial to be a denial of a concept of the individual as isolable from the collective. While de Certeau is opposed to viewing the individual as the atomic unit of all polities, he nonetheless posits an almost primal inability of living groups to control all their individual members, claiming to recognize this phenomenon in "the age-old ruses of fishes and insects that disguise or transform themselves in order to survive."

147. Lefebvre, *Production of Space*, 100.

148. De Certeau, *Practice of Everyday Life*, xix.

149. Ibid.

150. Ibid., 103.

151. Ibid., 106.

152. The notion that Jewish mysticism had a strong element of dissent from, and was subversive of, established orthodoxy was strengthened, in Scholem's view, by its later manifestations in Sabbateanism and Hasidism (see "Religious Authority and Mysticism," in Scholem, *On the Kabbalah and Its Symbolism*). Other scholars have theorized that even earlier trends were also characterized by alternative, dissenting stances relative to the established religious culture, elites and institutions of the time. See, e.g., Ithamar Gruenwald, "Meqoman shel mesorot kohaniot b'yetziratah shel ha-mistiqah shel ha-merqavah v'shel Shi'ur Qomah," *Jerusalem Studies in Jewish Thought* 6, no. 1–2 (1987): 65–120; Halperin, *Faces of the Chariot*; Yitzhak Baer, "Ha-Megamah ha-datit-ha-ḥevratit shel 'Sefer Ḥasidim,'" *Zion* 3 (1938): 1–50; Soloveitchik, "Three Themes."

153. See the summary in Tishby, *Mishnat*, 2:368–398. This view is echoed in Hellner-Eshed, *River Issues Forth* (in Hebrew), 141, referring to Y. Baer's seminal study, "Ha-Megamah." See, more extensively, Liebes, "Ha-*Zohar* v'ha-Tiqqunim—me-renesans l'mahapekhah." Giller tries to offer a corrective to this view in *Enlightened Will Shine*, 59–79. But his attack on Tishby seems overdrawn. The issue, as I shall argue, is not to be dichotomized into a test of observance or nonobservance of the halakhic system, but one of expressions of tensions within it.

154. Liebes, "Ha-*Zohar* ke-sefer halakhah," 598.

155. Lefebvre, *Production of Space*, 115.

156. Ibid., 163.

157. Ibid., 232.

158. See Lefebvre's discussion and critique of Panofsky's theory of the relation between Church ideology and the Gothic cathedral, ibid., 257–261.

159. For sources, see n. 128 above.

160. De Certeau, *Mystic Fable*, 9.

161. De Certeau, *Practice of Everyday Life*, 97–98.

162. De Certeau, *Mystic Fable*, 88. He elaborates: "Francis, walking in the fields, 'preaches' without needing words, those opaque mediators between man and nature" (316n24), citing Edward A. Armstrong, *Saint Francis: Nature Mystic; The Derivation and Significance of the Nature Stories in the Franciscan Legend* (Berkeley: University of California Press, 1973), 5–41.

163. De Certeau, *Mystic Fable*, 6.

164. Ibid., 14.

165. This is in contrast to the approach of Hellner-Eshed in *River Issues Forth*, who entitles her chapter on the walking motif "'While you walk on the way': The Locus of Mystical Experience" (in Hebrew).

166. See Septimus, "Piety and Power" and references cited n. 124 above.

167. See Idel, "Transmission in Thirteenth-Century Kabbalah"; Wolfson, "Beyond the Spoken Word" and "Anonymous Chapters." See also D. Abrams, "Orality in the Kabbalistic School of Nahmanides: Preserving and Interpreting Esoteric Traditions and Texts," *Jewish Studies Quarterly* 2 (1995): 85–102, now included as chap. 3, "The Textualization of Orality: The Reception and Interpretation of Nahmanides' Kabbalistic Traditions," in id., *Kabbalistic Manuscripts*, 198–223, and Fishbane, *As Light Before Dawn*, chap. 3, "Receiving Tradition, Constructing Authority" (49–76), and chap. 4, "Intention and the Recovery of Meaning" (77–100).

168. Pedaya, *Ha-Shem ve-ha-miqdash*, 61.

169. As cited in Scholem, *Origins*, 394. The original was published by Scholem in "Te'udah ḥadashah le-toldot reshit ha-qabbalah," in his *Meḥqerei qabbalah*, 7–38. See also Idel, *Kabbalah*, 20–22, and id, "Naḥmanides: Kabbalah, Halakhah, and Spiritual Leadership," 28–36; Wolfson, "Beyond the Spoken Word," 176; Pedaya, *Ha-Shem ve-ha-miqdash*, 59–66.

170. On the use of the claim for oral tradition as a source of authority, see Idel, "Transmission in Thirteenth-Century Kabbalah," 143–144. It may be that the *Zohar* is making such a claim when it ascribes its teachings to "the secret of our Mishnah" (1:55b). As Matt, *Zohar*, Pritzker ed., 1:314n1535, indicates, this reference is independent of the *Matnitin* sections of the *Zohar*. See his note for other places where this phrase is used.

171. Pedaya, *Ha-Shem ve-ha-miqdash*, 62–63.

172. Scholem, *Origins*. Scholem does mention this sentence of the epistle later in his discussion of it (395) though he omits the reference to "streets" and proceeds to refer to the problematic behavior of those whom R. Isaac opposed with the limited characterization "the literary propagation of their mystical ideas" (396). The argument here is that the additional problem is not one of literary propagation. Scholem cites the phrase fully in his discussion in "Te'udah ḥadashah," 23.

173. See Wolfson, "Beyond the Spoken Word," 174ff.

174. Yaakov Elman and Israel Gershoni, "Introduction—*Transmitting Tradition: Orality and Textuality in Jewish Cultures*," in their *Transmitting Jewish Traditions*, 14.

175. Ibid., 190.

176. See the studies of Matt and Liebes.

177. Wolfson, "Beyond the Spoken Word," 193.

178. See #73, cited above at n. 115. See also #96, where the *beit midrash* is the place that strictly enforces the textual integrity of the Torah scroll.

179. See Wolfson, "Beyond the Spoken Word," 170, citing *MTJM*, 174

180. E.g., #15, 47, *ZH* #21. See Megged, *Ha-Or sheneḥeshakh*, 28.

181. Oral transmission of esoteric Torah requires a spatial practice based on nearness between teacher and student. Publishing destroys the spatial limits that kabbalah had

previously assumed. Walking on the road is thus a statement about negotiating distances while engaged in spreading Torah. The negative attitude toward the book is compensated for by the alternative suggestion of spreading Torah through walking along.

182. De Certeau, *Mystic Fable*, 6.

183. See 140 above at n. 147 and ff.

184. Since the claim here is that this unique upending of the description of the production of Oral Torah is a conscious choice of this unique written text, one may say that the contemporary mystery of the composition of the *Zohar* is thus inherent in its nature, since it is based on an undisclosed, mysterious method of transforming the Oral to the Written. See Hellner-Eshed, *River Issues Forth*, pt. 4, chap. 5, 426–441 (in Hebrew; Eng., 365–378).

185. Lefebvre, *Production of Space*, 229.

186. Ibid., 52.

187. Ibid., 227. It should be noted that the distinction between speech and writing is not an absolute one in Lefebvre's usage. Speech tends toward writing, and both are subsumed under the concept of language, against whose powers of abstraction Lefebvre repeatedly warns. See, e.g., ibid., 28–29, 140, 403.

188. Ibid., 363.

Chapter 5. The Broad Dissemination of Torah

1. For a fundamental treatment of this theme, see Wolfson, "Circumcision," in his *Circle*, 29–48, 140–155, which includes references to his other studies of this rite. See also his "Re/membering," 222ff. Particularly relevant to the following discussion is the beginning of his study "Cut That Binds," 103–106.

2. As the *Zohar* declares, "The body wishes to walk on its way, and the culmination of the body is *brit*" (1:158a).

3. Particularly suggestive in this regard is a statement by David M. Levin, as cited by Wolfson in "Cut That Binds," 103: "Circumcision therefore corresponds to the breaking open of a path."

4. 3:21a (#80). For Smith on "the shift from a cosmological to an anthropological viewpoint," see, among other places, id., *Map*, 128, and *To Take Place*, 11.

5. 1:92b–96b (#12). See Matt's translation and notes, *Zohar*, Pritzker ed., 2: 82–115. And see Hellner-Eshed, *River Issues Forth*, 216–221 (in Hebrew; Eng., 183–188).

6. See Scholem, "She'elot be-viqoret," 53, for speculation as to the meaning and reading of this term. Matt, *Zohar*, Pritzker ed., 2: 82, translates as "castle," and see his n. 630.

7. See Scholem, "She'elot be-viqoret," 49–50. As he notes, Kfar Tarsha is also mentioned in *MH* 1:101a–b and identified with Mata Meḥasya, more familiar as a Babylonian locale. These two stories are clearly related in that they both report that the dedication to Torah learning in this village was an expression of repentance after a deadly plague that hit them. And see his *Kabbalah*, 222. R. Ḥayyim Vital, in Azulai, *Or ha-Ḥamah*, 1:83b, seems to consider them one story.

8. See Liebes, "Peraḳim be-milon," 350.

9. Such a mechanism was invented in Spain in the late thirteenth century. See Baer,

History, 1:267–268. And see further Matt, *Zohar*, Pritzker ed. 2:82nn634–635; Ashtor, *Jews in Moslem Spain*, 3:128–129.

10. On the phrase *ve'ishtadel be'oraita*, see R. Moshe de Leon, *Book of the Pomegranate*, ed. Wolfson, 47; Wolfson, "Female Imaging," in id., *Circle*, 18–19; id., *Through a Speculum*, 378n184. At 2:27a, the purpose of exertion in Torah is to clarify the law. At 3:98b, the purpose is to learn God's ways. At 3:112a, it is to know God and God's mysteries through the way of Wisdom. Using a similar term, the *Zohar* (2:246b) praises "those who exert themselves in Wisdom [*demishtadlei b'ḥokhm'ta*] to look at the Glory of their Master." This term can also be applied to rites and ceremonies (*ishtadlu bepulḥani, de-ishtadlu bepulḥani*), as at 3:159b.

11. The story, like other zoharic stories (see above chap. 2 at n. 18), does not record their reaching that destination. At the end of the story, R. Abba goes to Rashbi. See 31, 161–166 above.

12. This is a major motif in the *Zohar,* mentioned right before this text at 1:92a. See Wolfson, *Through a Speculum*, 372–374. See above, chap. 2 at n. 52.

13. See chap. 2, n. 34. For analysis of this gesture in another zoharic text, see Tene, "Darkhei," 150–152.

14. See Liebes, "Peraḳim be-milon," 136–167. The combination of light (*butzina*) and sound (*qala*) imagery is unique. I do not find reference in his entries to this phrase. As mentioned above, Liebes suggests that *butzina* may also occasionally mean a shofar. Perhaps this case is an additional instance of that meaning. In that case he would be encouraging the child to speak up (see 3:39ab). But the usual loaded meaning of the term remains in the background. (See Lavi, *Ketem Paz*, 1:227d, who tries to mitigate the clash between images.) The *butzina* (or *butzitza*) *d'qardinuta* is also the point of measurement that creates the spatial cosmic reality, as described in the section *Qav ha-Middah* (*ZH* 56d–58d). In that discourse, the mystic who engages in this study is said to "take the *butzina d'qardinuta* in his hand, to stretch it in all directions and make this measurement." In this sense, a Torah discourse might be called the voice of the spark, since it creates more cosmic reality. See Liebes, *Studies in the Zohar*, 68–69. On the space-creating function of the *butzina*, see below. On the *Zohar*'s uniting of light imagery with linguistic imagery, see Wolfson, "Letter Symbolism," 217n77.

15. This is a serious concern and frequently expressed lament in the *Zohar* (see chap. 2 at n. 85, chap. 3 at n. 224, chap. 6 at nn. 19, 36). The solution tended to be found in messianic expectations. See Liebes, "The Messiah of the *Zohar*," in *Studies in the Zohar*; id., "Ha-*Zohar* ke-renesans," 10; Huss, "Ḥakham 'adif mi-navi," 107–108. The *Tiqqunei Zohar* and *Ra'aya Meheimna* compositions should be seen as attempts to address this issue. See A. Goldreich, "Berurim bir'iyato ha-'atzmit shel ba'al *Tiqqunei ha-Zohar*," in *Massu'ot*, ed. Oron and Goldreich. The matter requires more study. On the status of Rashbi's generation, see Tishby, *Mishnat*, 1:27; Liebes, *Studies in the Zohar*, 5, 29–33; Hellner-Eshed, *River Issues Forth*, 77–104 (in Hebrew; Eng., 62–84).

16. Identified by the commentators with Elijah the prophet. See Liebes, "Peraḳim be-milon," 355–383, on the related term *qiyuma*. The associations run through notions of life, health, circumcision, place, phallus (see "Peraḳim be-milon," 266), naming, and understanding. See also Wolfson, *Along the Path*, 208n79. On Abraham's circumcision,

see 161 above. Liebes, *Studies in the Zohar*, 23, points out that the term *qiyuma* can also mean an "occasion" or "festive event."

17. See Wolfson, "Circumcision," in id., *Circle*, 154n91, on the connection between circumcision and seeing the Shekhinah.

18. 1:93a–b.

19. The role of women as actors in the *Zohar*—as distinct from the *Zohar*'s theory of women or the feminine—needs further study.

20. Wolfson analyzes the (Lurianic) connection between circumcision and seeing the face of God/Shekhinah in "Crossing Gender Boundaries," in id., *Circle*, 105–106. For the *Zohar*, the Companions themselves constitute the Face of the Shekhinah. See 2:163b (#70); Wolfson, *Through a Speculum*, 368–377; id., "Eunuchs," 171–172. And see also above chap. 2 at n. 78.

21. The teachings on gender relations build on each other. In some of the examples, the female is the active force instigating the performance of the mitzvah—the cases of Tzipporah and Deborah. In others, the female is the dangerous temptation who must be guarded against—the cases of Joseph and David. Finally the ideal of male and female conjunction is taught on the interpersonal level and on the level of human/divine conjunction. See Wolfson, "Crossing Gender Boundaries," *Through a Speculum*, and "Eunuchs."

22. 1:94a.

23. See *ZH* 77b (#24), and see 164–168 on the significance of this statement.

24. The word for "streams" of water and the word for "illumination" are the same: *naharei*, *naharin*.

25. Lavi, *Ketem Paz* 1:231b, takes this image literally, explaining that by living in a village, close to fields, the residents enjoyed better air than city dwellers who live in closed in spaces. But it seems more likely that the reference is to the sefirotic effluence generated by their Torah study. See also Wolski and Carmeli, "Those Who Know Have Wings," 103–104, regarding the possibility (rejected) that this refers to the use of entheogens for mystical purposes.

26. A term for rabbinic scholars. See BT *Berakhot* 27b—*ba'alei terisin*. The *Zohar* uses military imagery to refer to Torah study and sages in some important texts, such as *Sabba de Mishpatim* (2:209a–210a), *Yenuqa* (3:188b), *Idra Rabba* (3:127b), and *Idra Zuta* (3:296b). See Liebes, "Peraḳim be-milon," 383; id., *Studies in the Zohar*, 21–22; Wolfson, *Through a Speculum*, 371; Matt, *Zohar: The Book of Enlightenment*, 278. On the talmudic material, see Rubenstein, *Talmudic Stories*, 277–279.

27. 1:94a–b.

28. Traditional commentators explain that they sinned in neglecting Torah study. This is implied in the companion story of *MH* (1:101b), cited above. There, R. Aḥa stops the plague and calls on the town to repent and pledge never to neglect Torah study. But see 177–178 above.

29. This is a reversal of the famous story in the Passover Haggadah of the sages in Bene Beraq who sit all night discussing the Exodus until they are interrupted by their students, who tell them that day has dawned: "The time for morning recitation of *Sh'ma* has arrived." Matt, *Zohar*, Pritzker ed., 2:97, reads only, "Go out and see," omitting "if the day has dawned."

30. Lavi, *Ketem Paz*, 1:231c, interprets this phrase as an expression of R. Abba's fear, reading *qutra* as smoke, a sign of God's anger (on this meaning for *qutra*, see n. 32 below and chap. 6, n. 55). But it seems preferable to read this phrase differently. *Qutra* can also mean "knot" (see Liebes, "Peraḳim be-milon," s.v. *qeshara*, 394–402). The associations include divine emanation, divine forces such as the *sefirot* and their connections to each other, *brit*, the place or act of conjoining. I do not find the phrase *qutra de-hurmana* in Liebes. The term *hurmana* is known most widely in the phrase—*be-reish hormanuta di-malka*, which introduces some important zoharic texts dealing with the earliest stages of creation (see Giller, *Reading*, 69ff.). The term conveys authority, will, or decree. In the creation texts, the Divine Will sends out a *butzina de-qardinuta* (see Liebes, "Peraḳim be-milon," s.v. *butzina*; Giller, *Reading*; Wolfson, "Erasing the Erasure," in *Circle*, 49–78, 155–195, and "Woman," 178ff.). Thus, this phrase refers to Divine phallic activity. See also next note.

31. The Earth—*ar'a*—is often a symbol for Shekhinah. R. Abba's statement may thus be taken as referring to the conjoining of the Divine phallus (*Yesod*) with Shekhinah. This conjoining finds its manifestation in a number of phenomena, natural and human. Daybreak itself is a reprise of the initial breakthrough of light by the primordial spark. In *ZH* (61d) we read of Shekhinah (*ar'a*), whose light is enfolded within herself, "until the other light, outside that light, pounds it and penetrates her so that she is filled with that glow and shines in every direction" (cited by Wolfson, "Woman," 200n65). See 88, 107 above on the appearance of stars at daybreak, the sparks of the original act of creation. On the human level, the revelation of Torah by these sages and their children constitutes a powerful theurgical unification of the Upper Realms with Shekhinah, as the text immediately indicates.

32. The term *qitra* can refer to a knot or tie, with the sefirotic meanings associated with these words, as noted above. It also can be associated with the incense—*qetoret*—in the Tabernacle, with its associations to scent, fire and smoke. Indeed, the companion story to our text, *MH* 1:101a, has R. Aḥa advise the town that the recitation of the biblical texts about *qetoret* would protect them from the plague that had attacked this village, as Aaron stopped the plague in the Bible (Num. 17:12ff.). It should be noted that ordinarily the incense was offered, as the text at 2:219a points out, on the interior altar of the sanctuary (and it is brought into the Inner Sanctum by the High Priest on Yom Kippur), while here the house seems surrounded on the outside.

33. 1:94b. This scenario and these last words recall the story of Ben 'Azzai in *Shir ha-Shirim Rabbah* 1:10, 2 and parallels.

34. It is important to note, in contrast, that the walking texts do not report the Companions having such experiences. For another example, see 1:89a (*ST*) (#32 in list of texts outside the *guf ha-Zohar*).

35. 1:94b–96b.

36. It is treated extensively in the *Sabba de Mishpatim* section, among other places. There may be a connective hint to that section in the closing teaching of R. Abba, where he talks of the tower in the vineyard (Isa. 5:2), interpreted as referring to the conjoining of *Yesod* and *Malkhut*. Of course, the tower is the setting for the story in the *Sabba* text. The *Sabba*'s parable of the beautiful maiden without eyes who is hidden in a palace is related to many versions of the story that have her ensconced in a

tower. See Wineman, *Beyond Appearances*, 18–23: Liebes, *Studies in the Zohar*, 59–60. See Abrams, "Knowing the Maiden without Eyes" for further citations. On the further significance of the tower image, see 168–178 above. Liebes suggests that our text be read in light of zoharic golem traditions. The creative function of the Torah study at the time of circumcision is especially necessary for this child born of a levirate union. See his "Golem," 1320–1321.

37. For a discussion of the *Sabba* text as a meditation on dislocation, see Giller, *Reading*, 35–68.

38. The phrase *sidru milin*, "set forth these things," echoes talmudic phrases that convey the formal recitation, or the attempted organization, of teachings (aggadah, biblical verses, or halakhah—-cf. BT *Berakhot* 10a, *Megillah* 18b, 27a) or prayer (as in BT *Berakhot* 13a). But it does not appear in precisely this form in classical rabbinic literature. It appears in the zoharic imitation *Midrash Rut* in *Har Adonai*, reprinted in *Otzar Midrashim*, ed. Eisenstein (New York, 1915), 2:515: "set forth teachings on how the Holy Land and the Name were joined through *Teshuvah*" (on this work, see Scholem, *Kabbalah*, 219). In these various texts it does not seem to be used to refer to telling a narrative (see Matt, *Zohar*, Pritzker ed., 5:336n410). See further next note.

39. Here the narrative explicitly separates the story of R. Abba's experience from the teachings he heard. The phrase used above to describe his revelations to R. Ele'azar corresponds to the phrase used here for the Torah instruction only. Is this meant to convey that he shared the teachings but not the circumstances by which he learned them? Or perhaps the intent is that R. Abba rehearsed before R. Ele'azar how and when to reveal to his father what had happened. Thus it is not clear whether R. Eleazar is complicit with R. Abba in concealing information from Rashbi, or whether R. Abba has engaged in an elaborate plan of varying degrees of revelation and concealment. See 2:123b, where R. Ele'azar and R. Abba discuss the problem of whether to reveal Rashbi's teachings. See Matt, *Zohar*, Pritzker ed., 5:159–160nn57–58.

40. The term *gozarna* is related to the term for being circumcised—*gazir*.

41. This punishment is appropriate on a number of levels. Sometimes forgetting is necessary to protect Torah that is not ready to be revealed. See 1:118a (#15). Is that the case at Kfar Tarsha? It is noteworthy that for the whole day that they were circled by fire, there is no record of their Torah. True filiation requires remembering, as illustrated in the story of the forgetful R. Yose, 2:79ab. Forgetting is also the opposite of *zikkaron*—remembering—an important aspect of circumcision. See R. Moshe de Leon, "Shenei quntresim le-," 363; Liebes, *Studies in the Zohar*, 58; Wolfson, "Re/membering," 222ff., and his studies cited above, n. 2. Forgetting is also used as the justification for writing down esoteric Torah (see Wolfson, "Beyond the Spoken Word," 183–185). If walking along the road has to do with revealing and disseminating esoteric Torah, then R. Abba's "punishment" makes it all the more imperative to dislodge the Kfar Tarsha group that he was protecting.

42. There are several variants in this line, each changing the meaning of Rashbi's decree. One version has *d'oraita da yegalun be-bavel* (or, after the version cited in the body of the text, the addition of *vi-yegalun be-bavel*)—that this Torah will be revealed in Babylonia, and no longer be the sole possession of the sages of Kfar Tarsha. Another version

has *de-be-orta da yiglun le-bavel*—that they will be exiled this very night. See Azulai, *Or ha-Ḥamah*, 1:85c, and variants in R. Yehudah Ashlag's edition, *Zohar 'im Perush ha-Sulam*, ad loc. Matt, *Zohar*, Pritzker ed., 2:115, reads: "*d'b'oraita da yigalun l'bavel* . . . —with this Torah they will be exiled to Babylonia among all the Companions."

43. The reading according to Lavi, *Ketem Paz* 1:236b, translated as "pain [*ha-tza'ar*] in your heart." Matt, *Zohar*, Pritzker ed., renders it as "heart's configuration"; see his n. 887.

44. This is a reminder of the daybreak experience at Kfar Tarsha.

45. See 3:159a. See Liebes, *Studies in the Zohar*, esp. 23–26.

46. They call R. Abba *gavra rabba*—a great man (94b).

47. The righteous who rise at night to learn Torah are called God's sons. See 1:82a.

48. See 94b, where the formulae recited by "the earlier pietists, the elders of this place" at a *brit* are honored through use and study.

49. Based on Gen. 31:53. See, e.g., *Zohar* 1:213b.

50. See also 1:3b, where the *Zohar* dissects the word *Bereshit* into the components *bara* (create/son) and *shit* (six) and ties together revelation, concealment, filiation, and circumcision. See analysis of this text in "Christian Influences on the *Zohar*," in Liebes, *Studies*, 146ff.

51. Similarly, Tene, "Darkhei," 34, points out that in the zoharic story of R. Pinḥas's search for Rashbi (1:11ab), R. Pinḥas is located in a named place, but that he finds Rashbi, who has left his cave, in no specific place.

52. Lefebvre, *Production of Space*, 162.

53. Ibid., 170.

54. Ibid., 62. See also 179–180.

55. The *Zohar* sometimes characterizes the establishment of a place of Torah study as the building of a nest. See, e.g., 3:9a.

56. Deut. 22:6–7.

57. See BT *Berakhot* 33b; Maimonides, *Guide* 3:48; Naḥmanides on the Torah, ad loc.

58. *Sefer ha-Bahir*, ed. Abrams, ¶74, ed. Margaliot, ¶¶104–105. Naḥmanides cites the *Bahir*. R. Moshe de Leon, *Book of the Pomegranate,* ed. Wolfson, 339, begins to apply the *Bahir*'s interpretation to Shekhinah and lower entities.

59. In one text, however, the *Zohar* directly links the verses to the matter of filial devotion. See 3:304b (#115), where a distraught son argues that God should have spared his father and taken the children instead. See Tene's analysis of this story and her discussion of the motif of the bird's nest in "Darkhei," 159–167.

60. *ZH* (*Rut*) 77b (#24).

61. Ibid. See BT *Berakhot* 3a (in Greenstein, "Aimless Pilgrimage," talmudic walking text #1). The talmudic version constructs the phrase "Woe to My children, for on account of their sins I have destroyed," etc. The *Zohar*'s version leaves out blaming Israel for sinning and concentrates on the sorrow and pain of the catastrophe and its dislocating effects. See also R. Azriel's *Perush le-Shir ha-Shirim* 4:6, in *Kitvei ha-Ramban*, ed. Chavel (Jerusalem: Kook, 1964), 2:495.

62. The reading is unclear. Some read *heiman"a*, while some read *tevunah*. The first, more difficult reading is to be preferred, but, being difficult, its meaning is not clear. The term may refer to faith, as translated here. It may mean "a belt," signifying the com-

bination of all the knots or forces. The term *qitra* (or *qutra*) *de-heimana* is very similar to the term encountered above, when R. Abba exclaims that "the Knot of Will—*qutra de-hormana*—has been caught on Earth." See 160 above at n. 32.

63. See 3:159ab (#110), *ZH* 3d–4a (*MH*), 6d (*MH*). On the three worlds or levels of worlds, see Tishby, *Mishnat*, 1:387.

64. "All" can be a reference to Shekhinah.

65. *ZH* (*Rut*) 77b–c.

66. If the rationale for this mitzvah is tied to the Temple's destruction, the question arises why this should have been a mitzvah when the Temple stood. See Margaliot, *Sha'arei Zohar*, 122a, to *Ḥullin* 138b.

67. See "The Travails of Shekhinah," chap. 3 above.

68. See also 3:254ab. There it is explained that the six Divine potencies can only be drawn down to this world by Israel's sending away Shekhinah, the Mother, from Her nest. In that text, Israel accomplishes this through its recitation of prayers in synagogues and study halls, called *tziftzufa* (chirping). See 2:8a, where the Messiah is linked with the mother bird and the nest, hidden in the Garden of Eden. See Tene, "Darkhei," 165–167.

69. Gen. 11:1–9. Another disturbing association raised by this act is to Avtalyon's admonition in *Avot* 1:11: "Sages, be cautious in your words, lest you incur the punishment of exile," etc.

70. Gen. 11:4. The *Zohar* describes Shekhinah in Her future manifestation as "a tower of precious stone in the center [of other towers] that rises to the height of the firmament" (3:164a).

71. Medieval travel, especially under the influence of the Crusades, promoted an increased interest in the varieties of languages. This period saw the rise of language manuals to aid the traveler who needed to use a foreign tongue. See Sumption, *Pilgrimage*, 195.

72. M*Sanhedrin* 10:3 includes the generation of the Tower among other wicked groups, such as the Generation of the Flood and the inhabitants of Sodom, who have no share in the Coming World.

73. Josephus, *Antiquities of the Jews* 1:110–112, explains that God had ordered the inhabitants of the valley to spread across the earth, and that their decision to stay in one place was an act of defiance. Much later this explanation is put forth by Rashbam at Gen. 11:4. The order is presumably God's command to Noah, after the Flood, to have many children and populate the earth. Rashbam, however, cites the original command/blessing at Gen. 1:28. See also RaDaK ad loc. and next note.

74. Naḥmanides on Gen. 11:2, Hebrew text, ed. Chavel, *Torat Ḥayyim*, 1:140 (Jerusalem: Kook, 1986). Note that Naḥmanides records the view that the Generation of Division did not sin, citing Ibn Ezra, without refuting it in his sermon, "Torat ha-Shem temimah," *Kitvei ha-Ramban*, ed. Chavel, 1:174.

75. See R. Yosef Giqatilla, *Sha'arei Orah*, Gate X (ed. Ben-Shelomo, 122); *Sha'arei Tzedeq* (Kraków, 1881; Brooklyn, NY, 1986), 9b, 11b.

76. See Abulafia, *Sha'ar ha-Razim*, ed. Kushnir-Oron, 135. The editor cites Abulafia's *Otzar ha-Kavod*, Naḥmanides, and the *Ma'arekhet ha-Elohut*. One should also see Abulafia's remarks in *Otzar ha-Kavod* at *Ḥaggigah* 15, s.v. *Ayeh sofer*, 47b.

77. Menaḥem Reqanati, printed with R. Mordekhai Yaffe's commentary, *Sefer Levush Or Yaqrut* (reprint, Lublin, n.d.), 20b–c.

78. Baḥya, ed. Chavel (Jerusalem: Kook, 1994), 1:128.

79. *Ma'arekhet* (reprint of Mantua edition, Jerusalem, 1963), chap. 9, 122a–b, 125a. See Lavi, *Ketem Paz*, 1:185c–187c, who cites all these authorities except R. Todros in his polemic against R. Yehudah Ḥayyat.

80. The tenth chapter is *Sha'ar Ha-Adam*. There it is explained that the building refers to the *Shi'ur Qomah* seen through prophecy. See *Ma'arekhet*, 142b, 144a.

81. See *Ma'arekhet*, chap. 8, 105b.

82. Ibid., chap. 9, 122a–b, 125a.

83. See, similarly, the explanations of *Sefer ha-Peli'ah* and *Tziyyoni*, cited in *Yalqut Re'uveni* (Jerusalem: Vagshal, 1995), 145–146. The citation from *Sefer ha-Peli'ah* can be found in the recent printing, *Torat ha-Qanah: Sefer Ha-Peli'ah* (Jerusalem, 1997), 594; *Tziyyoni* (Lemberg [L'viv], 1882), 8cd.

84. Isaac of Acre, *Sefer Me'irat 'Eynayim*, ed. Goldreich, 40 (ed. H. A. Erlanger, 56).

85. The production of space is epitomized by the birth process, which brings about the separation of the fetus from the mother. Thus, the embrace of spatiality implies the acceptance of the need to distance oneself from the mother. Overattachment to the mother can be expressed in the desire for a limited, concentrated spatial practice. See de Certeau, *Practice of Everyday Life*, 109–110. Halperin, "Ascension or Invasion," 58, cites Erikson's research on the building of towers as an expression of Oedipal feelings.

86. 1:74a.

87. Note that, similarly, Rashbi (96b) suggests that Abraham was automatically circumcised.

88. 1:74a. See also #3.

89. See *Bereshit Rabbah* 38:7, ed. Theodor and Albeck, 356.

90. 1:74a–b.

91. See chap. 3 above at n. 26; Tishby, *Mishnat*, 1:387–388; G. Scholem, "Le-Ḥeqer qabbalat R. Yitzḥaq ben Ya'aqov ha-Kohen," *Tarbiz* 3 (1932): 36–39.

92. And see the parallel text of *Sitrei Torah*.

93. On the zoharic view of Babylonia, see 187–191 above.

94. 1:74b.

95. Ibid. We find here another association to the *Sabba de-Mishpatim* text. The *Sabba*, in the midst of struggling with his exposition, characterizes his experience to being on the sea in a boat without a captain. The Shekhinah is often characterized as the Great Sea, even with the detail of ships sailing Her. See, e.g., 1:124a. 2:48 (and Giqatilla's *Sha'arei Orah*, ed. Ben-Shelomo, 1:62). Since this grade is also identified with the Oral Torah, engaging in Torah can be pictured as sailing on the sea. The sage Rav Hamnuna Sabba is described as a fish who swam to all sides of the Great Sea (1:6a). The *Sabba de-Mishpatim* includes particularly striking examples of this: 2:98b, 100b, 103b. The same image that R. Ḥiyya uses to condemn the evil speech of the Tower builders thus serves the *Sabba* to describe his struggle over conceiving of and expounding the deepest truths of Torah. There are interesting parallels and differences to be found in the Christian mystical tradition. See McGinn, "Ocean and Desert." For instance, McGinn (163) quotes John Scotus

Erigena's use of the image of navigating difficult sea waters to refer to particularly profound theological investigations, an image reminiscent of the one used by the *Sabba.*

96. 1:75a.

97. 1:75b.

98. That the world derives its nourishment from the land of Israel and from Shabbat is a common idea in rabbinic and zoharic sources. Regarding Israel, see, e.g., *ZH* 9b (*MH*). For discussions of the significance of the land in rabbinic and kabbalistic sources, see Idel, "'Al Eretz Yisra'el ba-maḥashavah ha-yehudit ha-mistit" and "Land of Israel in Medieval Kabbalah," and Rosenberg, "Link to the Land of Israel in Jewish Thought." Regarding Shabbat, see, e.g., 2:88a. For a discussion of "Sabbath as the Source of Cosmic Blessing," see Elliot K. Ginsburg, *The Sabbath in the Classical Kabbalah* (Albany: State University of New York Press, 1989), 78–85.

99. 1:75b.

100. See *Livnat ha-Sappir*, 14d.

101. 1:75b.

102. For traditional commentaries, see Lavi, *Ketem Paz*, 1:188a–190b, and Cordovero, *Pardes Rimmonim*, "Sha'ar ABY" 'A," chap. 5, 79b–80a. In the following chap. 6, RaMaK ties together this theme with the theme of walking and the wandering bird and her nest.

103. 1:75b.

104. 1:76a. The teaching concludes with an assurance that at the end of time, all will be able to receive Divine Wisdom fully and serve God without doing harm to the world.

105. 1:94b.

106. See Liebes, *Studies in the Zohar*, 24–26.

107. Ibid., 26. It is noteworthy that the *Zohar* (3:200a), referring to Balaq's plan for Balaam, says: "And he did not know that the Holy Blessed One 'removes language from the faithful [*ne'emanim*], and takes away the sense of elders' [Job 12:20]. And all exists by His permission. 'Removes language from the faithful,'—these are the Generation of Division, for He confounded their language so that they should not control the matter [*milah*] at all."

108. See Huss, "Ḥakham 'adif mi-navi." This connection should be borne in mind with regard to the *Zohar*'s statement cited above, singling out Moses as the only biblical figure who could handle the esoteric Torah.

109. See Hellner-Eshed, *River Issues Forth*, 219 (in Hebrew; Eng., 187).

110. 2:86b (#62).

111. See, e.g., 1:64b (#7), 2:156a (#69), 3:22b (#80), 3:187a (#111), 3:206a (#115).

112. See "Studying the Zohar: A Unique Book and a Unique Motif" in "Two Introductions" above.

113. But see 2:149a (#67).

114. See 2:15a , 1:89a (*ST*) (#32 of texts outside *guf ha-Zohar*), and its parallel in *ZH* 25c (*MH* #18).

115. In the *MH* version of the walking text referred to in the previous note, the teacher is R. Ele'azar b. 'Arakh. This is another example of the *MH* not yet giving a central role to Rashbi and his son.

116. See 1:132a (#17). Rashbi predicts that he will meet someone with new words of

Torah to share. He encounters a Cappadocian who is seeking Rashbi in *titoreih*. The Cappadocian is introduced to Rashbi on the road, and questions him about rules of prayer. Rather than hearing new words from the Jew, Rashbi is the one who teaches new Torah. The word *titoreih* is translated in *Nitzotzei Orot,* in *Sefer ha-Zohar*, ed. Margaliot, as "his *beit midrash*." But the etymology is obscure. (See Scholem, "She'elot be-viqoret ha-*Zohar*," 42. And see Matt, *Zohar*, Pritzker ed., 2:241, who translates it as "amphitheater.") It is also unclear why Rashbi had to go out to meet the Jew instead of letting him come to him. If we read, instead, *timoreih*, we obtain "his hidden place" (see PT *Sh'vi'it* 9:1 [38d], "R. Shim'on ben Yohai *'avad tamir bim' 'arta . . .* "). The place of Rashbi's truly esoteric teaching is itself hidden. On Rashbi's relations with the Cappadocians, see Meroz, "R'qimato," 189–193.

117. See also Pachter's remarks cited in chap. 4 above at n. 19 with regard to #55.

118. See chap. 2 above at n. 37 and ff.

119. See chap. 2 above at n. 53 and ff.

120. Of course, the kabbalists also mourn over Shekhinah's exile and Israel's sinfulness and suffering. The argument here is that the complexity of the *Zohar*, noted in so many areas, is evident in this area as well.

121. See 2:157a (#69), "The Companions rejoiced on the road."

122. See "Spatiality and the Zohar: Places, Spaces, and Movement in and through Them" in "Two Introductions" above at n. 25 and ff.

123. The full range of meanings of the term *sha'ashu'a*, from mental contemplation to autoerotic and other sexual activity, has been analyzed by Wolfson, "Female Imaging" and "Erasing the Erasure," in id., *Circle*, 2, 124–125n6, and 69–72, 190–192nn175–180.

124. Liebes, "*Zohar* ve-eros," 81.

125. Ibid., 91.

126. The meaning is unclear. *Derekh Emet* translates: "Something slipped and came out of the pot he was cooking in, and the fat went onto the burning coals, so that smoke rose up from it." *Nitzotzei Orot* (in *Sefer ha-Zohar*, ed. Margaliot): "He was spreading spices on the fire and the smoke rose straight up." RaMaK (Azulai, *Or ha-ḥamah*, 1:170c): "*Mistamit*—roast, from the context." R. Abraham Galante (ibid., 170d): "The intended [meaning] is that he was roasting something fatty on coals and smoke was rising from it." Perhaps *safsina* can be read *safsera*—a sword or blade—hence, skewer. See Matt, *Zohar*, Pritzker ed., 3:66n449, who reads the word as *saspanya* and translates, "found R. Yose sizzling a dribbling bronchus [bronchial tube]."

127. 1:176b.

128. The *Zohar* reports elsewhere (3:79b) that when the Companions saw Rashbi, they would run after him and say this verse. See chap. 2, n. 78, above.

129. 1:223a (#34).

130. In light of this, the comments in chap. 4 above at n. 84 should be taken with a grain of salt.

131. See chap 4 above at n. 10.

132. See 1:41a. Through the secret of prayer the righteous know how "to bind together [*l'qashra qishrin*], to intoxicate his Master [with sweet fragrance] [*l'b'sumei l'mareih*] as is proper, and to know how to effect a complete union, and to tear firmaments [*le-miqr'a reqi'in*] and to open gates and doors, so that there will be no one to stop him."

133. 2:149a (#67), cited n. 113.

134. Liebes, "*Zohar* ve-eros," 82. There is a special palace, the fifth, reserved for the celestial supervisors in charge of bringing joy to the world, who are "the jesters for the world—[*badḥei 'alma*]" (2:256a). See also Baer, *History*, 1:269.

135. He traveled toward his unique quality of *Ḥesed*, located in the south (right, when facing east).

136. 1:118ab (#15). On this theme, see Wolfson, "Left Contained in the Right." See also Liebes, "*Zohar* ve-eros," 84–85.

137. Meyer Schapiro, *Late Antique, Early Christian and Mediaeval Art* (New York: G. Braziller, 1979), "Marginal Images and Drôlerie," 197–198, a review of Lilian M. C. Randall, *Images in the Margins of Gothic Manuscripts* (Berkeley: University of California Press, 1966), an extensive collection of such marginalia.

138. Burke, *Desire against the Law*, 18.

139. Ibid., 33–35.

140. Regarding the connection between humor and the forces of Evil in the *Zohar*, see Liebes, "*Zohar* ve-eros," 83–84. Despite Liebes's theory in "The Messiah of the *Zohar*" (in id., *Studies in the Zohar*), the this-worldly nature of the *Zohar*'s ironic humor indicates a very serious non-messianic side to it. Humor is not usually associated with fervent messianics. We would expect them to leave playfulness and laughter for the messianic era (see, e.g., R. Isaac Ha-Kohen in Scholem, *Qabbalot*, 263–264). On comfort and discomfort with the evil of the Other Side, see chap. 6, n. 23, below.

Chapter 6. Zoharic Geographics

1. See studies cited in chap 5, n. 98, above. See also Hallamish, "Qavim le-ha'arakhatah shel Eretz Yisra'el," and Liebes, "Ziqqat ha-*Zohar* l'Eretz Yisra'el."

2. See Scholem, "She'elot be-viqoret ha-*Zohar*," 40–46. Scholem showed that the *Zohar* was confused with regard to the town of Qapotqiya, but that it was clearly not referring to the place outside Israel, in Asia Minor.

3. See, e.g., 1:113a (*MH*), 1:237b, 1:145b (#18), 1:171b, 2:2b, 2:9b, 2:195b, 3:16a.

4. See, e.g., 1:74b, 2:34b. The land of Egypt is most often associated with this quality (see Wolfson, "Left Contained in the Right," 33–37). And all territories outside Israel were also seen in this light.

5. See, e.g., 1:260a, 2:7a (#44), 2:189b (#73), 2:239b. See 1:112 (*MH*) for reference to virtuous Babylonian bachelors who walk among the women without fear of temptation. On this problem in Spanish Jewish society, see Baer, *History*, 1:254–260.

6. See chap. 4 above at n. 122.

7. See, e.g., 1:85a, 1:149a, 3:2b, 3:66a. The presence of the Shekhinah in Babylonia became problematic with regard to the rule that God does not reveal Himself outside the land of Israel. Yet Ezekiel's vision took place in Babylonia. The *Zohar* seems to have two different ways of resolving this. In the second text cited, the *Zohar* sees the revelation as an ad hoc exception, specifically attributable to the merciful response of Shekhinah to the suffering of Israel in exile. However, in the first text cited, the *Zohar*, along with this argument, exegetically proves that the River Kevar is not really outside of sacred space, since it derives from the primeval river of Eden (but cf. 2:34b).

8. The Babylonian Talmud sometimes strives to equate Babylonia with Israel. See BT *Ketubot* 110b–111a.

9. See Huss, "Ḥakham 'adif mi-navi," 104–105, on the *Zohar*'s aspirations to become a canonical text, and 132–133, on the rivalry with Babylonia, and see Liebes, "Ziqqat ha-*Zohar*," 35–41. In "Ha-*Zohar* ke-renesans," 7, Liebes says that the Israel-based *Zohar*, inasmuch as it strove for a creative Jewish spiritual rebirth, considered the Babylonian Talmud a dry, uncreative, legalistic document.

10. See chap 3 above at n. 205.

11. 3:231b (#118). See Liebes, "Ziqqat ha-*Zohar*," 37–38, for another example of the *Zohar* criticizing the Babylonians' unworthiness regarding crying over the destruction of the Temple.

12. See Ta-Shma, *Ha-Nigleh she-ba-nistar*, 89–90, who cites Tishby and Scholem (and R. Margaliot's omission of a source citation here). Ta-Shma resolves the difficulty by suggesting that the *Zohar* refers to the Babylonian geonic polemic against the Karaites.

13. The *Zohar* recognizes them as a fellowship—*ḥavrayya*—parallel to the zoharic group. At 1:76b, the *Zohar* suggests that the Companions can learn about fellowship from the builders of the Tower. The term itself is applied to the Babylonians at 1:96b and 3:71b. On Rashbi's contact with Babylonian comrades, see 3:158a (#109).

14. 1:224b–225a.

15. Huss, "Ḥakham 'adif mi-navi," 132–133.

16. For an example of a Babylonian who learns to dispense with his fear after being in Israel for a while, see 2:168a (#71).

17. M*Ta'anit* 2:1. For a discussion of textual variants, see S. Lieberman, *Tosefta Ki-Fshutah*, pt. 5 (*Mo'ed*) (Jerusalem: Jewish Theological Seminary of America, 1992), 1071–1072. Some authorities had a reading that called for the ashes to be placed on the Torah scroll itself, not on the ark. The *Zohar* speaks of the Torah scroll.

18. BT *Ta'an*it 16a; PT *Ta'an*it 65a.

19. See chap. 5, n. 15, above, and references there, and n. 36 below.

20. 1:225a.

21. 3:71b. The text begins with R. Ele'azar reporting that the Companions forbid taking the Torah scroll out. But then he asks why it is taken out to the town square. Perhaps he means that this is forbidden as long as there is a righteous person for the generation such as Rashbi. Alternatively, he here refers to the Babylonians as *ḥavrayya*. Or, perhaps this is an expression of the transgressive, albeit necessary, nature of exposing the Torah.

22. 1:225b. On Rachel giving birth to Benjamin on the road, see chap. 3 above at n. 158 and ff.

23. The residents of Kfar Tarsha claim not to suckle from the Other Side. (1:95b). But perhaps, in keeping with their locative timidity, they are guilty of self-delusion here. On the other hand, Rashbi is intimately aware of the Other Side and masters it. See chap. 1 at n. 40.

24. Liebes, "*Zohar* ve-eros," 110, explains that they have been exiled to Babylonia because the revelation of secrets is allowed only in Israel.

25. 2:151b.

26. At 2:141a, the *Zohar* says that even someone who dies in Israel may incur corpse

impurity if the body is not buried (i.e., put in its proper place) that day, "for at night permission is given to the Unclean Spirit to roam." See also 1:61a.

27. See Gen. 28:19 where Luz and Bethel are identified. See Rashi and Ramban to vv. 11 and 17. See Josh. 16:2, 18:13 and Judg. 1:23, which indicate that the Luz and Bethel are close but not the same place. And Judg. 1:26 tells of a Canaanite man who helps the conquering Israelites and then goes off to build another city by that name.

28. *Bereshit Rabbah*, 69:7, ed. Theodor and Albeck, 798, in textual variants to line 1. The text is printed in the traditional Vilna editions. *Luz* is also the name of the bone in the human skeleton that is immortal (see *Vayiqra Rabbah* 18:1). However, L. Ginzberg, *The Legends of the Jews*, 5 (Philadelphia: Jewish Publication Society, 1946), 186n28, was not able to find a source that explicitly ties these traditions together.

29. "Nebuchadnezzar did not unsettle it [*ve-lo bilbelah*]" can be read as hinting that he did not incorporate it into Babylonia.

30. Perhaps a play on the words *met* (dead) and *mata* (place).

31. 2:151b.

32. By appealing to the possibility of the Canaanite founder, the *Zohar*, at this point is not identifying this place with the Temple Mount. Nevertheless, the associations with this prior, sacred site lurk in the background.

33. 2:151b.

34. Matt, *Zohar*, Pritzker ed., 5:384n554.

35. 2:149a.

36. See chap. 2 at n. 85 and citations there, and see E. Fishbane, "Scent," 334–336.

37. 2:151b–152a. This is different from the image offered at 1:56a, where letters are hanging, waiting for their final disposition, "depending" on whether Israel accepts the Torah or not.

38. 2:152a. See chap. 3 above at n. 136.

39. Shekhinah is identified with the altar, as noted chap. 3, n. 204, above. She encompasses all letters, from *alef* through *tav*. See 1:15b and innumerable other places (citations in n. 57 below).

40. The stationary Temple inherits its role from the traveling Tabernacle.

41. 2:152a.

42. Earlier in the discussion, the Angel of Death is called "very good" (2:149b). And, as opposed to Luz, the place of goodness in which no one can remain forever, the one place that no one can leave is that realm of Hell reserved for the unrepentant sinner (2:150b).

43. 1:3a.

44. See also 3:188b–189a (*Yenuqa*).

45. 1:3a. An interesting variant in these traditions is found in Baḥya's commentary to Lev. 7:30, ed. Chavel, 2:434–435.

46. See Azulai, *Or ha-ḥamah*, ad loc., 2:190, s.v. *ve-ha-RḤ"V*, and Matt, *Zohar*, Pritzker ed., 5:385n556. The implication is that this potency is the source of life in its eternal purity, while Shekhinah is the source of mortal life. See 199 above at nn. 60–61.

47. See Liebes, *Studies in the Zohar*, 73.

48. It should be recalled, as well, that the significance of the letter *tet* is explained in the *Sefer ha-Bahir* as a sign of the Divine womb. If it is impossible for anyone to stay in

Luz, though it is the very source of life, it may be because we are not allowed to stay in the womb forever. See *Bahir*, ed. Abrams (Scholem), §57 (ed. Margaliot, §84), §87 (ed. Margaliot, §124). The simplest association is to a potency that would correspond to Shekhinah. But at §75 (ed. Margaliot, §106), the *Bahir* groups the Womb—*beten*—(identified with *Galgal*) with *Teli* and Heart as three cosmic forces. Scholem speculates in his commentary to that section (*Das Buch Bahir* [Darmstadt: Wissenschaftliche Buchgesellschaft, 1970], 77n3) that this refers to the penultimate *sefirah*. However, as he points out in his later studies (e.g., *Origins*, 85), the *Bahir* cannot be understood through a strict theory of *sefirot*.

49. 2:151b.

50. Ibid.

51. See 3:174b–175a (*Ra'aya Meheimna*); *Sefer Mitzvot Qatan* (*Ammudei Golah*) (Kopust, 1810), 9b, §28; *Zohar ha-Raqi'a* (Vilna, 1879), 17ab, §18; *Sefer Ḥaredim* (Jerusalem, 1990), 7, §1.

52. 2:152b. The strap—*retzu'ah*—is seen as a tool of punishment, and hence as a synecdoche for the attribute of Judgment. See 2:149b, 2:190b. The positive role it plays in this passage is denied in 1:11b, where fear of punishment is called "evil fear" (*yir'ah ra'ah*). The strap also switches identity, since it is identified with the straps of the *tefillin*, the companion mitzvah to *tzitzit*. See 1:28b. For a more positive approach to *tekhelet*, see 3:175b.

53. M*Rosh Hashanah* 3:8.

54. 2:152b.

55. 1:75a.

56. See, e.g., 3:149a (#108), mentioned chap. 3 at n. 218 above, and see also n. 221 there.

57. See, e.g., #1, 26, 34, 35, 55, 6, 67, 80, 87, 89, 94, 96, 97, 108, 114, 123, 124, 125, *ZH* #11 (*MH*), 32 (*ST*).

58. Israel addresses Moses as feminine. *'At*—comprised of the first and last letters of the alphabet—also alludes to Shekhinah. See n. 39 above.

59. In the context of the passages in this section, this refers, not to the Other Side, but to Shekhinah. However, the associative connotation is noteworthy.

60. 3:261ab.

61. The passage continues that Moses is the exception. He stayed with God. Moses is identified with *tov*—good. He is able to remain (stand) in place, to stand on the holy place, also identified with *ki tov*—God's primordial declaration that the world was good. This quality of goodness, further identified as male, is the quality signified by the letter *tet*, that hovers over the place of immortality, as discussed above.

62. *Lam. Rab.* 9, cited by Margaliot, *Nitzotzei Zohar*, in *Sefer ha-Zohar*, ed. id., ad loc. See also *Zohar* 1:204b (#31). Also Rashi's citation of midrashim regarding Jacob's preparations for meeting Esau, Gen. 32:9, s.v., *v'haya ha-maḥaneh*.

63. 3:261b. This leads into a walking text (#122).

64. For a discussion of one such text, see 3:149a, discussed chap. 3 above at n. 218 and ff.

65. See chap. 1, n. 8, above.

66. 1:178a (#26). Shekhinah "walks to Her dwelling place"; the Companions walk on the road.

67. Ibid.

68. Ibid., a–b. On the phrase "going out and . . . coming in," see chap. 1, n. 41, above.

69. See online Appendix 3, A.10.a. and B.12.a.

70. In Hebrew *'etzah* (but the letter *heh* is not aspirated).

71. 3:202ab.

72. In this respect they imitate God, Who gives Israel *'ita*—advice (the Torah)—against the Serpent. See 1:190a.

73. See #41, 114, 115, 116, 117, *ZH* #5, 12, 22.

74. See chap. 3 above at n. 143 and ff.

75. The verse R. Ele'azar quotes to reassure R. Yitzḥaq concludes a psalm that promises God's protection against the rays of the sun (and moon). The appearance of the sun is also significant at the beginning of that story. Only when the sun appears does R. Ele'azar commence praying, confident that he is not interrupting the Divine union. His prayer facilitates his own union with Shekhinah in the mundane world. (See also 1:95b—the bad effects caused when the sun comes out and is worshipped.)

76. See 1:52b, cited chap. 3 above at n. 223.

77. #80. This text is discussed by Wolski, *Journey*, 185–214, but his reading does not deal with the concerns discussed here.

78. 3:21a.

79. See also 3:76b (#97), 3:269a (#124).

80. 3:45b (#87). See Hecker, "Face of Shame," for a full discussion of this text, including further elaboration of some of the issues raised here. He notes (see 61n83, 65n93) where our readings somewhat diverge.

81. The word refers to the Hebrew *'etzah*, which the *Zohar* associates with the word for tree, as noted above. The righteous are like a tree that gives supportive advice to turn people to repent and forsake their fears. The image of a tree recurs in this text. Before the Companions meet up with this man who stands under a tree, they see a different beautiful tree. They meet the ugly man after walking away from that tree because they do not want to enjoy its beauty after the Temple's destruction. The dimming effect of the destruction on their sight is called *'atifa de-qutra*, a tie of smoke. The leprous man accuses them of looking at him *be-qitra de'ita*—in a bond of counsel. He accuses them of being a group whose prejudices cause them to have clouded sight.

82. 3:46a.

83. See also 3:59b (#94).

84. The first occurrence of shame in the Torah is as a result of humans heeding the Serpent who speaks with Eve at the Tree.

85. On this word see chap 4. above, n. 85. Compare R. Ḥiyya's citation of Proverbs 1:21 with the complaint of R. Isaac the Blind, cited in chap. 4, above, n. 172.

86. See the Yom Kippur *Neilah* liturgy, "You have distinguished the human from the start," etc.

87. 3:46b. Perhaps this is why R. Ele'azar did not get involved in the Kfar Tarsha episode by telling his father of R. Abba's experience. This would have been an evil report.

Nor was it clear that R. Abba would not come before Rashbi after telling everything to R. Ele'azar. Therefore there was no reason to rebuke R. Abba. R. Ele'azar's role in this case was to remain silent and let R. Abba come forward. By avoiding evil speech, then, R. Ele'azar acts as a faithful son.

88. Hecker, "Face of Shame," argues that the son's words are more nuanced, for, while supporting the Companions' position, he avoids their unnecessary shaming of his father.

89. 3:47a.

90. On the issue of public reproof for social ills as advocated by the Spanish Jewish moralists and kabbalists, and with reference to this text, see Baer, *History*, 1:250–263, and Hecker, "Face of Shame," 35–46, esp. 45n41.

91. See the discussion in chap. 1 above.

92. See chap. 3 above, n. 27 and the discussion there at n. 49. And see Tishby, *Mishnat*, 1:289–292, 453.

93. 2:265a. See also 1:146a (#18), 3:60b (#94).

94. *Livnat ha-Sappir* (*Va-yera*) 26a. Cf. *Zohar* 1:171a. At the beginning of this sermon (25b), Angelino says he delivered it fourteen years after the expulsion from France in 1306.

95. See 1:178a–b, "there is a desolate place in the wilderness and that is their dwelling place," cited above at n. 68.

96. 3:205b (#115). The verse is Num. 27:3.

97. 3:206a (#115). On this text, see Tene, "Darkhei," 172–176. Wineman, *Mystic Tales*, 153–154.

98. 1:10b.

99. See *ZH* 8d (*MH*).

100. 2:183b (#72).

101. The term *taqifa* is used in various forms throughout this story with reference to the Other Side.

102. 2:184a.

103. A related idea is that "blessing is not found in an empty place" (2:153b).

104. See Hellner-Eshed, *River Issues Forth*, 101n114 (in Hebrew; Eng., 82 and 393n48). She does not differentiate sufficiently between the hermit's way and that of Rashbi and his students.

105. Note, for instance, that in the story recorded at 2:45b (#56), discussed chap. 3 above at n. 121, the Companions' response to the attack on a woman is avoidance, not intervention.

106. See Rubenstein, "Torah and the Mundane Life: The Education of R. Shimon bar Yohai (Shabbat 33b–34a)," in id., *Talmudic Stories*, 105–138.

107. See 1:128b–129a. See also *Zohar* #41, *ZH* #31.

108. See #41, 105, 124, 125. All these texts revolve around R. Ele'azar, Rashbi's son, who was with Rashbi in the cave of the original story. In #105, whose theme is that God accompanies Israel into even the most putrid places, it is clear that Rashbi has died. Perhaps there is here an exploration of the possibility that R. Ele'azar can be Rashbi's continuator, that Rashbi's death does not have to be of final significance. On this issue, see chap. 2 at n. 85 and citations there, and see E. Fishbane, "Scent," 334–336.

109. Rashbi's cave, *ZH* 59c (see R. Margaliot's note, ad loc.). See also #47, *ZH* #21.

110. See ##35, 89, 18, *ZH* #21. See also #80, where the mountain cave miraculously appears to offer refuge.

111. See Isa. 11:8. *Zohar* ##60, 79, 84, 94.

112. For other discussions of the cave motif, see Megged, *Ha-Or sheneḥeshakh*, 64–75, Wolski, *Journey*, 38 and passim. Megged mentions the Companions' fear only with regard to their concern over revealing concealed truths. Wolski does not mention the element of fear at all.

113. See online Appendix 3, A.10.f. and B.12.f.

114. 1:238b (#38). See Lavi, *Ketem Paz*, 2:425b, s.v. R. Yehudah, "When a person walks on the plain and in a straight path his heart broadens. And when he walks on a crooked path his heart is not with him. In order to widen their hearts to study Torah, he said, 'Let us go to that field which is a straighter path.' Perhaps the road they were walking on had rises and falls, so they chose to walk on the straight path."

115. But see the enigmatic text #53.

116. See, e.g., #79. In this story it seems that Rashbi cannot avert the evil decree until he actually leaves his place and goes out into the world, just as he is compelled to confront the mundane world when he leaves his cave.

117. 2:157a (#69).

118. 2:157b.

Conclusion

1. It is therefore important to forestall, for a while at least, the reading that sees these texts as a metaphor for a hermeneutical model. Anidjar, "Jewish Mysticism Alterable and Unalterable," 137, writes:

> [T]here is a recurring thread in some Zoharic texts that, loosely based on traditional phrases referring to the "ways of the Torah" (*darkhei orayta*), conceives of the text as a path. It is not only, as Charles Mopsik perceptively remarks, that "speech here is mostly exchanged on the way" but also that the very pursuit of reading is conceived of as an encounter *with the road*. Significantly enough, this text that reads and walks texts repeatedly tells its readers about the peripatetic wanderings of the rabbis. On almost every page of the *Zohar*, these rabbis are introduced with the recurring phrase: "Rabbi *x* and Rabbi *y* were walking on the road [*Rabi ploni ve-rabi palmoni havu azlei be-arha*]." This introduction, which one should refrain from reading as simply formulaic, already suggests that there are many possible (if not always responsible) ways of approaching toward, addressing, and encountering the path of textuality/ies.

2. The possibility emerges that the many times the *Zohar* says that the rabbis were walking "from *x* to *y*" should all be counted among the book's jokes.

3. Tene, "Darkhei," 180, on text #115.

4. Wolski, *Journey*, 11.

5. Ibid., 195.

6. See especially the works of Ronit Meroz and Daniel Abrams listed in the Bibliography.

Select Bibliography

The Zohar *and Commentaries*

Angelino, R. Joseph. *Livnat ha-Sappir.* Jerusalem, 1971. Reprint of the 1913 edition.

Azulai, Abraham ben Mordecai. *Or ha-Ḥamah.* 3 vols. Reprint. Yeshivat Be'erah shel Miriam, Israel, n.d.

Cordovero, R. Moshe. *Pardes Rimmonim.* Jerusalem, 1962. Reprint of the Munkács ed.

———. *Zohar 'im Perush Or Yaqar.* 15 vols. Jerusalem: Aḥuzat Yisra'el, 1972–1990.

Lavi, R. Shim'on. *Ketem Paz.* 2 vols. Djerba, Tunisia, 1940.

Sefer ha-Zohar. Edited by Reuven Margaliot. With notes, *Nitzotzei Orot* and *Nitzotzei Zohar*, etc. 3 vols. Jerusalem: Kook, 1984.

Sefer Zohar Ḥadash. Edited by Reuven Margaliot. With notes, *Nitzotzei Zohar.* Jerusalem: Kook, 1994.

The Zohar: Pritzker Edition. Translated with commentary by Daniel C. Matt. 12 vols. Stanford, CA: Stanford University Press, 2004–.

Writings of R. Moshe de Leon

The Book of the Pomegranate: Moses de Leon's "Sefer Ha-Rimmon." Edited by E. R. Wolfson. Atlanta: Scholars Press, 1988.

Sefer ha-Nefesh ha-Ḥakhamah. Jerusalem, 1969. Reprint of the 1608 Basel edition.

Sefer Sheqel ha-Qodesh. Edited by Charles Mopsik. Los Angeles: Cherub Press, 1996.

"She'elot u-Teshuvot le-R. Moshe de Leon be-'inyanei qabbalah." In Isaiah Tishby, *Ḥiqrei qabbalah u-sheluḥoteha*, 1: 36–75. Jerusalem: Magnes Press, 1982.

"Shenei quntresim le-R. Moshe de Leon yoẓ'im la-or 'al yedei Gershom Scholem." Edited by Gershom Scholem. *Qoveẓ 'al yad*, n.s., 8 (1976): 325–370; 371–384.

Other Kabbalistic Works

Abulafia, Todros ben Joseph, ha-Levi. *Sefer Otsar ha-Kavod.* Jerusalem: Maqor, 1970. Reprint of the 1879 Warsaw edition.

———. *Sha'ar ha-Razim.* Edited by M. Kushnir-Oron. Jerusalem: Bialik/Tel Aviv University, 1989.

Ibn Gaon, Shemtov. *Sefer Keter Shem Tov.* In Qovetz, *Sifrei ha-Qadmonim (Sefer Ma'or Va-Shemesh).* Jerusalem, 1997.

Giqatilla, R. Yosef. *Sha'arei Orah.* Edited by Y. Ben-Shelomo. 2 vols. Jerusalem: Bialik, 1981.

———. *Sod ha-naḥash u-mishpato.* Edited by R. Kohen. Jerusalem, 1998.

Joseph of Hamadan. *Sefer Tashak̦*. Edited by Jeremy Zwelling. Ph.D. diss., Brandeis University, 1975.

Perush ha-aggadot le-R. 'Azri'el. Edited by Isaiah Tishby. 1945. Jerusalem: Magnes Press, 1982.

Perush Rabbenu Menaḥem me-Reqanati. N.d. Reprint of the Lublin edition with *Be'ur ha-Levush* of R. Mordekhai Yaffe.

Rabbenu Baḥya 'al ha-Torah. Edited by R. Ḥayyim Dov Chavel. 3 vols. Jerusalem: Kook, 1994.

Sefer Mar'ot ha-Ẓove'ot [The Book of Mirrors]. R. David b. Yehudah he-Ḥasid, edited by D. C. Matt. Chico, CA: Scholars Press, 1982.

Sefer Ma'arekhet ha-Elohut. Jerusalem, 1963. Reprint of the 1558 Mantua edition.

"Sefer Me'irat 'Eynayim le-R. Yitzḥaq de-min 'Aqqo." Edited by Amos Goldreich. Ph.D. diss., Hebrew University, 1981.

Sefer Me'irat 'Eynayim le-R. Yitzḥaq de-min 'Aqqo. Edited by Ḥayyim Erlanger. Jerusalem, 1993.

Secondary Sources

Abrams, Daniel. "Ematai ḥubrah ha-Haqdamah le-Sefer ha-*Zohar*? Ve-Shinuiim Bitefasim Shonim shel ha-Haqdamah she-bidefus Mantovah." *Asufot* 8 (1994): 211–226.

———. *Kabbalistic Manuscripts and Textual History*. Jerusalem: Magnes Press; Los Angeles: Cherub Press, 2010.

———. "Knowing the Maiden without Eyes: Reading the Sexual Reconstruction of the Jewish Mystic in a Zoharic Parable." *Da'at* 50–52 (2003): lix–lxxxiii.

Altmann, Alexander. "Maimonides's Attitude toward Jewish Mysticism." In *Studies in Jewish Thought: An Anthology of German Jewish Scholarship*, ed. Alfred Jospe, 200–219. Detroit: Wayne State University Press, 1981.

Anidjar, Gil. "Jewish Mysticism Alterable and Unalterable: On Orienting Kabbalah Studies and the 'Zohar of Christian Spain.'" *Jewish Social Studies*, n.s., 3, no. 1 (Fall 1996): 89–157.

Ashtor, E. *The Jews of Moslem Spain*. Philadelphia: Jewish Publication Society, 1992.

Baer, Yitzhak. "Ha-Req'a ha-histori shel ha-Ra'aya Mehemna'." *Zion* 5 (1940): 1–44.

———. *A History of the Jews in Christian Spain*. 2 vols. Vol. 1, *From the Age of Reconquest to the Fourteenth Century*, trans. Louis Schoffman. Philadelphia: Jewish Publication Society, 1992.

Beinart, Haim, ed. *Moreshet Sepharad*. Jerusalem: Magnes Press, 1992.

Breuer, Mordekhai. "Nedudei talmidim va-ḥakhamim: aqdamut le-pereq mi-toldot ha-yeshivot." In *Tarbut ve-ḥevrah be-toldot Yisra'el biyemei ha-beynayim*, ed. R. Bonfils, M. Ben-Sasson, and J. Heker, 445–468. Jerusalem: Mercaz Zalman Shazar, 1989.

Brody, Seth Lance. "Human Hands Dwell in Heavenly Heights: Contemplative Ascent and Theurgic Power in Thirteenth Century Kabbalah." In *Mystics of the Book: Themes, Topics, and Typologies*, ed. R. A. Herrera, 123–158. New York: Peter Lang, 1993.

———. "Human Hands Dwell in Heavenly Heights: Worship and Mystical Experience in Thirteenth Century Kabbalah." PhD diss., University of Pennsylvania, 1991.

Buchanan, Ian. "Extraordinary Spaces in Ordinary Places: De Certeau and the Space of Postcolonialism." *Journal of the South Pacific Association for Commonwealth Literature and Language Studies* 36 (1993), wwwmcc.murdoch.edu.au/ReadingRoom/litserv/SPAN/36/Jabba.html.

Buchler, A. "Learning and Teaching in the Open Air in Palestine." *Jewish Quarterly Review*, n.s., 4 (1913–1914): 485–491.

Burke, James F. *Desire against the Law: The Juxtaposition of Contraries in Early Medieval Spanish Literature*. Stanford, CA.: Stanford University Press, 1998.

Carmeli, Merav. "'Mah 'osot ha-ayalot ba-laylah?' q'ri'at Yam Suf u-mitos ha-ayalah ha-yoledet v'ha-naḥash b'*Zohar* B'Shalaḥ." *Kabbalah: Journal for the Study of Jewish Mystical Texts* 23 (2010): 219–247.

Certeau, Michel de. "History and Mysticism." In *Histories: French Constructions of the Past*, ed. Jacques Revel and Lynn Hunt, trans. Arthur Golhammer et al., 437–447. New York: New Press, 1995.

———. *The Mystic Fable*. Vol. 1, *The Sixteenth and Seventeenth Centuries*, trans. Michael B. Smith. Chicago: University of Chicago Press, 1992.

———. *The Practice of Everyday Life*. Translated by Steven Rendall. Berkeley: University of California Press, 1984.

Chavel, Charles Ḥayyim Dov, ed. *Sefer ha-Hinnukh*. Jerusalem: Kook, 1990.

Chazan, Robert. "The Timebound and the Timeless: Medieval Jewish Narration of Events." *History and Memory* 6 (1994): 5–34.

Dan, Joseph, ed. *Meḥqerei Yerushalayim be-maḥashevet Yisra'el: Sefer ha-Zohar ve-doro 8* [Proceedings of the Third International Congress on the History of Jewish Mysticism, Hebrew University, Jerusalem, March 1987. Jerusalem Studies in Jewish Thought 8]. Jerusalem: Magnes Press, 1989.

———. "Min ha-semel el ha-mesumal: lehavanat 'Asarah Ma'amarim Bilti Historiim 'al ha-Qabbalah le-Gershom Scholem." *Meḥqerei Yerushalyim be-maḥashevet Yisra'el* 5 (1986): 363–385.

Eliade, Mircea. *A History of Religious Ideas*. 3 vols. Vol. 1, *From the Stone Age to the Eleusinian Mysteries*, trans. Willard R. Trask. Vol. 2, *From Gautama Buddha to the Triumph of Christianity*, trans. W. R. Trask. Vol. 3, *From Muhammad to the Age of Reforms*, trans. Alf Hiltebeitel and Diane Apostolos-Cappadona. Chicago: University of Chicago Press, 1978–1985.

———. *The Myth of the Eternal Return: Or, Cosmos and History*. Translated by Willard R. Trask. Princeton, NJ: Princeton University Press, 1954.

———. *Patterns in Comparative Religion*. Translated by Rosemary Sheed. Lincoln: University of Nebraska Press, 1958.

———. *The Quest: History and Meaning in Religion*. Chicago: University of Chicago Press, 1969.

———. *The Sacred and the Profane: The Nature of Religion*. Translated by Willard R. Trask. New York: Harper & Row, 1957.

Elman, Yaakov, and Israel Gershoni. *Transmitting Jewish Traditions: Orality, Textuality, and Cultural Diffusion*. New Haven, CT: Yale University Press, 2000.

Fine, Lawrence. "The Contemplative Practice of Yiḥudim in Lurianic Kabbalah." In *Jewish Spirituality: From the Sixteenth-Century Revival to the Present*, ed. Arthur Green, 64–98. New York: Crossroad, 1987.

———, ed. *Essential Papers on Kabbalah*. New York: New York University Press, 1995.
Fishbane, Eitan P. *As Light Before Dawn: The Inner World of a Medieval Kabbalist*. Stanford, CA: Stanford University Press, 2009.
———. "The Scent of the Rose: Drama, Fiction, and Narrative Form in the Zohar." *Prooftexts* 29 (2009): 324–361.
———. "Tears of Disclosure: The Role of Weeping in the Zoharic Narrative." *Journal of Jewish Thought and Philosophy* 11, no. 1 (2002): 25–47.
Fishbane, Michael. "The Book of Zohar and Exegetical Spirituality." In *Mysticism and Sacred Scripture*, ed. Steven T. Katz, 101–117. New York: Oxford University Press, 2000.
———. "Primordial Serpent and the Secrets of Creation." In id., *Biblical Myth and Rabbinic Mythmaking*, 273–292. New York: Oxford University Press, 2003.
———, ed. *The Midrashic Imagination: Jewish Exegesis, Thought, and History*. Albany: State University of New York Press, 1993.
Giller, Pinhas. *The Enlightened Will Shine: Symbolization and Theurgy in the Later Strata of the Zohar*. Albany: State University of New York Press, 1993.
———. "Love and Upheaval in the *Zohar*'s Sabba de-Mishpatim." *Journal of Jewish Thought and Philosophy* 7 (1997): 31–60.
———. *Reading the Zohar: A Sacred Text of Kabbalah*. New York: Oxford University Press, 2000.
———. "Recovering the Sanctity of the Galilee: The Veneration of Sacred Relics in Classical Kabbalah." *Journal of Jewish Thought and Philosophy* 4 (1994): 147–169.
Gottlieb, Efraim. *Ha-Qabbalah be-kitvei Rabbenu Baḥya b. Asher*. Jerusalem, 1970.
———. *Meḥqarim besifrut ha-qabbalah*. Edited by Joseph Hacker. Tel Aviv: Tel Aviv University, 1976.
Green, Arthur. *A Guide to the Zohar*. Stanford, CA: Stanford University Press, 2004.
———. "The Zohar: Jewish Mysticism in Medieval Spain." In *Essential Papers on Kabbalah*, ed. Lawrence Fine, 27–66. New York: New York University Press, 1995.
———, ed. *Jewish Spirituality from the Bible through the Middle Ages*. New York: Crossroad, 1987, 1994.
Greenstein, David. "Aimless Pilgrimage: The Quotidian Utopia of the Zohar." PhD diss., New York University, 2003.
Gruenwald, Ithamar. "Some Critical Notes on the First Part of *Sefer Yeẓira*." *Revue des Études Juives* 132 (1973): 475–512.
Guedemann, M. *Ha-Torah ve-ha-ḥayyim bi-yemei ha-beynayim be-Tzarfat u-ve-Ashkenaz*. Warsaw, 1896. Tel Aviv, 1968.
Hallamish, Moshe. "Qavim leha'arakhatah shel Eretz Yisra'el be-sifrut ha-qabbalah." In *Eretz Yisra'el ba-hagut ha-Yehudit b'yemei ha-beinayim*, ed. Moshe Hallamish and Aviezer Ravitzky, 215–232. Jerusalem: Yad Izhak Ben-Zvi, 1991.
Halperin, David J. "Ascension or Invasion: Implications of the Heavenly Journey in Ancient Judaism." *Religion* 18 (1988): 47–67.
———. *The Faces of the Chariot: Early Jewish Responses to Ezekiel's Vision*. Tübingen: J. C. B. Mohr (Paul Siebeck), 1988.
Hanawalt, Barbara A., and Michal Kobialka, eds. *Medieval Practices of Space*. Minneapolis: University of Minnesota Press, 2000.

Hecker, Joel. "The Face of Shame: The Sight and Site of Rebuke (*Zohar* 3:45b–47a)." *Kabbalah: Journal for the Study of Jewish Mystical Texts* 23 (2010): 29–67.

———. "Kissing Kabbalists: Hierarchy, Reciprocity and Equality." *Studies in Jewish Civilization* 15 (2008): 171–208. Also available at http://medievalists.net/files/11041301.pdf.

———. *Mystical Bodies, Mystical Meals: Eating and Embodiment in Medieval Kabbalah*. Detroit: Wayne State University Press, 2005.

———. "Mystical Eating and Food Practices." In *Judaism in Practice: From the Middle Ages through the Early Modern Period*, ed. L. Fine, 353–363. Princeton, NJ: Princeton University Press, 2001.

Hellner-Eshed, Melila. *A River Issues Forth from Eden: On the Language of Mystical Experience in the "Zohar."* In Hebrew. Tel Aviv: Am Oved, 2005. Translated by Nathan Wolski as *A River Flows from Eden: The Language of Mystical Experience in the "Zohar"* (Stanford, CA: Stanford University Press, 2009).

Huss, Boas. "Ḥakham 'adif mi-navi—R. Shim'on bar Yoḥai u-Moshe Rabbenu ba-*Zohar*." *Kabbalah: Journal for the Study of Jewish Mystical Texts* 4 (1999): 103–140.

———. "Hofa'ato shel Sefer ha-*Zohar*." *Tarbiz* 72, no. 2 (Spring 2002): 507–542.

———. *K'Zohar ha-raqi'a: p'raqim b'toldot hitqablut ha-Zohar u'v'havnayat 'erko ha-simli*. Jerusalem Yad Ben-Zvi/Bialik, 2008.

———. "NiSAN—The Wife of the Infinite: The Mystical Hermeneutic of Rabbi Isaac of Acre." *Kabbalah: Journal for the Study of Jewish Mystical Texts* 5, ed. D. Abrams and A. Elqayam, 155–181. Los Angeles: Cherub Press, 2000.

———. "*Sefer ha-Zohar* as a Canonical, Sacred and Holy Text: Changing Perspectives of the Book of Splendor between the Thirteenth and Eighteenth Centuries." *Journal of Jewish Thought and Philosophy* 7 (1998): 257–307.

Idel, Moshe. "'Al Eretz-Yisra'el ba-maḥashavah ha-mistit shel yemei ha-beinayim." In *Eretz Yisra'el ba-hagut ha-yehudit b'yemei ha-beinayim*, ed. M. Hallamish and A. Ravitzky, 193–214. Jerusalem: Yad Izhak Ben-Zvi, 1991.

———. "'Ḥalon ha-hizdamnuyot' shel ha-qabbalah: 1270–1290." *Da'at* 48 (Winter 2002): 5–32.

———. *Kabbalah: New Perspectives*. New Haven, CT: Yale University Press, 1988.

———. "The Land of Israel in Medieval Kabbalah." In *The Land of Israel: Jewish Perspectives*, ed. Lawrence A. Hoffman, 170–187. Notre Dame, IN: University of Notre Dame Press, 1986.

———. "Naḥmanides: Kabbalah, Halakhah, and Spiritual Leadership." In *Jewish Mystical Leaders and Leadership in the Thirteenth Century*, ed. M. Idel and Mortimer Ostow, 15–96. Northvale, NJ: Jason Aronson, 1998.

———. "On Mobility, Individuals and Groups: Prolegomenon for a Sociological Approach to Sixteenth-Century Kabbalah." *Kabbalah: Journal for the Study of Jewish Mystical Texts* 3 (1998): 145–173.

———. "Some Concepts of Time and History in Kabbalah." In *Jewish History and Jewish Memory: Essays in honor of Yosef Hayim Yerushalmi*, ed. Elisheva Carlebach, John M. Efron, and David N. Myers, 153–188. Hanover, NH: University Press of New England for Brandeis University Press, 1998.

———. "Transmission in Thirteenth-Century Kabbalah." In *Transmitting Jewish Tradi-*

tions: Orality, Textuality, and Cultural Diffusion, ed. Yaakov Elman and Israel Gershoni. New Haven, CT: Yale University Press, 2000.

———. "We Have No Kabbalistic Tradition on This." In *Rabbi Moses Naḥmanides (Ramban): Explorations in His Religious and Literary Virtuosity*, ed. Isadore Twersky, 51–73. Cambridge, MA: Harvard University Press, 1983.

———. "The Zohar as Exegesis." In *Mysticism and Sacred Scripture*, ed. Steven T. Katz, 87–100. New York: Oxford University Press, 2000.

Idel, Moshe, and Mortimer Ostow, eds. *Jewish Mystical Leaders and Leadership in the Thirteenth Century*. Northvale, NJ: Jason Aronson, 1998.

Jastrow, Marcus. *A Dictionary of the Targumim, the Talmud Babli and Yerushalmi, and the Midrashic Literature*. 2 vols. in 1. Peabody, MA: Hendrickson, 2005.

Jung, L. Shannon. "Feminism and Spatiality: Ethics and the Recovery of a Hidden Dimension." *Journal of Feminist Studies in Religion* 4, no. 1 (Spring 1988): 55–71.

Katz, Jacob. *Halakhah ve-qabbalah: meḥqarim be-toldot dat Yisra'el 'al madorehah ve-ziqatah ha-ḥevratit*. Jerusalem: Magnes Press, 1986.

Katz, Steven T., ed. *Mysticism and Religious Traditions*. New York: Oxford University Press, 1983.

———, ed. *Mysticism and Language*. New York: Oxford University Press, 1992.

Kedar, B. Z., and R. J. Z. Werblowsky, eds. *Sacred Space: Shrine, City, Land*. New York: New York University Press, 1998.

Lefebvre, Henri. *The Production of Space*. Translated by Donald Nicholson-Smith. Cambridge, MA: Blackwell, 1991.

Liebes, Yehuda. "de Natura Dei- 'al ha-mitos ha-Yehudi ve-gilgulo." In *Massu'ot*, ed. Michal Oron and Amos Goldreich, 243–297. Jerusalem: Bialik, 1994.

———. "Golem b'gimatria Ḥokhmah." *Kiryat Sefer* 63, no. 4 (1990–1991): 1305–1322.

———. "Ha-*Zohar* ke-renesans." *Da'at* 46 (Winter 2001): 5–11.

———. "Ha-Zohar ke-sefer halakhah." *Tarbiz* 64 (1995): 581–605.

———. *"Ha-Zohar* v'ha-Tiqqunim—me-renesans l'mahapekhah." In *Ḥiddushei Zohar: Meḥqarim ḥadashim b'sifrut ha-Zohar*, ed. R. Meroz, 251–301. Tel Aviv: Tel Aviv University, 2007.

———. "Kivunim ḥadashim be-ḥeqer ha-qabbalah." *Pe'amim* 50 (Winter 1991): 150–170.

———. "Peraḳim be-milon Sefer ha-*Zohar*." PhD diss. Jerusalem: Hebrew University, 1976.

———. *Studies in Jewish Myth and Jewish Messianism*. Translated by Batya Stein. Albany: State University of New York Press, 1993.

———. *Studies in the Zohar*. Translated by Arnold Schwartz, Stephanie Nakache, and Penina Peli. Albany: State University of New York Press, 1993.

———. "Ziqqat ha-*Zohar* l'Eretz Yisra'el." In *Tziyyon v'Tziyyonut b'qerev Y'hudei S'farad v'ha-Mizraḥ*, ed. W. Zeev Harvey et al., 31–44. Jerusalem: Misgav Yerushalayim, 2002.

———. "*Zohar* ve-Eros." *'Alpayim* 9 (1994): 67–119.

Margaliot, Reuven. *Sha'arei Zohar*. Jerusalem: Kook, 1994.

———. "She'elot be-viqoret ha-*Zohar* mitokh yedi'otav 'al Eretz Yisra'el." *Sinai* 54, no. 4 (1940): 237–240.

Matt, Daniel Chanan. "The Mystic and the *Mitzvot*." In *Jewish Spirituality from the Bible through the Middle Ages*, ed. Arthur Green, 367–404. New York: Crossroad, 1994.

———. "'New-Ancient Words': The Aura of Secrecy in the *Zohar*." In *Gershom Scholem's "Major Trends in Jewish Mysticism" 50 Years After: Proceedings of the Sixth International Conference on the History of Jewish Mysticism*, ed. Peter Schäfer and Joseph Dan, 181–207. Tubingen: J. C. B. Mohr, 1993.

———, ed. *Zohar: The Book of Enlightenment*. Mahwah, NJ: Paulist Press, 1983.

———, ed. and trans. *The Zohar: Pritzker Edition*. 12 vols. Stanford, CA: Stanford University Press, 2004–.

McGinn, Bernard. "Ocean and Desert as Symbols of Mystical Absorption in the Christian Tradition." *Journal of Religion* 74, no. 2 (April 1994): 155–181.

———. *The Foundations of Mysticism*. Vol. 1 of *The Presence of God: A History of Western Christian Mysticism*. New York: Crossroad, 1997.

Megged, Matti. *Ha-Or she-neḥeshakh: 'arakhim esteti'im be-Sefer ha-Zohar*. Tel Aviv: Vered, 1980.

Meroz, Ronit. "The Path of Silence: An Unknown Story from a Zohar Manuscript." *European Journal of Jewish Studies* 1 (2007): 319–42.

———. "R'qimato shel mittos: diyyun bishnei sippurim ba-*Zohar*." In *Limmud va-da'at ba-maḥashavah ha-Y'hudit*, vol. 2, ed. Hayyim Kreisel, 167–205. Tel Aviv: Bar-Ilan University, 2006.

———. "'Va-ani lo hayyiti sham?!' Qovlanotav shel Rashbi 'al pi sippur zohari bilti yadu'a." *Tarbiz* 71, no. 1–2 (2002): 163–193.

———. "Zoharic Narratives and Their Adaptations." *Hispania Judaica* 3 (2000): 3–62.

———, ed., *Ḥiddushei Zohar: meḥqarim ḥadashim b'sifrut ha-Zohar*. Tel Aviv: Tel Aviv University, 2007.

Oron, Michal. "'Simeni kha-ḥotam 'al libekha: 'iyyunim ba-po'etiqah shel ba'al ha-*Zohar* be-parashat 'Sabba de-Mishpatim." In *Massu'ot: meḥqarim be-sifrut ha-qabbalah u-ve-maḥashevet Yisra'el muqdashim le-zikhro shel Prof. Efrayim Gottlieb zal*, ed. Michal Oron and Amos Goldreich, 1–24. Jerusalem: Bialik, 1994.

———. "Sh'loshah perushim l'Ma'aseh B'reshit u-mashma'utam b'ḥeqer ha-*Zohar*." *Da'at* 50–52 (2003): 183–199.

Oron, Michal, and Amos Goldreich, eds. *Massu'ot: meḥqarim be-sifrut ha-qabbalah u-ve-maḥashevet Yisra'el muqdashim le-zikhro shel Prof. Efrayim Gottlieb zal*. Jerusalem: Bialik, 1994.

Otto, Rudolf. *The Idea of the Holy: An Inquiry into the Non-Rational Factor in the Idea of the Divine and Its Relation to the Rational*. Translated by John W. Harvey. New York: Oxford University Press, 1958.

Pachter, Mordekhai. "Beyn laylah le-voqer." In *Meḥqerei Yerushalayim be-maḥashevet Yisra'el: Sefer ha-Zohar ve-doro 8*, ed. J. Dan (1989): 311–346.

Patai, Raphael. *Man and Temple in Ancient Jewish Myth and Ritual*. London: Thomas Nelson & Sons, 1947.

Pedaya, Ḥaviva. *Ha-Shem ve-ha-Miqdash be-mishnat R. Yitzḥaq Sagi Nahor: 'iyyun mashveh be-kitvei rishonei ha-mequbalim*. Jerusalem: Magnes Press, 2001.

———. "The Divinity as Place and Time and the Holy Place in Jewish Mysticism." In

Sacred Space: Shrine, City, Land, ed. B. Z. Kedar, and R. J. Z. Werblowsky, 84–111. New York: New York University Press, 1998.

———. "Eretz shel ru'aḥ ve-eretz mamash: R. 'Ezra, R. 'Azriel ve-ha-Ramban." In *Eretz Yisra'el ba-hagut ha-Yehudit b'yemei ha-beinayim*, ed. Moshe Hallamish and Aviezer Ravitzky, 193–214. Jerusalem: Yad Izhak Ben-Zvi, 1991.

———. "Pegam ve-tiqqun shel ha-Elohut be-qabbalat R. Yitzḥaq Sagi Nahor." In *Meḥqerei Yerushalyim be-maḥshevet Yisra'el* 6, nos. 3–4 (1987): 157–285.

Rosenberg, Shalom. "The Link to the Land of Israel in Jewish Thought: A Clash of Perspectives." In *The Land of Israel: Jewish Perspectives*, ed. Lawrence A. Hoffman, 139–169. Notre Dame, IN: University of Notre Dame Press, 1986.

Rubenstein, Jeffrey L. *Talmudic Stories: Narrative Art, Composition, and Culture*. Baltimore: Johns Hopkins University Press, 1999.

Sack, Bracha. *B'Sha'rei ha-Qabbalah shel R. Moshe Qordovero*. Beer-Sheva, Israel: Ben Gurion University, 1995.

Schäfer, Peter, and Dan, Joseph, eds. *Gershom Scholem's "Major Trends in Jewish Mysticism" 50 Years After: Proceedings of the Sixth International Conference on the History of Jewish Mysticism*. Tübingen: J. C. B. Mohr, 1993.

Scholem, Gershom G. *Jewish Gnosticism, Merkabah Mysticism, and Talmudic Tradition*. New York: Jewish Theological Seminary, 1965.

———. *Kabbalah*. Jerusalem: Keter, 1974.

———. *Major Trends in Jewish Mysticism*. New York: Schocken Books, 1971.

———. *Meḥqerei Qabbalah* (I). Edited by Joseph ben Shelomo with supplementary revisions by Moshe Idel. Tel Aviv: Am Oved, 1998.

———. *The Messianic Idea in Judaism and Other Essays on Jewish Spirituality*. New York: Schocken Books, 1971.

———. *On the Kabbalah and Its Symbolism*. Translated by Ralph Mannheim. New York: Schocken Books, 1965.

———. *On the Mystical Shape of the Godhead: Basic Concepts in the Kabbalah*. Translated by Joachim Neugroschel. Edited and revised by Jonathan Chipman. New York: Schocken, Books 1991.

———. *Origins of the Kabbalah*. Edited by R. J. Zwi Werblowsky. Translated by Allan Arkush. Philadelphia: Jewish Publication Society; Princeton, NJ: Princeton University Press, 1987.

———. "Parashah ḥadashah min ha-Midrash ha-Ne'elam she-ba-*Zohar*." In *Jubilee Volume in Honor of Louis Ginzberg* (Hebrew Section), 425–446. New York: American Academy for Jewish Research and Jewish Publication Society, 1946.

———. "Qabbalot R. Ya'aqov ve-R. Yitzḥaq benei R. Ya'aqov ha-Kohen." *Mada'ei ha-Yahadut* 2. Jerusalem, 1927.

———. "She'elot be-viqoret ha-*Zohar* mitokh yedi'otav 'al Eretz Yisra'el." *Zion* 1 (1926): 40–55.

———. "Sitra Aḥra: Good and Evil in the Kabbalah." In Scholem, *On the Mystical Shape of the Godhead: Basic Concepts in the Kabbalah*. New York: Schocken, Books 1991.

Septimus, Bernard. "Piety and Power in Thirteenth Century Catalonia." In *Studies in*

Medieval Jewish History and Literature, ed. Isadore Twersky, 197–230. Cambridge, MA: Harvard University Press, 1979.

Signer, Michael A. "The Land of Israel in Medieval Jewish Exegetical and Polemical Literature." In *The Land of Israel: Jewish Perspectives*, ed. Lawrence A. Hoffman, 210–233. Notre Dame, IN: University of Notre Dame Press, 1986.

Smith, Jonathan Z. *Drudgery Divine: On the Comparison of Early Christianities and the Religions of Late Antiquity*. Chicago: University of Chicago Press, 1990.

———. *Imagining Religion: From Babylon to Jonestown*. Chicago: University of Chicago Press, 1982.

———. *Map Is Not Territory: Studies in the History of Religions*. Leiden: E. J. Brill, 1978.

———. *To Take Place: Toward Theory in Ritual*. Chicago: University of Chicago Press, 1987.

Soloveitchik, Haym. "Three Themes in the *Sefer Ḥasidim*." *AJS Review* 1 (1976): 311–357.

Sullivan, Richard E. "The Medieval Monk as Frontiersman." In *Christian Missionary Activity in the Early Middle Ages*, ed. Richard E. Sullivan, 25–49. Brookfield, VT: Variorum, 1994.

Sumption, Jonathan. *Pilgrimage: An Image of Medieval Religion*. Totowa, NJ: Rowman & Littlefield, 1975.

Ta-Shma, Israel M. *Ha-Nigleh she-ba-nistar: le-ḥeqer sheqi'ei ha-halakhah be-Sefer ha-Zohar*. Tel Aviv: Hakibbutz Hameuchad Publishing House, 1995.

———. "Hasidut Ashkenaz biSefarad: Rabbenu Yonah Girondi—ha-Ish u-fo'alo." In *Galut ahar golah: meḥqarim be-toldot 'am Yisra'el*, 165–194. Jerusalem: Makhon Ben-Zvi/Yad Ben-Zvi/Hebrew University, 1988.

———. "'Miqdash Me'at'—ha-semel ve-ha-mamashut." In *Knesset Ezra: Literature and Life in the Synagogue*, ed. S. Elizur, M. D. Herr, G. Shaked, and A. Shinan, 351–364. Jerusalem: Yad Izhak Ben-Zvi/Ben-Zvi Institute, 1994.

Tene, Naomi. "Darkhei 'itzuv ha-sippur be-Sefer ha-*Zohar*." PhD diss., Bar-Ilan University, 1993.

Tishby, Isaiah. *Mishnat ha-Zohar*. 2 vols. Jerusalem: Bialik, 1949, 1961. Translated by David Goldstein as *Wisdom of the Zohar: An Anthology of Texts*, 3 vols. (Oxford: Oxford University Press, 1991).

———, ed. *Perush ha-Aggadot le-R. 'Azri'el*. 1945. Jerusalem: Magnes Press, 1982.

Turner, Victor. *Blazing the Trail: Way Marks in the Exploration of Symbols*. Edited by Edith Turner. Tuscon: University of Arizona Press, 1992.

———. *Dramas, Fields, and Metaphors: Symbolic Action in Human Society*. Ithaca, NY: Cornell University Press, 1974.

Turner, Victor, and Edith Turner. *Image and Pilgrimage in Christian Culture: Anthropological Perspectives*. New York: Columbia University Press, 1978.

Twersky, Isadore, ed. *Rabbi Moses Nahmanides (Ramban): Explorations in His Religious and Literary Virtuosity*. Cambridge, MA: Harvard University Press, 1983.

Verman, Mark. *The Books of Contemplation: Medieval Jewish Mystical Sources*. Albany: State University of New York Press, 1992.

Wineman, Aryeh. *Beyond Appearances: Stories from Kabbalistic Ethical Writings*. Philadelphia: Jewish Publication Society, 1988.

———. *Mystic Tales from the Zohar.* Philadelphia: Jewish Publication Society, 1997.

Wolfson, Elliot R. *Along the Path: Studies in Kabbalistic Myth.* Albany: State University of New York Press, 1995.

———. "The Anonymous Chapters of the Elderly Master of Secrets—New Evidence for the Early Activity of the Zoharic Circle." *Kabbalah: Journal for the Study of Jewish Mystical Texts* 19 (2009): 143–278.

———. "Beautiful Maiden without Eyes: *Peshat* and *Sod* in Zoharic Hermeneutics." In *The Midrashic Imagination*, ed. Michael Fishbane, 155–203. Albany: State University of New York Press, 1993.

———. "Beyond the Spoken Word: Oral Tradition and Written Transmission in Medieval Jewish Mysticism." In *Transmitting Jewish Traditions: Orality, Textuality, and Cultural Diffusion*, ed. Yaakov Elman and Israel Gershoni, 166–224. New Haven, CT: Yale University Press, 2000.

———. "By Way of Truth: Aspects of Naḥmanides' Kabbalistic Hermeneutic." *AJS Review* 14, no. 2 (Fall 1989): 103–178.

———. *Circle in the Square: Studies in the Use of Gender in Kabbalistic Symbolism.* Albany: State University of New York Press, 1995.

———. "Circumcision and the Divine Name: A Study in the Transmission of Esoteric Doctrine." *Jewish Quarterly Review* 78, nos. 1–2 (July–October 1987): 77–112.

———. "Coronation of the Sabbath Bride: Kabbalistic Myth and the Ritual of Androgynisation." *Journal of Jewish Thought and Philosophy* 6 (1997): 301–343.

———. "Crossing Gender Boundaries in Kabbalistic Ritual and Myth." In id., *Circle in the Square*, 79–121, 195–232. Albany: State University of New York Press, 1995.

———. "The Cut That Binds: Time Memory, and the Ascetic Impulse (Reflections on Bratslav Hasidism)." In *God's Voice from the Void: Old and New Studies in Bratsav Hasidism*, ed. Shaul Magid, 103–154. Albany: State University of New York Press, 2002.

———. "Dimmui Antropomorfi ve-Simboliqah shel ha-Oti'ot be-Sefer ha-*Zohar*." *Meḥqerei Yerushalyim be-Maḥshevet Yisra'el* 8 (1989): 147–182.

———. "Erasing the Erasure/Gender and the Writing of God's Body in Kabbalistic Symbolism." In id., *Circle in the Square.* Albany: State University of New York Press, 1995.

———. "Eunuchs Who Keep the Sabbath: Becoming Male and the Ascetic Ideal in Thirteenth-Century Jewish Mysticism." In *Becoming Male in the Middle Ages*, ed. Jeffrey Jerome Cohen and Bonnie Wheeler, 151–185. New York: Garland, 1997.

———. "The Face of Jacob in the Moon: Mystical Transformations of an Aggadic Myth." In *The Seductiveness of Jewish Myth: Challenge or Response?*, ed. S. Daniel Breslauer, 235–270. Albany: State University of New York Press, 1997.

———. "Forms of Visionary Ascent as Ecstatic Experience in *Zoharic* Literature." In *Gershom Scholem's "Major Trends in Jewish Mysticism" 50 Years After: Proceedings of the Sixth International Conference on the History of Jewish Mysticism*, ed. Peter Schäfer and Joseph Dan, 209–238. Tubingen: J. C. B. Mohr, 1993.

———. "From Sealed Book to Open Text: Time, Memory and Narrativity in Kabbalistic Hermeneutics." In *Interpreting Judaism in a Postmodern Age*, ed. Steven Kepnes, 145–178. New York: New York University Press, 1996.

———. "Images of God's Feet: Some Observations on the Divine Body in Judaism." In *People of the Body: Jews and Judaism in Embodied Perspective*, ed. Howard Eilberg-Schwartz, 143–181. Albany: State University of New York Press, 1992.

———. "Left Contained in the Right: A Study in Zoharic Hermeneutics." *AJS Review* 11 (1986): 27–52.

———. "Letter Symbolism and *Merkavah* Imagery in the *Zohar*." In *'Alei Shefer: Studies in the Literature of Jewish Thought Presented to Rabbi Dr. Alexandre Safran*, ed. Moshe Hallamish, 195–236. Tel Aviv: Bar-Ilan University Press, 1990.

———. "Light through Darkness: The Ideal of Human Perfection in the *Zohar*." *Harvard Theological Review* 81 (1988): 78–84.

———. "Mystical Rationalization of the Commandments in *Sefer ha-Rimmon*." *Hebrew Union College Annual* 59 (1988): 217–251.

———. "Mystical-Theurgical Dimensions of Prayer in *Sefer ha-Rimmon*." In *Approaches to Judaism in Medieval Times*, ed. David R. Blumenthal, 3: 41–79. Atlanta: Scholars Press, 1988.

———. "Negative Theology and Positive Assertion in the Early Kabbalah." *Da'at* 32–33 (1994): iii–xxii.

———. "Occultation of the Feminine and the Body of Secrecy in Medieval Kabbalah." In *Rending the Veil: Concealment and Secrecy in the History of Religions*, ed. E. R. Wolfson, 13–154. New York: Seven Bridges Press, 1998.

———. "Re/membering the Covenant: Memory, Forgetfulness, and the Construction of History in the *Zohar*." In *Jewish History and Jewish Memory: Essays in Honor of Yosef Hayim Yerushalmi*, ed. Elisheva Carlebach, John M. Efron, and David N. Myers, 214–246. Hanover, NH: University Press of New England for Brandeis University Press, 1998.

———. *Through a Speculum that Shines: Vision and Imagination in Medieval Jewish Mysticism*. Princeton, NJ: Princeton University Press, 1994.

———. "Woman—The Feminine as Other in Theosophic Kabbalah." In *The Other in Jewish Thought and History: Constructions of Jewish Culture and Identity*, ed. Laurence J. Silberstein and Robert L. Cohn, 166–204. New York: New York University Press, 1994.

———, ed. *The Book of the Pomegranate: Moses de Leon's "Sefer Ha-Rimmon."* Atlanta: Scholars Press, 1988.

Wolski, Nathan. *A Journey into the Zohar: An Introduction to the Book of Radiance*. Albany: State University of New York Press, 2010

Wolski, Nathan, and Merav Carmeli. "Those Who Know Have Wings: Celestial Journeys with the Masters of the Academy." *Kabbalah: Journal for the Study of Jewish Mystical Texts* 16 (2007): 83–114.

Index

teachings of, 47–48; Oral, 72, 73, 88, 148–50, 153; punishment of Kfar Tarsha sages concerning, 159–63, 276*n*41; revelation of, 49, 162–63, 165; on serpent's punishment, 69; Shekhinah and, 38, 156; spatial existence of, 89; theurgy and the study of, 39–40; walking as context for teachings of, 24, 31–41, 52, 105, 107, 109, 125–27, 241*n*48; wilderness as site for study of, 209–12; Written, 72, 148–50, 153. *See also Beit midrash*
Tosafists, 135, 137
Tower of Babel, 169–78, 180, 186
Travel: of Abraham, 13–17; dangers and temptations of, 18–20, 80, 101, 111–12, 199–200; excitement of, 113, 181; and language, 278*n*71; Shekhinah as company in, 13–22, 80, 88; of Spanish Jews, 112–13. *See also* Paths and roads; Walking
Trees, 61. *See also* Cosmic Tree
Truth, 208
Turner, Edith, 121
Turner, Victor, 121–23
Tzaddiq, 80, 120
Tzaḥuta, 126, 205
Tzitzit, 194–98

Unification: as contraction of space, 74–75; counteraction to, 90, 93; divine, 61; of male and female, 38; sacrifice and, 90–92; in spiritual experience, 39; walking and, 40–41
Union-separation duality, 14–22, 25, 174–76, 180, 186
Upper Female, 14, 19, 21
Upper Male, 14
Upper Mother, 15, 18
'Uvda (act, story, geste), 90, 95–99, 125

Verticality: horizontality in relation to, 57, 60–61, 70, 83; human body and, 27; the sacred associated with, 10, 12, 70
Vitry, Jacques de, 124

Walking: being place-bound vs., 160; as context for teachings of Torah, 24, 31–41, 52, 105, 107, 109, 125–27, 241*n*48; expressive character of, 146, 153; with God, 28–29, 36–37; instructions for, 199; meanings and purposes of, 106, 127; mundane nature of, 145–46, 215–16; mysticism and, 6, 29, 118, 138–39, 147, 179–80, 184, 215–16, 219–20; pure act of, 12, 42–43, 106–10, 146, 214, 215; redemption associated with, 29; as resistance, 12, 142, 145–47; Serpent's incapacity for, 207–8; and space, 57, 127–28, 216–17; as a tactic, 140–48, 153, 154, 182–83; thematization of, 42–43, 52, 109, 118; and theurgy, 40–41; and truth, 208; and union of male and female potencies, 73; as wandering, 41–42, 51. *See also* Speech act; Travel
Walking motif: innovative use of, 145, 220; as motif, 4–5; uncertain significance of, 12, 42, 52, 109–10, 218–19
Walking stories: assumptions underlying, 12; Companions in, 32, 236*n*31; defining, 4–5, 29–32, 232*n*3, 238*n*10; deflected journeys in, 110; destinations not the focus of, 31, 42, 47, 110, 215, 218; emotions connected with, 42; fear in, 198; fellowship in, 32–43, 123; locations of, in *Zohar*, 5–6, 234*n*3; meaning of, 3, 12; meetings in, 20, 47, 51, 202; and mystical practice, 6, 29; number of, 30, 238*n*13; paradoxical nature of, 5–6, 217–18; in rabbinic literature, 238*n*13; Rashbi in, 32, 236*n*31; redemptive significance of, 29; relationship of spiritual and mundane in, 54–55, 117–21, 217–20; scholarship on, 3–4, 220; Shekhinah in, 242*n*69; significance of space and motion in,